TM

References for the Rest of Us!®

BESTSELLING BOOK SERIES

Are you intimidated and confused by computers? Do you find that traditional manuals are overloaded with technical details you'll never use? Do your friends and family always call you to fix simple problems on their PCs? Then the For Dummies® computer book series from Wiley Publishing, Inc. is for you.

For Dummies books are written for those frustrated computer users who know they aren't really dumb but find that PC hardware, software, and indeed the unique vocabulary of computing make them feel helpless. For Dummies books use a lighthearted approach, a down-to-earth style, and even cartoons and humorous icons to dispel computer novices' fears and build their confidence. Lighthearted but not lightweight, these books are a perfect survival guide for anyone forced to use a computer.

> *"I like my copy so much I told friends; now they bought copies."*
> — Irene C., Orwell, Ohio

> *"Quick, concise, nontechnical, and humorous."*
> — Jay A., Elburn, Illinois

> *"Thanks, I needed this book. Now I can sleep at night."*
> — Robin F., British Columbia, Canada

Already, millions of satisfied readers agree. They have made For Dummies books the #1 introductory level computer book series and have written asking for more. So, if you're looking for the most fun and easy way to learn about computers, look to For Dummies books to give you a helping hand.

Wiley Publishing, Inc.

Starting an Online Business

FOR

DUMMIES®

3RD EDITION

Starting an Online Business

FOR

DUMMIES®

3RD EDITION

by Greg Holden

Wiley Publishing, Inc.

Starting an Online Business For Dummies®, 3rd Edition

Published by
Wiley Publishing, Inc.
10475 Crosspoint Blvd.
Indianapolis, IN 46256

www.wiley.com

Copyright © 2002 by Wiley Publishing, Inc., Indianapolis, Indiana

Published by Wiley Publishing, Inc., Indianapolis, Indiana

Published simultaneously in Canada

No part of this publication may be reproduced, stored in a retrieval system or transmitted in any form or by any means, electronic, mechanical, photocopying, recording, scanning or otherwise, except as permitted under Sections 107 or 108 of the 1976 United States Copyright Act, without either the prior written permission of the Publisher, or authorization through payment of the appropriate per-copy fee to the Copyright Clearance Center, 222 Rosewood Drive, Danvers, MA 01923, (978) 750-8400, fax (978) 750-4744. Requests to the Publisher for permission should be addressed to the Legal Department, Wiley Publishing, Inc., 10475 Crosspoint Blvd., Indianapolis, IN 46256, (317) 572-3447, fax (317) 572-4447, e-mail: permcoordinator@wiley.com.

Trademarks: Wiley, the Wiley Publishing logo, For Dummies, the Dummies Man logo, A Reference for the Rest of Us!, The Dummies Way, Dummies Daily, The Fun and Easy Way, Dummies.com and related trade dress are trademarks or registered trademarks of Wiley Publishing, Inc., in the United States and other countries, and may not be used without written permission. All other trademarks are the property of their respective owners. Wiley Publishing, Inc., is not associated with any product or vendor mentioned in this book.

For general information on our other products and services or to obtain technical support, please contact our Customer Care Department within the U.S. at 800-762-2974, outside the U.S. at 317-572-3993, or fax 317-572-4002.

Wiley also publishes its books in a variety of electronic formats. Some content that appears in print may not be available in electronic books.

Library of Congress Cataloging-in-Publication Data:

Library of Congress Control Number: 2002107896

ISBN: 0-7645-1655-8

Manufactured in the United States of America

10 9 8 7 6 5 4 3 2 1

Wiley Publishing, Inc. is a trademark of Wiley Publishing, Inc.

About the Author

Greg Holden is founder and president of a small business called Stylus Media, which is a group of editorial, design, and computer professionals who produce both print and electronic publications. The company gets its name from a recording stylus that reads the traces left on a disk by voices or instruments and translates those signals into electronic data that can be amplified and enjoyed by many.

One of the ways Greg enjoys communicating is through explaining technical subjects in nontechnical language. The first edition of *Starting an Online Business For Dummies* was the ninth of his twelve computer books. Recently, Greg was named a contributing editor of *Computer Currents* magazine, where he writes a monthly column. He also contributes to *PC World* magazine. Other projects have included preparing documentation for an electronics catalog company in Chicago and creating online courses on Windows 2000 and Microsoft Word 2000.

Greg balances his technical expertise and his entrepreneurial experience with his love of literature. He received an M.A. in English from the University of Illinois at Chicago and also writes general interest books, short stories, and   poetry. Among his editing assignments is the monthly newsletter for his daughters' grade school.

After graduating from college, Greg became a reporter for his hometown newspaper. Working at the publications office at the University of Chicago was his next job, and it was there that he started to use computers. He discovered, as the technology became available, that he loved desktop publishing (with the Macintosh and LaserWriter) and, later on, the World Wide Web.

Greg loves to travel, but since his two daughters were born, he hasn't been able to get around much. However, through the Web, he enjoys traveling vicariously and meeting people online. He lives with his family in an old house in Chicago that he has been rehabbing for — well, for many years now. He is a collector of objects such as pens, cameras, radios, and hats. He is always looking for things to take apart so that he can see how they work and fix them up. Many of the same skills prove useful in creating and maintaining Web pages. He is an active member of Jewel Heart, a Tibetan Buddhist meditation and study group based in Ann Arbor, Michigan.

Dedication

To my best friend Ann Lindner, who makes everything possible.

Author's Acknowledgments

One of the things I like best about this book is that it's a teaching tool that gives me a chance to share my knowledge — small business owner to small business owner — about computers, the Internet, and communicating your message to others in an interactive way. As any businessperson knows, most large-scale projects are a team effort.

In the course of writing this book, I met a lot of businesspeople. I was struck by the fact that the most successful entrepreneurs also tended to be the ones who were the most generous with their time and experience. They taught me that the more helpful you are, the more successful you'll be in return.

I want to thank all those who were profiled as case studies, particularly Dan Podraza of CollectibleX.com, who pops up all through the book. Thanks also go to John Counsel of The Profit Clinic; Caroline Dauteuille, Jeffrey E. Edelheit, and Mike Gearhart of CMStat Corporation; Dave Hagan, Jr. and Ernie Preston of General Tool and Repair; Doug Laughter of The Silver Connection; John Moen of Graphic Maps; Brennan Mulligan of Timbuk2 Designs; John Raddatz of SoftBear Shareware; Sarah-Lou Reekie of Alfresco; Michael Rosenberg of Health Decisions; Judy Vorfeld of Office Support Services; and Marques Vickers.

I would also like to acknowledge some of my own colleagues who helped prepare and review the text and graphics of this book and who have supported and encouraged me in other lessons of life. Thanks to my friend and Stylus Media partner John Casler (jcasler@lucent.com), who taught me multitasking, and Ann Lindner, whose teaching experience proved invaluable in suggesting ways to make the text more clear.

For editing and technical assignments, I was lucky to be in the capable hands of the folks at Wiley Publishing: my project editors Paul Levesque and Kala Schrager, my copy editor Nicole Laux, and technical editor Jim McCarter.

Thanks also to Neil Salkind and David and Sherry Rogelberg of Studio B, and to Terri Varveris of Wiley Publishing for helping me to add this book to the list of those I've authored and, in the process, to broaden my expertise as a writer.

Last but certainly not least, the future is in the hands of the generation of my two daughters, Zosia and Lucy, who allow me to learn from the curiosity and joy with which they approach life.

Publisher's Acknowledgments

We're proud of this book; please send us your comments through our online registration form located at `www.dummies.com/register/`.

Some of the people who helped bring this book to market include the following:

Acquisitions, Editorial, and Media Development

Project Editors: Kala Schrager, Paul Levesque

Acquisitions Editor: Theresa Varveris

Copy Editor: Nicole Laux

Technical Editor: Jim McCarter

Editorial Director: Mary Corder

Media Development Manager: Laura VanWinkle

Media Development Supervisor: Richard Graves

Editorial Assistant: Amanda Foxwoth

Production

Project Coordinator: Maridee Ennis

Layout and Graphics: Kristin McMullan, Jackie Nicholas, Jacque Schneider, Jeremey Unger, Erin Zeltner

Quality Control Technicians: Andy Hollandbeck, Linda Quigley

Proofreaders: TECHBOOKS

Indexer: TECHBOOKS

General and Administrative

Wiley Publishing Technology Publishing Group: Richard Swadley, Vice President and Executive Group Publisher; Bob Ipsen, Vice President and Group Publisher; Joseph Wikert, Vice President and Publisher; Barry Pruett, Vice President and Publisher; Mary Bednarek, Editorial Director; Mary C. Corder, Editorial Director; Andy Cummings, Editorial Director

Wiley Publishing Manufacturing: Ivor Parker, Vice President, Manufacturing

Wiley PublishingMarketing: John Helmus, Assistant Vice President, Director of Marketing

Vice President of Production Services: Gerry Fahey

Wiley Publishing Composition for Branded Press: Debbie Stailey, Composition Director

Wiley Publishing Sales: Michael Violano, Vice President, International Sales and Sub Rights

Contents at a Glance

Cartoons at a Glance

By Rich Tennant

"See? I created a little felon figure that runs around our Web site hiding behind banner ads. On the last page, our logo puts him in a non lethal choke hold and brings him back to the home page."

page 189

"Can someone please tell me how long 'Larry's Lunch Truck' has had his own page on the intranet?"

page 9

"Just how accurately should my Web site reflect my place of business?"

page 85

"They were selling contraband online. We broke through the door just as they were trying to flush the hard drive down the toilet."

page 257

"Sales on the Web site are down. I figure the server's chi is blocked, so we're fudgin' around the feng shui in the computer room, and if that doesn't work, Ronnie's got a chant that should do it."

page 309

"So far our Web presence has been pretty good. We've gotten some orders, a few inquiries, and nine guys who want to date our logo."

page D-1

Cartoon Information:
Fax: 978-546-7747
E-Mail: richtennant@the5thwave.com
World Wide Web: www.the5thwave.com

Table of Contents

Introduction

You've been thinking about starting your own business, but until now, it's been just a dream. After all, you're a busy person. You have a full-time job, whether it's running your home or working outside your home. Or perhaps you've been through some life-changing event and are ready to take off in a new direction. Then, the economy took a turn for the worse, and you were understandably reluctant to make a big career change.

Well, I have news for you: *Now* is the perfect time to turn your dream into reality by starting your own online business — even now that the euphoria surrounding dot-com startups has passed and people are taking a more realistic look at e-commerce. Many people just like you are making money and enriching their lives by operating businesses online. The clock and your location are no longer limiting factors. Small business owners can now work any time of the night or day in their spare bedroom, local library, or neighborhood coffee shop.

If you like the idea of being in business for yourself, but you don't have a particular product or service in mind at the moment, relax and keep yourself open for inspiration. Many different kinds of commercial enterprises can hit it big on the Internet. Among the entrepreneurs I interviewed for this book are a woman who sells her own insect repellent, a mapmaker, a woman who provides office services for the medical community, a hardware salesman, a sculptor and painter, and several folks who create Web pages for other businesses. With the help of this book, you can start a new endeavor and be in charge of your own cyberbusiness, too.

You Can Do It!

What's that? You say you wouldn't know a merchant account, profit-and-loss statement, or clickthrough advertising rate if it came up to you on the street and introduced itself? Don't worry: The Internet (and this book) level the playing field, so a novice has just as good a chance at succeeding as MBAs who love to throw around business terms at cocktail parties.

The Internet is pretty much an accepted part of the business landscape these days. Whether you've been in business for 20 years or 20 minutes, the keys to success are the same:

✔ **Having a good idea:** If you have something to sell that people have an appetite for, and if your competition is slim, your chances of success are hefty.

✔ **Working hard:** When you are your own boss, you can make yourself work harder than any of your former bosses ever could. But if you put in the effort and persist through the inevitable ups and downs, you will be a winner.

✔ **Preparing for success:** One of the most surprising and useful things I learned from the online businesspeople that I interviewed was that if you believe that you will succeed, you probably will. Believe in yourself and proceed as though you're going to be successful. Together with your good ideas and hard work, your confidence will pay off.

If you're the cautious type who wants to test the waters before you launch your new business on the Internet, let this book lead you gently up the learning curve. After you're online, you can master techniques to improve your presence. This book includes helpful hints for doing market research and reworking your Web site until you get the success you want. Even if you aren't among the lucky small business owners who make a fortune by connecting to the Net, the odds are very good that you will make new friends, build your confidence, and have fun, too.

The Water's Still Fine

When I first started revising this new edition in early 2002, I posed some hard questions to business consultants and business owners alike. I was concerned about the future of e-commerce for the very entrepreneurs this book seeks to help — individuals who are starting their first businesses on the Web.

My fears quickly evaporated when I began to interview friends and colleagues who do business online. They're either thriving or at least treading water, and they enthusiastically encourage others to jump right in — the water's fine.

This is still a great time to start an online business. People who are getting into e-commerce today have advantages over those who started out three or four years ago. Simply put, both consumers and businesses are smarter. "There are more experts in the field so that it is easier to make things happen," says Sarah-Lou Reekie, an online entrepreneur I profile in Chapter 10. "The world is far more *au fait* and switched on to the Web. The percentage of people able to competently order is far higher. People aren't as nervous as they were to put through credit cards. After an amazingly short time, the Web has changed from an unknown and somewhat scary medium to something as easy as ABC for most users."

"I feel the best time to start an online business is when you are positioned to begin. I do not feel that there is an advantage/disadvantage to waiting for a 'better time' to start," says Mark Cramer, whose own online business and Web site are profiled in Chapter 16.

Where This Book Is Coming From

Online business isn't just for large corporations, or even just for small businesses that already have a storefront in the "real" world and simply want to supplement their marketability with a Web site.

The Internet is a perfect place for individuals who want to start their own business, who like using computers, and who believe that cyberspace is the place to do it. You don't need much money to get started, after all. If you already have a computer and an Internet connection and can create your own Web pages (which this book will help you with), making the move to your own business Web site may cost only $100 or less. After you're online, the overhead is pretty reasonable, too: You may pay only $15 to $75 per month to a Web hosting service to keep your site online.

With each month that goes by, the number of Internet users increases exponentially. To be precise, in early 2002 the U.S. Commerce Department released census data indicating that (as of September 2001) more than 143 million individuals in the U.S. (more than 50 percent of the population) used the Internet, and that Internet use in 2001 grew at a rate of *two million* new users per month. We have now reached that critical mass where *most* people are using the Internet regularly for everyday shopping and other financial activities. The Internet is already becoming a powerhouse for small businesses.

So why wait to fall behind your competition? The goal of this book is to help you open your fledgling business on the Internet now. Let this book guide you through the following steps:

- ✔ Preparing a business plan, defining your target market, and setting goals
- ✔ Purchasing the hardware and software you need to run your business
- ✔ Making your Web pages content-rich and interactive
- ✔ Marketing to customers around the world
- ✔ Creating a secure environment for shopping and receiving payments online
- ✔ Keeping your business records and observing legal requirements

How to Use This Book

Want to get an overview of the whole process of going online and be inspired by one family's online business success story? Zip ahead to Chapter 1. Want to find out how to accept credit card payments? Flip ahead to Chapter 9. Feel free to skip back and forth to chapters that interest you. I've made this book into an easy-to-use reference tool that you will be comfortable with, no matter what your level of experience with computers and networking. You don't have to scour each chapter methodically from beginning to end to find what you want. The Net doesn't work that way and neither does this book!

If you're just starting out and need to do some essential business planning, see Chapter 2. If you want to prepare a shopping list of business equipment, see Chapter 3. Chapters 4 through 11 are all about the essential aspects of creating and operating a successful online business, from organizing and marketing your Web site to providing effective online customer service. Later chapters get into security, legal issues, and accounting. The fun thing about being online is that continually improving and redoing your presentation is easy. So start where it suits you and come back later for more.

What This Book Assumes

This book assumes that you have never been in business before but that you're interested in setting up your own commercial site on the Internet or America Online. I also assume that you're familiar with the Internet, have been surfing for a while, and may even have put out some information of your own in the form of a home page.

It also assumes that you have or are ready to get the following:

- ✔ **A computer and a modem:** Don't worry, Chapter 3 explains exactly what hardware and software you need.

- ✔ **Instructions on how to think like a businessperson:** I spend a good amount of time in this book encouraging you to set goals, devise strategies to meet those goals, and do the sort of planning that successful businesspeople need to do.

- ✔ **Just enough technical know-how:** You don't have to do it all yourself. Plenty of entrepreneurs decide to partner with someone or hire an expert to perform design and technical work. This book can help you understand your options and give you a basic vocabulary so that you can work productively with the consultants you hire.

What's Where in This Book

This book is divided into five parts and an Internet Directory.

Part 1: Starting Your Own Online Business

In Part I, I describe what you need to do and how you need to *think* in order to start your new online business. The first chapter follows the story about how a business started by an 11-year-old boy and his family has grown into an Internet success story. Subsequent chapters also present case studies profiling other entrepreneurs and describing how they started their online businesses. Within these pages is where I also describe the software that you need in order to create Web pages and perform essential business tasks, along with any computer upgrades that will help your business run more smoothly.

Part II: Putting Your Web Site to Work

Even if you use an online service that isn't technically part of the Web, such as America Online, you need to create a Web site — a series of interconnected Web pages that everyone in cyberspace can view with a Web browser. As far as online business is concerned, the Web is where it's at. This part explains how to create a compelling and irresistible Web site, one that attracts paying customers around the world and keeps them coming back to make more purchases. This part also includes options for accepting electronic cash or credit card payments from your customers.

Part III: Promoting Your Online Business

Your work doesn't end after you put your Web site online or start to make a few sales. In fact, what you do after you open your cyberdoors for business can make the difference between a site that says "Wow!" and one that says "Ho-hum." In this part, I describe cost-effective marketing and advertising techniques that you can do yourself to increase visibility and improve customer satisfaction.

Part IV: Law, Security, and Accounting

This part delves into some less-than-sexy but essential activities for any online business. Find out about general security methods designed to make commerce more secure on the Internet. I also discuss copyrights, trademarks, and other legal concerns for anyone wanting to start a company in the increasingly competitive atmosphere of the Internet. Finally, you get an overview of basic accounting practices for online businesses and suggestions of accounting tools that you can use to keep track of your e-commerce activities.

The Starting an Online Business For Dummies Internet Directory

If you're running your online business in your off-hours or between other activities, you don't have time to scour the Web for help. Not to fear: You can find everything you need in this directory. It's a collection of Web sites and other Internet resources of special interest to individuals starting an online business — especially if you're working alone or at home and need to find people to help you.

Part V: The Part of Tens

Filled with tips, cautions, suggestions, and examples, the Part of Tens presents many tidbits of information that you can use to plan and create your own business presence on the Internet.

Conventions Used in This Book

In this book, I format important bits of information in special ways to make sure that you notice them right away:

- **In This Chapter lists:** Starting at the very beginning, every chapter begins with a list of the topics that I cover in that chapter. This list represents a kind of table of contents in miniature.

- **Numbered lists:** When you see a numbered list, follow the steps in a specific order to accomplish a given task.

- **Bulleted lists:** Bulleted lists (like this one) indicate things that you can do in any order or list related bits of information.

✔ **Web addresses:** When I describe activities or sites of interest on the World Wide Web, I include the address, or Uniform Resource Locator (URL), in a special typeface like this: `http://www.wiley.com/`. Because the newer versions of popular Web browsers, such as Netscape Navigator and Microsoft Internet Explorer, don't require you to enter the entire URL, this book uses the shortened addresses. For example, if you want to connect to the Wiley Publishing site, you can get there by simply entering the following in your browser's Go To box: `www.wiley.com`.

Don't be surprised if your browser can't find an Internet address you type or if a Web page that's depicted in this book no longer looks the same. Although the sites were current when the book was written, Web addresses (and sites themselves) can be pretty fickle. Try looking for a missing site by using an Internet search engine. Or try shortening the address by deleting everything after the `.com` (or `.org` or `.edu`).

Icons Used in This Book

Starting an Online Business For Dummies, 3rd Edition, also uses special graphical elements called *icons* to get your attention. Here's what they look like and what they mean:

This icon points out some technical details that may be of interest to you. A thorough understanding, however, isn't a prerequisite to grasping the underlying concept. Non-techies are welcome to skip items marked by this icon altogether.

This icon calls your attention to interviews I conducted with online entrepreneurs who provided tips and instructions for running an online business.

This icon flags practical advice about particular software programs or about issues of importance to businesses. Look to these tips for help with finding resources quickly, making sales, or improving the quality of your online business site. This icon also alerts you to software programs and other resources that I consider to be especially good, especially for the novice user.

This icon points out potential pitfalls that can develop into more major problems if you're not careful.

This icon alerts you to facts and figures that are important to keep in mind as you run your online business.

We're in It Together

Improving communication is the whole point of this book. My goal is to help you express yourself in the exciting new medium of the Internet and to remind you that you're not alone. I'm a businessperson myself, after all. So I hope that you'll let me know what you think about this book by contacting me. Check out the Wiley Publishing Book Registration page at the back of this book for information about registering this book and sending your feedback. And remember to check out the *For Dummies* Web site at www.dummies.com.

You're also welcome to contact me directly if you have questions or comments. Visit my personal Web page at www.gregholden.com, or send e-mail to me at gholden@interaccess.com.

Part I
Starting Your Own Online Business

The 5th Wave   By Rich Tennant

"Can someone please tell me how long 'Larry's Lunch Truck' has had his own page on the intranet?"

In this part . . .

What all does starting an online business involve? In this part, I answer that question with a brief overview of the whole process. The following chapters help you set your online business goals and draw up a blueprint for meeting those goals.

And just as dentists prepare their drills and carpenters assemble their tools, you need to gather the necessary hardware and software to keep your online business running smoothly. So, in this part, I discuss the business equipment that the online store owner needs and suggest ways that you can meet those needs even on a limited budget.

Let the step-by-step instructions and real-life case studies in this part guide you through the process of starting a successful business online.

Chapter 1

Opening Your Own Online Business in Ten Easy Steps

In This Chapter

▶ Taking one step at a time toward starting an online business

▶ Developing practical strategies for turning your ideas into realities

▶ Getting connected and creating a commercial Web site

▶ Marketing your business to your targeted customers

▶ Evaluating your success and revising your site

*T*hese days, virtually every existing company seems to be adding a Web site with an address like www.company.com to its arsenal of business tools. But the steps required to conduct commerce online are well within the reach of individuals like you and me who have no prior business experience. Companies are continually releasing new programs or starting up new services that make creating Web pages and transacting online business easier than ever. All you need is a good idea, a bit of start-up money, some computer equipment, and a little help from your friends.

One of my goals in this book is to be one of the friends who provides you with the right advice and support to get your business online and make it a success. In this chapter, I give you a step-by-step overview of the entire process of starting an online business.

Step 1: Identify a Need

A lot of people are buying and selling online. (See the sidebar "A hotbed of commerce" if you don't believe me.) Still, all this cyber-buying doesn't mean that starting an online business is a sure thing. After all, you can't expect Web surfers to patronize your online business unless you identify services or items that they really need. Your first job is to get in touch with your market (the people who'll be buying your stuff or using your services) and determine how you can best meet its needs.

A hotbed of commerce

Statistically, the Internet is a hotbed of commerce — and it just keeps getting hotter. Listen to what the experts are saying:

✔ **BizRate** (www.bizrate.com), in early 2002, raised its online retail sales estimates from what it had previously projected. The company estimated that consumer online sales in the U.S. would jump 44 percent between 2001 and 2002. BizRate also found that shoppers spent an average of $127 per purchase in the first quarter of 2002, up from an average $120 spent in the first quarter of 2001.

✔ **Statistics Canada** (www.statcan.ca), the Canadian government's central statistical agency, recently reported that e-commerce sales in Canada more than doubled, jumping from $417 million in 1999 to $1.1 billion in 2000.

✔ **eMarketer** (www.emarketer.com) predicts that worldwide revenues from e-commerce will hit $75 billion in 2002 and reach $155.6 billion by 2005.

Check out the *Starting an Online Business For Dummies*, 3rd Edition, Internet Directory, later in this book for more sites where you can gather "fast facts" and background information on doing business online.

Understanding the marketplace

The Internet is a worldwide, interconnected network of computers to which people can connect either from work or home, and through which people can communicate via e-mail, receive information from the Web, and buy and sell items using credit cards or other means.

Many people decide to start an online business with little more than a casual knowledge of the Internet. But when you decide to get serious about going online with a commercial endeavor, it pays to get to know the environment in which you plan to be working.

One of your first steps should be to find out what it means to do business online and to determine the best ways for you to fit into the exploding field of electronic commerce. For example, you need to realize that the Internet is a personal place; that customers are active, not passive, in the way they absorb information; and that the Net was established within a culture of people sharing information freely and helping one another.

Some of the best places to learn about the culture of the Internet are the newsgroups, chat rooms, and bulletin boards where individuals gather and exchange messages online. Visiting discussion forums devoted to topics that interest you personally can be especially helpful, and you're likely to end up participating yourself. Also visit commerce Web sites, such as online marketplaces, and take note of ideas and approaches that you may want to use.

Seeing what's out there

The more information you have about the following aspects of the online world, the more likely you are to succeed in doing business online:

- **Competition:** Familiarize yourself with other online businesses that already do what you want to do.

- **Customers:** Investigate the various kinds of customers who shop online and who might visit your site.

- **Environment:** Explore the special language and style of online communication — in other words, know the culture of the Internet.

As you take a look around the Internet, notice the kinds of goods and services that tend to sell in the increasingly crowded, occasionally disorganized, and sometimes complex online world. The things that sell best in cyberspace include the following:

- Items sold at a discount

- Hard-to-find or unique items

- Items that are easier to buy online than at a "real" store, such as a rare book that you can order in minutes from Amazon.com (www.amazon.com), or an electronic greeting card that you can send online in seconds (www.greeting-cards.com)

- Publications available by subscription, such as newspapers and magazines, or electronic publications (*ezines*) that exist only online

Visit one of the tried-and-true indexes to the Internet, such as Yahoo! (www.yahoo.com), or a search service, such as Google (www.google.com). Enter a word or phrase in the site's home page search box that describes the kind of goods or services you want to provide online. Find out how many existing businesses already do what you want to do. Better yet, determine what they *don't* do, and set a goal of meeting that specialized need yourself.

Figuring out what's missing

After you take a look at what's already out there, the next step is to find ways to make your business stand out from the crowd. Direct your energies toward making your site unique in some way and providing things that others don't offer. The things that set your online business apart from the rest can be as tangible as half-price sales, contests, seasonal sales, or freebies. They can also involve making your business site higher in quality than the others.

What if you can't find other online businesses doing what you want to do? Lucky you! In electronic commerce, being first often means getting a head start and being more successful than latecomers, even if they have more resources than you do. (Just ask the owners of the online bookstore Amazon.com.) Don't be afraid to try something new and outlandish. It just might work!

CASE STUDY

The Podraza family finds its online niche

When 11-year-old Michael Podraza received his first two Beanie Babies as gifts in the fall of 1996, he decided to become an avid collector. In case you don't know, Beanie Babies are little plush animals produced by Ty Inc. (www.ty.com). In the years since they first appeared in 1996, Beanies have become hot items, especially those that Ty strategically "retired" before the retirement of the entire Beanie line was announced in 1999. Although the critters retail for about $5, some scarce varieties can sell for as much as $800 or even up to $5,000.

Michael's father, Dan Podraza, drove him to flea markets and swap meets, where they looked long and hard for particular Beanies. Dan started to think that there must be a better way to locate these little treasures — and that there must also be lots of collectors like Michael who were eager to buy and sell them.

One day, Michael heard two women in a store discussing how difficult it was to find certain varieties of Beanie Babies, and how much they might pay for the Beanies if they could find them. Michael ended up selling the toys, which had originally cost $5, to the women for $25 and $30.

Dan Podraza's 15-year-old son, Christopher, introduced him to the Web. The Podrazas didn't know much about the Internet or online commerce at the time they jumped on the cybercommerce bandwagon. "I've been a high school math teacher for 29 years," Dan explains. "I've never sold anything before."

Although Beanie Baby publications, businesses, and Web sites are plentiful these days, in mid-1997, no Web sites at all were set up to exchange Beanie Babies. "We visited other Beanie Baby Web sites, but none of them sold Beanies," says Dan Podraza. "We knew that lots of people were interested, though. We often saw messages that people left on electronic bulletin boards, asking where they could go to find these things."

The family decided to start the Collectible Exchange, Ltd., a Web site that brought buyers and sellers together to make transactions. (They have recently changed the name to CollectibleX.com.) They had no idea how well it would do, but they had determined two essential things: There was a market for this product, and there was a need for a service that did not yet exist online.

CollectibleX.com now employs six full-time and three part-time workers (all family members and neighbors), and its Web site (www.collectiblex.com) receives 50,000 visits each day. When I spoke to Dan Podraza in early 2002, he was in the midst of redesigning the site for a new look and more automated online transaction system. It's an investment of $60,000 in the face of an economic slowdown. The business has now expanded to trade in many different kinds of collectibles.

E-commerce can be complex and expensive; it depends on your goals for your online business. But not so long ago, the Podrazas, like you, were just starting out, and they, too, had only a dream and the courage to explore something new. I hope that their story will inspire you to turn your own online business into a reality as well.

Step 2: Determine What You Have to Offer

What business is all about, either online or off, is identifying customers' needs and figuring out exactly what goods or services you're going to provide to meet those needs. (Often, you perform this step before or at the same time that you scope out what the business needs are and figure out how you can position yourself to meet those needs, as I explain in the earlier section "Step 1: Identify a Need.")

To determine what you have to offer, make a list of all the items you have to put up for sale, or all the services you plan to provide to your customers. Next, you need to decide not only what goods or services you can provide online, but also where you're going to obtain them. Are you going to create sale items yourself? Are you going to purchase them from another supplier? Jot down your ideas on paper and keep them close at hand as you develop your business plan.

The Internet is a personal, highly interactive medium. Be as specific as possible with what you plan to do online. The medium favors businesses that specialize. After all, the more specific your business, the more intimate you can be with your customers.

Step 3: Set Your Cyberbusiness Goals

The process of setting goals and objectives and then designing strategies for attaining them is essential when starting a new business. What you end up with is called a *business plan*. A good business plan applies not only to the start-up phase but also to a business's day-to-day operation. It can also be instrumental in helping a small business obtain a bank loan.

Creating a business plan

To set specific goals for your new business, ask yourself these questions:

- ✔ Why do you want to start a business?
- ✔ Why do you want to start it online?
- ✔ What would you want to buy online?
- ✔ What would make you buy it?

Sure, I can give you plenty of reasons for setting up virtual shop on the Internet. But only *you* can answer these questions for yourself. Make sure that you have a clear idea of where you're going so that you can commit to making your venture successful over the long haul. (See Chapter 2 for more on setting goals and envisioning your business.)

To carry your plan into your daily operations, observe these suggestions:

- ✔ Write a brief description of your company and what you hope to accomplish with it.
- ✔ Draw up a marketing strategy. (See Chapters 8 and 11 for tips.)
- ✔ Keep track of your finances. (See Chapter 14 for specifics.)

Consider using specialized software to help you prepare your business plan. Programs such as Business Plan Pro by Palo Alto Software (`www.palo-alto.com`) lead you through the process by asking you a series of questions as a way of identifying what you want to do. The program retails for $99.95.

If you set aside part of your home for business purposes, you are eligible for tax deductions. Exactly how much you can deduct depends on how much space you use. (For example, I have a nine-room house, and one room serves as my office, so I am able to deduct one-ninth of my utility and other housing costs.) You can depreciate your computers and other business equipment, too. On the other hand, your municipality may require you to obtain a license if you operate a business in a residential area; check with your local authorities to make sure that you're on the up-and-up. You can find out more about tax and legal issues, including local licensing requirements, in Chapters 13 and 14 of this book.

Step 4: Assemble Your Equipment and Set Up Your "Store"

Not all businesses cost thousands of dollars to start up. As many of the entrepreneurs that I profile in the case studies throughout this book report, you can start an online business with an investment of only a few hundred dollars, or perhaps even less.

In addition to your virtual storefront, you also have to find a real place to do your business. You don't necessarily have to rent a large space with both men's and women's bathrooms, as the Podrazas did. Many online entrepreneurs use a home office or perhaps a corner in a room where computers, books, and other related equipment reside.

Finding a Web host

Any business needs a place to call home. Although doing business online means that you don't have to rent space in a mall or open a real, physical store, you do have to set up a virtual space for your online business. You do so by creating a Web site and finding a host for your site. In cyberspace, your landlord is called a Web hosting service. A Web *host* is a company that, for a fee, makes your site available 24 hours a day by maintaining it on a special computer called a Web *server*.

A Web host can be as large and well-known as America Online, which gives all its customers a place to create and publish their own Web pages. Some Web sites, such as Yahoo! GeoCities (`geocities.yahoo.com`), or Tripod (`www.tripod.lycos.com`), act as hosting services and provide easy-to-use Web site creation tools as well. In addition, the company that gives you access to the Internet — your Internet service provider (ISP) — may also publish your Web pages.

Make sure that your host has a fast connection to the Internet and can handle the large numbers of simultaneous visits, or *hits*, that your Web site is sure to get eventually. You can find a detailed description of Web hosting options in Chapter 4.

In Chapter 2, I describe two methods for selling your wares online that don't require a Web site — online classifieds and auctions. But most online businesses find having a Web site indispensable for generating and conducting sales. And hosts like America Online and Yahoo! make it easier than ever to create your own site, as I discuss in Chapter 4.

Getting the hardware you need

For doing business online, your most important piece of equipment is your computer. Other hardware, such as scanners, modems, and monitors, are essential, too. You need to make sure that your computer equipment is up to snuff because you're going to be spending a lot of time online: answering e-mail, checking orders, revising your Web site, and marketing your product.

The Podrazas, profiled earlier in this chapter, decided to make a substantial commitment to the success of their online business by investing in a solid hardware system. Dan Podraza says they spent about $6,000 purchasing and setting up computers to handle orders. They have six computers in their business that are networked together so that they can all access the company's database.

Keeping track of your inventory

As Dan Podraza points out, making sure that you have sufficient inventory to meet demand is important. Having too many items for sale is preferable to not having enough. "We operated on a low budget in the beginning, and we didn't have the inventory that people wanted," Dan points out. "People online get impatient if they have to wait for things too long. Make sure you have the goods you advertise. Plan to be successful."

CollectibleX.com keeps track of its inventory by using a PostgreSQL database that's connected to its Web site. When someone orders a product from the Web site, that order is automatically recorded in the database, which then produces an order for replacement stock.

In this kind of arrangement, the database serves as a so-called *back end* or *back office* to the Web-based storefront. This is a sophisticated arrangement that's not for beginners. However, if orders and inventory get to be too much for you to handle yourself, consider hiring a Web developer to set up such a system for you. If you're adventurous and technically oriented, you can link a database to a Web site by using a product such as FrontPage or Dreamweaver.

Computer-related equipment will probably be your main expense. It pays to shop wisely and get the best setup you can afford up front so that you don't have to purchase upgrades later on. (For more suggestions on buying business hardware and software, see Chapter 3.)

Choosing your software

For the most part, the programs you need in order to operate an online business are the same as the software you use to surf the Internet. You do, however, need to have a wider variety of tools than you would use for simple information gathering.

Because you're going to be in the business of information *providing* now, as well as information gathering, you need programs such as the following:

- ✔ **A Web page editor:** These programs, which you may also hear called *Web page creation tools* or *Web page authoring tools,* make it easy for you to format text, add images, and design Web pages without having to learn HyperText Markup Language (HTML), the set of instructions that Web browsers use to present those pages the way you want them.

- ✔ **Graphics software:** If you decide to create your business Web site yourself, rather than find someone to do it for you, you need a program that can help you draw or edit images that you want to include on your site.

✔ **Storefront software:** You can purchase software that leads you through the process of creating a full-fledged online business and getting your pages on the Web.

✔ **Accounting programs:** To keep track of expenses and income, you can use software that acts as a spreadsheet, helps you with billing, and even calculates sales tax.

Step 5: Find the Support You Need

Conducting online business does involve relatively new technologies, but they aren't impossible to learn. In fact, the technology is becoming more accessible all the time, thanks to more powerful and affordable software.

Many of the people who start online businesses learn how to create Web pages and promote their companies by reading books, attending classes, or networking with friends and colleagues. Of course, just because you *can* do it all doesn't mean that you have to. Often, you're better off hiring help, either to advise you in areas where you aren't as strong or simply to help you tackle the growing workload.

Hiring technical consultants

It often pays to have professionals point you in the right direction and help you develop an effective Web presence. Many businesspeople who usually work alone (myself included) hire knowledgeable individuals to do design or programming work that they would find impossible to tackle otherwise.

Don't be reluctant to hire professional help in order to get your business online. The Web is full of development firms that perform several related functions: providing customers with Web access, helping to create Web sites, and hosting sites on their servers. The expense for such services may be considerable at first (Dan Podraza estimates that CollectibleX.com's start-up costs were $12,000, not counting hardware purchases), but they can pay off in the long term. Choose a designer carefully, he says. "Thoroughly check out sites they've done before. Tell them your business plan, and spell out clearly what you want each page to do. It pays to surround yourself with the right people and let them handle the technical aspects of your site."

Another area where you may want to find help is in networking and computer maintenance. As Dan Podraza points out, "Along with having the knowledge of your product, you have to know how to keep your computers running. Find out if you have a computer expert in your neighborhood."

Who are the people in your neighborhood?

Try to find an expert or helper right in your own neighborhood. In my own case, I work with a graphic designer who lives right around the corner from me, and he uses a consultant who lives across the street from him. Ask around your school or church, as well as other social venues. Your neighbors may be able to help you with various projects, including your online business . . . and your online business just may be able to help them, too.

Businesspeople who provide professional services also commonly recommend other consultants in the course of e-mail communications. Don't work in a vacuum. Participate in mailing lists and discussion groups online. Make contacts and strike up cooperative relationships with individuals who can help you.

If you do find a business partner, make sure that the person's abilities balance your own. If you're great at sales and public relations, for example, find a writer or Web page designer to partner with.

Gathering your team members

Many entrepreneurial businesses are family affairs. For example, a husband-and-wife team started Scaife's Butcher Shop in England, which has a successful Web site (www.jackscaife.co.uk). CollectibleX.com is another example: Besides Dan Podraza, his wife, Diana, and their children, Bradley and Jennifer, the company employs Grandfather John (bill payments), Grandma Jean (receiving), and son Christopher (straightening up and day-to-day maintenance). (Michael is too young to be a paid employee.) Two friends of the Podrazas, Veronique and Mike, function as CollectibleX.com's office managers, performing essential functions, such as downloading orders and answering e-mail inquiries.

Early on, when you have plenty of time to do planning, you probably won't feel a pressing need to hire others to help you. Many people wait to seek help until they have a deadline to meet or are in a financial crunch. Waiting to seek help is okay — as long as you realize that you will need help, sooner or later.

Of course, you don't need to hire family and friends, but you do need to find people who are reliable and can make a long-term commitment to your project. Keep these things in mind:

- ✔ Because the person you hire will probably work online quite a bit, pick someone who already exhibits high-tech experience.

- ✔ Online hiring practices work pretty much the same as those offline: You should always review a resume, get at least three references, and ask for samples of the candidate's work.

✔ Pick someone who responds promptly and courteously and who provides the talents you need.

✔ If your only contact is by phone and e-mail, references are even more important.

Step 6: Build a Web Site

A Web site is pretty much indispensable for any online business these days. Fortunately, Web sites are becoming easier to create. You don't have to know a line of HTML in order to create an effective Web page yourself. Chapter 6 walks you through the specific tasks involved in organizing and designing Web pages. Also, see Chapter 7 for tips on making your Web pages content-rich and interactive.

Make your business easy to find online. Pick a Web address (otherwise known as a URL, or Uniform Resource Locator) that's easy to remember. You can purchase a short domain-name alias, such as `www.company.com`, to replace a longer one like `www.internetprovider.com/~username/companyname/index.html`. See "What's in a name?" in Chapter 4 for more information on domain name aliases.

Creating compelling content

Content is the most important part of any Web site. The more useful information you provide, the more visits your site will receive. By compelling content, I'm talking about words, headings, or images that induce visitors to interact with your site in some way. You can make your content compelling in a number of ways:

✔ Provide a call to action, such as "Click Here!" or "Buy Now!".

✔ Explain how the reader will benefit by clicking a link and exploring your site ("Visit our News and Specials page to find out how to win 500 frequent flyer miles").

✔ Briefly and concisely summarize your business and its mission.

✔ Scan or use a digital camera to capture images of your sale items (or of the services you provide) as I describe in Chapter 6, and post them on a Web page called Products.

Don't forget the personal touch when it comes to connecting with your customers' needs. People who shop online don't get to meet their merchants in person, so anything you can tell about yourself helps to personalize the process and put your visitors at ease, as shown in Figure 1-1. Let your cybervisitors know that they're dealing with real people, not remote machines and computer programs.

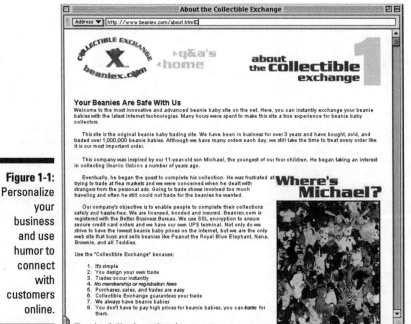

Figure 1-1:
Personalize your business and use humor to connect with customers online.

Peeking in on other businesses' Web sites — to pick up ideas and see how they handle similar issues — is a natural practice. In cyberspace, you can visit plenty of businesses from the comfort of your home office that are comparable to yours, and the trip takes only minutes.

Establishing a graphic identity

A site with an identity looks a certain way. For example, take a look at Figure 1-2, as well as Figure 1-3 later in this chapter. Both pages are from the CollectibleX.com Web site. Notice how each has the same white background, the same company logo, and similar heading styles. Using such elements consistently from page to page creates an identity that gives your business credibility and helps viewers find what they're looking for.

CollectibleX.com's Web pages look simple because they are uncluttered and use a clean white background. But the pages, which a consultant creates, are actually pretty complex. The pages employ advanced layout options, such as image maps (images that have been divided into clickable regions), tables, headings that are actually graphic images, and interactive forms. See Chapter 6 for more about such advanced layout options.

Figure 1-2:
Through careful planning and design, the CollectibleX.com site maintains a consistent look and feel, or graphic identity, on each page.

Step 7: Set Up Systems for Handling Sales

Many businesses go online and then are surprised by their own success. They don't have systems in place for finalizing sales and tracking finances and inventory.

Early on, CollectibleX.com found itself in just such a predicament. It operated on a low budget and initially suffered from insufficient inventory. To reiterate Don Podraza's point (see the "Keeping track of your inventory" sidebar earlier in this chapter), make sure that you have the goods you advertise. Plan to be successful.

An excellent way to plan for success is to set up ways to track your business finances and to create a secure purchasing environment for your online customers. That way, you can build on your success rather than be surprised by it.

Providing a means for secure transactions

Getting paid is the key to survival as well as success. When your business exists only online, the payment process is not always straightforward. Make your Web site a safe and easy place for customers to pay you. Provide different payment options and build customers' level of trust any way you can.

Although the level of trust among people doing shopping online is increasing steadily, some Web surfers are still squeamish about submitting credit card numbers online. Make them feel at ease by explaining what measures you're taking to ensure that their information is secure. Such measures include signing up for an account with a Web host that provides a *secure server*, a computer that uses software to encrypt data and uses digital documents called certificates to ensure its identity. (See Chapters 9 and 12 for more on Internet security and secure shopping systems.)

Becoming a credit card merchant

The words *electronic commerce* or *e-commerce* bring to mind visions of online forms and credit card data that is transmitted over the Internet. Do you have to provide such service in order to run a successful online business? Not necessarily. Being a credit card merchant makes life easier for your customers, to be sure, but it also adds complications and extra costs to your operation.

To become a credit card merchant, you have to apply to a bank. Small and home-based businesses can have difficulty getting their applications approved. (Some businesses specialize in granting credit card merchant status to small businesses, however; see Chapter 9 for suggestions.)

If you do get the go-ahead to become a credit card merchant, you have to pay the bank a *discount rate*, which is a fee (typically, 2 to 3 percent of each transaction) to the bank. You sometimes have to pay a monthly premium charge of $10 to $25 as well. Besides that, you may need special software or hardware to accept credit card payments.

In the early stages of your business, you may find it easier to take orders over the phone. Remember that most of your customers probably don't have a second phone line for Internet access, however. They have to disconnect from the Internet to call and place their orders. Also invite them to send you an e-mail message that provides contact information and states what they want to order. Then, if your business takes off, you can present your sales records to the bank and be more likely to get your merchant application approved. See Chapter 9 for more on electronic commerce options for your business.

To maximize your sales by reaching users who either don't have credit cards or don't want to use them on the Internet, provide low-tech alternatives, such as toll-free phone numbers and fax numbers, so that people can provide you with information by using more familiar technologies.

One reason that the Podrazas' business succeeds is that it inspires the trust and confidence of its customers. The home page of the CollectibleX.com Web site, for example, contains the message "A Better Business Bureau Program." The site also provides a secure way for people to make electronic purchases by providing online forms, such as the one in Figure 1-3, where people can safely enter credit card and other personal information. The Sample Order page (`www.collectiblex.com/exchange/SampleOrder.jsp`) contains instructions on how to place orders and check on the status of those orders.

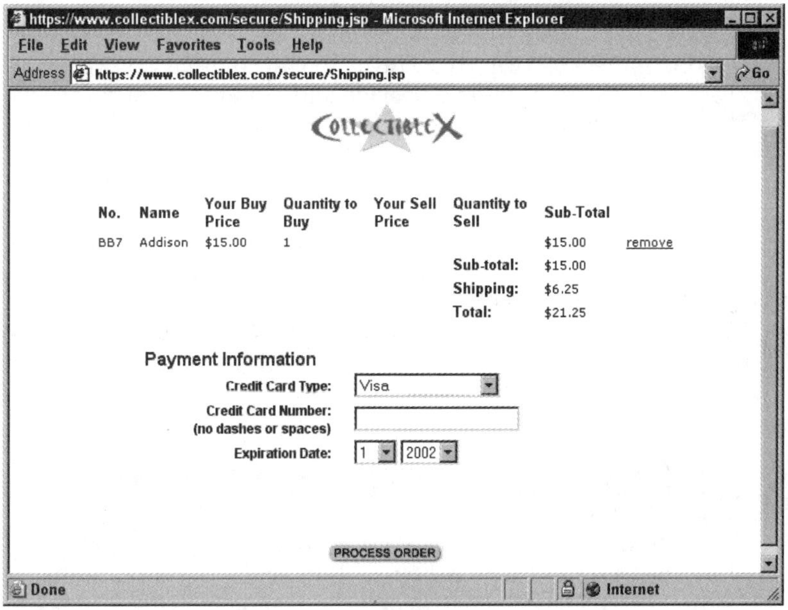

Figure 1-3:
A secure
electronic
commerce
site lets
shoppers
submit
information
that is
encrypted
so that
criminals
can't
access it.

				https://www.collectiblex.com/secure/Shipping.jsp - Microsoft Internet Explorer

File   Edit   View   Favorites   Tools   Help

Address https://www.collectiblex.com/secure/Shipping.jsp   Go

CollectibleX

No.	Name	Your Buy Price	Quantity to Buy	Your Sell Price	Quantity to Sell	Sub-Total	
BB7	Addison	$15.00	1			$15.00	remove
					Sub-total:	$15.00	
					Shipping:	$6.25	
					Total:	$21.25	

Payment Information

Credit Card Type: Visa

Credit Card Number:
(no dashes or spaces)

Expiration Date: 1   2002

PROCESS ORDER

Done   Internet

Safeguarding your customers' personal information is important, but you also need to safeguard yourself. Many online businesses get burned by bad guys who submit fraudulent credit card information. If you don't verify the information and submit it to your financial institution for processing, you're liable for the cost. Strongly consider signing up with a service that handles credit card verification for you in order to cut down on lost revenue.

Keeping your books straight

What does "keeping your books" mean, anyway? In the simplest sense, it means recording all financial activities that pertain to your business, including any expenses you incur, all the income you receive, as well as your equipment and tax deductions. The financial side of running a business also entails creating reports, such as profit-and-loss statements, that banks require if you apply for a loan. Such reports not only help meet financial institutions' needs but also provide you with essential information about how your business is really doing at any given time.

You can record all this information the old-fashioned way, by writing it down in ledgers and journals, or you can use accounting software. (See Chapter 14 for some suggestions of easy-to-use accounting packages that are great for financial novices.). Because you're making a commitment to using computers on a regular basis by starting an online business, it's only natural for you to use computers to keep your books, too. Accounting software can help you keep track of expenses and provide information that may save you some headaches at tax time. And after you've saved your financial data on disk, make backups so that you don't lose information you need to do business. See Chapter 12 for ways to back up and protect your files.

CollectibleX.com uses a popular program called QuickBooks to pay the salaries of its employees. The rest of the financial matters are handled with online banking services. Other businesses that I profile in subsequent chapters use popular programs, such as Quicken and Peachtree First Accounting, to keep their books.

Step 8: Provide Customer Service

The Internet, which runs on wires, cables, and computer chips, may not seem like a place for the personal touch. But technology didn't actually create the Internet and all its content; *people* did that. In fact, the Internet is a great place to provide your clients and customers with outstanding, personal customer service.

By helping your customers get their questions answered and problems resolved, you help yourself, too. You build loyalty as well as credibility among your clientele. For many small businesses, the key to competing effectively with larger competitors is by providing superior customer service. See Chapter 10 for more ideas on how you can do this.

Sharing your expertise

Your knowledge and experience are among your most valuable commodities. So you may be surprised when I suggest that you give them away for free. Why? It's a "try before you buy" concept. Helping people for free builds your credibility and makes them more likely to pay for your services down the road.

When your business is online, you can easily communicate what you know about your field and make your knowledge readily available. One way is to set up a Web page that presents the basics about your company and your field of interest in the form of Frequently Asked Questions (FAQs). Another technique is to become a virtual publisher/editor and create your own newsletter in which you write about what's new with your company and about topics related to your work. See Chapter 10 for more on communicating your expertise through FAQs, newsletters, and advanced e-mail techniques.

Becoming a resource for customers

Many *ontrepreneurs* (online entrepreneurs) succeed by making their Web sites not only a place for sales and promotion but also an indispensable resource, full of useful hyperlinks and other information, that customers want to visit again and again. For example, the CollectibleX.com, which I profile earlier in this chapter, acts as a resource, a meeting place, and a place to do buying and selling.

John Moen, a cartographer, knows the importance of making your site a resource for potential customers. He saw visits to his Graphic Maps business site (www.graphicmaps.com/ and www.graphicmaps.com/custmaps.htm) jump from 30 a day to 1,000 a day after he decided to give away free art (called *clip art*) that he had created. Today, he reports, "We are so busy, we literally can't keep up with the demand for custom maps. Almost 95 percent of our business leads come from the Web, and that includes many international companies and Web sites. Web page traffic has grown to more than 3 million hits per month, and banner advertising now pays very well."

John first took his business, Graphic Maps, online in 1995 for start-up costs of only $300. He now has six employees, receives many custom orders for more than $10,000, and has done business with numerous Fortune 500 companies. To promote his site, which is shown in Figure 1-4, John gives away free maps for nonprofit organizations, operates a daily geography contest with a $60 prize to the first person with the correct answer, and answers e-mail promptly. His site now includes an online store. "I feel strongly that the secret on the Web is to provide a solution for a problem, and for the most part, do it free," he suggests. "If the service is high-quality, and people get what they want . . . they will tell their friends and all will beat a path to your URL, and then, and only then, will you be able to sell your products to the world, in a way you never imagined was possible."

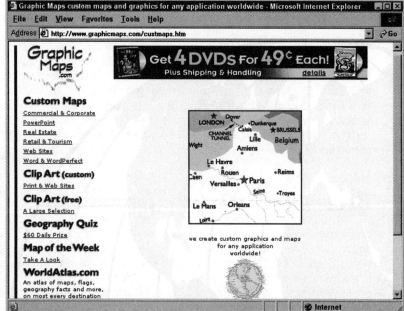

Figure 1-4:
This site
uses free
art, a
mailing list,
and daily
prizes to
drum up
business.

Another way to encourage customers to congregate at your site on a regular basis is to create a discussion area. In Chapter 10, I show you how to provide a discussion page right on your own Web site.

Becoming an e-mail expert

E-mail is, in my humble opinion, the single most important marketing tool that you can use to boost your online business. Becoming an expert e-mail user increases your contacts and provides you with new sources of support, too.

The two best and easiest e-mail strategies are the following:

- ✔ Check your e-mail as often as possible.
- ✔ Respond to e-mail inquiries immediately.

Additionally, you can e-mail inquiries about co-marketing opportunities to other Web sites similar to your own. Ask other online business owners if they will provide links to your site in exchange for your providing links to theirs.

And always include a signature file with your message that includes the name of your business and a link to your business site. See Chapter 10 for more information on using e-mail effectively to build and maintain relations with your online customers.

Step 9: Advertise Your Business

In order to be successful, small businesses need to get the word out to the people who are likely to purchase what they have to offer. If this group turns out to be only a narrow market, so much the better; the Internet is great for connecting to specialized "niche" markets that share a common interest. (See Chapters 8 and 11 for more on locating your most likely customers on the Internet and figuring out how best to communicate with them.)

The Internet provides many unique and effective ways for small businesses to advertise, including search services, e-mail, newsgroups, electronic mailing lists, and more.

Registering with Internet search services

How, exactly, do you get listed on the search engines such as Yahoo! and Lycos? Frankly, it's getting more difficult. Many of the big search services charge for listings. But some let you contribute a listing for free, though there's no guarantee if or when you'll see your site included in their database.

You can increase the chances that search services will list your site by including special keywords and site descriptions in the HTML commands for your Web pages. You place these keywords after a special HTML command (the <META> tag), making them invisible to the casual viewer of your site. Turn to Chapter 11 for details.

Reaching the entire Internet

Your Web site may be the cornerstone of your business, but if nobody knows it's out there, it can't help you generate sales. Perhaps the most familiar form of online advertising are *banner ads*, those little electronic billboards that seem to show up on every popular Web page that you visit.

But banner advertising can be expensive and may not be the best way for a small business to advertise online. In fact, the most effective marketing for CollectibleX.com hasn't been traditional banner advertising or newspaper/magazine placements. Rather, the Podrazas and their Web marketing consultants targeted electronic bulletin boards (such as the one shown in Figure 1-5) and mailing lists where people exchanged inquiries regarding where they could find Beanie Babies. When the Podrazas went online, they posted notices on the bulletin boards and sent e-mail messages to the same Beanie Baby collectors they had found on the bulletin boards and mailing lists, notifying them that their trading services were now available.

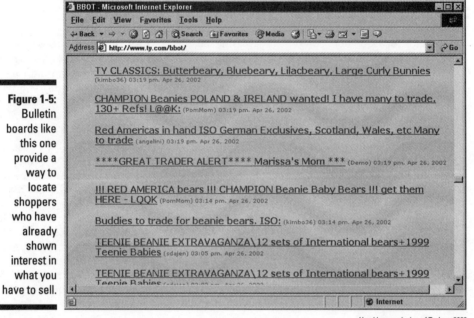

Figure 1-5: Bulletin boards like this one provide a way to locate shoppers who have already shown interest in what you have to sell.

Used by permission of Ty, Inc., 2002

This sort of direct, one-to-one marketing may seem tedious, but it's often the best way to develop a business on the Internet. Reach out to your potential customers and strike up an individual, personal relationship with each one.

Chapter 11 contains everything you need to know about advertising with mailing lists, newsgroups, and even traditional banner ads.

Step 10: Evaluate Your Success and Move On

For any long-term endeavor, you need to establish standards by which you can judge its success or failure. You must decide for yourself what you consider success to be. After a period of time, take stock of where you are, and then take steps to do even better.

Taking stock

After 12 months online, the Podrazas took stock. After paying their employees' salaries, they still had more than five times their initial investment in the bank. They had provided full- or part-time employment to nine people. That alone was one of their goals. The extra income means that their business was a rousing success.

When all is said and done, your business may do so well that you can reinvest in it by buying new equipment or increasing your services. You may even be in a position to give something back to the community. The Podrazas raised more than $10,000 for the Cystic Fibrosis Foundation by selling ten pairs of collectible Beanie Babies at the Fairmont Hotel in Chicago. Perhaps you'll have enough money left over to reward yourself, too — as if being able to tell everyone "I own my own online business" isn't reward enough!

Money is only one form of success. Plenty of entrepreneurs are online for reasons other than making money. That said, it *is* important from time to time to evaluate how well you're doing financially. Accounting software, such as the programs that I describe in Chapter 14, makes it easy to check your revenues on a daily or weekly basis. The key is to establish the goals you want to reach and develop measurements so that you know when and if you reach those goals.

Updating your data

Getting your business online now and then updating your site regularly is better than waiting to unveil the perfect Web site all at one time. In fact, seeing your site improve and grow is one of the best things about going online. Over time, you can create contests, strike up cooperative relationships with other businesses, and add more background information about your products and services.

CollectibleX.com isn't about to rest on its laurels. Its resident business genius, Michael Podraza, is now 16 years old and ready to conquer new worlds. At the time of this writing, Michael was busy designing his own line of collectible bears. He's creating his own prototype bears and sending them overseas to be manufactured. He has designed bears for American Cancer Society, Batten Disease Research and Support Association, Save a Life Foundation, and Snap-On Tools.

Dan Podraza recently hired a Webmaster and a publicist and dramatically expanded the business. The new site has improved inventory tracking as well as shipping and order tracking.

Not all of CollectibleX.com's promotions have been successful. Advertisements in online magazines proved expensive and provided few results, for example. A single large display ad on the back cover of a print magazine has brought results, as well as no-cost link exchanges, however. But trial and error is the name of the game when it comes to business start-ups. Taking a chance and learning from your mistakes is better than not trying in the first place.

Chapter 2

Setting Your Sights on Success

*S*tarting your own online business is like restoring a vintage car —
something I undertook back in those long-ago college days when I had
plenty of time on my hands. Both projects involve a series of recognizable
phases:

✔ **The idea phase:** First, you tell people about your great idea. They see
the stars dance in your eyes, nod their heads, and say something like,
"Gee, that sounds great." It's unusual, it's crazy, it's adventurous, and
they don't know how to react.

✔ **The decision phase:** Undaunted, you begin honing your plan. You read
books (like this one), ask questions, and shop around until you find a
diamond in the rough, be it a sketchy business plan or a rusting hulk
of an automobile. Of course, when the project is staring you down in
your own workshop, you may start to panic, asking yourself whether
you're really up for the task.

✔ **The assembly phase:** Still determined to proceed, you forge ahead.
You gather your tools and go to work. Drills spin, sparks fly, and metal
moves.

✔ **The test-drive phase:** One fine day, out of the smoke and fumes, your
masterpiece emerges. You take it for a spin around the block. All those
who were skeptical before are now full of admiration. You clean and
polish your treasure, tune it up from time to time, and get enjoyment
from it for years to come.

If the automotive analogy doesn't work for you, think about building a house,
planning a wedding, or devising an adventurous rafting excursion in Brazil.
The point is that starting an online business is no mystery. It's a project like

any other — one that you can understand and accomplish in stages. Right now, you're at the first stage of launching your new cyberbusiness. You and your muse are working overtime. You have some rough sketches that only a mother could love.

This chapter helps you get from idea to reality. Your first step is to dream up how you want your business to look and feel. Then you can begin to develop and implement strategies for achieving your dream. You've got a big advantage over those who started new businesses a few years ago: You've got plenty of examples of what works and what doesn't. With the right combination of inspiration and perspiration, you'll be driving your shiny new online business around the Net for years to come.

Don't let anyone rush you into signing a contract to host your online business before you're ready. I've encountered experienced businesspeople who prepaid for a year's worth of Web hosting and had no idea what to do next. Be sure that you know your options and have a business strategy, no matter how simple, before you sign anything.

Envisioning Your Online Business

How do you get to square one? Start by envisioning the kind of business that is your ultimate goal. Ask yourself: How would my business look if it were humming along like a well-oiled machine and I were totally happy with it? Envisioning your business is a creative way of asking yourself the all-important question: Why do I want to go into business online? What are my goals? Table 2-1 illustrates some possible goals and suggests how to achieve them.

Table 2-1	Online Business Models	
Goal	*Type of Web Site*	*What to Do*
Make Big Bucks	Sales	Sell items/gain paying advertisers
Gain credibility and attention	Marketing	Put your résumé and samples of your work online
Promote yourself	Personal	Promote yourself so that people will hire you or want to use your goods or services
Turn an interest into a source of income	Hobby/Special Interest	Invite like-minded people to share your passion, participate in your site and generate traffic so that you can gain advertisers

By envisioning the final result you want to achieve, you can determine your online business goals.

Finding inspiration

What's that you say? Your imaginative powers are on the blink, or, in Internet-speak, your bandwidth is a little clogged? Sometimes, just half an hour of surfing the Net can stimulate your own mental network. Find sites with qualities you want to emulate. Throughout this book, I suggest good business sites you can visit to bolster your own inspiration.

Keep a low-tech pencil and stack of paper handy while you surf for ideas. Draw out ideas that occur to you for logos, Web page designs, snappy slogans, and the like. That way, you won't be scratching your head trying to remember your inspirations later on.

Standing out from the crowd

The Web and other parts of the online world are getting to be crowded places. According to Internet Software Consortium's Domain Survey (www.isc.org), in January 2002, 147.3 million computers were connected to the Internet, compared with 109.5 million the year before and 72.4 million the year before that. Thirty percent of those computers have Web addresses that end with the commercial (.com) designation.

As an *ontrepreneur* (online entrepreneur), your goal is to stand out from the crowd — or to "position yourself in the marketplace," as business consultants like to say. Consider the following tried-and-true suggestions if you want your company to really turn heads:

- ✔ **Pursue something you know well.** The more you know about your business, the more valuable the information that you provide will be. In the online world, expertise sells.

- ✔ **Make a statement.** On your Web site, include a positioning statement that says what you do, whom you hope to reach, and how you're different from your competitors.

- ✔ **Give something away for free.** Giveaways and promotions are sure-fire ways to gain attention and develop a loyal customer base. In fact, there are entire Web sites devoted to providing free stuff online, like iWon (www.iwon.com) or WebStakes (www.webstakes.com). The "something" you give away doesn't have to be an actual product; it can be words of wisdom based on your training and experience.

✔ **Find your niche.** Web space is a great place to pursue niche marketing. In fact, it often seems that the quirkier the item, the better it sells. Don't be afraid to target a narrow audience and direct all your sales efforts to a small group of devoted followers.

✔ **Do something you love.** Having fun is optional, I suppose. But, given the choice, wouldn't you rather promote something you're passionate about and love to discuss? The more you love your business, the more time and effort you're apt to put into it and, therefore, the more likely it is to be successful. In fact, some of the most successful Web sites capitalize on the love affair — the obsession — people have with something. Such businesses take advantage of the Internet's worldwide reach, which makes it easy for people with the same interests to gather at the same virtual location.

High Point Solutions (www.highpt.com), the top-ranked company in Inc. Magazine's 500 List for 2001, found success by following all these strategies. High Point (a small, high-tech company specializing in networking hardware) was started by two brothers who skipped college and began the business in their home in Sparta, New Jersey. Younger brother Tom decided to pursue High Point at the lowest point in his life, when he was struggling to support his family and with $20,000 in credit card debt. The company posted sales of $200,000 in its first year, 1996, but it's now the fastest-growing company in the United States, with $60 million in revenue in 2000. The small sales force focuses on a niche: helping corporate customers iron out the logistical details of buying network hardware. They find good prices on new and used equipment, and deliver products fast. They have cultivated a small (only 50 or so clients provide 80 percent of sales) but highly satisfied group of customers.

Sizing up commercial Web sites

Commercial Web sites — those whose Internet addresses end with .com or .biz — are the fastest-growing segment of the Net. This is the area you'll be entering, too. But not all commercial Web sites are created equal. They come in many different sizes and levels of complexity. Like Goldilocks with her porridge, you want to create a Web site that's "just right."

A big company Web site . . . too big

Lots of big companies create Web sites with the primary goal of supplementing a product or business that's already well known and well established. Just a few examples are the Ragu Web site (www.ragu.com), the Pepsi World Web site (www.pepsiworld.com), and the Toyota Web site (www.toyota.com).

True, these commercial Web sites were created by large corporations with many thousands of dollars to throw into Web design, and so they're too big for you to use as a model for your Web site. But you can still look at them to get ideas for your own site.

Always keep this very important fact in the forefront of your consciousness: In the online world, all business sites are new, and they all contain the same basic elements. On the Web, big companies and small communicate with the same tools (Web pages joined by hyperlinks), and they're all listed in the same indexes (such as Yahoo!). So in terms of technology, you compete on a level playing field — even with much larger companies. As a result, you can do what the Big Players do . . . only better. Often, big companies don't use the Web as well as individual entrepreneurs like you.

A mid-size company Web site . . . still too big

The Web is an ideal place for a small business of ten to twelve employees to provide customer service, disseminate information, and post a sales catalog. I describe many of these functions in my book *Small Business Internet For Dummies*. Yet this sort of online business may also be too extensive and complex to serve as a model for your new endeavor. Chances are that you don't need press releases, messages from the president, employee e-mail accounts, or a firewall for Internet security.

Nevertheless, some features that mid-size companies use, such as a Frequently Asked Questions (FAQ) page or a sales catalog, may be useful to you. Look at the Golfballs.com site (www.golfballs.com) for a bounty of good ideas.

A home-grown entrepreneurial business . . . just right

Many businesses start entirely on the Web and are run by a single person, couple, or family with little or no prior business experience — in other words, people just like you.

If you're nodding in agreement that the company described in the previous paragraph is "just right" for you, you'll be pleased to know that the story doesn't end there. In fact, the rest of this book is devoted to helping you and your Web site live together happily ever after. This chapter gets you off to a good start by examining the different kinds of businesses you can launch online and some business goals you can set for yourself.

Types of Online Businesses You Can Start

As you comb the Internet for ideas to help you give your online business a definite shape and form, you can easily get confused by the dizzying array of Web sites already out there. Luckily, you can reduce this throng to a few general categories and then hone in on the ones most like your own. Use the following brief descriptions of online businesses to keep your options in mind without getting overwhelmed.

Selling consumer products

Leading Internet research firm Jupiter Media Metrix (`www.jmm.com/xp/jmm/press/industryProjections.xml`) predicts that by the year 2004, shopping online will grow to $82.9 billion. If you have products to sell (such as auto parts, antiques, jewelry, or food), the online marketplace is a great place to find customers who are ready to buy. This is especially true if the products you have for sale are unique in some way and attract the narrow, passionately interested audiences that have always gone online. Consider taking your wares online if one or more of the following applies to you:

- ✔ Your products are high in quality.

- ✔ You create your own products; for example, you design jewelry, bake cookies, or prepare gift baskets.

- ✔ You specialize in some aspects of your product that larger businesses can't achieve. Perhaps you sell regional foods, such as Texas barbecue sauce or New England chowder.

One of my favorite commercial Web sites is Ben and Jerry's (`www.benjerry.com`). Years ago, these guys were entrepreneurs, starting out just like you. Their Web site, like the rest of their business, conveys their personality and mission. It focuses on the unique flavors and high quality of their ice cream, as well as their commitment to their employees, their shareholders, and the communities to which they belong.

The Internet still has plenty of room for talented individuals to set up shop and develop online markets for their wares. The key is to find your niche, as many small-but-successful businesses have done. Believe in what you have to sell and make use of your Web space to express why you love your products (and, by implication, why your customers will love them, too).

Selling your professional services

Chances are that, at one time or another, you've found yourself scratching your head and wondering, "Where do I find the best _____ in the business?" (Fill in the blank with accountant, lawyer, stockbroker, insurance agent, health care provider . . . the list goes on and on.)

Simply finding a good professional (or being found, if you're the one hanging out your virtual shingle) is half the battle. Making yourself available in cyberspace, either through a Web site or through listings in indexes and directories, can help people find you.

Offering your professional services online can expand your client base dramatically. It also gives existing clients a new way to contact you: through e-mail. Here are just a few examples of professionals who are offering their services online:

- **Attorneys:** Immigration attorney Kevin L. Dixler is based in Chicago. Through his Web site (`www.dixler.com`), he can reach individuals around the world who want to come to the United States.

- **Psychotherapists:** Carole Killick, a music psychotherapist, has a simple, nicely designed Web site (`www.eclipse.co.uk/pens/killick`) that explains her work and courses she teaches.

- **Physicians:** Dr. Peter J. Dorsen, a physician in Minneapolis, Minnesota, has a Web site (`www.housecalldocs.com`) that explains what he does that sets him apart from other doctors: His practice is based entirely on making "house calls."

- **Consultants:** Experts who keep their knowledge up-to-date and are willing to give advice to those with similar interests and needs are always in demand. Consultants in a specialized area often find a great demand for their services on the Internet. The Yahoo! consulting page (`dir.yahoo.com/business_and_economy/business_to_business/consulting`) is crowded with fields in which online consultants are available. Here are examples of consultants and experts who have enhanced their professional reputations by creating their own successful businesses in Web-space:

  - Dr. Walter Bortz (`www.thirdage.com/bortz/`) writes a regular column for the ThirdAge Web site, which targets individuals age 50 and older.

  - Freelance writer David Barlow supplements his print, TV, and radio advertising copy with his Web site (`www.writer.com.hk`).

  - Publisher and product developer Bill Myers (`www.bmyers.com`) has a busy Web site that emphasizes his videos and other products.

Tips are a great addition to any publication, online or in print. (You're reading this one, aren't you?) Any tips you can provide your online customers/clients help you build credibility and make visitors feel as though they're getting "something for free." One way you can put forth this professional expertise is by starting your own online newsletter. You get to be editor, writer, and mailing-list manager. Plus, you get to talk as much as you want, network with tons of people who are interested enough in what you have to say to subscribe to your publication, and put your name and your business before lots of people. John Counsel (profiled in Chapter 16) puts out a regular newsletter called Network Ink that supplements her online business site (`www.profnet.org`), as do Marques Vickers and many of the other online businesspeople I mention in this chapter.

Selling information

The need to share knowledge via computers was the whole reason the Internet was born. And similar to how high-protein baby food works for babies, information is the commodity that has fueled cyberspace's rapid growth. As the Internet and commercial online networks continue to expand, information remains key.

Finding valuable information and gathering a particular kind of resource for one location online can be a business in itself. If you've been working in a specific field for some time, you may be qualified to provide information to those interested in that field. For example, if you have a great deal of experience with the college application process, you can sell your expertise to students and parents who need help sorting through the procedures involved and the data required to apply for college. (See educational consultant Cornelia Nicholson's Web site, www.collegecounselor.com, for example.)

Other online businesses provide gathering points or indexes to more specific areas. What kinds of areas? The sky's the limit. Here are just a few examples:

- ✔ **Search engines:** Some businesses succeed by connecting cybersurfers with companies, organizations, and individuals that specialize in a given area. Yahoo! (www.yahoo.com) is the most obvious example. Originally started by two college students, Yahoo! has practically become an Internet legend by gathering information in one index so that people can easily find things online.

- ✔ **Links pages:** On her "Grandma Jam's I Love to Win" sweepstakes site, (www.grandmajam.com), Janet Marchbanks-Aulenta gathers links to current contests along with short descriptions of each one. Janet says her site receives as many as 22,000 visits per month, and generates income through advertising and affiliate links to other contest Web sites. She says she loves running her own business despite the hard work involved with keeping it updated. "The key to succeeding at this type of site is to build up a regular base of users that return each day to find new contests — the daily upkeep is very important," she says.

- ✔ **Personal recommendations:** The personal touch sells. Just look at About.com (www.about.com). This guide to the online world provides Web surfers with a central location where they can locate virtually anything. It works because real people do the choosing and provide evaluations (albeit brief) of the sites they list.

How can information resource sites such as these make money? In some cases, individuals pay to become members; sometimes, businesses pay to be listed on a site; other times, a site attracts so many visitors on a regular basis that other companies pay to post advertising on the site. Big successes — such as About.com — carry a healthy share of ads and strike lucrative partnerships with big companies, as well.

Selling technology or computer resources

The online world itself, by the very fact that it exists, has spawned all kinds of business opportunities for entrepreneurs. Just think of all the hardware and software you need in order to get online:

- ✔ **Computers:** Some discount computer houses have made a killing by going online and offering equipment for less than conventional retail stores. Being on the Internet means that they save on overhead, employee compensation, and other costs, and they are able to pass those savings on to their customers.

- ✔ **Internet Service Providers:** These are the businesses that give you a dial-up or direct connection to the Internet. Many ISPs, such as Netcom or UUNET, are big concerns. But smaller companies — such as YourNET Connection (www.ync.net), which is based in Schaumburg, IL and offers free online Web training for its customers, are succeeding, as well.

- ✔ **Browsers:** The obvious example of a company that made it big by offering its browser (software for viewing the World Wide Web) online is Netscape Communications Corp., which is battling giant Microsoft for the lion's share of the Web browser market.

- ✔ **Software:** Matt Wright is well-known on the Web for providing free computer scripts that add important functionality to Web sites, such as processing information that visitors submit via online forms. Matt's Script Archive site (worldwidemart.com/scripts) now includes an advertisement for a book on scripting that he co-authored, as well as a Web postcard system for sale and an invitation to businesses to take out advertisements on his site.

Selling your creative work

Starving artists, as well as those with a little bit of nourishment in their bellies, need to find wide exposure for little or no money. Where better to turn than the Internet? If you're simply looking for exposure and feedback on your creations, you can put samples of your work online. Consider the following suggestions for virtual creative venues (and revenues):

✔ **Host art galleries.** Thanks to online galleries, artists whose sales were previously only regional can get inquiries from all over the world. Art Xpo (www.artxpo.com) reports thousands of dollars in sales through its Web site and aggressive marketing efforts. The personal Web site created by artist Marques Vickers (www.marquesv.com), has received worldwide attention; see Figure 2-1. (The upcoming sidebar, "Painting a new business scenario," profiles Vickers' site.)

✔ **Sell your art.** Tony Barker is an Australian graphic designer. His company, Moving Pixels, sells a computer drawing program called Art for Kids from its Web site (www.bigearth.com.au).

✔ **Publish your writing.** Blogs (Weblogs, or online diaries) are all the rage these days. To find out how to create one yourself, check out Blogger (www.blogger.com). You can find links to lots of electronic literary journals at www.usd.edu/engl/journals.html. Many journals, such as American Literary Review (www.engl.unt.edu/alr) and BeeHive (beehive.temporalimage.com/index.html) provide forums for writers.

✔ **Sell your music.** Singer-songwriter Michael McDermott sells his own CDs, videos, and posters through his online store (www.michael-mcdermott.com).

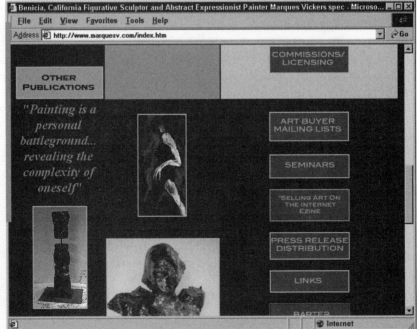

Figure 2-1:
A California artist created this Web site to gain recognition and sell his creative work.

One-to-One Marketing Strategies

After you review your options and check out any Web sites that already conduct the sorts of business ventures that you hope to tackle yourself, it's time to put your goals into action. You do so by developing marketing strategies that are well-suited to expressing your unique talents and services and by encouraging customers to explore your business and place orders with you.

The most effective online marketing strategies are those that run counter to the widespread image of cyberspace as a place where millions of lonely, disconnected people interact without really getting to know one another.

Quite the contrary: Online communities are often close-knit, long-standing groups of people who get to be great friends. The best way to promote your business is to reach out to people and help them, to communicate with them as individuals. The Web, newsgroups, and e-mail enable you to accomplish this goal in ways that other media can't match.

Get to know your audience

Remember the days of the corner drugstore and the local market whose proprietors knew each of their customers by name and did their best to provide them with personal service? Are those days really gone? Well, of course, to a large extent, they are. But old-fashioned business practices are alive and well in cyberspace. Your number one business strategy, when it comes to starting your business online, sounds simple: Know your audience.

What's not so simple about this little maxim is that, in cyberspace, it takes some work to get to know exactly who your customers are. Web surfers don't leave their names, addresses, or even a random e-mail address when they visit your site. Instead, when you check the raw, unformatted records (or *logs*) of the visitors who have connected to you, you see pages and pages of what appears to be computer gobbledygook. You need special software to interpret the information, such as the program WebTrends, which I mention in Chapter 16.

The surprising thing is this: You *can* get to know the individuals who come to your Web site. You can develop long-standing relationships in which your customers come to trust you and return to your site on a regular basis.

Painting a new business scenario

Marques Vickers is an artist based in Benicia, California. Through his self-named Web site (www.marquesv.com), as well as 15-20 "mini-sites," he markets his own painting, sculpture, and photography as well as his books on marketing and buying fine art online. He first went online in November 1999 and spends about 20 hours a week working on his various Web sites. His sites receive anywhere from 25,000 to 40,000 visits per month.

Q. What are the costs of running all your Web sites and doing the associated marketing?

A. Out of pocket expense is approximately $39 monthly for a Web site hosting and Internet access package. New domain name registrations and renewals probably add another $15.

Q. What would you describe as the primary goals of your online business?

A. My initial objective was to develop a personalized round-the-clock global presence in order to recruit sales outlets, sell directly to the public, and create a reference point for people to access and view my work. I also have an intuitive sense that an online Web site presence will be a marketing necessity for any future visual artist and a lifelong exposure outlet. Having an online presence builds my credibility as a fine artist and positions me to take advantage of the evolution of the fine arts industry, too.

Q. Has your online business been profitable financially?

A. Absolutely — but make no mistake, achieving sales volume and revenue is a trial and error process and involves a significant time commitment. I'm still perfecting the business model and it may require years to achieve the optimum marketing plan.

Q. How do you promote your site?

A. With the Internet, you are layering a collective web of multiple promotional sources. Experimentation is essential because recognition is not always immediate but may ultimately be forthcoming since postings in cyberspace are often stumbled across from unforeseen resources. I try multiple marketing outlets from direct television promotion to traded banner ads to trade magazine advertisements. Some have had moderate success, some unforeseen and remarkable exposure. Unlike traditional advertising media that have immediate response times, the Internet may lag in its response. It is a long-term commitment and one that cannot be developed by short-term tactics or media blitzes.

Q. Do you create your Web pages yourself or do you work with someone to do that?

A. I'm too particular about the quality of content to subcontract the work out. Besides, I know what I want to say, how and am capable of fashioning the design concepts I want to integrate. The rectangular limitations of HTML design make color a very important component and the very minimal attention span of most Web viewers means that you'd better get to the point quickly and concisely. The more personalized, timely and focused your content, the more reason an individual has to return to your Web site and ultimately understand your unique vision of what you're trying to create. A Web site is an unedited forum for telling your version of a story and a means for cultivating a direct support base.

Q. What advice would you give to someone starting an online business?

A. Don't hesitate one minute longer than necessary. Read substantially and from a diverse selection of sources on the subject. Subscribe to ezines on related subject matter (such as my own "Selling Art On The Internet" at www.ArtsInAmerica.com). Go to informational seminars; ask questions. Experiment with marketing ideas and by all means, consider it a lifelong project. The Internet is continuing to evolve and the opportunities have never been more prevalent.

How do you develop relationships with your customers?

- ✔ **Get your visitors to identify themselves.** Have them send you e-mail messages, place orders, enter contests, or provide you with feedback. (For more specific suggestions, see Chapter 7.)

- ✔ **Become an online researcher.** Find existing users who already purchase goods and services online that are similar to what you offer. Visit newsgroups that pertain to what you sell, search for mailing lists, and participate in discussions so that people can learn about you.

- ✔ **Keep track of your visitors.** Count the visitors who come to your site and, more important, the ones who make purchases or seek out your services. Manage your customer profiles so that you can sell your existing clientele the items they're likely to buy.

- ✔ **Help your visitors get to know you.** Web space is virtually unlimited. Don't be reluctant to tell people about aspects of your life that don't relate directly to how you hope to make money. Consider Judy Vorfeld, who does Internet research, Web design, and office support. Her Web site (www.ossweb.com) includes the usual lists of clients and services; however, it also includes a link to her personal home page and a page that describes her community service work. (See Figure 2-2.)

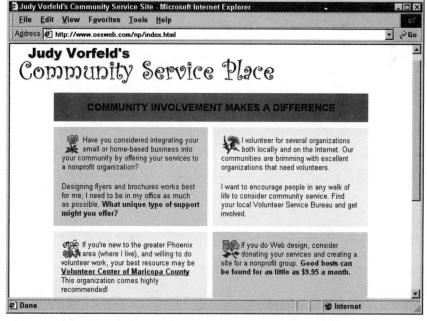

Figure 2-2: Telling potential customers about yourself makes them more comfortable telling you about themselves.

I recommend doing your own Internet research so that you can learn more about the culture of the online world: how the most successful Web sites look and feel, and how many Web sites use a hip, techno-savvy tone when presenting information. But if you don't have scads of time to spend online, you can hire researchers to do the job for you. A company called Leafworks (www.leafworks.com) says that it will search the Web for you and report on quick facts for $5 each, or perform more complicated custom research for hourly fees.

The more clearly you target your market and focus your sales pitches, the more successful your online business will be.

Catch a wave: Grab Web surfers' attention

Imagine yourself standing in the front door of your store on Main Street, arms folded, watching cars zoom by. How do you stop traffic so that people will at least look at you?

On the Web, people move quickly, jumping from site to site. After you get to know your audience, job number two in your marketing strategy is to catch their attention. You have two ways to do this:

✔ **Make yourself visible.** In Web-space, the problem isn't so much that potential customers are surfing right past your site. Rather, your task is simply making them aware that you exist at all. You do this by getting yourself included in as many indexes, search sites, and business listings as possible; Chapter 11 outlines some strategies for doing so. You can also do a bit of self-promotion in your own online communications: John Counsel of the Profit Clinic (www.profitclinic.com) appends this interesting teaser, followed by a link to his Web site, to his e-mail messages:

```
"90% of all small business owners are PRE-PROGRAMMED to
    FAIL. Are you one of them? Find out now with our Quick
        Quiz"
```

✔ **Make your site an eye-catcher.** Getting people to come to you is only half the battle. The other half is getting them to do some shopping or investigating after they're there. You encourage this participation by combining striking images with promotions, useful information, and ways for them to interact with you. (See Chapters 6 and 7 for details.)

Promote your expertise

You know just how knowledgeable you are in your area of business. You may have been plumbing, painting, selling insurance, or trading collectibles for many years. Even if you're just starting out doing business online, you're still an expert, right?

Marketing task number three is to transfer your confidence and sense of authority about what you do to anyone who visits you online. Make people believe that you're an expert and a good person with whom to do business.

The Web has been around only since the mid '90s. Everyone is a relative newcomer to online commerce. Many individuals pretend to be experts, making it difficult to know for sure who's reliable and worth visiting.

Here, too, you can do a quick two-step in order to market your expertise.

Show your credentials

List any honors, awards, or professional affiliations you have that relate to your online work. If you're providing professional or consulting services online, you might even make a link to your online resume. Tell people how long you've been in your field and how you got to know what you know about your business.

Of course, if you're just starting to sell pet supplies or homemade pottery, you won't have this sort of information available; in that case, move to the all-important technique that I describe next.

Convince with authoritative information

Providing useful, practical information about a topic is one of the best ways to market yourself online. One of the great things about starting an online business is that you don't have to incur the design and printing charges to get a brochure or flyer printed. You have plenty of space on your online business site to talk about your sales items or services in as great detail as you want.

Most Internet service providers give you 10 to 20MB (megabytes, that is) of space for your Web pages and associated files. Because the average Web page occupies only 5 to 10K (that's kilobytes) of space, it'll take a long time before you begin to run out of room.

What, exactly, can you talk about on your site? I'm glad you asked. Here are some ideas:

- ✔ Provide detailed descriptions and photos of your sale items.
- ✔ Include a full list of clients you have worked for previously.
- ✔ Publish a page of testimonials from satisfied customers.
- ✔ Give your visitors a list of links to Web pages and other sites where people can find out more about your area of business.
- ✔ Toot your own horn: Tell why you love what you do and why you're so good at it.

When the job is done, be sure to get someone to give you a good testimonial. Ask someone for a sentence or two you can use on your Web site.

A site that is chock-full of compelling, entertaining content will become a resource that online visitors bookmark and return to on a regular basis — and that, of course, is any online business owner's dream.

Encourage potential customers to interact

A 16-year-old cartoonist named Gabe Martin put out his cartoons on his Web site, called The Borderline. Virtually nothing happened. But when his dad put up some money for a contest, young Gabe started getting hundreds of visits and inquiries. He went on to create 11 mirror sites around the world, develop a base of devoted fans, and sell his own cartoon book.

Cybersurfers are used to getting things for free online. They regularly download shareware or freeware programs. They get free advice from newsgroups, and they find free companionship from chat rooms and online forums. Having already paid for network access and computer equipment, they actually *expect* to get something for free.

Help meet your customers' expectations by devising as many promotions, giveaways, or sales as possible. You can also get people to interact through online forums or other tools, as I describe in Chapter 7.

In online business terms, anything that gets your visitors to click links and enter your site is good. Provide as many links to the rest of your site as you can on your home page. Many interactions that don't seem like sales do lead to sales or help your fledgling business in some way.

See Chapters 6 and 7 for instructions on how to create hyperlinks and add interactivity to your Web site. For more about creating Web sites, check out *Creating Web Pages For Dummies*, 4th Edition, by Bud Smith and Arthur Bebak.

Be a joiner

You may be physically alone, tapping away at your keyboard or peering at your monitor in your home office, but that doesn't mean that you really are alone. Thousands of home office workers and entrepreneurs just like you connect to the Net every day and share many of the same concerns, challenges, and ups and downs as you.

Starting an online business isn't only a matter of creating Web pages, scanning photos, and taking orders. Marketing and networking are essential to making sure that you meet your goals. Participate in groups that are related either to your particular business or to online business in general. Here are some ways you can make the right connections and get support and encouragement at the same time.

Be a newsgroupie

Newsgroups are discussion groups that occupy an extensive and popular part of the Internet called Usenet, as well as appear on America Online and other online services. Many large organizations such as universities and corporations run their own internal newsgroups, too.

Businesspeople tend to overlook newsgroups because of admonitions about spam (unsolicited messages sent by people trying to sell something to newsgroup participants who don't want it) and other violations of *Netiquette*, the set of rules that govern newsgroup communications. However, when you approach newsgroup participants on their own terms (not by spamming them but by answering questions and participating in discussions), newsgroups can be a wonderful resource for businesspeople. They attract knowledgeable consumers who are strongly interested in a topic: just the sorts of people who make great customers.

A few newsgroups (in particular, the ones with `biz` at the beginning of their names) are especially intended to discuss small business issues and sales. Here are a few suggestions:

- ✔ `misc.entrepreneurs`
- ✔ `biz.marketplace.discussion`
- ✔ `biz.marketplace.international.discussion`
- ✔ `biz.marketplace.services.discussion`
- ✔ `alt.business.home`
- ✔ `alt.business.consulting`
- ✔ `alt.business.franchise`
- ✔ `aol.commerce.general`

The easiest way to access newsgroups is to use the newsgroup software that comes built into the two most popular Web browser packages, Netscape Communicator and Microsoft Internet Explorer. Each browser or newsgroup program has its own set of steps for enabling you to access Usenet. Use your browser's online help system to find out how you can access newsgroups.

Be sure to read the group's FAQ (frequently asked questions) page before you start posting. It's a good idea to *lurk before you post* — that is, simply read messages being posted to the group in order to find out about members' concerns before posting a message yourself. Stay away from groups that seem to consist only of get-rich-quick schemes or other scams. When you do post a message, be sure to keep your comments relevant to the conversation and give as much helpful advice as you can.

The most important business technique in communicating by either e-mail or newsgroup postings is to include a signature file at the end of your message. A *signature file* is a simple text message that newsgroup and mail software programs automatically add to your messages. A typical one includes your name, title, and the name of your company. You can also include a link to your business's home page. A good example is Judy Vorfeld's signature file, shown in Figure 2-3. (Chapter 10 tells how to create your own signature file.)

Figure 2-3:
A descriptive signature file on your messages serves as an instant business advertisement.

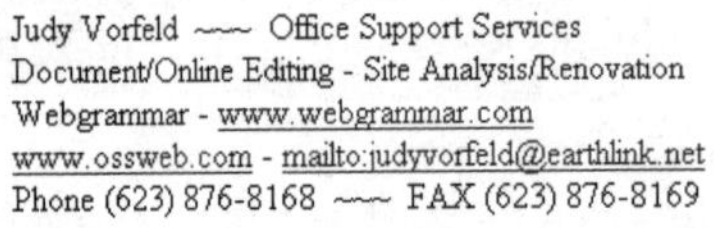

Judy Vorfeld ~~ Office Support Services
Document/Online Editing - Site Analysis/Renovation
Webgrammar - www.webgrammar.com
www.ossweb.com - mailto:judyvorfeld@earthlink.net
Phone (623) 876-8168 ~~ FAX (623) 876-8169

Be a mailing list-ener

A *mailing list* is a discussion group that communicates by exchanging e-mail messages between members who share a common interest and who have subscribed to join the list. Each e-mail message sent to the list is distributed to all of the list's members. Any of those members can, in turn, respond by sending e-mail replies. The series of back-and-forth messages develops into discussions.

The nice thing about mailing lists is that they consist only of people who have subscribed, which means that they really want to be involved and participate.

An excellent mailing list to check out is the Small and Home-Based Business Discussion List (www.talkbiz.com/bizlist/index.html). This list is *moderated,* meaning that someone reads through all postings before they go online and filters out any comments that are inappropriate or off-topic. Also, try searching the Topica directory of discussion groups (www.topica.com). Click Small Business (under Choose from Thousands of Newsletters and Discussions) to view a page full of discussion groups and other resources for entrepreneurs.

The number of groups you join and how often you participate in them is up to you. The important thing is to regard every one-to-one-personal contact as a seed that may sprout into a sale, a referral, an order, a contract, a bit of useful advice, or another profitable business blossom.

It's not a newsgroup or a mailing list, but a Web site called iVillage.com (www.ivillage.com) is designed to bring women together by providing chat rooms where they can type messages to one another in real time, as well as message boards where they can post messages. (Men, of course, can partici- pate, too.) Experts (and some who just claim to be experts) often participate in these forums. The work-from-home section (www.ivillage.com/work) is a good one for online entrepreneurs like yourself.

Find more than one way to sell

Many successful online businesses combine more than one concept of what constitutes electronic commerce. Chapter 8 discusses ways to sell your goods and services on your Web site, but the Internet offers other venues for promoting and selling your wares, too.

Free income for your Web site

You can make money on your Web site without having anything to sell. Sound too good to be true? Believe me, it's for real. It's all because the Web is get- ting so competitive. Some sites will pay you for building your page with them or linking to them. You'll find out more in Chapter 7, but following are some quick suggestions:

- **We'll pay you to join:** Usually, you pay a membership fee to join some- thing. Some online businesses are giving that principle the old switcheroo. Build your Web site on Tripod (www.tripod.com). If you get enough visits, they'll pay you cash through a program called Builder Bucks.

- **Lucrative links:** If you become a member of Yahoo! GeoCities (www.geocities.com) and locate your Web site there (see Chapter 4), you can join the Pages that Pay Affiliate Program, in which you make links to specified business Web sites. You receive commissions for each visitor who goes to the business's Web site from yours. Amazon.com (www.amazon.com) has had a similar program for years.

Selling through online classifieds

If you're looking for a quick and simple way to sell products or promote your services online without having to pay high overhead costs, it's hard to beat taking out a classified ad in an online publication or other site.

The classifieds work the same way online as they do in print publications: You pay a fee and write a short description along with contact information, and the publisher makes the ad available to potential customers. However, online classifieds have a number of big advantages over their print equivalents:

- ✔ **Audience:** Instead of hundreds or thousands who might view your ad in print, tens of thousands or perhaps even millions can see it online.

- ✔ **Searchability:** Online classifieds are often indexed so that customers can search for particular items with their Web browser. This makes it easier for shoppers to find exactly what they want, whether it's a three-bedroom house or a Betty Boop cookie jar.

- ✔ **Time:** On the Net, ads are often online for a month or more.

- ✔ **Cost:** Some sites, such as Commerce Corner (www.comcorner.com), let you post classified ads for free.

On the downside, classifieds are often buried at the back of online magazines or Web sites, just as they are in print, so they're hardly well-traveled areas. Also, most classifieds don't make use of the graphics that help sell and promote goods and services so effectively throughout Web-space.

Use classifieds if you're short on time or money. Stick with traditional media or your own online business site where you can provide more details to customers and not have to spend a cent.

Selling via online auctions

Many small businesses, such as antique dealerships or jewelry stores, sell individual merchandise through online auctions. Increasingly popular auction sites provide effective ways to target sales items at highly motivated collectors who are likely to pay top dollar for especially scarce or desirable goodies.

Sellers often make far more money on desirable single items through auctions than they could by putting the items on a garage-sale table or even in a consignment shop. Why? Auctions attract buyers from all over the world rather than from around the neighborhood. Auctions also attract buyers who are passionate about a particular kind of item and who know its value.

Know what you're selling. Pick out the antiques or collectibles from the junk when you go to a garage sale. Research them so you know roughly what they're worth. Chances are the people who will be bidding on your items know as much as (or more than) you do. The more knowledge you display about an item, the more interest you'll get and the better the chances that the bids will go higher, as well.

The best way to discover what you can sell and how much a particular goodie might fetch is to visit the auction yourself. Keep track of prices and look at the photos and descriptions to see which items are likely to attract the next bidder. Here are some places you can visit:

- **Amazon.com Auctions** (`auctions.amazon.com`): The online bookselling giant's auction service continues to thrive, selling everything from Karaoke machines to land in Oregon.
- **eBay** (`www.ebay.com`): This is one of the best-known auction companies on the Web, dealing in all sorts of items sold person-to-person.
- **uBid** (`www.ubid.com`): This site specializes in auctioning off computer equipment but also offers housewares and other general consumer goods.

Each auction house works differently, but the basic elements have been part of the online world for years: trust, honesty, and courtesy. The buyer trusts you to put out an honest description, you trust the buyer to send in the payment, and the auction house trusts you to pay your share and treat people well. Infractions are documented in reports that can ruin your reputation and prevent you from selling again. On the other hand, those who make lots of successful transactions get gold stars by their names that attract more customers.

Typically, you sign up with the auction house and agree to pay a fee for each item sold. You either put the item online and let the marketplace determine how much it's worth or, if you want to protect your investment, you specify a "reserve" amount that covers how much you paid for it. If your reserve isn't met, you don't have to sell. On the other hand, if the reserve is met, you're obligated to sell. You also specify how long the item is to be offered for sale — usually a few days or a week. You also tell people how you want to be paid — postal money orders are common, although some sellers accept credit cards or personal checks.

Web-based auctions are great ways for individuals to make money online. Find out how to buy and sell wisely in *Internet Auctions For Dummies*, by yours truly.

Chapter 3

Your Online Business Equipment List

*O*ne of the many exciting aspects of launching a business online is the absence of something: You don't have to encounter much *overhead* (that is, operating expenses). Many non-cyberspace businesses must take out loans, pay rent, remodel their storefronts, pay license fees, and purchase store fixtures. Only then can they stock the shelves, hire employees, and open for business.

When you start a business online, many (though not all) of these tasks are unnecessary. Instead of patching plaster and painting walls, you pick colors and graphics for your Web pages. Rather than write checks to a landlord, you (sometimes, though not always) pay Web hosting and registration fees.

The primary overhead for an online business is computer hardware and software. Internet appliances, and wireless e-mail, networking, and Web-enabled communications devices are all the rage these days. Although it's great if you can afford top-of-the-line equipment, you'll be happy to know that the latest bells and whistles aren't absolutely necessary in order to get a business site online and maintain it effectively

The one silver lining in the dark economic cloud that's been hanging over the economy lately is that computers continue to get better and at the same time more affordable. And new digital devices, such as Web-enabled cell phones, are making it easier than ever to stay connected no matter where you are. Even if you're on a tight budget, you're sure to be able to find a computer or other device that will get your business up and running.

As a lone entrepreneur, you're on a limited budget. If you already have an Internet connection and enough equipment to surf the Web, you're probably asking yourself: "Do I have to spend thousands of dollars on upgrading my equipment and new software to start an online business?"

Short answer: Nope!

Long answer: No, but to streamline the technical aspects of connecting to the online world and creating a business Web site, some investment may be a wise and profitable idea. Read on for more details.

Hardware and Software Rules to Live By

Some general principles apply when assembling machinery and programs for an online endeavor. First and foremost, look on the Internet for what you need. You can find just about everything you want to get you started.

If you're looking for hardware and software that's tailored to the needs of a small business or home office, check out the Apple Computer Running Your Business Web site (www.apple.com/smallbusiness/ryb/). Also visit the ZDNet Hardware area (www.zdnet.com/products/hardwareuser) for reviews of the latest products.

Be sure to pry before you buy! Don't pull out that credit card until you get the facts on what warranty and technical support your hardware or software vendor provides. Make sure that your vendor provides phone support 24 hours a day, 7 days a week. Also ask how long the typical turnaround time is in case your equipment needs to be serviced.

If you purchase lots of new hardware and software, remember to update your insurance by sending your insurer a list of your new equipment. Also consider purchasing insurance specifically for your computer-related items from a company such as Safeware (www.safeware.com). And don't forget that you can record all hardware purchases as business expenses on your tax returns. As I point out in Chapter 14, when you run a business, it makes sense to itemize computer and other business expenses on IRS form Schedule C when tax time comes.

Easyware (Not Hardware) for Your Business

Sure, you have a computer. You dial up the Net. You surf the Web. Isn't that the end of the story?

Indeed, your existing hardware setup may work just fine for you as a consumer. But becoming an information provider on the Internet places an additional burden on your computer and peripheral equipment, such as your modem. When you're "in it for the money," you may very well start to go online everyday, and perhaps several times a day. The better your computer setup, the more e-mail messages you can download, the more catalog items you can store, and so on. In this section, I introduce you to any upgrades you may need to make to your existing hardware configuration.

The right computer for your online business

You very well may already have an existing computer setup that's adequate to get your business online and start the ball rolling. Or you may be starting from scratch and looking to purchase a computer for personal and/or business use. In either case, it pays to know what all the technical terms and specifications mean. That way, when you go to the computer store (either online or down the street), the spec sheets and manuals won't seem ike so much alphabet soup to you. Here are some general terms you need to understand:

- **Megahertz (MHz):** This unit of measure indicates how quickly a computer's processor can perform functions. The central processing unit (CPU) of a computer is where the computing work gets done. In general, the higher the processor's internal clock rate, expressed in megahertz, the faster the computer. Taking other variables (such as available memory, the programs you're running, and your Internet connection) into account, an 866 MHz processor operates roughly twice as fast as one that has a clock rate of 433 MHz.

- **Random access memory (RAM):** This is the memory that your computer uses to temporarily store information needed to operate programs. RAM is usually expressed in millions of bytes, or megabytes (MB), of information. The more RAM you have, the more programs you can run simultaneously. If you don't have enough RAM to operate all the programs you have open at any one time, your computer slows to a crawl.

- **Synchronous dynamic RAM (SDRAM):** Many ultra-fast computers use some form of SDRAM, which is synchronized with a particular clock rate of a CPU so that a processor can perform more instructions in a given time.

- **Double data rate SDRAM (DDR SDRAM):** This is a type of SDRAM that can dramatically improve the clock rate of a CPU to at least 200 MHz.

- **Auxiliary storage:** This term refers to physical data-storage space on a hard disk, tape, CD-ROM, or other device.

- **Virtual memory:** This is a type of memory on your hard disk that your computer can "borrow" to serve as extra RAM.

✔ **Network interface card (NIC):** You need this hardware add-on if you have a cable modem or if you expect to connect your computer to others on a network. Having a NIC usually provides you with Ethernet data transfer to the other computers. (*Ethernet* is a network technology that permits you to send and receive data at very fast speeds.)

The Internet is teeming with places where you can find good deals on hardware. A great place to start is the CNET Shopper.com Web site (`shopper.cnet.com`). Also visit the auction site uBid.com (`www.ubid.com`). And if you're looking for bargains on used hardware, don't forget the newsgroups devoted to equipment for sale, such as `comp.sys.mac.forsale` and `misc.forsale.computers.pc-specific.systems`.

Processor speed: Don't be dazzled

Computer processors are getting faster all the time. Every month, it seems, some manufacturer comes out with a faster chip that is supposed to make games leap off the screen, perform all your functions in half the time, and wax the kitchen floor, besides.

Don't be overly impressed by a computer's clock speed (measured in megahertz or even gigahertz). Sure, purchasing the fastest computer you can afford is a wise move, but don't obsess about getting the latest and fastest processor on the block. By the time you get your computer home, another, faster chip will already have hit the streets.

A super-fast Pentium 4 or Advanced Micro Devices (AMD) chip primarily helps if you have to perform scads of calculations, fill out spreadsheets, and deal with other number-crunching tasks. For basic business needs, Web surfing, and viewing graphics, concentrate on getting lots of memory — not speed — for your computer. The newest computers also have their own processor and memory allocated to graphics, which frees up the system's main processor to perform other tasks.

A Pentium chip is a popular processor introduced in the early 1990s by the Intel Corporation to replace its own 486 processor. Faster versions of the original Pentium — Pentium III and Pentium 4 chips — are now available. The AMD Athlon XP runs at 2.1 GHz (that's gigahertz, which is equivalent to 1000 MHz), while the AMD Duron for laptops clocks in at 1.2 and 1.3 GHz. Although you can conceivably surf the Web, exchange e-mail messages, and update Web pages with a 486 processor in your computer, it's really ancient technology now, and you should upgrade to at least a Pentium III, which is becoming more practical and reasonable in cost as time goes on.

Hello, Computer Central? Get me more RAM!

The single most important item on your business-equipment shopping list is memory. After you go online and start assembling a Web site, your memory requirements go up dramatically. Think about the memory required to run the types of applications shown in Table 3-1. (Note that these are only estimates, based on the Windows versions of these products that were available at the time of this writing.)

Table 3-1	Memory Requirements	
Type of Application	*Example*	*Amount of RAM Recommended*
Web browser	Internet Explorer	32MB
Web page editor	Macromedia Dreamweaver	64MB
Word processor	Microsoft Word	136MB (on Windows XP)
Graphics program	Paint Shop Pro	32MB
Accounting software	Microsoft Excel	8MB (if you are already running an Office application)
Animation/Presentation	Macromedia Director Shockwave Studio	64MB

The sample applications in Table 3-1 add up to a whopping 336MB of RAM. And it doesn't stop there. As the number of Web pages you view and graphics you download increases, your RAM requirements also go up. The Task Manager utility included with Windows 2000 or XP contains a long list of processes that are consuming your memory at any one time. The list shown in Figure 3-1 indicates that Netscape Communicator (which has the program name netscape.exe) is using 4.7 megabytes of memory, for instance. This is an older version of the program; more recent ones require more memory.

Applications such as those shown in Figure 3-1 easily consume more than half of my PC's 256MB of RAM. If I try to start a Web page editor or other program, my system may slow down, freeze, or I will see the dreaded Windows "blue screen" forcing me to restart and possibly lose data.

Virtual memory (VM) may seem like a good solution, but it's not a long-term substitute for "real" RAM that you or a service person physically adds to your computer in the form of memory chips. The problem is that VM only *simulates* more memory than your computer actually has. It breaks a program into small sections, called *pages*, and in some instances, widely separates these pages on your computer disk. As a result, the program needs to switch back and forth to your disk in order to run, which slows down your general computer operation.

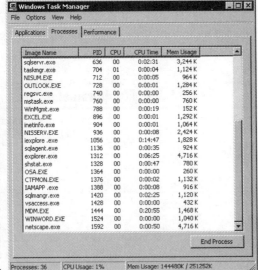

Figure 3-1:
A few
Internet
applications
can quickly
consume
your
computer's
available
RAM.

If you plan to work online on a regular basis, be sure to get at least 256MB of RAM — more if you can swing it. Don't believe the Windows XP box that says you can get along with 64MB of RAM. Windows XP is a hungry beast that consumes lots of food. Memory is cheap nowadays, and the newer PCs will allow you to install as much as 2GB (that's 2000 megabytes, or 2 gigabytes) of RAM (and probably more by the time you read this).

Don't try to perform memory upgrades yourself unless you've done it before. You can easily cause serious damage to your computer through static electricity discharge. Take the machine to a service center at a computer or electronics store and pay the nominal service fee to get more memory installed.

Hard disk storage

Random access memory is only one type of memory your computer uses; the other kind, *hard disk*, stores information, such as text files, audio files, programs, and the many essential files that your computer's operating system needs in order to boot up and function the way you want.

Most of the new computers on the market come with hard disk drives that store multiple GB (that's *gigabytes*; a gigabyte is a thousand megabytes) of data. Any hard disk of a gigabyte or more should be adequate for your business needs if you don't do a lot of graphics work. But most new computers come with hard disks of 40 or more GB in size. Whether you're buying new or used equipment, be sure to get a machine that has as many gigabytes of storage space as possible; you'll still run out of room before long.

If you want to ensure that you *never* run out of disk space, purchase a removable disk drive for your computer. Iomega Systems makes the most popular removable disk drives. The Iomega Zip disk holds a cartridge that gives you either 100MB or 250MB of storage, depending on the version you obtain. The Jaz drive is available in 1GB and 2GB versions per cartridge. Other such devices are on the market, but the advantage in going with the popular ones is that printers and service bureaus are likely to have their own Zip and Jaz drives that you can use to transmit graphics and other files.

A Web-based service called PriceSCAN.com (`www.pricescan.com`) gives you a quick way to compare prices on hard disk drives and other computer hardware devices. You look up the type of device you want and fill out an online form that lets you specify criteria, such as the maximum price you're willing to spend for it. PriceSCAN searches its database of vendors and presents you with a list of currently available items.

CD-ROM/DVD drive

Although a CD-ROM drive may not be the most important part of your computer for business use, it can perform essential installation, storage, and data communications functions, such as

- **Installing software:** A CD-ROM drive is pretty much a must-have item for installing sophisticated Internet software of the sort that I describe throughout this book. A wide range of entertainment software is available only on CD, and so are general reference materials, such as online encyclopedias, that can help you prepare documentation for your products.

- **Recording data:** Some newer CD-ROM drives let you record data yourself onto disc. In terms of storage, a writeable CD lets you store 650MB or more of data on a single disc.

- **Sharing data:** As a mode of data communications, CDs are lightweight and easy to ship. If you work in music or multimedia, writeable CDs can be a terrific way to present a digitized copy of your work to your customers. CDs are also a great way to deliver your product to customers if you work in the software industry.

The *speed* of a CD-ROM drive is a measurement of how fast the drive can transfer data to or from a CD. The earliest CD-ROM drives transferred data at 150KB per second. A double (or 2X) drive works twice that fast, a 4X drive works four times as fast, and so on. These days, 40X drives are common. Usually, the speed of the drive is printed right on the front of your computer.

Every computer comes with a CD-ROM drive these days; the current ones are rated at a speed of 16X or 24X. 16X is the minimum that your machine should have. If your drive works more slowly than you want, you can upgrade it at the same service center where you obtain a memory upgrade.

A growing number of machines are now being made available with a drive that operates a new type of CD called a *digital versatile disc* (DVD). These discs can hold many gigabytes of information, compared with the 600MB or so that a conventional CD-ROM can handle. If you can find a new computer that includes a DVD drive at an additional cost that you can afford, by all means go for it. You'll be able to view an entire motion picture on your computer's CD, for example.

Another attractive option is a writeable CD — a CD-ROM on which you can write or record data. Your computer needs a special CD-R drive in order to use writeable CDs. Writeable CDs provide you with loads of storage space, but the downside is that the information on a writeable CD cannot be changed after it's written. You can only add more data to the disc. CD-RW (compact disc-rewriteable) compact discs, such as the ZipCD or HP CD-Writer, let you write and change information contained on them, just as you can with a floppy disk or hard disk.

Before you trade it, upgrade it!

Let's face it: It's almost impossible to have the fastest and best-equipped computer for very long. As soon as you buy one model, another one comes out with a faster processor and more memory.

One way to keep up while staying within your budget is to upgrade your existing machine rather than scrapping it and buying an entirely new model. Before you plunk down the big bucks for a new machine, check with your local computer retailer for prices on the following essentials:

- **A speedier processor:** Replacing your motherboard and/or CPU gives you a new lease on life and lets you run the latest and greatest office or operating system software.

- **More RAM:** If you tend to run many applications at the same time, don't scrimp on RAM. See if you can get as much as 256 MB, if not more.

- **More storage:** A second hard disk can be installed easily and give you many gigabytes of space if you like to run multimedia files, work with digital photos, and do other graphics-intensive things.

You can also add a DVD drive, a Zip drive, or lots of other features, but simply beefing up one or more of the preceding three computing must-haves will improve your ability to surf the Web, download software, and run the latest database or accounting software without breaking the bank.

Safety devices

You can spend all the money you want on top-notch computer equipment, but if you plug your expensive machines into a substandard electrical system, your investment can (almost literally) go up in smoke.

Be sure to protect your equipment against electrical problems that can result in loss of data or substantial repair bills. What kinds of problems? A *power surge* or *spike* is a sudden increase in voltage that can damage your equipment. Electrical storms can damage ungrounded equipment, and blackouts can put you offline and prevent you from getting work done, which can hit you in your pocketbook.

At the very least, make sure that your home office has grounded three-prong outlets. (Even if the rest of your house has the old-fashioned outlets, it's worth paying an electrician to upgrade the line to your office.) Upgrading doesn't just mean changing the outlets themselves, however; it means that you use a three-wire cable to bring electricity to the outlet. The third wire, the *ground wire*, should literally connect to the ground. Usually, electricians do this by burying a copper spike in the ground near your house. This causes shorts or lightning strikes to go into the ground, rather than into your computer equipment.

Another must-have is a *surge suppressor*, a device that guards your equipment against power surges and other electrical problems. A common variety is a five- or six-outlet strip that has a protection device built in. You can find surge suppressors at your neighborhood hardware store.

Also consider the option of an uninterruptible power supply (UPS). These hardware add-ons can get expensive, but they're reliable. Plus, they don't generate heat inside your computer and take up a PCI slot, like the PowerCard by Guardian On Board (www.guardian-ups.com). The PowerCard is available at most computer retail outlets, and costs about $149. Whether it's hardware- or software-based, a UPS keeps devices from shutting off immediately in the event of blackouts or on/off flickering that frequently occurs during electrical storms. You get a few extra minutes of operation during which you can save your data and shut down programs.

Multimedia add-ons

If multimedia is important to your business, be sure that you have a sound card, speakers, and a microphone. Usually, these features are included with computers that you purchase in retail outlets.

If you aren't sure whether your computer is equipped with these devices, here's how to check:

✔ **If you're a Windows 95 (or higher) user,** follow these steps:

1. **Right-click My Computer and select Properties from the context menu that pops up.**

   The System Properties dialog box appears.

2. **Click the Device Manager tab to bring it to the front. (If you use Windows 2000, click the Hardware tab in System Properties and then click the Device Manager button.)**

   The Device Manager dialog box presents a list of the hardware available on your computer, arranged by the type of device.

3. **Use this list to check for devices.**

   For example, to see whether your computer has a built-in sound card, click the plus sign (+) next to the Sound, video, and game controllers category. If your system already has a sound card, it will be listed beneath the category name, along with other sound, video, or game hardware you have.

✔ **If you're a Macintosh user,** be aware that many Macs don't come with a built-in mike, although virtually all have built-in speakers and sound cards. System software called *extensions* enable the Mac to record audio and play video files. To find out what extensions you have, follow these steps:

   1. **Choose Control Panel⇨Extensions Manager from the Apple menu.**

      Your currently available extensions appear under the Extensions heading, and those that are currently enabled have a check mark.

   2. **Choose Control Panel⇨Sound from the Apple menu to see whether you have a microphone.**

   3. **Make sure that the Mute check box is unchecked in the Volumes Sound options.**

   4. **Select Sound In from the drop-down menu near the top of the Sound dialog box.**

If you know exactly what type of device you need to buy and are only looking for the best price, check one of the online auction services that specialize in computer and other digital equipment, such as CNET Auctions (`auctions. cnet.com/`). If you don't know what you need, talk to a consultant at a computer store or check out a computer buying guide at a newsstand.

You probably don't need to worry about purchasing special sound cards, external speakers, or audio-video goodies when you're first starting out. At a later stage, when your online business site becomes more sophisticated, you may want to try Web browser add-ons that require you to be able to listen to audio and conduct voice communications online, such as the conferencing and whiteboard technologies that are built into the major browser packages: Netscape Communicator and Microsoft Internet Explorer. (Conferencing enables you to communicate by voice with other Internet users in real time, almost as though you're using your computer to make an online phone call.)

Keyboard

All keyboards aren't created alike. Some have 101 keys. Some add special keys that perform special Windows functions. Some are straight and old-fashioned, whereas others are curved in a "natural" style that some users prefer.

One of the coolest new keyboards for computer users who continually surf the Web, Microsoft Natural Keyboard Pro, adds six keys that control your Web browser as well as control your computer's CD-playing software. (You can use keys to change the volume or jump forward or back from one CD track to another.) One special button can be configured to launch your e-mail software of choice.

Microsoft Natural Keyboard Pro has a list price of $75; you can find it for $53 or so at online hardware outlets, such as Buy.com (www.buy.com) or Beyond.com (www.beyond.com). You can save money big time by choosing a conventional (straight, not contoured) keyboard, Microsoft Internet Keyboard, which has ten special Internet keys; I saw it on sale at a discount retailer for $24.99.

Monitor

In terms of your online business, the quality or thinness of your monitor doesn't affect the quality of your Web site directly. Even if you have a poor-quality monitor, you can create a Web site that looks great to those who visit you. The problem is that you won't know how good your site really looks to those customers who have high-quality monitors. It's a good idea to view your Web site on several different kinds of monitors to see how it will look to people with small, poor-quality monitors and to those with bigger, high-quality ones.

As I'm writing this, the new flat-panel LCD (liquid crystal display) monitors are the hot item, and they're becoming more affordable, too. You've got a real choice between a traditional CRT (cathode-ray tube) monitor and a flat LCD. Whether you choose flat or traditional, the quality of a monitor depends on several factors:

✓ **Resolution:** The resolution of a computer monitor refers to the number of pixels it can display horizontally and vertically. A resolution of 640 x 480 means that the monitor can display 640 pixels across the page and 480 pixels down the page. Higher resolutions, such as 800 x 600 or 1,024 x 768, make images look sharper but require more RAM in your computer. Anything less than 640 x 480 is unusable these days.

✔ **Size:** Monitor size is measured diagonally, as with TVs. Sizes such as 14 inches, 15 inches, and up to 21 inches are available. (Look for a 17-inch monitor, which can display most Web pages fully, and which are now available for less than $200.)

✔ **Refresh rate:** This is the number of times per second that a video card redraws an image on-screen. Look for a monitor with a refresh rate of at least 60 Hz (hertz).

Scrimping on computer monitors is tempting, especially for bargain hunters like me. You can find cheap monitors for $100 or even less if you want to go with a used device. I've been known to buy recycled 14-inch monitors myself. However, if I had to do it over again today, I'd probably get at least a 17- or 21-inch monitor instead of the smaller variety. Even an extra inch makes a huge difference in terms of viewing word processing documents and Web pages. Lots of Web pages seem to have been designed with 17-inch or 21-inch monitors in mind. The problem isn't just that some users have 15-inch monitors, but you can never control how wide the viewer's browser window will be. The problem is illustrated in the page from the Yale Style Manual, one of the classic references of Web site design, shown in Figure 3-2.

Figure 3-2:
This page from the Yale Style Manual fits easily into a 15-inch monitor's display space, thus practicing what it preaches.

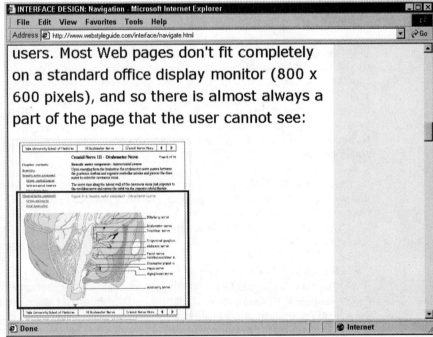

It's annoying when you can't read an entire line of type or see an extra column full of hyperlinks without having to scroll to the right. Besides making your Web surfing more difficult, a small monitor can slow down the process of viewing Web pages that you have created and want to view, either before or after you put them online.

Computer monitors display graphic information that consists of little units called *pixels*. Each pixel appears on-screen as a small dot — so small that it's hard to perceive with the naked eye, unless you magnify an image to look at details close up. Together, the patterns of pixels create different intensities of light in an image, as well as ranges of color. A pixel can contain one or more bytes of binary information. The more pixels per inch (ppi), the higher a monitor's potential resolution. The higher the resolution, the closer the image appears to a continuous-tone image such as a photo. When you see a monitor's resolution described as 1,280 x 1,024, for example, that refers to the number of pixels that the monitor can display. *Dot pitch* refers to the distance between any two of the three pixels (one red, one green, and one blue) that a monitor uses to display color. The lower the dot pitch, the better the image resolution that you obtain. A dot pitch of 0.27 mm is a good measurement for a 17-inch monitor.

Modem

A *modem* is a hardware device that translates your computer's digital data to the analog signals carried over ordinary telephone lines. Modems can do more than just connect computers on the Internet; *fax modems* can also send and receive fax transmissions with other computers or fax machines. Fax modems also let you exchange programs and data files with other computers that are equipped with fax modems.

If you already have a modem that you use to connect your computer to the Internet, you don't necessarily need to purchase a new and faster one just because you're starting an online business. But you should look into a direct connection to the Internet, such as a DSL or cable modem line. (For more information, see "Internet Connection Options" later in this chapter.)

Fax equipment

A fax machine is an essential part of many home offices. If you don't have the funds available for a standalone machine, you can install software that helps your computer send and receive faxes.

Modern modems come in many models

Bandwidth refers to the amount of data that you can transmit through an Internet connection. This amount is usually measured in bits per second (bps). Different kinds of modems provide varying amounts of bandwidth:

✔ **Analog modems:** These devices, either external or built into your computer, are used for dialup connections to the Internet. Modems that transmit 56 Kbps (kilobits per second) of data are common at this writing, though you can probably get by with a 36.6 Kbps modem.

✔ **ISDN modems:** You use a digital ISDN modem if you have an ISDN line installed to your home or business. ISDN modems can deliver 56 Kbps or 128 Kbps of data and are just about obsolete thanks to the two following high-speed options.

✔ **Cable modems:** These modems can receive data from the Internet through a cable TV company's existing underground fiber-optic cable. They are extremely fast and an attractive option — if they available in your area. (See the section "Cable modem" later in this chapter.)

✔ **DSL modems:** Digital Subscriber Line (DSL) modems let conventional telephone lines transfer data at very high rates and are becoming common in many areas. (See the section "DSL" later in this chapter.)

When you're trying to decide on the best Internet connection for your needs, keep in mind that all of these connections require modems that you'll either have to purchase or rent. But don't focus on the modem itself. In the case of cable and DSL, the provider usually picks out a modem for you (though some providers do let you purchase your own modem and even do your own installation if you want to save a few bucks). The important thing is the speed of your connection, the reliability of the provider, and the level of customer service you get.

You have three options for fax communications via your computer:

✔ You can install a fax modem, a hardware device that usually works with fax software. The fax modem can either be an internal or external device.

✔ You can use your regular modem but install software that enables your computer to exchange faxes with someone else's computer or fax machine.

✔ You can sign up for a service that receives your faxes and sends them to your computer in the body of an e-mail message. (See the Fax Services section of this book's Internet Directory for more information.)

If you want to send faxes from your computer, look into WinFax PRO by Symantec, Inc. (www.symantec.com/winfax/index.html). I found the program easy to set up, and software reviewers frequently recommend it. Your Windows computer needs to be equipped with a modem in order to send or receive faxes with WinFax.

After you configure your computer to handle faxes, your computer can do just about anything that a real fax machine can do. For example, you can broadcast faxes to multiple destinations. You can also print faxes to your regular laser printer, thus avoiding the flimsy fax paper that many fax machines use.

Another option is to purchase a multifunction machine, which acts as a fax machine, printer, and photocopier, among other things. (See the upcoming section, "Scanners," for more information on multifunction machines.)

 If you plan to do fax transmissions and access the Internet from your home office, you really should get a second phone line or a direct connection, such as DSL or cable modem. That way, people won't get a busy signal when they're trying to phone or fax you, in case you're already on the phone or the Internet.

Image capture devices

When you're ready to move beyond the basic hardware and on to a frill, think about obtaining a tool for capturing photographic images. (By *capturing*, I mean *digitizing* an image or, in other words, saving it in computerized, digital format.) Photos are often essential elements of business Web pages: They attract a customer's attention, they illustrate items for sale in a catalog, and they can provide before-and-after samples of your work. If you're an artist or designer, having photographic representations of your work is especially important.

Most marketing gurus agree that a picture is worth a thousand megabytes of information. Including a clear, sharp image on your Web site greatly increases your chances of selling your product or service. You have two choices for digitizing:

- ✔ Taking photos with a conventional camera and then processing the prints with a scanner
- ✔ Taking photos with a digital camera and saving the image files on your computer

The choice depends on your budget and your needs; the following sections discuss the advantages and disadvantages of each.

Digital camera

The advantage of using a digital camera instead of a scanner to capture images for your Web site is that it's portable and convenient. A digital camera connects directly to your computer, so you can save images right to disk. You can get photos online in a matter of minutes, without spending money or time having them processed and printed conventionally and then scanning them in.

Not so long ago, digital cameras cost thousands of dollars. These days, you can find a good digital camera made by a reputable manufacturer, such as Nikon, Fuji, Canon, Olympus, or Kodak, for $275–$600. You have to make an investment up front, but this particular tool can pay off for you in the long run. Not only can you use the camera for your business but with the addition of a color printer, you can even print your own photos, which could save you a pile in photo lab costs.

Don't hesitate to fork over the extra dough to get a camera that gives you good resolution. Cutting corners doesn't pay when you end up with images that look fuzzy, but you can find many low-cost devices with good features. For example, the Canon PowerShot A20, which I spotted for $279, has a resolution of more than 2 megapixels — fine enough to print on a color printer and enlarge to a size such as 5 x 7 inches — and a zoom feature. *Megapixels* are calculated by multiplying the number of pixels in an image — for instance, when actually multiplied, 1,984 x 1,488 = 2,952,192 pixels or 2.9 megapixels. But keep in mind that the higher the resolution, the fewer photos your camera is able to store at any one time because each image file requires more memory.

Online material is primarily intended to be displayed on computer monitors (which have limited resolution), so having super-high resolution images isn't critical when it comes to Web pages. Besides, in order to be displayed by Web browsers, images must first be compressed by using the GIF or JPEG formats. (See Chapter 6 for more scintillating technical details on GIF and JPEG.) Also, smaller and simpler images (as opposed to large, high-resolution graphics) generally appear more quickly on the viewer's screen. If you make your customers wait too long to see any given image, they're apt to get bored and go to someone else's online store.

When shopping for a digital camera, look for the following features:

✔ The ability to download images to your computer via a serial port or a USB connection

✔ Bundled image-processing software

✔ The ability to download image files directly to a floppy disk so that you can easily transport them to another location

✔ An included LCD screen that lets you see your images as soon as you take them

On the downside, because of optical filtering that's intended to reduce *color artifacts* — distortions of an image caused by limitations in hardware — photos taken with digital cameras tend to be less sharp than conventional

35mm photos. You can correct this problem in a graphics program, but that can be time consuming. If you want high-quality close-ups and your budget is limited, try a scanner instead.

Scanners

Scanning is the process of turning the colors and shapes contained in a photographic print or slide into digital information (that is, bytes of data) that a computer can understand. You place the image in a position where the scanner's camera can pass over it, and the scanner turns the image into a computer document that consists of tiny bits of information called *pixels*.

The best news about scanners is that they've been around for a while, which, in the world of computing, means that prices are going down at the same time that quality is on the rise. The bargain models are well under $100, and I've even seen a couple priced as low as $49.95 after a rebate.

Scanners come in many different types. Some devices scan slides, but most accept photographic prints. The one that I find easiest to use is a flatbed scanner. You place the photo or other image on a flat glass bed, just like what you find on a photocopier. An optical device moves under the bed and scans the photo.

A type of scanner that has lots of benefits for small or home-based businesses is a multifunction device. You can find these units, along with conventional printers and scanners, at computer outlets. I have a multifunction device myself, in my home office. It sends and receives faxes, scans images, acts as a laser printer, and makes copies — plus it includes a telephone and answering machine. Now, if it could just make a good cup of espresso. . . .

A low-budget alternative

If you only want to get a computerized version of your smiling face on your Web site and you don't want to invest in any of the hardware that I mention here, not to worry. Just call your local photo shop or copy center. Many Kinko's Copies outlets, for example, provide computer services that include scanning photos. If you do your photo processing through Kodak, you can have the images placed online or on a CD. If you're a member of America Online, you can get your photos online through a program called "You've Got Pictures" and delivered to a location that you set up with AOL.

Wherever you go, be sure to tell the technician that you want the image to appear on the Web, so it should be saved in GIF or JPEG format. Also, if you have an idea of how big you want the final image to be when it appears online, tell that to the technician, too. The person can save the image in the size that you want, so you don't have to resize it later in a graphics program.

Video capture devices

Some of the top-of-the-line digital video cameras capture still images that you can port to your computer. But in general, the image quality of these still video images isn't as sharp as an image from a good digital camera. Additionally, digital video cameras may be small in size, but they're hefty in terms of price.

If you already have a video camera for home use and you need a way to get images on the Web, consider a neat little device called Snappy Video Snapshot, which enables you to select still images from your videotapes and save them in digital format so that you can show them on your Web pages.

Snappy is a software and hardware package that works only with PCs, not Macs. You plug the hardware module into your printer port, install the software, and then plug your camcorder into the hardware module by using the cables that come with the product. The taped images appear on your computer screen through the Snappy software window. When you find the image you want, you can adjust contrast and brightness and then save it as a computer file. Snappy's original manufacturer, Play Incorporated, no longer supports the product, but at the time of this writing, you could still find Snappy for less than $20 at the computer store CDW (www.cdw.com).

You can even convert a VHS videotape to CD or DVD format by sending it to a company called YesVideo.com (or you can drop off your tape with many Target and Walgreens stores, which will send them to YesVideo). You can then isolate still images from the digital file and convert them to Web page format by using a graphics program. Visit www.yesvideo.com for more information.

Internet Connection Options

After you purchase the computer hardware that you need, telephone bills are likely to be the biggest monthly expense you'll encounter in connection with your online business. At least, they are for me: I pay for local service, long-distance service, cell phone service, plus DSL service over my phone lines. It pays to choose your *telco* (telephone company) connection wisely.

A second phone line

First and foremost, you should strongly consider obtaining a second phone line for your office. Having a second line is pretty much a given if you plan to do business online regularly — or if your children and significant other use your existing phone line even on a semi-regular basis.

Because you'll be using your modem to dial the same one or two access numbers provided by your Internet service provider, confirm with your telco that your Internet access number is truly local — not a number for which you're required to pay any kind of a toll fee.

Ask your telco whether a call pack is available. Call packs allow you to make a large number of calls to the same number for the same rate: 100 calls per month for a flat $10 fee, for example.

Beyond dialup

Fewer and fewer people I know, even those who are on a budget, use a regular dialup modem connection to get online. This is the simplest and most straightforward way to connect to the Internet — though it's also the slowest. A far better way to connect to the Internet is through a *direct line*, which means that, rather than be connected to the Internet for the length of your modem's phone call, you're connected all the time. Besides freeing up a phone line, a direct connection is typically light-years faster than a dialup modem connection.

If you have a modem and a dialup connection already, fine; go ahead and use it. But when your e-mail messages begin to mount and you start surfing the Web more often to market your online business, you may find that your old connection is slow and cumbersome. In that case, consider upgrading to a direct connection. But if you haven't signed up with a provider, first look around to see whether the following attractive options are available.

Cable modem

Cable modem connections offer a really attractive way to get a high-speed connection to cyberspace. So go ahead and ask your local cable TV providers whether they provide this service. Turmoil erupted when the largest cable provider, @Home, ceased operations in early 2002. But other options, such as AT&T Broadband Internet (www.attbroadband.com) and EarthLink (www. earthlink.net/home/broadband/cable) provide high-speed Internet access through affiliations with cable TV providers in many parts of the country. In my neighborhood in Chicago, a company called RCN Chicago (rcnchicago.com) offers Internet access via cable modem for $45.95 plus a $75 installation fee that includes the cable modem device itself. AT&T Broadband Internet (www.attbroadband.com), however, offers similar service for $39.95.

The advantages of having a cable modem connection are many: It's a direct connection, it frees up a phone line, and it's super fast. Cable modems have the capacity to deliver 4 or 5MB of data per second. In reality, of course, the speed is going to be less than this because you're sharing access with other users. Plus, you have to purchase or lease the cable modem itself, pay an installation fee, and purchase an Ethernet card. But a cable modem is still almost certainly going to be far faster than your dialup connection.

You can find out which cable modem and DSL providers cover your area by using the Service Availability tool provided by Cable-Modem.net (`www.cable-modem.net/gc/service_availability.html`).

DSL

Wouldn't it be great if you could use conventional telephone lines to connect to the Internet all the time? Wouldn't it be even better if the connection were really fast — say, 100 times as fast as a 56 Kbps dialup modem?

If your telephone company offers its customers Digital Subscriber Line (DSL) connections, these aren't just pie-in-the-sky questions. DSLs "borrow" the part of your phone line that your voice doesn't use, the part that transmits signals of 3,000 Hz (hertz) or higher. DSLs can *upload* (send) data to another location on the Internet at 1.088 Mbps (megabits per second), and *download* (receive) data at more than twice that rate: 2.560 Mbps.

Of course, you can't just use your existing telephone to connect via DSL. DSL requires you to buy and install special hardware at your end of the telephone line. The telephone company needs to have the same piece of DSL hardware at its end. Where you live also makes a difference: You must be located relatively close to a telephone switch that supports DSL technology.

DSL comes in different varieties. Asymmetrical Digital Subscriber Line (ADSL) transmits information at different speeds depending on whether you're sending or receiving data. Symmetrical Digital Subscriber Line (SDSL) transmits information at the same speed in both directions. As DSL gets more popular, it becomes more widely available and the pricing drops. As I'm writing this, EarthLink DSL is available for $49.95 per month with free DSL modem and installation. Your local phone provider might offer DSL, too. In the Chicago area, Ameritech has a DSL option for $49 per month plus $99 to purchase the DSL modem.

MSN TV Service

Since Microsoft purchased it, WebTV has changed its name to MSN TV Service and has received a big boost in attention and the services it offers. It's an option that a home-based entrepreneur might well consider as an alternative to owning two computers. With MSN TV Service, you purchase a set-top box, a hand-held controller, and a keyboard. You sign up with the MSN TV Service network and pay a monthly fee for access. Although MSN TV Service uses a regular telephone jack, you don't necessarily need to install a second phone line. Classic service MSN TV Service uses call waiting to put the Internet "on hold" while your phone calls come through.

The advantage of MSN TV Service is that it gives you a way to surf the Web and use Internet software without having to purchase a computer. It frees up your regular computer so that someone else in the family can do homework — or you can work on your business site while someone else surfs the Web. At this writing, MSN TV Service Classic service costs $21.95 per month if you need a dialup Internet connection or $11.95 per month if you want to use the service with an existing connection.

ISDN

ISDN (Integrated Services Digital Network) service is becoming a far less attractive option now that DSL and cable modems are becoming more available and affordable. ISDN is still an alternative for many rural Web surfers, however, who don't have access to DSL or cable modem. ISDN enables your computer to connect to the Net at 64 or 128 Kbps by means of a special phone line and line-switching equipment that your phone company must install. You have to check with your phone company to find out whether it provides ISDN service.

Internet and Other Software

One of the great things about starting an Internet business is that you get to use Internet software. As you probably know, the programs you use online are inexpensive (sometimes free), easy to use and install, and continually being updated.

Although you probably already have a basic selection of software to help you find information and communicate with others in cyberspace, the following sections describe some programs you may not have as yet and that will come in handy when you create your online business.

Web browser

A *Web browser* is software that serves as a visual interface to the images, colors, links, and other content contained on the Web. The most popular such program is Microsoft Internet Explorer, with Netscape Navigator (part of the Communicator suite) coming in a distant second place.

Your Web browser is your primary tool for conducting business online, just as it is for everyday personal use. When it comes to running a virtual store or consulting business, though, you have to run your software through a few more paces than usual. You need your browser to

✔ Preview the Web pages you create

✔ Display frames, animations, movie clips, and other goodies you plan to add online

✔ Support some level of Internet security, such as Secure Sockets Layer (SSL), if you plan to conduct secure transactions on your site

In addition to having an up-to-date browser with the latest features, installing more than one kind of browser on your computer is a good idea. For example, if you use Microsoft Internet Explorer because that's what came with your operating system, be sure to download the latest copy of Netscape Navigator, as well. That way, you can test your site to make sure that it looks good to all your visitors.

Another reason to have more than one Web browser available is that certain Web sites work well with one browser and not at all with others. Try using Netscape Navigator to connect to the Microsoft Web site and you're likely to end up with nothing because its pages have actually been configured to block out Netscape users. Recently, when I tried to view some of the EarthLink pages in Internet Explorer, I came up blank, but the same pages showed up fine in Navigator. Also consider using a freely available browser called Opera by Opera Software (www.opera.com).

Web page editor

HyperText Markup Language (HTML) is a set of instructions used to format text, images, and other Web page elements so that Web browsers can correctly display them. But you don't have to learn HTML in order to create your own Web pages. Plenty of programs called *Web page editors* are available to help you format text, add images, make hyperlinks, and do all the fun assembly steps necessary to make your Web site a winner.

In many cases, Web page editors come with electronic storefront packages; QuickSite, which I discuss in Chapter 4, comes with Microsoft FrontPage Express. Sometimes, programs that you use for one purpose can also help you create Web documents: Microsoft Word has an add-on called Internet Assistant that enables you to save text documents as HTML Web pages, and Microsoft Office 98 (for the Mac) or 2000 (for Windows) enables you to export files in Web page format automatically.

Taking e-mail a step higher

You're probably very familiar with sending and receiving e-mail messages. But when you start an online business, you should make sure that e-mail software has some advanced features:

- **Autoresponders:** Some programs automatically respond to e-mail requests with a form letter or document of your choice.

- **Mailing lists:** With a well-organized address book (a feature that comes with some e-mail programs), you can collect the e-mail addresses of visitors or subscribers and send them a regular update of your business activities or, better yet, an e-mail newsletter.

- ✔ **Quoting:** Almost all e-mail programs let you quote from a message to which you're replying, so you can respond easily to a series of questions.

- ✔ **Attaching:** Attaching a file to an e-mail message is a quick and convenient way to transmit information from one person to another.

- ✔ **Signature files:** Make sure that your e-mail software automatically includes a simple electronic signature at the end. Use this space to list your company name, your title, and your Web site URL.

Both Outlook Express, the e-mail component of Microsoft Internet Explorer, and Netscape Messenger, which is part of the Netscape Communicator suite of programs, include most or all of these features. Because these functions are all essential aspects of providing good customer service, I discuss them in more detail in Chapter 9.

Discussion group software

A *newsgroup* is a collection of messages about a particular subject. Newsgroups are part of Usenet, an extensive and popular part of the Internet. In order to read and post messages to Usenet discussion groups, you need newsgroup software, which is built into Netscape Communicator and Microsoft Internet Explorer.

However, when your business site is up and running, consider taking it a step further by creating your own discussion area right on your Web site. This sort of discussion area isn't a newsgroup as such; it doesn't exist in Usenet, and you don't need newsgroup software to read and post messages. Rather, it's a Web-based discussion area where your visitors can compare notes and share their passion for the products you sell or the area of service you provide.

Programs such as Microsoft FrontPage enable you to set up a discussion area on your Web site. See Chapter 9 for more information.

FTP software

FTP (File Transfer Protocol) is one of those acronyms you see time and time again as you move around the Internet. You may even have an FTP program that your ISP gave you when you obtained your Internet account. But chances are you don't use it that often.

In case you haven't used FTP yet, start dusting it off. When you create your own Web pages, a simple, no-nonsense FTP program is the easiest way to transfer them from your computer at home to your Web host. If you need to correct and update your Web pages quickly (and you will), you'll benefit by having your FTP software ready and set up with your Web site address, user-name, and password so that you can transfer files right away. See Chapter 4 for more on using File Transfer Protocol.

Image editors

You need a graphics editing program either to create original artwork for your Web pages or to crop and adjust your scanned/digitally photographed images. In the case of adjusting or cropping photographic image files, the software you need almost always comes bundled with the scanner or digital camera, so you don't need to buy separate software for that.

In the case of graphic images, the first question to ask yourself is, "Am I really qualified to draw and make my own graphics?" If the answer is yes, think share-ware first. Two programs I like are LView Pro by Leonardo Haddad Loureiro (www.lview.com) and Paint Shop Pro by Jasc, Inc. (www.jasc.com). You can download both of these programs from the Web to use on a trial basis. After the trial period is over, you'll need to pay a small fee to the developer in order to register and keep the program. LView Pro version 2001 costs $40; Paint Shop Pro, which is shown in Figure 3-3, costs $99 for Version 7 or $49 if you're upgrading from an earlier version.

Figure 3-3:
Paint Shop Pro enables you to crop, resize, re-color, and save images for the Web.

The ability to download and use free (and almost free) software from share-ware archives and many other sites is one of the nicest things about the Internet. Keep the system working by remembering to pay the shareware fees to the nice folks who make their software available to individuals like you and me.

IRC

Internet Relay Chat (IRC) is a form of real-time computer conferencing between Internet users. Users communicate by typing messages and submitting them to a central computer, called a *chat server*, using special chat software. Chances are you don't have to download a special chat program because chat function-ality is integrated into the latest versions of Microsoft Internet Explorer and Netscape Communicator. The difference between Internet Relay Chat and newsgroups is that participants in a chat room can read messages and respond with their own within a matter of seconds.

Chatting is one of the most popular features of the Internet and a great source of fun and recreation. But it's not just a way for teenagers to share their angst. Some ways that you can use chat for business include conducting an online meeting with a group of customers or clients, or connecting with people who are interested in your area of expertise.

Instant messaging

You may think that MSN Messenger, AOL Instant Messenger, ICQ, and PalTalk are just for social "chatting" online, but instant messaging has its business applications, too. Here are a few suggestions:

- ✔ If individuals you work with all the time are hard to reach, you can use a messaging program to tell you if those people are logged on to their computers. This allows you to contact them the moment they sit down to work (provided they don't mind your greeting them so quickly, of course).

- ✔ You can cut down on long-distance phone charges by exchanging mes-sages with far-flung colleagues.

- ✔ With a microphone, sound card, and speakers, you can carry on voice conversations through your messaging software.

MSN Messenger enables users to do file transfers without having to use FTP software or attaching files to e-mail messages.

Internet phone

Some businesspeople regularly use Internet phone to communicate in real time with colleagues and customers across the country and around the world. You can use Conference, included in the Netscape Communicator suite of applications, or NetMeeting, which comes with Microsoft Internet Explorer, to make Internet phone calls.

Other Business Software

Besides benefiting from the software that lets you navigate and communicate online, your business can benefit from programs that help you keep track of accounts, solve technical problems, and get your words online. The following sections briefly present some suggestions for business software that you can use.

Building an online presence takes time

Judy Vorfeld, who goes by the *nom de Net* Webgrammar, started the online version of her business Office Support Services (www. ossweb.com) from her home in Arizona in early 1998. She now has a second Web site (www.webgrammar.com), which serves as a resource for students, educators, writers, and Web developers.

As far as equipment goes, Judy estimates that each year she spends about $1,000 to $1,500 on computer hardware and $350 on software related to her business. She has two desktop computers — one of which is her primary machine, the other serves as a backup — and each computer has a Pentium III processor, which she upgrades once a year. Her data files are stored on an MR27 Mobile Rack that she can use with either machine. She also has a Seagate tape backup. Her 6-lb. laptop, which she uses whenever she travels, has a CD-RW/DVD-ROM drive, and 256 MB/RAM. For software, she uses the Web page editor Macromedia HomeSite to create Web pages,

Paint Shop Pro to work with graphics, and Microsoft Word for most of her book editing.

Q. What would you describe as the primary goal of your online business?

A. To help small businesses achieve excellent presentation and communication by copy-editing their print documents, books, and Web sites.

Q. How many hours a week do you work on your business site?

A. Three to six hours, which includes my syndicated writing tips, surveys, and newsletter, Communication Expressway (www.ossweb.com/ezine-archive-index.html).

Q. How do you promote your site?

A. Participating in newsgroups, writing articles for Internet publications, adding my URLs to good search engines and directories, moderating discussion lists and forums for others, and offering free articles and tips on my sites.

Q. Has your online business been profitable financially?

A. I continue to break even, and am able to upgrade hardware and software regularly. I rarely raise my rates because my skills seem best suited to the small business community, and I want to offer a fee these people can afford.

Q. Who creates your business's Web pages?

A. I create them myself. I tried having others do it, but I wanted the ability to make extensive and frequent changes in text and design. I do hire someone to format my e-zine pages and graphics.

Q. What advice would you give to someone starting an online business?

A. I have a bunch of suggestions to give, based on my own experience:

✔ **Network.** Network with small business people who have complementary businesses and with those who have similar businesses. Also, network by joining professional associations participating in the activities. Volunteer time and expertise. Link to these organizations from your site.

✔ **Join newsgroups.** Study netiquette first. Lurk until you can adequately answer a question or make a comment. Also, keep on the lookout for someone with whom you can build up a relationship, someone who might mentor you and be willing to occasionally scrutinize your site, a news release, and so on. This person must be brutally honest, but perhaps you can informally offer one of your own services in return.

✔ **Learn Web development and the culture.** Even if you don't do the actual design, you have to make decisions on all the offers you receive regarding how to make money via affiliate programs, link exchanges, hosts, Web design software, etc. It's vital that you keep active online and make those judgments yourself, unless you thoroughly trust your Webmaster. Find online discussion lists that handle all areas of Web development and keep informed.

✔ **Include a Web page that shows your business biography or profile.** Mention any volunteer work you do, groups to which you belong, and anything else you do in and for the community. You need to paint as clear a picture as possible in just a few words. Avoid showcasing your talents and hobbies on a business site unless they are directly related to your business.

✔ **In everything you write, speak to your visitors.** Use the word "you" as much as possible. Avoid the words "I," "we," and "us." You, as a businessperson, are there to connect with your visitors. You can't give them eye contact, but you can let them know that they matter, that they are (in a sense) the reason for your being there.

✔ **Become known as a specialist in a given field.** Be someone who can always answer a question or go out and find the answer. Your aim is to get as many potential clients or customers to your site as possible, not to get millions of visitors. Forget numbers and concentrate on creating a site that grabs the attention of your target market.

✔ **Get help.** If you can't express yourself well with words (and/or graphics), and know little about layout, formatting, etc., hire someone to help you. You'll save yourself a lot of grief if you get a capable, trustworthy editor or designer.

She concludes: "Don't start such a business unless you are passionate about it, and willing to give it some time and an initial investment. But when you do start, there are resources everywhere — many of them free — to help people build their businesses successfully."

Voice recognition software

Personally, I like to type. It gives my hands something to do while thoughts are cooking inside my brain. But I realize that, for lots of other people, typing is akin to sitting in the dentist's chair listening to the drill whine. Many small-business people are interested in voice recognition software that automatically turns their spoken words into typed computer text. Here are two suggestions:

- **Dragon Naturally Speaking:** This program, by ScanSoft (`www.dragonsys.com/naturallyspeaking/`), has been around for several years and comes in many specialized versions. The Essentials version costs $59.99 and requires a 400 MHz or higher Pentium processor, 64MB of RAM, and 300MB of hard disk space.

- **IBM ViaVoice Personal Edition:** This program, which lists for just $29, ($171 in the version for Mac OS X users) lets you dictate directly into a Microsoft Word document. To use this program, IBM recommends that you have 64MB of RAM and 460MB of hard disk space. Spanish-language versions are also available. Find out more at `www-3.ibm.com/software/speech/desktop/w9-prs.html`.

Microsoft Office XP also has voice recognition, though personally I've found that it makes too many mistakes to replace my flying fingers.

Antivirus and troubleshooting software

Lots of good things can come to you from cyberspace, but, unfortunately, some bad things can invade your computer space, as well. These include harmful programs called *viruses*, destructive *macros*, or *Trojan horses*, each of which can rob you of data or disable your computer in some way.

Every computer that is connected regularly to the Internet needs to be equipped with some sort of virus protection software. Such programs have the ability to detect a virus if it is downloaded to your machine from the Internet. Usually, the software notifies you when it detects a virus and disables the virus as well.

Because new viruses keep cropping up, I suggest that you buy a program (or, in the case of VirusScan, an online service) that provides you with free upgrades to catch the latest harmful things that could invade your computer. Here are some good bets:

- ✔ **VirusScan Online** by McAfee.com (`www.mcafee.com/products/#VirusScan`). You purchase a subscription that enables you to download the software, then update it periodically to keep up with new viruses. A one-year subscription costs $29.95; a two-year subscription costs $49.90.

- ✔ **Dr. Solomon's Anti-Virus** (`www.drsolomon.com`). This, too, is owned by McAfee.com; it costs $49.95.

One way to deal with computer trouble, in case you do encounter it, is to record serial numbers and make/model information for all of your equipment. This practice is important for insurance purposes, in case something is lost or stolen, and it also helps if your computer is down and you need to talk to service people about exactly how much memory and what kind of peripheral hardware you have attached to the machine.

Backup software

Losing copies of your personal documents is one thing, but losing files related to your business can hit you hard in the pocketbook. That makes it even more important to make backups of your online business computer files.

Iomega Zip or Jaz drives come with software that lets you automatically make backups of your files. If you don't own one of these programs, I recommend you get really familiar with the backup program included with Windows XP, or look into Backup Exec by VERITAS Software Corporation (`www.veritas.com`).

If you need help . . .

Your wires are crossed, your computers aren't speaking to one another on your network, and your browser is freezing up. Don't suffer in silence.

I can think of no better place to look for free help than the Internet itself. After you restart your computer, try to connect to the Internet and consult newsgroups. If you can't get your computer to work, use another computer; you may have to visit your local library to use a public computer that can access the Internet. Turn to any newsgroup that relates to the problem you're having.

Check out the `comp.infosystems` hierarchy for computer issues. Groups in the `news.software.misc` category address software problems.

When all else fails, find out whether the computer store where you purchased your equipment will help you. They may charge a fee, but in the long run, the expense may be worthwhile, especially if a qualified technician can get your computer to run faster or your browser to operate better every time you go online.

Internet storefront software

If you plan to present lots of catalog items for sale on the Web, and you envision a full-fledged online business that includes customer service options and online purchases, you may want to look into software that guides you through the process of creating an online store.

Electronic storefront programs take much of the work out of designing Web pages and putting them online. These programs often provide you with predesigned Web pages, called *templates*, that you can customize with your own content. They usually also provide space on a Web server that will host your site, and they lead you through the process of transferring your files from your computer to the server.

Chapter 4 examines some of the more affordable storefront programs, but if you're curious, check out some Web sites that give you space on a Web server and also let you create a storefront online:

- ✔ **Microsoft bCentral** (www.bcentral.com)**:** bCentral provides you with forms that you can use to create a sales catalog of products that you can subsequently sell through the Microsoft Network or other sales channels.

- ✔ **Yahoo! Store** (store.yahoo.com)**:** The Yahoo! storefront option is easy to use and you can try it out for free. You pay a flat fee of $100 per month to offer up to 50 items for sale on your site. More expensive pricing options are available for larger storefronts.

Accounting software

Because you're essentially creating and operating your online business through your computer, keeping track of your finances on your computer only makes sense.

You don't necessarily have to purchase special accounting software to do this. You can set up a table in Word or Word Perfect, or use Microsoft Works or Excel. But with luck, you will need to keep track of lots of orders and will want a more powerful financial software package. For something more elaborate, try programs such as QuickBooks, Quicken, Peachtree Accounting, or one of the other popular software packages that I describe in Chapter 14.

Part II
Putting Your Web Site to Work

The 5th Wave   By Rich Tennant

"Just how accurately should my Web site reflect my place of business?"

In this part . . .

Just as business owners in the real world have to rent or buy a facility and fix it up to conduct their businesses, you have to develop an online storefront to conduct your online business. In this part, I explain how to put a virtual roof over your store and light a cyberfire to welcome your customers. In other words, it focuses on the nuts and bolts of your Web site itself.

The World Wide Web is the most exciting and popular place to open an online store. But merely creating a set of Web pages isn't enough to succeed online. Your site needs to be compelling — even irresistible. This part shows you how to organize your site and fill it with useful content that attracts customers in the first place and encourages them to stay to browse. I also show you ways to open your Web site to an international audience, to get your pages up and running quickly, and to equip your site (and yourself) to handle many different kinds of electronic purchases.

Chapter 4

Choosing Your Web Host and Design Tools

*A*lthough you can sell items online without having a Web site, doing real online business without one is nearly impossible. The vast majority of online commercial concerns use their Web sites as the primary way to attract customers, convey their message, and make sales. A few ambitious capitalists use online auction sites such as eBay (www.ebay.com) to make money, but the serious auctioneers often have their own Web pages, too.

Two of the most important factors in determining a Web site's success are where it's hosted and how it's designed. These factors affect how easily you can create and update your Web pages, what special features such as multimedia or interactive forms you can have on your site, and even how your site looks. Some hosting services provide Web page creation tools that are easy to use but that limit the level of sophistication you can apply to their design. Other services leave the creation and design up to you. In this chapter, I provide an overview of your Web hosting options as well as different design approaches that you can implement.

A growing number of Web sites and CD-ROMs say that they can have your Web site up and running online "in a matter of minutes" using a "seamless" process. The actual construction may indeed be quick and smooth — as long as you've done all your preparation work beforehand. This preparation work includes identifying your goals for going online, deciding on the market that you want to reach, deciding what products you want to sell, writing descriptions and capturing images of those products, and so on. Before you jump over to Yahoo! Store or bCentral and start assembling your site, be sure that you've done all the groundwork that I discuss in Chapters 2 and 3, such as identifying your audience and setting up your hardware.

Finding a Host with the Most

An Internet connection and a Web browser are all you need if you're simply intending to surf through cyberspace, consuming information and shopping for online goodies. But when you're starting an online business, you're no longer just a consumer; you're becoming a provider of information and consumable goods. Along with a way to connect to the Internet, you need to find a hosting service that will make your online business available to your prospective customers.

A *Web hosting service* is the online world's equivalent of a landlord. Just as the owner of a building gives you office space or room for a storefront where you can hang your shingle, a hosting service provides you with space online where you can set up shop.

A Web host provides space on special computers called *Web servers* that are connected to the Internet all the time. Web servers are equipped with software that makes your Web pages visible to people who connect to them by using a Web browser. The process of using a Web hosting service for your online business works roughly like this:

1. **You decide where you want your site to appear on the Internet.**

   Do you want it to be part of a virtual shopping mall that includes many other businesses? Or do you want a standalone site that has its own Web address and doesn't appear to be affiliated with any other organization?

2. **You sign up with a Web host.**

   Sometimes you pay a fee, and sometimes no fee is required, which is increasingly unusual. In all cases, you're assigned space on a server. Your Web site gets an address, or *URL*, that people can enter in their browsers to view your pages.

3. **You create your Web pages.**

   Usually, you use a Web page editor to do this.

4. **After creating content, adding images, and making your site look just right, you transfer your Web page files (HTML documents, images, and so on) from your computer to the host's Web server.**

   You generally need special File Transfer Protocol (FTP) software to do the transferring. (The most popular Web editors, such as Macromedia Dreamweaver, will let you do this too.)

5. **You access your own site with your Web browser and check the contents to make sure that all the images appear and that any hypertext links you created go to the intended destinations.**

   At this point, you're open for business — visitors can view your Web pages by entering your Web address in their Web browser's Go to field.

6. **You market and promote your site to attract potential clients or customers.**

Carefully choose a Web host because the Web host will affect which software you'll use to create your Web pages and get them online. The Web host also affects the way your site looks, and it may determine the complexity of your Web address. (See the "What's in a name?" sidebar later in this chapter for details.)

If you have a direct connection to the Internet such as a DSL line and are really good with computers (or if you have access to someone who is), you can host your own site on the Web. However, turning your own computer into a Web server is a lot more complicated than signing up with a hosting service. (Your ISP may not allow you to set up your own server anyway; check your user agreement first.) You need to install server software and set up a domain name for your computer. You may even have to purchase a static IP address for your machine. (An *IP address* is a number that identifies every computer that's connected to the Internet, and that consists of four sets of numerals separated by dots, such as 206.207.99.1. A *static IP address* is one that doesn't change from session to session.) If you're just starting a simple home-based or part-time business, hosting your own Web site is probably more trouble than you care to handle, but you should be aware that it's an option.

Shopping for a Web Server to Call Home

Hi! I'm your friendly World Wide Web real estate agent. Call me Virtual Larry. You say you're not sure exactly what kind of Web site is right for you, and you want to see all the options, from a tiny storefront in a strip mall to your own landscaped corporate park? Your wish is my command. Just hop into my 2002-model Internet Explorer, buckle your seat belt, and I'll show you around the many different business properties available in cyberspace.

Here's a road map of our tour:

- ✔ **Online Web-host-and-design-kit combos:** Yahoo! Store, Yahoo! GeoCities, and bCentral, among others.
- ✔ **America Online:** My Place and Hometown AOL.
- ✔ **Electronic merchant CD-ROMs:** ShopSite and WebSite Complete, to name two.

✔ **eBay:** A site that lets its users create their own About Me Web pages.

✔ **Auxiliary companies:** These folks do something that doesn't seem directly related to e-commerce, but they let you build a store online, like FedEx eCommerce Builder.

✔ **An online shopping mall:** You can rent a space in these virtual malls.

✔ **Your current Internet service provider (ISP):** Many ISPs are only too happy to host your e-commerce site — for an extra monthly fee in addition to your access fee.

✔ **Companies devoted to hosting Web sites full-time:** These are businesses whose primary function is hosting e-commerce Web sites and providing their clients with associated software, such as Web page building tools, shopping carts, catalog builders, and the like.

The first four options combine Web hosting with Web page creation kits. Whether you buy these services or get to use them on the Web for free, you simply follow the manufacturer's instructions. Most of these hosting services enable you to create your Web pages by filling in forms; you never have to see a line of HTML code if you don't want to. Depending on which service you choose, you have varying degrees of control over how your site ultimately looks.

The last three options (ISPs, online malls, and full-time Web hosts) tend to be do-it-yourself projects. You sign up with the host, you choose the software, and you create your own site. However, the distinction between this category and the others is blurry. As competition between Web hosts grows keener, more and more companies are providing ready-made solutions that streamline the process of Web site creation for their customers. For you, the end user, this is a good thing: You have plenty of control over how your site comes into being and how it grows over time.

If you simply need a basic Web site and don't want a lot of choices, go with one of the kits. Your site may look like everyone else's and seem a little generic, but setup is easy and you can concentrate on marketing and running your business.

However, if you're the independent type who wants to control your site and have lots of room to grow, consider taking on a do-it-yourself project. The sky's the limit as far as the degree of creativity you can exercise and the amount of sweat equity you can put in (as long as you don't make your site so large and complex that shoppers have a hard time finding anything, of course). The more work you do, the greater your chances of seeing your business prosper.

Web site homesteading for free

Free Web hosting is still possible for small businesses. If you're on a tight budget and looking for space on a Web server for free, turn first to your ISP, which probably gives you server space to set up a Web site. You can also check out one of a handful of sites that provide customers with hosting space for no money down and no monthly payments, either. Instead of money, you pay in terms of advertising: you might have to look at ads or other things, but if you don't mind, here are some good deals you can enjoy:

✔ **Netfirms (www.netfirms.com):** This site places ads on your Web pages but gives you 25MB of server space where you can set up a business Web site for free and get CGI processing for your forms, too. CGI (Common Gateway Interface) provides a way for a Web server to interact with an application, such as a computer script, that receives the information from a form and processes it in a form that you can read easily.

✔ **Freeservers (www.freeservers.com):** In exchange for banner ads, which you view on its site, and Freeservers Special Offers, which are sent to your e-mail address, this site gives you several tools. You have the choice of two free editors, add-ons (such as guest books and hit counters), and an online Web page building tool for creating your site — not to mention 12MB of server space.

You'll find more free Web hosting services on Yahoo! at `dir.yahoo.com/Business_ and_Economy/Business_to_Business/ Communications_and_Networking/ Internet_and_World_Wide_Web/ Network_Service_Providers/Hosting/ Web_Site_Hosting/Free_Hosting/`. Be sure that the site you choose lets you set up for-profit business sites for free.

Using online Web site creation kits

A new class of Web sites has caught on to the concept of making things easy and affordable for would-be ontrepreneurs (online entrepreneurs). These sites act as both a Web host and a Web page creation tool. You connect to the site, sign up for service, and fill out a series of forms. Submitting the completed forms activates a script on the host site that automatically generates your Web pages based on the data you entered.

In this section, I show you how to set up a business Web site using Yahoo! Store, a popular "kit" service. Many such sites are available, and investigating all your options is always smart. Some other Web site creation packages are available at the following sites:

✔ **Yahoo! GeoCities** (`geocities.yahoo.com`)**:** Yahoo! GeoCities is a popular spot for individuals who want to create home pages and full-fledged personal and business Web sites at a low cost. The site charges a $15 setup fee plus an $8.95 per month hosting fee.

✔ **AOL Hometown** (`hometown.aol.com`)**:** America Online hosts this Web site where individuals can create their own Web pages for business or personal use. A "neighborhood" within AOL Hometown, called Business Park, is set aside for commercial sites, and an area within the Business Park area hosts home-based businesses. (See the upcoming section, "Setting up shop with America Online," for more information.)

Yahoo! Store makes setting up an online business easy. The hard part is deciding what you want to sell, how best to describe your sales items, and how to promote your site. Getting your words and images online is remarkably straightforward:

1. **Connect to the Internet, start up your Web browser, and go to** `store.yahoo.com`**.**

   The Yahoo! Store home page appears in your browser window.

2. **Click the link just beneath the introductory text. (The exact text changes; when this book was written, the link was called <u>30 Days Free Sign Up Now!</u>)**

   The Welcome to Yahoo! Store page appears. Before creating a store, you need to register with Yahoo! and obtain a username and password (if you haven't done so already).

3. **Enter your password and click the Sign In button, or, if you haven't registered yet, click the <u>Sign up now</u> link and follow the steps to obtain a username and password.**

   After you sign in, the Build Your Own Yahoo! Store page appears.

4. **Verify your personal information on the Build Your Own Yahoo! Store page; be sure to click Yes in reply to the question, "Do you need help building your Yahoo! Store?"**

5. **When you're done, click the Create my Yahoo! Store button at the bottom of the page.**

   Another Yahoo! Store page appears, this one with the heading Yahoo! Store Test Drive — Free 30-Day Trial.

6. **Enter a name for your store as well as your contact information. When you're done, click the <u>Create My Yahoo! Store!</u> link.**

   The front page (or home page) of your store appears, the first in a series of "guided tour" Web pages of your site. These pages contain messages that explain how to create your store.

7. **Click the Edit button at the bottom of the screen.**

A page with a Message text box appears.

8. **Enter a Welcome message in the Message box and click Update.**

   Your store's Welcome page reappears with your message visible.

9. **Click Variables.**

   A page entitled Colors and Typefaces appears. The default text color, black, is displayed.

10. **Either click Update to accept the default color or click the <u>Choose a color</u> link to select a new one.**

    This step assumes you click Update. Your store's Welcome page reappears.

11. **Click the New Section button.**

    A simple Web form appears with the instructions "Enter a name for the section" at the top of the page.

12. **Type a name for a major section of your Web site, and then click Update.**

    Your new section heading appears on your Web-page-in-progress, as shown in Figure 4-1.

Figure 4-1:
After you fill out a simple form, Yahoo! Store gives you instant results, such as this sample home page.

13. **Click the Up button at the bottom of the page to return to the front page of your store, and then click the button that bears the name of the heading you created in Step 12.**

    The section heading page appears for the section you created in Step 12.

14. **Click the New Page button.**

    Another Web form appears, this one with Name, Image, Headline, and Caption fields where you can enter information about the merchandise you want to sell within this section of your store. The caption field contains a description of the merchandise.

15. **Fill out the information, and then click Update.**

    Your updated Web page appears with the description of your item. If you want to add a new item, click Up to go back to the section you created in Step 14, and then click the New Page button again.

16. **If you want to add an image, click the Image button.**

    A new Web page form appears.

17. **If you know the name of the image file you want to add, type the pathname (in other words, the directory structure) and filename in the text box next to File. If you don't remember the name and the directory in which the image file is located, click Browse.**

    If you click Browse, a dialog box appears enabling you to navigate through the directories or folders on your computer. When you locate the file you want to add, single-click the file to select it and then click Open. The name of the image file appears in the text box next to File.

18. **Click Send.**

    After a few seconds, the Web page you're working on reappears, with the image included in a predetermined location to the left of the item name and description.

    The Yahoo! Store wizard has plenty of other options. By clicking the Special button at the bottom of a page, you can feature an item for sale as a "special" item on your site's home page.

19. **When you finish adding sale merchandise, click the Info button.**

    A page appears that lets you add your address, phone number, or other contact information for your online business.

20. **Click Edit.**

    A form appears that lets you add information about your site as well as contact information.

21. **Add your contact information to the form that appears, and then click Update to see the results.**

22. **When you're satisfied with your Web page, click Publish to transfer your new Web page files to the Yahoo! Store site.**

You can visit your new site by entering your own Web address, which takes the form `http://store.yahoo.com/`*storename* (where *storename* is the name you entered in Step 6).

Setting up shop with America Online

If you're one of the millions of folks who already have an account with America Online, by all means consider setting up your online store with AOL as your host. Even if you don't have an account with AOL presently, you might consider signing up in order to create and publish a simple Web site. Plenty of entrepreneurs either started an online business with AOL and then moved on to another Web host, or continue to maintain their business Web sites on one of AOL's Web servers.

When you sign up for an account with America Online, you're entitled to 2MB of space for your own Web pages. That may not seem like a lot of room, but consider that the average Web page is only 5 to 10K in size. Even if each page contains images that are perhaps 10 to 20K in size, which still means you have room for 70 to 100 Web pages. Besides that, an account with AOL provides for seven separate usernames. Each username is entitled to 2MB of Web site space. In theory, at least, you have 10MB of space at your disposal. This is more than enough to accommodate most moderately sized Web sites.

If AOL is so great, why doesn't everyone publish Web sites with it? Well, AOL has its downsides, too. For one thing, its servers seem (to me, at least) to be noticeably slower than others, perhaps because of the sheer volume of users. AOL has had problems with members being unable to get online during busy times. And unless you pay AOL's flat monthly rate for unlimited access, you're liable to run up some sizable hourly access charges in the course of creating, revising, and maintaining your business site. Finally, there's a subtle but important difference between AOL and a Web host that's on the Internet: AOL isn't really part of the Internet. It's on its own online network. E-mail sent from an AOL user to someone on the Internet has to go through a computer connection called a *gateway*. If the gateway goes down or if some other aspect of AOL's operation experiences a problem, all AOL users are suddenly inaccessible from the Internet. Your business may be inaccessible to many potential customers for a time. Although AOL does seem to be getting more reliable, the fact that it's separate from the Internet is an important consideration to keep in mind if you're thinking about setting up shop there.

America Online presents several resources for customers who want to publish Web pages for their business or personal use. Some of these resources are accessible only through America Online, but because AOL is making an effort to branch out onto the Web itself, other resources are located on the Web, not within AOL.

Collectively, the AOL Web page publishing options are known as My Place or My FTP Space, shown in Figure 4-2.

Figure 4-2:
My FTP
Space
and AOL
Hometown
are the
primary
resources
that AOL
offers
members
who want to
publish their
own Web
sites.

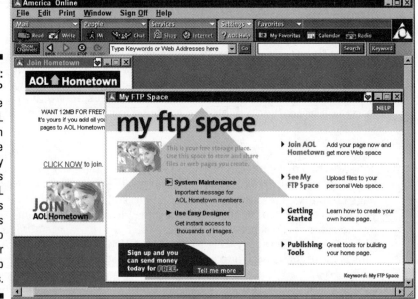

Within My FTP Space, you can find plenty of resources, including

- **1-2-3 Publish:** This is a service that performs roughly the same function as the Web page generators provided by Yahoo! GeoCities, CNET WebSite Builder, or Yahoo! Store. You fill out a form using your AOL browser. The information on the form is presented in the form of a very rudimentary Web page. The information requested is personal, however, and not intended for business use. (AOL Keyword: 1-2-3 Publish.)

- **Easy Designer:** This is AOL's graphic Web page design tool for publishing sites on AOL Hometown (which I discuss in a later bullet). It lets you create and preview your own pages without having to learn HTML. Versions are available for both Windows and Macintosh users.

- **Other Web page editors:** AOL also provides links to shareware and commercial Web editors that you can download and use to create your business site.

- **My FTP Space:** This is the service that transfers Web pages you have already made to your directory on one of AOL's servers using FTP (File Transfer Protocol). My FTP Place doesn't create your Web pages for you, but you can use any Web page authoring tool to do that. (AOL Keyword: My FTP Space.)

✔ **AOL Hometown:** After you publish your Web site on AOL by using My FTP Space, you can add the site to the AOL online community on the Web. AOL Hometown (`hometown.aol.com`) is a "real" Web site on the Internet: It's not part of AOL's own domain the way My Place is. AOL Hometown is open to America Online members and other Internet users alike. AOL members who go through the extra effort of including their sites on AOL Hometown get double exposure. Their sites are accessible both within AOL (through My FTP Space) and on the Web itself (through AOL Hometown).

✔ **Verio:** AOL has entered into an agreement to promote this well-known Web-based business-Web site hosting service. Verio has a variety of plans for hosting your site on the Web (not within AOL's own network, but on the wider Internet), listing your site on AOL's business indexes, and helping you get a user-friendly domain name such as `www.mycompany.com`. Find out more at `www.verioprimehost.com`.

If you're an AOL customer and you want to start a home-based business for virtually nothing, you've got two options: My FTP Space or AOL Hometown. Which one is best? AOL Hometown gives you more space (either 4MB or 12MB, depending on how many files you keep online). Getting your files online is also easier with AOL Hometown. With My FTP Space, you create the pages by using one of the AOL Web page tools or another Web editor. You then upload the files, following the instructions in the My FTP Space Help files. But if you use one of the AOL Web page creation tools (1-2-3 Publish or Easy Designer) to create your site, you can upload the files from within the same program.

To set up your site at AOL Hometown by using 1-2-3 Publish, follow these steps:

1. **Create a new screen name.**

   The first step is to pick a screen name for your site. This doesn't need to be the same as your usual AOL username. AOL lets you use as many as five different screen names, and I recommend reserving one for your personal use and one for your business site. To create a new screen name, connect to AOL by using your master screen name, enter the keyword **Names**, and then follow the instructions for creating a new screen name.

   Your choice of screen name is important when you use My FTP Space as your Web site host. The screen name appears as part of your Web site URL. For example, if your business is called WidgetWorld, you might choose the screen name *widgets*. When you transfer your files online by using My FTP Place, you and your visitors can then access your site by using the URL `members.aol.com/widgets`. If you want AOL to give you a shorter domain name, such as `www.widgets.com`, you have to sign up for the Verio PrimeHost service.

2. **Start using 1-2-3 Publish (keyword 1-2-3 Publish).**

   The Welcome page, entitled Get a Free Page in Minutes!, appears. A number of predesigned page templates appear on this page.

   You don't have to be using AOL software to use 1-2-3 Publish; you don't even have to be an AOL subscriber. If you're not a subscriber, you do have to sign up for a screen name, but it's free to do so. Go to home-town.aol.com to find out more.

3. **Click My Business Page to begin designing your Web page.**

   The My Business Page Template page appears.

4. **Choose a color and background for your page, and assign a name to the page by filling out this page's form; then click the Save this Page button.**

   A preview of your page appears.

5. **If you want to make changes, click Modify. When you're satisfied with your page's appearance, click Done.**

   When you click Done, a page appears with the message Congratulations — You've Got a Home Page! and a link to the site that you just created.

6. **Click the link to view your new Web site.**

It's as easy as that. If you ever want to edit your page, click the <u>Edit My Page</u> link that appears above any AOL Hometown page.

You don't have to use 1-2-3 Publish to create a Web site, but it's a great tool for beginners. More experienced users can create a complete Web site by using a Web editor. After you've completed your pages, go to AOL Hometown and click the <u>Create</u> link that appears above any page on the site. You'll go to a page entitled Create or Edit Pages. Click Upload to move your already-created files to AOL Hometown, or click Add to add your pages to an AOL Hometown site that you've previously created.

Investigating electronic storefront software

All the other options that this chapter provides for publishing your business site are ones that you access and utilize online. Yet another option for creating a business site and publishing it online is to purchase an application that carries you through the entire process of creating an electronic storefront.

Like hosting services such as Yahoo! Store, Tripod, and CNET WebBuilder, electronic storefront software is designed to facilitate the process of creating Web pages and to shield you from having to learn HTML. Most storefront software provides you with predesigned Web pages, called *templates*, that you customize for your particular business. Some types of electronic storefront options go a step or two beyond the other options by providing you with shopping cart systems that enable customers to select items and tally the cost at checkout. They may also provide for some sort of electronic payment option, such as credit card purchases.

Usually, you purchase the software on disk or CD-ROM, install the package like any other application, and follow a series of steps that detail the primary aspects of a business:

- ✔ **The storefront:** These are the Web pages that you create. Some packages, such as WebSite Complete, include predesigned Web pages that you can copy and customize with your own content.

- ✔ **The inventory:** You can stock your virtual storefront shelves by presenting your wares in the form of an online catalog or product list.

- ✔ **The delivery truck:** Some storefront packages streamline the process of transferring your files from your computer to the server. Rather than using FTP software, you publish information simply by pushing a button in your Web editor or Web browser.

- ✔ **The checkout counter:** Most electronic storefront packages give you the option to accept orders by phone, fax, or credit card.

CASE STUDY

Finding a host that makes your business dynamic

Whether you choose America Online or another ISP, which Web host you choose can have a big impact on how easy it is to get online and run your business successfully. Just ask Doug Laughter. He and his wife Kristy own The Silver Connection, LLC, which sells sterling silver jewelry imported from India, Asia, and Mexico. They began their endeavor when Kristy brought back some silver jewelry from Mexico. The Silver Connection went online in April 1998 at www.silverconnection.com and is hosted by CrystalTech Web Hosting, Inc. (www.crystaltech.com).

Q. Why did you choose CrystalTech as your Web host?

A. CrystalTech is my second Web host. I didn't have any problems with my previous host, but the issue of changing Web hosts came down to the Web development technology I wanted to choose for my site. I settled on CrystalTech because they supported the Web Application Server that I chose, which was a Windows platform running Internet Information Server. I also wanted to use Access or SQL Server for my database solution to support the development of Active Server Pages (ASP).

(continued)

(continued)

Q. What makes CrystalTech such a good Web host?

A. What makes CrystalTech particularly good is that they give their clients access to a Control Center that allows complete administrative control for the domain. Included in this are mail, FTP, and Domain Name System with automatic ODBC (Open Database Connectivity) for databases. The client also gets to use Media House Statistics, which is a utility that analyzes traffic to your Web site. I also use their comprehensive knowledge base and online forums that carry on discussions about programming, Web site design, databases, networking, and other topics.

Q. What kinds of customer service features do you use that other business owners should look for?

A. One feature that CrystalTech is very good with is notification. If Web hosting or mail services will be offline for a certain amount of time, I receive an e-mail in advance specifying exactly what is going to happen and when. I have always been treated very well by tech support when I have needed to call.

Q. What kinds of questions should small business owners and managers ask when they're shopping around for a hosting service? What kinds of features should they be looking for initially?

A. I would first suggest considering how you want to develop your Web site. Today's e-commerce site needs to be dynamic in nature, so the business needs to research and determine what

Web server application they will use. A Web server application consists of the following:

- **Server Side Technology:** Active Server Pages, ColdFusion, Java Server Pages, PHP
- **Database Solution:** Microsoft SQL Server, MS Access, MySQL, Oracle
- **Server Application:** IIS, Apache, iPlanet, Netscape Enterprise
- **Operating Platform:** Windows, UNIX

So the decision on how the e-commerce site will be developed and in what technology is a very key decision to make from the onset. Once this is decided, choose a Web host that supports your Web server application of choice.

Q. After the development platform is determined, what features should you look for?

A. Look for dedicated disk space for database applications. 250MB or 500MB of disk space might be fine for your Web site files, but throw in a highly developed Microsoft SQL Server relational database management system and you'll be paying for some additional space.

Also ask about how much data transfer you can do in a given period, how many e-mail addresses are given with the domain, and whether there's an application that lets you control and administer your entire Web site. If you don't have a shopping cart, ask your host what they offer in this area. Finally, make sure there's an application that can analyze traffic, such as WebTrends or Media House Services.

Besides providing you with all the software that you need to create Web pages and get them online, electronic storefronts instruct you on how to market your site and present your goods and services in a positive way. In addition, some programs provide you with a backroom for your business, where you can record customer information, orders, and fulfillment.

The problem with many electronic storefront packages is that they're very expensive — some cost $5,000 to $10,000 or more. They're not intended for individuals starting their own small businesses, but rather for large corporations that want to branch out to the Web. However, a few packages (two of which I describe in the following sections) provide a Ford-type alternative to the Rolls-Royce storefronts.

ShopSite

ShopSite, by ShopSite, Inc., isn't software that you purchase and install on your computer. Rather, you find a Web hosting service that runs ShopSite on its servers. You then set up an account with the host and use the ShopSite software over the Internet using your Web browser. This kind of setup, which is called a *hosted application*, means you don't have to worry about having enough memory or disk space to run the program yourself. You also don't have to bother with updating or troubleshooting the software; that, too, is the hosting service's responsibility.

In order to find a hosting service that runs ShopSite, you go to the ShopSite Web site (www.shopsite.com) and scan a list of hosts. You pick a company and arrange for an account. Pricing varies depending on the host and the version of the service that you want. ShopSite comes in three varieties: Lite, Manager, and Pro. ShopSite Lite lets you create a catalog of only 12 items for sale and 5 Web pages. ShopSite Manager gives you an unlimited number of pages, plus templates, themes, a shopping cart, and real-time credit card processing. ShopSite Pro adds the ability to create a searchable database of products. One host I saw was offering ShopSite Lite for free with its hosting packages, the Manager version for $30 per month, and the Pro version for $125 per month. Rather than renting the software on a monthly basis, you can also buy a lifetime license. I saw ShopSite Lite advertised for $135, Manager for $495, and Pro for $1,295.

WebSite Complete

WebSite Complete, by GoDaddy Software, Inc. (www.godaddy.com), is software that you purchase and install on your computer. You either download the program from the GoDaddy Software Web site or purchase it on a CD-ROM. The software makes it easy for you to create not only basic Web pages, but to make a site searchable by keyword, to set up password-protected pages, and set up a shopping cart.

The WebSite Complete software costs only $14.95, but you're also charged a licensing fee for each site you create with the software and then post online ($35 for the first Web site and $49.95 for each additional site). You can then host your site with GoDaddy Software for $9.95 to $12.95 per month. You can find out more about these options at www.godaddy.com/gdshop/webhosting.asp.

WebSite Complete comes with more than 450 templates and 2,500 stock photo images; it works with Windows 98 or later.

Moving into an online mall

In addition to Web site kits, Internet service providers, and businesses that specialize in Web hosting, online shopping malls provide another form of Web hosting. You set up your site, either on your own or using special Web page authoring utilities that some malls provide. You pay a monthly fee, you transfer your files to the mall's Web site, and your store appears online. The basic steps are the same with an online mall as with any of the other hosting businesses that I mention in this chapter.

What's the difference, then, between a shopping mall that does Web hosting, an Internet service provider that does hosting, and a Web hosting service? Their names and the features they offer differ slightly, but the important thing to remember is that they all do essentially the same thing. After you open your virtual business on the Web, your customers can't always tell whether you're part of America Online, a mall, or a Web host such as EarthLink.

What *is* an online shopping mall, anyway? It's a collection of online businesses that are listed in a directory or index provided by a single organization. The directory may be a simple list of stores on a single Web page. For larger malls with a thousand stores or more, the online businesses are arranged by category and can be found in a searchable index.

In theory, an online shopping mall helps small businesses by giving them additional exposure. A customer who shops at one of the mall's stores might notice other businesses on the same site and visit it, too. Some malls function as Web hosts that enable their customers to transfer Web page files and present their stores online, using one of the mall's Web servers. Other malls let people list their business in the mall with a hyperlink, even if the store is actually hosted by another company.

Perhaps the only thing that really distinguishes online malls from other hosting services is presentation:

- Some malls, such as Downtown Anywhere (www.awa.com), use the metaphor of a town square to organize their businesses. Stores are presented as being on particular streets; visitors browse the shops as though walking around the streets of a small town.

- Another online mall to look into is Microsoft bCentral Marketplace (www.bcentral.com/marketplace/), which gathers in one location a number of small businesses that are hosted by bCentral. bCentral, like its rival Yahoo! Store, lets you test the service first, trying the Web page creation system for free. Then you pay a monthly fee to locate your business with the site permanently. The difference is that, when you create a site with bCentral, you can choose whether to sell products on bCentral Marketplace or other sales channels, such as MSN Marketplace (marketplace.msn.com), MSN Auctions (auctions.msn.com), or your own Web site.

Consider joining an online mall if you find one that offers an attractive hosting package, particularly if it has Web page forms that will help you set up your site or create an online catalog quickly. But remember that, to Web shoppers, it doesn't matter who your host is; what's more important is that you develop compelling content for your site to attract customers and encourage sales.

Amazon.com doesn't look like an online mall, but it has instituted some new opportunities for entrepreneurs to sell items on its site. You can create a virtual storefront called a zShop with Amazon.com as your host. If you don't want to create an entire storefront, you also have the option of selling items individually or auctioning them on the Amazon.com Auctions site. You pay fees to list items for sale and for completed sales as well. Find out more by going to the Amazon.com home page (www.amazon.com) and clicking the Sell Items link at the bottom of the page.

Turning to your ISP for Web hosting

People sometimes talk about Internet service providers (ISPs) and Web hosts as two separate types of Internet businesses, but that's not necessarily the case. Providing users with access to the Internet and hosting Web sites are two different functions, to be sure, but they may well be performed by the same organization.

In fact, it's only natural to turn to your own ISP first to ask about its Web hosting policies for its customers. Like John Raddatz (see the section "Holding a Contest" in Chapter 11), if you already go online with AOL, trying out its Web hosting facilities makes sense. If you have an Internet access account with the popular ISP EarthLink (www.earthlink.net), by all means, consider EarthLink as a Web host for your business site.

EarthLink has different Web hosting options depending on the kind of account you have. Like most ISPs, however, EarthLink provides Web space to its customers so that they can publish Web pages that are primarily personal in nature. Yes, you *can* publish a business Web site, and EarthLink won't complain or cancel your account. But it really suggests that business users "spring" for special business services that include oodles of Web space, support for forms and CGI scripts, and a "vanity" URL of the www.company.com variety.

EarthLink offers A StarterSite package ($19.95 per month plus $25 setup fee), which provides individual users with the following Web hosting options:

- 200MB of storage space
- 30 separate e-mail accounts for personal or family members' use
- Free CGI scripts that you can run to capture information submitted in a Web page form to either an e-mail message or a file that you can read

- ✔ Click-n-Build, the EarthLink Web page editing tool

- ✔ Urchin, a reporting service that analyzes traffic to your site

- ✔ A Web page URL that takes the form
  `http://www.earthlink.com/~username`

What should you look for in an ISP Web hosting account, and what constitutes a "good deal"? For one thing, price: A rate of $19.95 per month for unlimited access and 50 to 100MB (or even 200MB with StarterSite) of Web site space is currently a pretty good deal. Look for a host that doesn't limit the number of Web pages that you can create. Also find one that gives you at least one e-mail address with your account and that lets you add extra addresses for a nominal fee. Finally, look for a host that gives you the ability to include Web page forms on your site so that visitors can send you feedback.

What to expect from an ISP Web hosting service

The process of setting up a Web site varies from ISP to ISP. Here are some general features that you should look for, based on my experience with my own ISP:

- ✔ **Web page editor:** You don't necessarily need to choose a provider that gives you a free Web page editor. You can easily download and install the editor of your choice. I tend to use one of two programs, either Microsoft FrontPage or Macromedia Dreamweaver, to create Web pages. (I describe both programs later in this chapter.)

- ✔ **Password and username:** When my Web pages are ready to go online, I get to use the same username and password to access my Web site space that I use when I dial up to connect to the Internet. Although you don't need to enter a password to view a Web site through a browser (well, at least at most sites), you do need a password to protect your site from being accessed with an FTP program. Otherwise, anyone can enter your Web space and tamper with your files.

- ✔ **FTP software:** When I signed up for an account with Interaccess, I received a disk containing a basic set of software programs, including a Web browser and an FTP program. FTP is the simplest and easiest-to-use software to transfer files from one location to another on the Internet. When I access my Web site space from my Macintosh, I use an FTP program called Fetch. From my PC, I use a program called WS-FTP. CuteFTP (`www.cuteftp.com`) is another program that many Web site owners use, which costs $39.95. Most FTP programs are either available for free on the Internet or can be purchased for a nominal fee.

- ✔ **URL:** When you set up a Web site using your ISP, you're assigned a directory on a Web server. The convention for naming this directory is `~username`. The `~username` designation goes at the end of your URL for your Web site's home page. However, you can (and should) register a shorter URL with a domain name registrar, such as Network Solutions. You can then "point" the domain name to your ISP's server so that it can serve as an "alias" URL for your site. (See Chapter 5.)

After you have your software tools together and have a user directory on your ISP's Web server, it's time to put your Web site together. Basically, when I want to create or revise content for my Web site, I open the page in my Web page editor, make the changes, save the changes, and then transfer the files to my ISP's directory with my FTP program. Finally, I preview the changes in my browser.

What's the ISP difference?

What's the big difference between using a kit, such as Yahoo! Store, to create your site and using your own inexpensive or free software to create a site from scratch and post it on your ISP's server? It's the difference between putting together a model airplane from a kit and designing the airplane yourself. If you use a kit, you save time and trouble; your plane ends up looking pretty much like everyone else's, but you get the job done faster. If you design it yourself, you have absolute control. Your plane can look just the way you want. It takes longer to get to the end product, but you can be sure you get what you wanted.

On the other hand, three differences lie between an ISP-hosted site and a site that resides with a company that does *only* Web hosting, rather than provide Internet dialup access and other services:

- A business that does only Web hosting charges you for hosting services, whereas your ISP may not.

- A Web hosting service lets you have your own domain name (www. company.com), whereas an ISP may not. (Some ISPs require that you upgrade to a business hosting account in order to obtain the vanity address. See the "What's in a name?" sidebar for more about how Web hosting services offer an advantage in the domain-name game.)

- A Web hosting service often provides lots of frills, such as super-fast connections, one-button file transfers using Web editors such as Microsoft FrontPage, and tons of site statistics, as well as automatic backups of your Web page files.

To find out more about using a real, full-time Web hosting service, see the section "Going for the works with a Web hosting service" later in this chapter.

Where to find an ISP

What if you don't already have an Internet service provider, or you're not happy with the one you have? On today's Internet, you can't swing a mouse without hitting an ISP. How do you find the one that's right for you? In general, you want to look for the provider that offers you the least expensive service with the fastest connection and the best options available for your Web site.

Bigger doesn't necessarily mean cheaper or better; many regional or local ISPs provide good service at rates that are comparable to the giants such as

Verio or EarthLink. When you're shopping around for an ISP, be sure to ask the following types of questions:

- ✔ What types of connections do you offer?
- ✔ How many dialup numbers do you have?
- ✔ What is your access range? (Do you provide only local coverage, or regional or international coverage as well?)
- ✔ What type of tech support do you offer? Do you accept phone calls or e-mail inquiries around the clock or only during certain hours? Are real human beings always available on call or are clients sent to a phone message system?

Some Web sites are well known for listing ISPs by state or by the services they offer. Here are a few good starting points in your search for the ideal ISP:

- ✔ **The List** (thelist.internet.com): This site lists about 8,000 ISPs. You can search the list by area code or by country code, or you can focus on the United States or Canada.
- ✔ **Providers of Commercial Internet Access** (www.celestin.com/pocia): This site lists more than 1,700 ISPs around the world. It also has a section for Web hosting companies.
- ✔ **Yahoo's List of Internet Access Providers** (http://dir.yahoo.com/ Business_and_Economy/Business_to_Business/Communications_ and_Networking/Internet_and_World_Wide_Web/Network_Service _Providers/Internet_Service_Providers__ISPs_/): This is a good source for directories of national and international ISPs.

Going for the works with a Web hosting service

After you've had your site online for a while with a free Web host, such as AOL (which is free if you have an AOL account) or Yahoo! GeoCities, you may well decide that you need more room, more services (such as Web site statistics), and a faster connection that can handle many visitors at one time. In that case, you want to locate your online business with a full-time Web hosting service.

As the preceding sections attest, many kinds of businesses now host Web sites. But in this case, I'm defining *Web hosting service* as a company whose primary mission is to provide space on Web servers for individual, nonprofit, and commercial Web sites.

What's in a name?

Most hosts assign you a URL that leads to your directory (or folder) on the Web server. For example, my account with my ISP includes space on a Web server where I can store my Web pages. The address is as follows:

```
http://homepage.interaccess.
    com/~gholden
```

This is a common form of URL that many Web hosts use. It means that my Web pages reside in a directory called ~gholden on a computer named homepage. The computer, in turn, resides in my provider's domain on the Internet: interaccess.com.

However, for an extra fee, some Web hosts allow you to choose a shorter domain name, provided that the one you want to use isn't already taken by another site. For example, if I'd paid extra for a full-fledged business site, my provider would have let me have a catchier, more memorable address, like this:

```
http://www.gregholden.com
```

What to look for in a Web host

Along with providing lots of space for your HTML, image, and other files (typically, you get anywhere from 50 to 500MB of space), Web hosting services offer a variety of related services, including some or all of the following:

- ✔ **E-mail addresses:** You're likely to be able to get several e-mail addresses for your own or your family members' personal use. Besides that, many Web hosts give you special e-mail addresses called *auto-responders*. These are e-mail addresses, such as info@yourcompany.com, that you can set up to automatically return a text message or a file to anyone looking for information.

- ✔ **Domain names:** Virtually all of the hosting options that I mention in this chapter give customers the option of obtaining a short domain name, such as www.mycompany.com. But some Web hosts simplify the process by providing domain-name registration in their flat monthly rate.

- ✔ **Web page software:** Some hosting services include Web page authoring/editing software, such as Microsoft FrontPage. Some Web hosting services even offer Web page forms that you can fill out online in order to create your own online shopping catalog. All you have to provide is a scanned image of the item you want to sell, along with a price and a description. You submit the information to the Web host, who then adds the item to an online catalog that's part of your site.

- ✔ **Multimedia/CGI scripts:** One big thing that sets Web hosting services apart from other hosts is the ability to serve complex and memory-intensive content, such as RealAudio sound files or RealVideo video clips. They also let you process Web page forms that you include on your site by executing computer programs called *CGI scripts*. These programs receive the data that someone sends you (such as a customer service request or an order form) and present the data in readable form, such as a text file, e-mail message, or an entry in a database. See Chapter 7 for more about how to set up and use forms and other interactive Web site features.

✔ **Shopping cart software:** If part of your reason for going online is to sell specific items, look for a Web host that can streamline the process for you. Most organizations provide you with Web page forms that you can fill out to create sale items and offer them in an online shopping cart, for example.

✔ **Automatic data backups:** Some hosting services automatically back up your Web site data to protect you against data loss — an especially useful feature because disaster recovery is important. The automatic nature of the backups frees you from the worry and trouble of doing it manually.

✔ **Site statistics:** Virtually all Web hosting services also provide you with site statistics that give you an idea (perhaps not a precisely accurate count, but a good estimate) of how many visitors you have received. Even better is access to software reports that analyze and graphically report where your visitors are from, how they found you, which pages on your site are the most frequently viewed, and so on.

✔ **Shopping and electronic commerce features:** If you plan to give your customers the ability to order and purchase your goods or services online by using their credit cards, be sure to look for a Web host that provides you with secure commerce options. A *secure server* is a computer that can encrypt sensitive data (such as credit card numbers) that the customer sends to your site. For a more detailed discussion of secure electronic commerce, see Chapter 12.

Having so many hosting options available is the proverbial blessing and curse. It's good that you have so many possibilities and that the competition is so fierce because that could keep prices down. On the other hand, deciding which site is best for you can be difficult. In addition to asking about the preceding list of features, here are a few more questions to ask prospective Web hosts about their services to help narrow the field:

✔ **Do you limit file transfers?** Many services charge a monthly rate for a specific amount of electronic data that is transferred to and from your site. Each time a visitor views a page, that user is actually downloading a few kilobytes of data in order to view it. If your Web pages contain, say, 1MB of text and images and you get 1000 visitors per month, your site accounts for 1GB of data transfer per month. If your host allocates you less than 1GB per month, it will probably charge you extra for the amount you go over the limit.

> ✔ **What kind of connection do you have?** Your site's Web page content appears more quickly in Web browser windows if your server has a super-fast T1 or T3 connection, as opposed to sharing an ISDN line with hundreds of other Web sites. (See Chapter 3 for explanations of ISDN, T1, and other connection options.)
>
> ✔ **Will you promote my site?** Some hosting services (particularly online shopping malls) help publicize your site by listing you with Internet search indexes and search services so that visitors are more likely to find you.

Besides these, the other obvious questions that you would ask of any contractor apply to Web hosting services as well. These include questions like: "How long have you been in business?" and "Can you suggest customers who will give me a reference?"

The fact that I include a screen shot of a particular Web hosting service's site in this chapter or elsewhere in this book doesn't mean that I'm endorsing or recommending that particular organization. Shop around carefully and find the one that's best for you. Check out the hosts with the best rates and most reliable service. Visit some other sites that they host and e-mail the owners of those sites for their opinion of their hosting service.

Competition is tough among hosting services, which means that prices are going down. But it also means that hosting services may seem to promise the moon in order to get your business. Be sure to read the fine print and talk to the host before you sign a contract, and always get statements about technical support and backups in writing.

What's it gonna cost?

Because of the ongoing competition in the industry, prices for Web hosting services vary widely. If you look in the classified sections in the back of magazines that cover the Web or the whole Internet, you'll see adds for hosting services costing from $14.95 to $24.95 per month. Chances are, these prices are for a basic level of service: Web space, e-mail addresses, domain name, and software. This may be all you need.

The second level of service provides CGI script processing, the ability to serve audio and video files on your site, regular backups, and extensive site statistics, as well as consultants who can help you design and configure your site. This more sophisticated range of features typically runs from $39 per month up to $200 or more per month. At Hosting.com, for instance, you can conduct secure electronic commerce on your site as part of hosting packages that cost between $39 and $199 per month. MySQL database support starts at $59 per month.

Choosing a Web Page Editor

A woodworker has his or her favorite hammer and saw. A cook has an array of utensils and pots and pans. Likewise, a Web site creator has software programs that facilitate the presentation of words, colors, images, and multimedia in Web browsers.

A little HTML is a good thing — but just a little. Knowing HTML comes in handy when you need to add elements that Web page editors don't handle. Some programs, for example, don't provide you with easy buttons or menu options for adding <META> tags, which enable you to add keywords or descriptions to a site so that search engines can find them and describe your site correctly.

If you really want to get into HTML or to find out more about creating Web pages, read *HTML 4 For Dummies*, 3rd Edition, by Ed Tittel, Natanya Pitts, and Chelsea Valentine, or *Creating Web Pages For Dummies*, 6th Edition, by Bud Smith and Arthur Bebakc.

It pays to spend time choosing a Web page editor that has the right qualities. What qualities should you look for in a Web page tool, and how do you know which tool is right for you? To help narrow the field, I've divided this class of software into different levels of sophistication. Pick the type of program that best fits your technical skill.

For the novice: Use your existing programs

A growing number of word processing, graphics, and business programs are adding HTML to their list of capabilities. You may already have one of these programs at your disposal. By using a program with which you're already comfortable, you can avoid having to install a Web page editor.

Here are some programs that enable you to generate one type of content and then give you the option of outputting that content in HTML, which means that your words or figures can appear on a Web page:

- ✔ **Microsoft Word 2000 or 2002:** The most recent versions of the venerable word processing standby work pretty much seamlessly with Web page content. You can open Web pages from within Word and save Word files in Web page format.

- ✔ **Adobe PageMaker/Quark Xpress:** The most recent versions of these two popular page layout programs let you save the contents of a document as HTML — only the words and images are transferred to the Web, however; any special typefaces become generic Web standard headings.

✔ **Microsoft Office 2000 or XP:** Word, Excel, and PowerPoint all give users the option of exporting content to Web pages.

✔ **Corel Presentations 10:** You can save each slide of a Corel presentation as an HTML page, a GIF image, or a Macromedia Flash presentation that you can present on the Web. If you have chosen to present one slide per Web page, the program adds clickable arrows to each slide in your presentation so that viewers can skip from one slide to another.

Although these solutions are convenient, they probably won't completely eliminate the need to use a Web page editor. Odds are, you'll still need to make corrections and do special formatting after you convert your text to HTML.

For intermediate needs: User-friendly Web editors

If you're an experienced Web surfer and eager to try out a simple Web editor, try a program that lets you focus on your site's HTML and textual content, provides you with plenty of functionality, and is still easy to use. Here are some user-friendly programs that are inexpensive (or, better yet, free), yet allow you to create a functional Web site.

The following programs don't include some of the bells and whistles you need to create complex, interactive forms, format a page using frames, or access a database of information from one of your Web pages. These goodies are served up by Web page editors that have a higher level of functionality, which I describe in the upcoming section for advanced commerce sites.

BBEdit

If you work on a Macintosh and you're primarily concerned with textual content, BBEdit is one of the best choices you can make for a Web page tool. It lives up to its motto: "It doesn't suck." BBEdit is tailored to use the Mac's highly visual interface, and Version 6.5 will run on the Mac OS 8.6 or later, including Mac OS X. You can use Macintosh drag-and-drop to add an image file to a Web page in progress by dragging the image's icon into the main BBEdit window, for example. Find out more about BBEdit at the Bare Bones Software, Inc. Web site (www.barebones.com/products/bbedit.html).

Other good choices of Web editors for the Macintosh are World Wide Web Weaver by Miracle Software Inc. (www.miracleinc.com/Products/W4) or PageSpinner by Optima System (www.optima-system.com).

Macromedia HomeSite

HomeSite is an affordable tool for Web site designers who feel at ease working with HTML code. However, HomeSite isn't just an HTML code editor. It provides a visual interface so that you can work with graphics and preview your pages layout. HomeSite also provides you with step-by-step utilities called *wizards* to quickly create pages, tables, frames, and JavaScript elements. The program works with Windows 98 or later; find out more about it at www.macromedia.com/software/homesite.

Microsoft FrontPage Express

Microsoft doesn't support FrontPage Express any more, but if you still use Windows 98 and you're on a tight budget, give it a try. The software comes bundled with Windows 98 and you don't have to do a thing to install it. Just choose Start➪Programs➪Internet Explorer➪FrontPage Express to open FrontPage Express.

CoffeeCup HTML Editor

CoffeeCup HTML Editor, by CoffeeCup Software, is a popular Windows Web site editor that contains a lot of features for a small price ($49). You can begin typing and formatting text by using the CoffeeCup HTML Editor menu options. You can add an image by clicking the Insert Image toolbar button, or use the Forms toolbar to create the text boxes and radio buttons that make up an interactive Web page form. You can even add JavaScript effects and choose from a selection of clip art images that come with the software.

CoffeeCup HTML Editor doesn't let you explore database connectivity, add Web components, or other bonuses that come with a program like FrontPage or Dreamweaver. But it does have everything you need to create a basic Web page.

Netscape Composer

When I read reviews of Web page software, I don't often see Netscape Composer included in the list. But to me, it's an ideal program for an entrepreneur on a budget. Why? Let me spell it out for you: F-R-E-E.

Netscape Composer is the Web page editing and authoring tool that comes with Netscape 6.2 or Netscape Communicator 4.79. All you have to do is download one of these packages from the Netscape Browser Central page (browsers.netscape.com/browsers/main.tmpl), and Composer is automatically installed on your computer along with Navigator (the Netscape Web browser) and several other Internet programs.

With Composer, you can create sophisticated layout elements, such as tables (which I discuss further in Chapter 6), with an easy-to-use graphical interface. After you edit a page, you can preview it in Navigator with the click of a button. Plus, you can publish all your files by choosing a single menu item. If you already have Communicator installed, check out Composer right now!

Editors that'll flip your whizzy-wig

Web browsers are multilingual; they understand exotic-sounding languages such as FTP, HTTP, and GIF, among others. But one language browsers don't speak is English. Browsers don't understand instructions such as "Put that image there" or "Make that text italic." HyperText Markup Language, or HTML, is a translator, if you will, between human languages and Web languages.

If the thought of HTML strikes fear into your heart, relax. Thanks to modern Web page creation tools, you don't have to learn HTML in order to create Web pages. Although knowing a little HTML does come in handy at times, you can depend on these special user-friendly tools to do almost all your English-to-HTML translations for you.

The secret of these Web page creation tools is their WYSIWYG (pronounced whizzy-wig)

display. WYSIWYG stands for "What You See Is What You Get." A WYSIWYG editor lets you see on-screen how your page will look when it's on the Web, rather than force you to type (or even see) HTML commands like this:

```
<H1> This is a Level 1 Heading
    </H1>
<IMG SRC = "lucy.gif"> <BR>
<P>This is an image of
    Lucy.</P>
```

A WYSIWYG editor, such as CoffeeCup HTML Editor for Windows (www.coffeecup.com), shows you how the page appears even as you assemble it. Besides that, it lets you format text and add images by means of familiar software shortcuts such as menus and buttons.

For advanced commerce sites: Programs that do it all

If you plan to do a great deal of business online, or even to add the title of Web designer to your list of talents (as some of the entrepreneurs profiled in this book have done), it makes sense to spend some money up front and use a Web page tool that can do everything you want — today and for years to come.

The advanced programs that I describe here go beyond the simple designation of Web page editors. They not only let you edit Web pages but also help you add interactivity to your site, link dynamically updated databases to your site, and keep track of how your site is organized and updated. Some programs (notably, FrontPage) can even transfer your Web documents to your Web host with a single menu option. This way, you get to concentrate on the fun part of running an online business — meeting people, taking orders, processing payments, and the like.

Macromedia Dreamweaver

What's that you say? You can never hear enough bells and whistles? The cutting edge is where you love to walk? Then Dreamweaver, a Web authoring tool by Macromedia (www.macromedia.com), is for you. Dreamweaver is a feature-rich, professional piece of software.

Dreamweaver's strengths aren't so much in the basic features such as making selected text bold, italic, or a different size; rather, Dreamweaver excels in producing Dynamic HTML (which makes Web pages more interactive through scripts) and HTML style sheets. Dreamweaver has ample FTP (File Transfer Protocol) settings, and it gives you the option of seeing the HTML codes you're working within one window and the formatting of your Web page within a second, WYSIWYG window. The latest version, Dreamweaver MX, is a complex and powerful piece of software. It lets you create Active Server pages, connect to the ColdFusion database, and lots of templates and wizards. Dreamweaver is available for both Windows and Macintosh computers; find out more at the Macromedia Web site (www.macromedia.com/software/dreamweaver).

Microsoft FrontPage

FrontPage (www.microsoft.com/frontpage) is a powerful Web authoring tool that has some unique e-commerce capabilities. For one thing, it provides you with a way to organize a Web site visually. The main FrontPage window is divided into two sections. On the left, you see the Web page on which you're currently working. On the right, you see a tree-like map of all the pages on your site, arranged visually to show which pages are connected to each other by hyperlinks.

Another nice thing about FrontPage — something that you're sure to find helpful if you haven't been surfing the Web or working with Web pages for very long — is the addition of wizards and templates. The FrontPage wizards enable you to create a discussion area on your site where your visitors can post messages to one another. The wizards also help you connect to a database or design a page with frames. (See Chapter 6 for more about creating frames.)

If you want to create an e-commerce Web site hosted by Microsoft bCentral, you can download and install an auxiliary program FrontPage called an add-in that enables you to create a sales catalog and upload the files to bCentral, all from within FrontPage.

Adobe GoLive

GoLive, a highly popular Web page tool by Adobe Systems Incorporated (www.adobe.com/products/golive/main.html), is an especially good choice if you want to exert a high level of control over how your Web page looks. It helps you make use of the latest HTML style-sheet commands that precisely control the positioning of text and images on a page.

GoLive (which is available in versions for Windows 95/98/NT and for the Macintosh) is especially well integrated with Adobe Photoshop and Illustrator, two popular and sophisticated graphics programs. Like Dreamweaver, GoLive supports server technologies such as ASP, JSP, and PHP, which enable you to create active, dynamic Web sites. You can even create Web pages that are especially formatted for wireless devices, such as PDAs and Web-enabled cell phones.

Chapter 5

Online Shortcuts to Success

*O*ne of the nice things about starting an online business now, after e-commerce has been around for a few years, is the abundance of experts, services, and online tools that make your job easier. After all, everyone needs a little help getting a business up and running, and you've got a lengthy laundry list of decisions to make and tasks to tackle.

You don't have to go it alone when it comes to the technical side of starting up a site. You don't have to be a programmer. Plenty of utilities are available to help you create Web pages, make links, keep your books, and do other tasks online.

As time goes on, the range of software "shortcuts" grows larger and more user-friendly. You can create forms that will process data and send it to you. You can keep track of your business expenses online, create banner ads and animations, hold videoconferences, and more. In this chapter, I suggest practices that you can implement to reduce your business time-to-market as well as ways to share information more efficiently so that you can concentrate on what you're here to do: business.

What makes a good Web host?

Time and again, I hear successful entrepreneurs extol the virtues of the companies that enable their businesses to go online. Why all the praise? Some Web hosting services or ISPs go beyond the basic tasks of providing space on a Web server and keeping the server functioning smoothly.

If you're a computer novice or just technically challenged, look for a full-service host that can help set up a Web site, make it easy to process forms or run scripts, and perform similar tasks. One of the best shortcuts to success is to find a good Web host, and then depend on that company's software tools and service reps when you need help building your Web site.

Before you sign up with a host, check out customer service options. Specifically, find out when the service staff is available by telephone. Also ask if telephone support costs extra. If you're working alone and don't have a technical person you can call, being able to speak to a technical support person about a problem you're encountering on your site can be invaluable.

It might seem surprising to think of your Web host as one of the reasons for your success. After all, you do most of the work. At the most basic level, a hosting service is just a company that provides you with space on a server. You only call them when you have a problem or a billing question. At least, that's how most people look at their Web host.

However, whether you use the server space given to you by your ISP or sign with a full-time Web host, the relationship can be much more.

For example, pair Networks (www.pair.com), which offers a pretty typical selection of hosting options and which has been praised by some technical writers I know, offers the following kinds of e-commerce services that go above and beyond the basic $49.95 per month hosting arrangements:

- ✔ **Secure server:** You can pay an extra charge and have your site hosted on a secure server — a computer that encrypts traffic — so that you can protect the information that your customers send you.

- ✔ **Shopping cart:** For an extra $15 per month, you can add shopping cart functionality to your site.

- ✔ **Credit card authorization:** For an extra $29.95 plus a $249 setup fee, customers can set up credit card processing and address checking through the Authorize.net payment program. (See Chapter 9 for more information on setting up online credit card systems.)

- ✔ **Dedicated server:** The basic hosting option for almost all hosting services is to put your site on a computer that hosts many different Web sites. In other words, you're on a shared server. When traffic to your site gets really heavy, you can get your own, dedicated server. The dedicated server options that pair Networks offers start at $249 per month, but you get unlimited telephone support as well as faster access for your customers because you're running your own server.

Don't get locked in to a two- or three-year contract with a Web host. Go month to month or sign a one-year contract. Even if you're initially happy with your host, this gives you a chance to back out and go elsewhere if the company takes a turn for the worse or your needs change.

Domain name registration

People frequently get confused when I try to explain how to register a domain name and how to "point" the name at the server that hosts their Web sites. This is a perfect place for an ISP to help you. In addition to giving you an Internet connection and Web server space, some ISPs also function as domain name registrars: The ISP provides a service that enables anyone to purchase the rights to use a domain name for one, two, or more years. It's a kind of one-stop-shopping: You can set up your domain name and, if the same company hosts your site, you can easily have the name associated with your site rather than having to go through an extra step or two of "pointing" the name at the server that holds your site.

By "pointing" your domain name at your server, I mean the following: You purchase the rights to a domain name from a registrar. You then need to associate the name with your Web site so that, when people connect to your site, they won't have to enter a long URL such as http://username.home. mindspring.com. Instead, they'll enter http://www.mybusiness.com. To do this, you tell the registrar that your domain name should be assigned to the IP address of your server. Your ISP or Web host will tell you the IP address to give to the registrar.

When you're registering your site, don't focus solely on the dot-com (.com) domain. Some new domains have been made available that can provide you with alternate names in case your ideal dot-com name is unavailable. Even if you do get a dot-com name (.com is still the most recognizable and desirable domain name extension), you may want to buy up the same name with .biz at the end so that someone else doesn't grab it.

Marketing utilities

Some people are great at promotion and marketing. Others excel at detail work. Only a few lucky people can do both kinds of business tasks well and enjoy it. If, like me, your promotional talents are a bit weak, find a hosting service that will help you get noticed.

Some hosts, such as Microsoft bCentral (www.bcentral.com), give you access to a variety of marketing services if you sign with it as your host. Not all of the services are free of course. For instance, the bCentral optional List Builder marketing package gives you access to a selection of Web page templates that enable you to create your own newsletter and then send it to a mailing list of customers. This service costs an extra $29.99 per month in addition to the usual bCentral Web hosting fee of $29.95 per month. (See the section "Yahoo! Store Versus bCentral" later in this chapter for more about hosting solutions that Microsoft offers.)

Catalog creators

Some of the biggest Web hosts (such as Yahoo! Store, which I describe in Chapter 4 and later in this chapter) give you software that enables you to create an online sales catalog by using your Web browser. In other words, you don't have to purchase a Web design program, learn to use it, and create your pages from scratch.

On the down side, a Web-based catalog creation tool doesn't give you the ultimate control over how your pages look. You probably can't pull off fancy layout effects with tables or layers. (See Chapter 6 for more on using tables and layers to design your site's Web pages.) On the plus side, however, if you have no interest in Web design and don't want to pay a designer, you can use one of these tools to save time and money by getting your pages online quickly all by yourself.

Database connectivity

If you plan on selling only five, ten, or even twenty or so items at a time, your e-commerce site can be a *static* site, which means that every time a customer makes a sale, you have to take the time to manually adjust inventory. A static site also requires you to update descriptions and revise shipping charges or other details by hand, one Web page at a time. In contrast, a *dynamic* e-commerce site presents catalog sales items "on the fly" (dynamically) by connecting to a database whenever a customer requests a Web page. Suppose, for example, that a customer clicks a link for shoes. On a dynamic site, the customer sees a selection of footwear gathered instantly from the database server that's connected to the Web site. The Web page data is live and up-to-date because it's created every time the customer makes a request.

If you need to create a dynamic Web site, another factor in choosing a Web host is whether or not it supports the Web page and database software that you want to use. For Doug Laughter of The Silver Connection, LLC (which I profile in Chapter 4), the choice of host was essential. He wanted to develop his site himself by using technologies he was familiar with and regarded highly: Microsoft Active Server Pages (ASP) language and Macromedia UltraDev Web site creation software. If you use a database program such as MySQL, for instance, you may want to sign up with a Web host that allows you to run SQL Server on one of its servers.

Payment plans

Handling real-time online transactions is one of the most daunting of all e-commerce tasks. Some Web hosts can facilitate the process of obtaining a merchant account and processing credit card purchases made online. Yahoo! Store, for one, says you can receive a merchant account in just one to three days by applying through its site.

NTT/Verio, one of the best-known Web hosts/ISPs, has several hosting plans especially for e-commerce Web sites. The company's Gold Hosting Plan, which costs $50 to set up and $99.95 per month, includes access to a Merchant Payment Center as well as a shopping cart that you set up by following a tutorial. You still have to set up your Web site, catalog, and shopping cart pages, and you still have to ship out your items and answer your customers' questions. But having your Web host provide you with the sales and payment tools and be available to answer your questions, removes part of the burden of setting up a payment system.

Yahoo! Store versus bCentral

A few years ago, there were lots of Web hosts. The ranks have thinned somewhat, and currently two big companies, Yahoo! Store and Microsoft bCentral, dominate. Lots of smaller hosting services are available that can meet your needs. Because of their size, however, these two are likely to be around for the foreseeable future, and each can provide you with a range of services that the others can't. Which one is right for you? Table 5-1 looks at the pros and cons of each company.

Table 5-1	Comparing Yahoo! Store with Microsoft bCentral		
Feature	*Yahoo!*	*bCentral*	*Greg's Pick*
Cost	$49.95 per month, $0.10 per item listed per month, 0.5% transaction fee on all transactions, and 3.5% revenue share on transactions that originate on the Yahoo! Network.	$24.95 per month or $224.95 per year	bCentral is less expensive to start, but add-on services can pile up.
Bells and whistles	Database connectivity	FrontPage e-commerce add-in	It's a draw.

(continued)

Table 5-1 *(continued)*

Feature	Yahoo!	bCentral	Greg's Pick
Customer service	Lots of FAQs plus Yahoo! Advice area where (for a per-minute fee) you can speak to "expert" users. The rate varies by advisor	FAQs and chat; phone support costs $9.95 per month or $99.95 per year.	It's a draw.
Software	Web browser	Web browser or FrontPage	bCentral gives you more control.
Term of contract	You can cancel anytime	You sign up for one or two years.	Yahoo! Store
Traffic analyzer	Sophisticated, including referring sites, click trails, etc.	Primitive; a simple "hit" counter	Yahoo! Store
Worldwide access	U.S., Canada, New Zealand, Australia only	No restrictions	bCentral

Both Yahoo! Store and bCentral have a list of e-commerce success stories. Yahoo! Store, in particular, can boast the San Francisco Museum of Modern Art, Ben and Jerry's, Cirque du Soleil, Miramax Films, and the list goes on. bCentral doesn't talk about "famous" clients on its Web site, but prefers to profile its successful small business. Both sites give their customers access to an online marketplace, and both have tools that submit site listings to search engines.

Some of the advantages of using a big Web host are that they're competent, well-known, and reliable. However, the large size can be a disadvantage, too. With a big Web host, you're just one of thousands of customers. You might not get the individual attention that you would with a smaller host, and customer service can be impersonal. With bCentral, for instance, if you decide not to pay a monthly fee for phone support, you have to send questions to the customer service area by chatting: typing messages in a form and sending your comments to the company. In my experience, this is a slow and cumbersome process.

Efficient Communication Means Better Business

In the earlier sections of this chapter, I show you how ISPs can help you create catalogs, process payments, obtain domain names, and perform other business tasks. However, sometimes the tasks that aren't directly related to marketing and sales can actually enable you to improve your sales by giving you more time to do marketing and sales. If you can use the Internet to communicate with vendors, coworkers, and other business partners, you increase efficiency, which, in turn, enables you to take care of business.

Efficiency involves getting everyone on the same page and working together, if not at the same time, at least at the *right* time. Standing in the hallway with a megaphone and announcing a group meeting is going to disturb people who are working — and besides, you'll miss employees who are out running errands or taking a lunch break.

A less intrusive tool for getting people together is an online *personal information manager* (PIM). An online PIM provides the tools, such as a calendar, an address book, a to-do list, and e-mail, so that members of a workgroup can coordinate their schedules.

An example of an online PIM is ScheduleOnline (`www.scheduleonline.com`). ScheduleOnline received high marks from the online news service CNET, particularly for its calendar, which enables multiple users to share lists of tasks and meetings, as shown in Figure 5-1. Users can invite others to meetings (guests confirm with a single click), send meeting announcements by e-mail, and check for conflicts to ensure that everyone's schedule has an opening during the time selected.

Figure 5-1:
An online personal information manager lets you share schedules and set up meetings with coworkers and customers alike.

Collaboration boosts efficiency

Health Decisions (www.healthdec.com), a clinical research and development company based in Chapel Hill, North Carolina, manages an office in Oxford, England by using the Internet. The company posts its company's benefits, travel, and orientation information for new employees on its intranet. Staff can also purchase travel vouchers and record purchases made with company credit cards online.

Improved communication and workflow — thanks to e-mail, the intranet, and access to the wider Internet — enables the company's 50 staff members to collaborate and communicate with the aid of only two administrative staff. Health Decisions doesn't even have a receptionist.

CEO Michael Rosenberg estimates that Health Decisions would require 5–7 additional people if it used conventional communications. At an average salary of 35K plus benefits, he believes the company's intranet is saving them about $175K to 245K per year.

"A lot of the administrative questions you get are very predictable. How do I check the status of my 401K plan, or enter time for a project? We try to put it all on our intranet. Why pay someone to do these repetitive tasks when we can put the relevant information on the intranet, and people can access the data quickly. We save time; the employee saves time. I look on it as a means of empowering people."

The Internet also enables Health Decisions to handle critical procedures far more quickly when compared with industry standards:

- The time required to process a questionnaire averages 3.9 hours, compared with weeks or months typically required of clinical research companies.

- The error rate for databases is less than five per 10,000 database fields, compared with about 5 per 1,000 incurred by other companies.

- The time required to submit one 10,000-page regulatory application is three months, compared with about a year for companies that don't collaborate online.

Health Decisions conducts tests of pharmaceutical drugs. Such tests are expensive and collect an extensive amount of data. It's critical for staff to get the data in the system quickly and get the information in the field. When a study has been completed, Health Decisions uses standard forms stored on its intranet to present the data, which is then submitted via the Internet.

"While a study is still being done, we can tell how it's progressing because the data is put on the intranet in real time in a database," says Rosenberg. "We set up a Web site for each study. At other organizations, it might take a week to gather the data. On the Net, you can do it instantly."

Monitoring Your Web Site's Performance

It's tempting to just get your Web site online, and then forget about it. It's up to your hosting service or ISP to monitor traffic and make sure everything's up and running. That's their job, right?

It *is* their job, to be sure, but unless you keep an eye on your site and its avail-ability to your customers, you may not be aware of technical problems that can scare potential business away. If your site is offline periodically or your server crashes or works slowly, it doesn't just waste your customers' time — it can cut into your sales directly. Luckily, some shortcuts are available to help you monitor your Web site that don't take a lot of time and effort or technical know-how.

If your site doesn't work well, another site whose pages load more quickly can be found just a few mouse-clicks away. Outages can be costly, too. Internet Week reported back in 1999 that if the Dell Computer site was down for just one minute, it would cost the hardware giant $10,000. A 90-minute outage would cost the company nearly a million dollars — and the rate is probably even higher these days.

Using software to monitor performance

A number of programs are available for between $30 and $200 that continu-ally keep an eye on your Web site and notify you of any problems. Such pro-grams take some effort to install. But the effort required to get them up and running has a big benefit — you know about setbacks at least as soon as your customers do, if not before.

WebCheck is a utility that monitors the performance of your Web site. It auto-matically checks your site and alerts you if your site goes down or if a page has been accidentally renamed or deleted. You configure WebCheck to check your site's URLs; you can have the program load the URLs once a minute, or even once every second (faster checking may slow down your site's perfor-mance, however). You can be notified by e-mail, fax, pop-up browser window, or taskbar icon. You can download WebCheck from the ZDNet Web site (www.zdnet.com/downloads). Another application, SiteScope, by Freshwater Software (www.sitescope.com/SiteScope.htm), runs on Microsoft Windows NT or 2000 and checks sites every five to ten minutes.

You don't have to install your own software in order to monitor your Web site's performance, of course. You can sign up with a company that offers such monitoring as a service. In this case, you use the company's software, which resides on its computers, not yours. For example, @watch (www.atwatch.com) provides an online service that checks your site's images and links periodically to see if everything is working correctly. The company offers several levels of service. The @watch Lite version costs $19.95 per month and checks your site once every 60 minutes. Other versions can check your site as frequently as every five minutes.

Dealing with service outages

Ideally, your Web host will provide a page on its Web site that keeps track of its network status and records any recent problems. *One* site monitoring notification (from a program you install yourself or one that you "rent" as a service from an ASP — see the next section "Outsourcing Your Business Needs") probably shouldn't be cause for concern. However, when you receive a *series* of notifications, call your Web hosting service and talk to its technical staff. Be courteous, but be specific. Tell them exactly what the problems are/were. You might even want to print out the reports you receive so that you can be aware of the exact nature of the problems. If you find that such outages are occurring on a regular basis, exercise patience but be firm in dealing with technical problems that have an impact on your business.

If the problem with your site is a slow response to requests from Web browsers rather than a complete outage, the problem may be that your server is slow because you're sharing it with other Web sites. Consider moving from shared hosting to a different option. In *co-location*, you purchase the server on which your files reside, but the machine is located at your Web host's facility rather than at your own location. Your site is the only one on your machine. You also get the reliability of the host's technical support and high-speed Internet connection.

If you really need bandwidth, consider a *dedicated server*. In this case, you rent space on a machine that is dedicated to serving your site. This arrangement is far more expensive than sharing a Web server, and you should choose it only if the number of visits to your site at any one time becomes too great for a shared server to handle. You'll know a shared server is becoming overtaxed if your site is slow to load. Discuss the situation with your host to see whether a move to a dedicated server makes sense.

Outsourcing Your Business Needs

One of the most effective ways to save time and money doing business online is to let someone else install and maintain the computer software that you use. *Outsourcing* is a fancy word for the practice of using an online service to perform various tasks for you, such as Web hosting, form creation, or financial record keeping, rather than installing software and running it on your own computer. Outsourcing isn't anything mysterious, however: It simply refers to the practice of having an outside company provide services for your business.

One of the companies that provide Web-based services on an outsourced basis is called an Application Service Provider (ASP). An ASP is a company that makes business or other applications available on the Web. You and your coworkers can then use those applications with your Web browser rather than having to purchase and install special software. For instance, when you fill out a form and create a Web page on Yahoo! Store (which I describe in Chapter 4), you're using Yahoo! as an ASP. Rather than create your Web page on your own computer by using a program, such as Microsoft FrontPage, you use an application on the Yahoo! site, and store your Web page information there.

How ASPs can help your company

You have to pay a monthly fee to use an ASP's services. You might incur installation fees, and you might have to sign a one- or two-year contract. In return, ASPs provide a number of benefits to your company. Here are the kinds of business processes they can help you perform:

- **Payroll and administration:** AquaPrix, Inc. (www.aquaprix.com), a small Hayward, California, water systems distribution company, out-sources some of its payroll functions to a company called QuikPay. AquaPrix, which doesn't have a large administrative staff, sends payroll data to QuikPay, which calculates salary and issues checks to all employees for about $100 per month.

- **Tech support:** ComponentControl (www.componentcontrol.com), a 55-person company with offices in San Diego and New York, licenses software that enables aerospace companies to locate and trade aviation parts. Rather than having to travel all over the country to solve every problem that users encounter with its software, ComponentControl's tech support staff use an online application called DesktopStreaming that enables them to "see" the problem a customer is encountering. ComponentControl can also show customers how to use the software from its own offices, which saves on travel costs and has reduced the time to solve problems by 30 percent.

- **Creating forms online:** FormSite.com (www.formsite.com) is a leader in creating a variety of forms that can help online shoppers provide such essential functions as subscribing to newsletters or other publications, asking for information about your goods and services, or providing you with shipping or billing information. The sample pizza order form shown in Figure 5-2 is an example of the type of form that this particular ASP can help you create.

- **Gathering marketing and survey data online:** LeadMaster (www.leadmaster.com) calls itself a "Web-based data mining tool." You store your customer information with LeadMaster, and LeadMaster provides you with an online database that you can access any time with your Web browser. It enables you to develop mailing lists based on your customer database. You can use LeadMaster's online tools to do sales forecasting and develop surveys that give you a better idea of what your customers need and want.

Figure 5-2:
An ASP like
FormSite.
com lets you
create a
database-
backed
Web page
feature
such as a
feedback
form without
having to
purchase,
install, and
learn a
database
program.

Although ASPs can help you in many ways, they require research, interviewing, contract review, and an ongoing commitment on your part. When does the extra effort make sense? I illustrate the potential plusses and minuses of outsourcing in Table 5-2.

Table 5-2 Outsourcing Benefits and Risks

Pros	Cons
Time saving: Saving time can save you money in the long run.	**ASPs are relatively new:** Many are start-ups, and they may have just as little business experience as you do. Take extra care before you sign a contract for service.
Better customer service: By outsourcing scheduling or other functions, businesses give customers increased options for interacting with them online. Customers don't have to call or e-mail the company; in the case of online scheduling, customers can schedule or cancel appointments by accessing the company's online calendar.	**A contract is required:** When ASPs first began to appear in the late '90s, they spoke in terms of "renting" software. These days, ASPs usually allow customers to try out their services for a while, but then offer long-term contracts. The terms of these contracts can range from one to three years. Don't get yourself locked in to a long-term arrangement that will prevent you from trying out cheaper or better alternatives down the road.

Pros	Cons
Greater Web site functionality: ASPs enable your site to provide better service to your customers and allow you to get more work done.	**ASPs face stiff competition:** Many ASPs have failed in recent years. Make sure the companies that you sign agreements with will be around for a while by talking to current customers and reviewing resumes of senior staff and key employees. Scan the Web for any press releases or articles that serve as warning signs about the ASP's financial health.
Expanded scope: You don't have to become proficient in subjects that aren't part of your core business or expertise.	**Security risks:** The moment you hand over your business data to another online firm or give outside companies access to your internal network, you risk theft of data or virus infections from hackers. Make sure that the ASPs you work with use encryption and other Internet security measures. (See Chapter 12 for more on Web site security.)

In many cases, ASPs can provide a software solution and customize it to your needs. Outsourcing not only improves your company's bottom line, but also helps you convey your message to potential customers that you might never reach otherwise.

ASPNews.com (`www.aspnews.com`) provides an overview of the current state of the ASP industry. ASP observer Phil Wainewright and his staff publish regular articles about ASPs and industry trends. The site also includes a directory of ASPs (`http://linksmanager.com/aspnews/`). To check out a very good ASPNews.com article on what to look for in an ASP, go to the following URL:

```
www.aspnews.com/analysis/analyst_cols/article/0,,4431_425751,
                    00.html
```

Before you sign on the dotted line . . .

After you try out the software or other service that you want to lease (and any reputable ASP should let you try it out first), you usually need to sign a contract to keep using the service. This is the time to slow down and read the fine print.

Videoconferencing: Being in two places at once

One of the best and most useful types of ASP-based services you can use is videoconferencing, which can allow you to hold live meetings with your customers or business partners by using a Web-based conferencing service. It works like this: Participants need a computer that's equipped with a microphone and a camera that takes photos of them while they're sitting in front of their computers. They connect to a central location on the Web — the conferencing service — by using their Web browsers. After they're connected to the same location on the server, they can communicate in real time.

CMstat Corporation, a configuration management company with 20 employees based in San Diego, provides enterprise information management software to businesses around the world. Demos are essential for clients to decide if they want to make a purchase. In the past, CMstat would send a team of employees to visit each prospective customer one or more times. "We were making approximately eight trips per month for a total cost of $12,000," says Mike Gearhart, Marketing Manager for CMstat. "Our

dilemma was how to increase sales, yet keep expenses low. In addition, we wanted to shorten the sales cycle, which can be 6–12 months between demos." WebEx charged CMstat a $2,500 setup fee and $900 per month to provide online demos. All told, CMstat estimates that it's saving $26,000 per month in total sales travel and tech support costs.

What's that you say? You think that videoconferencing is too difficult to set up and expensive to use? WebEx (www.webex.com), one of the leaders in the field of Web-based conferencing, now offers a pay-as-you-go plan. You can use the company's services for a whopping twenty cents per user per minute. It's a great way to try out the service to see how it works for you.

Keep in mind, though, that the quality of any real-time activity on the Web, depends on the speed of the participants' respective Internet connections. Because of time lags, videoconferencing is really ideal for users with direct connections, such as T1 or T3 lines, cable modems, or DSL connections.

"It's a huge commitment for people to go into an ASP arrangement," says Dana Danley, an analyst with Current Analysis of Reston, Virginia. "The lengths of contracts can range from 12 to 50 months. Sometimes you can choose the length of a contract, but most often you're offered one contract. It's important not to get one that's too long. You don't even know for sure if the ASP will be around in three years, for instance."

Don't be in a hurry, even if you're experiencing the time-to-productivity pressures, merger upheavals, or lack of IT resources that drive many companies to outsource. In the following list, I present some suggestions to help you get the service you think you're getting:

 ✔ **Understand pricing schemes:** The pricing schemes that ASPs use to charge for their Web-based services are downright confusing. For instance, some ASPs charge on a "per-employee" basis, which means you pay according to the number of individuals in your company. But others charge "per-seat" fees based on each registered user, not every employee. Still others charge "per-CPU," which means you're charged for each machine that runs the hosted application. Make sure you understand what your prospective ASP plans to charge by asking questions and getting detailed information.

✔ **Pin down startup fees:** Virtually all ASPs charge a startup fee, also called a service implementation fee, when you sign the contract. Make sure the fee covers installation and any customization that you'll need.

✔ **Don't accept just any SLA:** Obtaining a service level agreement (SLA), a document that spells out what services you expect an ASP (or other vendor) to provide, is essential. But regard the SLA as a dynamic document. Don't stand for the boilerplate. Think of SLA as standing for Stop, Look, and Adjust.

Paula M. Hunter, vice-president of sales & marketing for cMeRun Corp (an ASP) and the president of the ASP Industry Consortium, says, "The SLA and/or hosting contract should outline additional monthly fees for data backup and recovery (often these items are included). It's also important to review the contract regarding help desk support and any fees which would be associated with placing support calls to the ASP."

✔ **Avoid "gotcha" fees:** Pricing arrangements are hardly standard with regard to ASPs. Some of the big hidden costs involve personalizing or customizing the service to adapt to legacy systems. Here are some questions you can ask in order to avoid wincing at gotchas when you open up the bill from your ASP:

- Is there an additional cost for customizing or personalizing the application?

- Does it cost extra to back up my company's data and recover it if one of my computers goes down?

- Is help desk support included in my monthly fee, or will you charge me every time I call with a question or problem?

✔ **Make sure you have security:** Having information reside on someone else's system is a double-edged sword. Putting this data on the Web makes it accessible from anywhere. But some huge security risks are associated with transmitting your information across the wide-open spaces of the Net. Make sure that your ASP takes adequate security measures to protect your data by asking informed questions, such as

- Is my data protected by SSL encryption?

- Do you run a virtual private network?

- How often do you back up your customers' data?

If the answer to any of these questions seems inadequate, move on to the next ASP — plenty are out there, and competition among ASPs is fierce. So right now at least, it's a buyer's market, and you should be able to get what you want.

Increase Accounting Efficiency

Time is money, and anything that can reduce the time your accounting staff spends entering data that employees can enter themselves frees them up to create reports and projections, deal with taxes, and handle responsibilities that no one else can do.

Expense account reporting, timesheet recording, and the tracking of "billable time" can all be expedited with the help of intranet Web pages and special time-management software. The same sorts of Web page forms that your customers fill out to make purchases or register for services on your external Web site can be created for employees who need to record their daily activities in your internal database.

An intranet, equipped with the right software, allows your employees to record their billable hours and other work-related activities by filling out a Web page form and submitting the data to a central server. That way, you can easily track how much time your employees have spent on specific projects. This is one of the great advantages of the Internet. Electronically networked information is available and can be updated anytime, day or night.

Should you hire an accountant?

It may be a good idea to hire someone to help you with your taxes and advise you from time to time on financial planning, at the very least. Enlisting the help of an accountant can be particularly helpful if you're self-employed and don't have sources of financial advice through your place of employment.

How do you find an accountant? I found mine through a personal recommendation, which is always a good way to find professionals. Here are some things to look for:

✔ Look for a CPA: Of the two groups of accountants — Public Accountants and Certified Public Accountants (CPAs) — CPAs are the best-qualified candidates.

✔ Try a small accounting firm rather than a big corporate firm: The small players probably have more experience with small business concerns. They tend to charge lower fees, too.

✔ Get recommendations: If you can't find a personal recommendation, ask your state CPA society for a list of accountants in your area.

When you interview accountants, find out whether they're familiar with the type of business that you run. Also ask about any small business clients that they have and especially any online businesses they may handle.

Chapter 6

Organizing and Designing Your Business Site

*T*he business bandwagon known as the World Wide Web is getting so crowded that it's in danger of tipping over. As cyberspace fills up with small businesses trying to find their niches, standing out from the crowd and attracting attention on the Internet becomes increasingly difficult.

How do you gain the attention of Web surfers who are increasingly mobile and increasingly accustomed to sophisticated content? Keep your site simple, well organized, and content rich.

In this chapter, I discuss one of the best ways for a new business to attract attention online: through a clearly organized and eye-catching Web site. (Another strategy for attracting visitors — developing promotions and content that encourages interaction — is the subject of Chapter 7.)

Organizing Your Web Site

Although you may be tempted to jump right into the creation of a cool Web page, take a moment to plan. Whether you're exploring the Alaskan wilderness or building a playhouse for the kids, you'll progress more smoothly by drawing a map of where you want to go. I mean that literally: Grab a pencil and a sheet of paper and make a list of the elements you want to have on your site.

Look over the items on your list and try to break them into two or three main categories. These main categories will branch off your *home page*, which functions as the welcome mat for your online business site. You can then draw a map of your site that assumes the shape of a triangle, as shown in Figure 6-1.

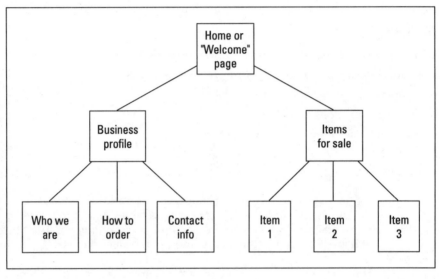

Figure 6-1: A home page is the point from which your site branches into more specific levels of information.

Think of your home page as a person at the door of your store who greets all the guests attending your grand opening and who hands folks a sheet listing sale items or a map of the departments in the store. Remember to include the following items on your home page:

- ✔ The name of the store or business

- ✔ Your logo, if you have one

- ✔ Links to the main areas of your site or, if your site isn't overly extensive, to every page

- ✔ Contact information, such as your e-mail address, phone/fax numbers, and (optionally) your address so that people know where to find you in the Land Beyond Cyberspace

Making a good first impression

First impressions are critical on the Web, where shoppers jump from site to site with a click of the mouse button. In this atmosphere, a few extra seconds of downtime waiting for complex images or mini-computer programs called *Java applets* to download can make the difference between a purchase and a rejection.

How do you make your welcome page a winner rather than a dud? Here are some suggestions:

✔ **Keep it simple:** Don't overload any one page with more than three or four images. Keep all images 20K or less in size.

✔ **Find a fast host:** Web servers are not created equal. Some have super-fast connections to the Internet and others use slower lines. Test your site; if your pages take 10 or 20 seconds or more to appear, ask your host company why and find out whether they can move you to a faster machine.

✔ **Provide sales hooks:** Nothing attracts attention as a contest, a giveaway, or a special sales promotion does. If you have anything that you can give away, either through a contest or a deep discount, do it. See Chapter 7 for more ideas.

✔ **Keep it short:** Make sure that your most important information appears at or near the top of your page. Readers on the Web don't like having to scroll through several screens worth of material in order to get to the information they want.

Establishing Your Store's Identity — Visually

Designing Web pages may seem complicated if you haven't tried it before, but it really boils down to a simple principle: effective visual communication that conveys a particular message. The first step in creating graphics is not to open a painting program and start drawing, but rather to plan your page's message. Next, determine the audience you want to reach with that message and think about how your graphics can best communicate what you want to say. Following are some ways to do this:

✔ Gather ideas from Web sites that use graphics well — both award-winning sites and sites created by designers who are using graphics in new or unusual ways. To find some award-winners, check out The Webby Awards (www.webbyawards.com/main) and The International Web Page Awards (www.websiteawards.com).

✔ Use graphics consistently from page to page to create an identity.

✔ Know your audience. Create graphics that meet visitors' needs and expectations. If you're selling skateboards to teenagers, go for neon colors and out-there graphics. If you're selling insurance to senior citizens, choose a distinguished and sophisticated typeface.

How do you "get to know" your audience when you can't actually see them face-to-face in cyberspace? Find newsgroups and mailing lists in which potential visitors to your site are discussing subjects related to what you plan to publish on the Web. Read the posted messages to get a peek into the concerns and vocabulary of your intended audience.

Choosing your Web page wallpaper

The technical term for the wallpaper that sits behind the contents of a Web page is its *background*. Most Web browsers display the background of a page as light gray unless you specify something different. If you don't change that plain ol' gray wallpaper, viewers are likely to get the impression that the page is poorly designed or that the author of the page hasn't put a great deal of thought into the project. So changing the background of all your pages is a good idea — even if you only make them a neutral color, such as white.

You can change the background of your Web page by tinkering with the HTML source code — but why bother? Most Web page creation programs offer a simple way to specify a color or an image file to serve as the background of a Web page. For example, in CoffeeCup HTML Editor, a popular Web page design tool, you use the Document Properties dialog box (see Figure 6-2) to set your Web page wallpaper.

Figure 6-2: Most Web page editors let you specify background image/color options in a dialog box like this.

Using color to convey your message

You can use colors to elicit a particular mood or emotion and also to convey your organization's identity on the Web. The right choice of color can create impressions ranging from elegance to professionalism to the energy of youth.

The conservative colors chosen by package-delivery company United Parcel Service (www.ups.com) assure customers that it is a staid and reliable company, and the U.S. Postal Service (www.usps.gov) sticks to the solid-citizen choice of red, white, and blue. In contrast, the designers of the HotHotHot hot sauce site (www.hothothot.com) combine fiery colors and original art to convey a spicy, mouth-watering atmosphere.

When selecting colors for your own Web pages, consider the tastes of your target audience. Ask yourself what emotions or impressions different colors evoke in you. Try to determine which colors best convey the mission or identity of your business.

The best color choices for Web backgrounds are ones that don't shift dramatically from browser to browser or platform to platform. The best palette for use on the Web is a set of 216 colors that is common to all browsers. These are called *browser-safe colors* because they appear pretty much the same from browser to browser and on different monitors. The palette itself appears on Victor Engel's Web site (the-light.com/netcol.html).

Keep in mind that the colors you use must have contrast so that they don't blend into one another. For example, you don't want to put purple type on a brown or blue background, or yellow type on a white background. Remember to use light type against a dark background, and dark type against a light background. That way, all your page's contents will show up.

As long as your type and graphics are visible, there is no right or wrong color choice. Go with your instincts and then get feedback from your colleagues and a sample of your audience before you make your final decision.

Tiling images in the background

You can use an image instead of a solid color to serve as the background of a page. You specify an image in the HTML code of your Web page (or in your Web page editor), and browsers automatically *tile* the image, reproducing it over and over to fill up the current width of the browser window.

Background images only work when they're subtle and don't interfere with the page contents. Be careful to choose an image that doesn't have any obvious lines that will create a distracting pattern when tiled. It should literally look like wallpaper.

Any background image, if not chosen correctly, can make the page unreadable. Visit the Maine Solar House home page (`www.solarhouse.com`) shown later in Figure 6-7 for a rare example of a background image that is faint enough to not interfere with foreground images and that actually adds something to the page's design.

Using special Web typefaces

If you create a Web page and don't specify that the text be displayed in a particular font, the browser that displays the page will use its default font — which is usually Times or Helvetica (although individual users can customize their browsers by picking a different default font).

However, as a Web page designer, you can exercise a degree of control over the appearance of your Web page by specifying that the body type and headings be displayed in a particular nonstandard font, such as Arial, Garamond, Century Schoolbook, and so on. But you don't have ultimate control over whether a given browser will display the specified typeface because you don't know for sure whether the individual user's system has access to your preferred typefaces. If the particular font you specified is not available, the browser will fall back on its default font (which, again, is probably Helvetica or Times).

That's why, generally speaking, when you design Web pages, you want to pick a generic typeface that is built into virtually every computer's operating system. This convention ensures that your Web pages look more or less the same no matter what Web browser or what type of computer displays them.

Where, exactly, do you specify type fonts, colors, and sizes for the text on a Web page? Again, special HTML tags tell Web browsers what fonts to display, but you don't need to mess with these tags yourself if you're using a Web page creation tool. The specific steps you take depend on what Web design tool you're using. In Macromedia Dreamweaver, you have the option of specifying a group of preferred typefaces rather than a single font in the Property Inspector (see Figure 6-3). If the viewer doesn't have one font in the group, another font is displayed. Check the Help files with your own program to find out exactly how to format text and what typeface options you have.

 When I was a print publications manager, I was taught the conventional wisdom that serif typefaces, such as Times Roman, are more readable than sans-serif fonts, such as Helvetica. An article on the Web Marketing Today Web site (`www.wilsonweb.com/wmt6/html-email-fonts.htm`) found that by a whopping 2 to 1 margin, the sans-serif font Arial is more readable online than Times Roman.

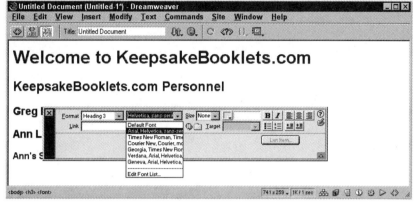

Copying and using clip art

Clip art is a quick and economical way to add graphic interest to Web pages, particularly if you don't have the time or resources to scan photos or create your own original graphics. Many Web page designers add clip-art bullets, diamonds, or other small images next to list items or major Web page headings to which they want to call special attention. You can also use clip art to provide a background pattern for a Web page or to highlight sales headings such as Free! New! or Special!

Clip art gets its name from the catalogs of illustrations that publishers can buy to clip out art and paste it down. In keeping with the spirit of exchange that has been a part of the Internet since its inception, some talented and generous artists have created icons, buttons, and other illustrations in electronic form and offered them free for downloading.

Here are some suggestions for sources of clip art on the Web:

- ✔ Barrys Clip Art Server (www.barrysclipart.com)
- ✔ ArtToday.com (www.arttoday.com)
- ✔ The Yahoo! page full of links to clip art resources (dir.yahoo.com/Business_and_Economy/Business_to_Business/Computers/Software/Graphics/Clip_Art/)

If you use Microsoft Office, you have access to plenty of clip art images that come with the software. If you're using Word, just choose Insert➪Picture➪ Clip Art to view clip art images as displayed in the Insert Picture dialog box. If these built-in images aren't sufficient, you can also connect to a special

Microsoft Clip Gallery Live Web site by clicking the Clips Online toolbar button in the Insert Clip Art dialog box. Web page editors — such as Microsoft FrontPage and CoffeeCup HTML Editor — come with their own clip art libraries, too.

Be sure to read the copyright fine print before you copy graphics. All artists own the copyright to their work. It's up to them to determine how they want to give someone else the right to copy their work. Sometimes, the authors require you to pay a small fee if you want to copy their work, or they may restrict use of their work to nonprofit organizations.

Adding digital images

Unless your customers are looking for something very specific, such as a particular variety of silverware or a carburetor for a 1956 Edsel, you need to add images to help entice them into your site and encourage them to move from one item or catalog page to another.

Even if you use only some basic clip art, such as placing spheres or arrows next to sale items, your page will likely be the better for it. A much better approach, though, is to scan or take digital images of your sale items and provide compact, clear images of them on your site.

Step 1: Choose images to scan

After you purchase a scanner or digital camera (see the suggestions in Chapter 3), the next step is to select images (if you're going to scan) or take images (if you're using a camera) that have the following qualities:

- **Moderate brightness:** Whenever possible, select images that are well illuminated. Subtle images may come out dark and unrecognizable on a computer screen.

- **Good contrast:** Select images that display a clear difference between light and dark areas.

- **Small in size:** Snapshots work well on Web pages. If you scan an entire 8½" x 11" sheet of paper, you end up with an image that's far too big to display on the average 7" x 10" computer screen. Inline images on Web pages are generally less than 7 inches wide. Often, photos are only 1 to 4 inches wide and perhaps 1 to 5 inches tall.

The overall quality of the image is just as important as how you scan or retouch it. Images that appear murky or fuzzy in print will be even worse when viewed on a computer screen.

Step 2: Preview the image

Virtually all digital cameras let you preview an image so that you can decide whether to save it or retake it before you save it to disk. If you're working with a scanner, scanning programs let you make a quick *preview* scan of an image so that you can get an idea of what it looks like before you do the actual scan. When you press the Preview button, you hear a whirring sound as the optical device in the scanner captures the image. A preview image appears on-screen, surrounded by a *marquee box* (a rectangle made up of dashes), as shown in Figure 6-4.

After you have a digital image (whether you have taken a photo or scanned a photo or other object), you need to do some editing. If you're scanning, you can edit the image by using the scanning software. If you're working with a digital photo, you can save the image file to disk and then open it in a graphics program to crop and adjust the brightness and other qualities. The following steps focus on scanning, but the general concepts apply to both scanned images and digital photographs.

Figure 6-4:
The marquee box lets you crop a preview image to make it smaller and reduce the file size.

Step 3: Crop the image

Cropping an image is highly recommended because it highlights the most important contents and reduces the file size. Reducing the file size of an image should always be one of your most important goals — the smaller the image, the quicker it appears in someone's browser window. *Cropping* means that you resize the box around the image in order to select the portion of the image that you want to keep and leave out the parts of the image that aren't essential.

Almost all scanning and graphics programs present separate options for cropping an image and reducing the image size. By cropping the image, you eliminate parts of the image you don't want, and this *does* reduce the image size. But it doesn't reduce the size of the objects within the image. Resizing the overall image size is a separate step, which enables you to change the dimensions of the entire image without eliminating any contents.

Step 4: Select an input mode

After you crop your image, the next step is to tell the scanner or graphics program how you want it to save the visual data. Select one of the following options in your scanning software's Mode menu:

- ✔ **Color:** When scanning a color photo, choose this option.
- ✔ **Line art:** Use this setting to scan black-and-white drawings, signatures, cartoons, or other art.
- ✔ **Grayscale:** If you want to present a black-and-white photo on your Web page, choose this option.

No one's going to turn you in to the Web design police if you scan a black-and-white drawing in color mode. You'll just end up with an image file that's far larger than it needs to be. It'll use up more space on your hard disk and take longer to appear on-screen.

Accommodating your viewers

Lack of bandwidth is one of the major roadblocks to presenting such content as live video, teleconferencing, and complex graphics files on the Web. This is changing: Recent surveys indicate that, for the first time, the number of Web surfers with broadband connections (such as cable modem or DSL) is just beginning to outnumber those with dialup modem connections. But the many Web surfers who still have very slow Internet connections (or very low tolerances for waiting) may not have the bandwidth to display even ordinary images quickly enough. After many minutes or even just seconds of waiting, the surfer is likely to hit the browser's Stop button, with the result that no graphics appear at all.

How do you prevent customers from slamming the door on your graphics like this? Some alternatives include

- ✔ Creating low-resolution alternatives to high-resolution graphics, such as thumbnails (postage-stamp sized versions of larger images)

- ✔ Cropping images to keep them small
- ✔ Using line art whenever possible, instead of high-resolution photos

By using the same image more than once on a Web page, you can give the impression of greater activity while speeding up the appearance of the entire page. Why? If you repeat the same image three times, your customer's browser has to download the image file only once. It stores the image in a storage area, called *disk cache*, on the user's hard disk. To display the other instances of the image, the browser retrieves the file from the disk cache, so the second and third images appear much more quickly than the first one did.

Users can also disable image display altogether, so they don't see graphics on any of the sites they visit. The solution: Always provide a simple textual alternative to your images so that, if the user has disabled the display of a particular image, a word or two describing that image appears in its place.

Step 5: Set the resolution

In Chapter 3, I note that digital images are made up of little bits (dots) of computerized information called *pixels*. The more pixels per inch, the higher the level of detail. When you scan an image, you can tell the scanner to make the dots smaller (creating a smoother image) or larger (resulting in a more jagged image). This adjustment is called *setting the resolution* of the image. (When you take a digital photo, the resolution of the image depends on your camera's settings.)

 How many dots per inch (dpi) do you want your image to be? When you're scanning for the Web, you expect your images to appear primarily on computer screens. Because many computer monitors can display resolutions only up to 72 dpi, 72 dpi — a relatively rough resolution — is an adequate resolution for a Web image. By contrast, many laser printers print at a resolution of 600 dots per inch. But using this coarse resolution has the advantage of keeping the image's file size small. Remember, the smaller the file size, the more quickly an image appears when your customers load your page in their Web browsers.

Step 6: Adjust contrast and brightness

You're probably aching to make your scan by this point, but wait! You have one final step. The more preparatory work you do up front, the better your image will appear when it gets online.

 Take a look at your preview image. Does the image seem dark or muddy? Virtually all scanning programs and graphics editing programs provide brightness and contrast controls that you can adjust with your mouse to improve the image. If you're happy with the image as is, leave the brightness and contrast set where they are. (You can also leave the image as is and adjust brightness and contrast later in a separate graphics program, such as Paint Shop Pro, which you can try out by downloading it from the JASC Web site, www.jasc.com.)

Step 7: Reduce the image size

You can do even one *more* thing to improve your digital image. Just keep repeating this mantra to yourself: "Make my image small . . . make my image small. . . ." If you're scanning and the preview image is much larger than you want the image to be when it appears on the Web, you can tell your scanner to reduce the size as it scans the image.

Do some quick math and estimate how much the image has to be reduced. For example, if an image is 8" x 10" and you're sure that it needs to be about 4" x 5" when it appears on your Web page, scan it at 50 percent of the original size. This step reduces the file size right away and makes the file easier to transport, in case you have to put it on a floppy disk to move it from one computer to another.

Step 8: Scan away!

Finally, you get to flex your mouse-clicker finger and choose your scanning program's Scan button. Listen to your scanner whir away as it turns those colors into pixels. Because you're scanning only at 72 dpi, your image shouldn't take too long to scan. When the machine finishes, the image appears again in your scanning program's window. (If you're editing an image captured with a digital camera, skip ahead to the next step.)

Step 9: Save the file

Now you can save your image to disk. Most programs let you do this by choosing File⇨Save. In the dialog box that appears, enter a name for your file and select a file format. (Because you are working with images to be published on the Web, remember to save either in GIF or JPEG format.)

When you give your image a name, be sure to add the correct filename extension. Web browsers recognize only image files with extensions such as `.gif`, `.jpg`, or `.jpeg`. If you name your image product and save it in GIF format, call it `product.gif`. If you save it in JPEG format and you're using a PC, call it `product.jpg`. On a Macintosh, call it `product.jpeg`.

GIF versus JPEG

Web site technology and HTML may have changed dramatically over the past several years, but for the most part, Web pages still display only two types of images: GIF and JPEG. Both formats use compression methods that compress computer image files so that the visual information contained within them can be transmitted easily over computer networks. (PNG, a third format designed a few years ago as a successor to GIF, is appearing online more and more, but it still isn't as widely used as GIF.)

GIF (pronounced either "jiff" or "giff") stands for Graphics Interchange Format. GIF is best suited to text, line art, or images with well-defined edges. Special types of GIF allow images with transparent backgrounds to be interlaced (broken into layers that appear gradually over slow connections) and animated. JPEG (pronounced "jay-peg") stands for Joint Photographic Experts Group, the name of the group that originated the format. JPEG is better suited for large photos and continuous tones of grayscale or color that need greater compression.

Creating a logo

An effective logo establishes your online business's graphic identity in no uncertain terms. A logo can be as simple as a rendering of the company name that imparts an official typeface or color. Whatever text it includes, a logo is a small, self-contained graphic object that conveys the group's identity and purpose. Figure 6-5 shows an example of a logo.

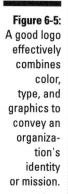

Figure 6-5:
A good logo
effectively
combines
color,
type, and
graphics to
convey an
organiza-
tion's
identity
or mission.

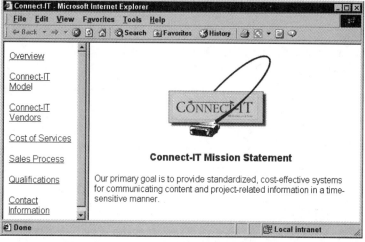

A logo doesn't have to be a fabulously complex drawing with drop-shadows and gradations of color. A simple, type-only logo often works just fine. See the logo for the Collectible Exchange in Chapter 2, for example. Pick a typeface you want, choose your graphic's outline version, and fill the letters with color.

Using Advanced Web Page Layouts

If you're just starting out and creating your first Web site, I advise you to stay away from more complicated ways of designing Web pages, such as frames and tables. On the other hand, you're the adventurous type; that's why you want to start an online business in the first place, right? So this section includes some quick explanations of what tables and frames are so that you know where to start if the time comes when you do want to use them.

TECHNICAL STUFF

A quick HTML primer

Thanks to Web page creation tools, you don't have to learn HyperText Markup Language in order to create your own Web pages, although some knowledge of HTML is helpful when it comes to editing pages and understanding how they're put together.

HTML is a markup language, not a computer programming language. You use it in much the same way that old-fashioned editors marked up copy before they gave it to typesetters. A markup language allows you to identify major sections of a document, such as body text, headings, title, and so on. A software program (in the case of HTML, a Web browser) is programmed to recognize the markup language and to display the formatting elements that you have marked.

Markup tags are the basic building blocks of HTML as well as its more complex and powerful cousin, eXtensible Markup Language (XML). Tags enable you to structure the appearance of your document so that, when it is transferred from one computer to another, it will look the way you described it. HTML tags appear within carrot-shaped brackets. Most HTML commands require a *start tag* at the beginning of the

section and an *end tag* (which usually begins with a backslash) at the end.

For example, if you place the HTML tags <B> and </B> around the phrase "This text will be bold," the words appear in bold type on any browser that displays them, no matter if it's running on a Windows-based PC, a UNIX workstation, a Macintosh, an Amiga, or any other computer.

Many HTML commands are accompanied by *attributes,* which provide a browser with more specific instructions on what action the tag is to perform. In the following lines of HTML, SRC is an attribute that works with the <IMG> tag to identify a file to display:

```
<IMG SRC="house.jpg">
```

Each attribute is separated from an HTML command by a single blank space. The equal sign (=) is an operator that introduces the value on which the attribute and command will function. Usually, the value is a filename or a directory path leading to a specific file that is to be displayed on a Web page. The straight (as opposed to curly) quotation marks around the value are essential for the HTML command to work.

Setting the tables for your customers

Tables give designers another means to present information in a graphically interesting way on a Web page. Tables were originally intended to present "tabular" data in columns and rows, much like a spreadsheet. But by using advanced HTML techniques, you can make tables a much more integrated and subtle part of your Web page.

Because you can easily create a basic table by using Web page editors, such as HotDog, Netscape Composer, and FrontPage, starting with one of these tools makes sense. Some HTML tinkering is probably unavoidable, however, especially if you want to use tables to create blank columns on a Web page (as I explain later in this section). Here is a quick rundown of the main HTML tags used for tables:

- ✔ `<TABLE> </TABLE>` encloses the entire table. The `BORDER` attribute sets the width of the line around the cells.

- ✔ `<TR> </TR>` encloses a table row, a horizontal set of cells.

- ✔ `<TD> </TD>` defines the contents of an individual cell. The `HEIGHT` and `WIDTH` attributes control the size of each cell. For example, the following code tells a browser that the table cell is 120 pixels wide:

```
<TD WIDTH=120> Contents of cell </TD>
```

Don't forget that the cells in a table can contain images as well as text. Also, individual cells can have different colors from the cells around them. You can add a background color to a table cell by adding the `BGCOLOR` attribute to the `<TD>` table cell tag.

The clever designer can use tables in a hidden way to arrange an entire page, or a large portion of a page, by doing two things:

- ✔ Set the table border to 0. Doing so makes the table outline invisible, so the viewer sees only the contents of each cell, not the lines bordering the cell.

- ✔ Fill some table cells with blank space so that they act as empty columns that add more white space to a page.

An example of the first approach, that of making the table borders invisible, appears in Figure 6-6: David Nishimura's Vintage Pens Web site (`www.vintagepens.com`) where he sells vintage writing instruments.

Framing your subject

Frames are subdivisions of a Web page, each consisting of its own separate Web document. Depending on how the designer sets up the Web page, visitors may be able to scroll through one frame independently of the other frames on the same page. A mouse click on a hypertext link contained in one frame may cause a new document to appear in an adjacent frame.

Simple two-frame layouts such as the one used by one of my personal favorite Web sites, Maine Solar House (see Figure 6-7), can be very effective. A page can be broken into as many frames as the designer wants, but you typically want to stick with only two to four frames because they make the page considerably more complex and slower to appear in its entirety.

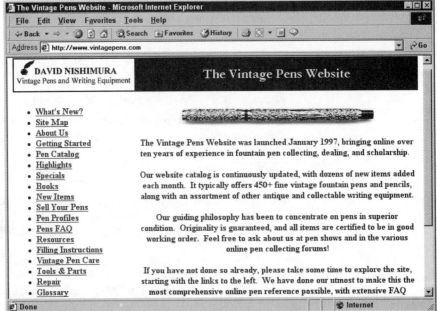

Figure 6-6:
This page
is divided
into table
cells, which
give the
designer a
high level of
control over
the layout.

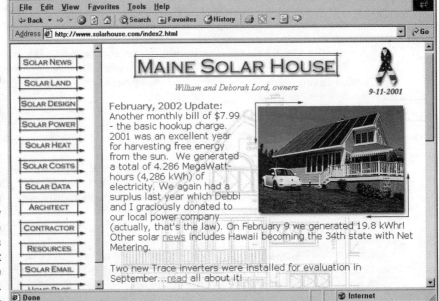

Figure 6-7:
This site
uses a
classic
two-frame
layout:
A column
of links in
the narrow
frame on the
left changes
the content
in the frame
on the right.

Frames fit within the BODY section of an HTML document. In fact, the `<FRAMESET>` `</FRAMESET>` tags actually take the place of the `<BODY>` `</BODY>` tags and are used to enclose the rest of the frame-specific elements. Each of the frames on the page is then described by `<FRAME>` `</FRAME>` tags.

Only the more advanced Web page creation programs provide you with menu options and toolbar buttons that enable you to create frames without having to enter the HTML manually. Most of the popular Web page editors do this, including Macromedia Dreamweaver and HotDog Professional by Sausage Software. See each program's Help topics for specific instructions on how to implement framing tools.

Frames add interactivity and graphic interest to a page, but many users dislike the extra time they require. As a Web page designer, be sure to provide a "no frames" alternative to a "frames" layout.

Break the grid with layers

Tables and frames bring organization and interactivity to Web pages, but they confine your content to rows and columns. If you feel confined by the old up-down, left-right routine, explore layers for arranging your Web page content.

Layers, like table cells and frames, act as containers for text and images on a Web page. Layers are unique because they can be moved around freely on the page — they can overlap one another, and they can "bleed" right to the page margin.

Layers carry some big downsides: You can't create them with just any Web editor. Macromedia Dreamweaver is the Web editor of choice, and it's not free (at this writing, Dreamweaver version MX costs $399). Layers are only supported by Versions 4.0 or later of Microsoft Internet Explorer or Netscape Navigator. However, Dreamweaver lets you create a layout in frames and then convert it to tables, which are supported by almost all browsers.

With Dreamweaver, you can draw a layer directly on the Web page you're creating. You add text or images to the layer, and then resize or relocate it on the page by clicking and dragging it freely. The result: some innovative page designs that don't conform to the usual grid.

Turning to a Professional Web Designer

Most of the entrepreneurs I interviewed in the course of writing this book do their own Web page design work. They learned how to create Web sites by reading books or taking classes on the subject. But in many cases, the initial cost of hiring someone to help you design your online business can pay off in the long run. For example:

✔ If you need business cards, stationery, brochures, or other printed material in addition to a Web site, hiring someone to develop a consistent look for everything at the beginning is worth the money.

✔ You can pay a designer to get you started with a logo, color selections, and page layouts. Then you can save money by adding text yourself.

✔ If, like me, you're artistically impaired, consider the benefits of having your logo or other artwork drawn by a real artist.

Most professional designers charge $40 to $60 per hour for their work. You can expect a designer to spend five or six hours to create a logo or template, but your company may use that initial design for years to come.

Chapter 7

Adding Content and Interactivity to Your Site

· ·

· ·

*P*eople often say that Content Is King when it comes to the Web, and although I believe that to be true, I would add that not just any content makes an online business work. You need the *right* content, presented in the *right* way, to make prospective clients and customers want to explore your site the first time and then come back for more later on.

So what's the *right* content? you ask. Well, that's the subject of this chapter. However, because one of my primary points in this chapter is that you need to express your main message on your business site up front, I'll do the same by explaining what I consider to be the right content for an online business. The material that you include on your site should

✔ Consider the way people absorb information online *(fast)*

✔ Make it easy for visitors to find out who you are and what you have to offer

✔ Be friendly and informal in tone, concise in length, and clear in its organization

✔ Help develop the all-important one-to-one-relationship with customers and clients by inviting dialogue and interaction, both with you and with others who share the same interests

There you have the main topics of this chapter in a nutshell. Here's another important point: You need to be straightforward about who you are and where you're coming from on your business site. Accordingly, my "mission statement" for this chapter is to get you to think, not so much about writing for the Web, but about being a provider of useful, exciting, well-organized, and easily digestible information. Now, on to the specifics of how you can put these goals into action.

Give 'Em What They Want!

Long ago, when mail-order merchandising was revolutionizing retail commerce (much the way the Internet is today), Marshall Field uttered his famous quote, "Give the lady what she wants." Today, on the Internet, the message is the same, albeit in a gender-free, 21st century sort of way: "Give your Web surfers what they want." Half the battle with developing content for a business Web site is knowing what shoppers online want and determining strategies for providing it to them.

Studies of how people absorb the information on a Web page indicate that people don't really read the contents from top to bottom (or left to right, or frame to frame) in a linear way. In fact, most Web surfers don't *read* in the traditional sense at all. Instead, they browse. They "flip through pages" by clicking link after link. As more Internet users connect using broadband technologies, such as DSL and cable, they can absorb complex graphics and multimedia. On the other hand, lots of users are beginning to use palm devices, pocket PCs, Web-enabled cell-phones, even Internet-ready automobiles to get online. They don't necessarily have tons of computing power or hours worth of time to explore your site. The best rule: Keep it simple.

People who are looking for things on the Web are often in a state of hurried distraction. Think about the stock trader, checking his hand-held device while waiting in line at the diner to grab a bite to eat. Think about the office worker at 4 p.m. on a Friday, waiting for the week to end. Imagine this person surfing with one hand on a mouse, the other on a cookie or a cup of coffee. Imagine the noise of the office in the background: phones ring, voices mumble. This person isn't in the mood to read ten pages of beautifully written prose describing your life story, why you started your business, and what you love about your field of expertise. Here's what this shopper is probably thinking:

"Look, I don't have time to read all this. I'm on my coffee break. My boss gets out of that meeting in ten minutes. I'm not supposed to be surfing the Web, anyway."

"What's this? Why does this page take so long to load? And I have a direct con-
nection here at the office. I swear, sometimes I wish the Web didn't have any
graphics. Here, I'll click this. No, wait! I'll click that. . . ."

The following sections describe some ways to attract the attention of the dis-
tracted and point their tired, jittery eyes where you want them to go.

Get it all out in the open

Don't make anyone wait to find out who you are and what you do. Keep in
mind that people who come to a Web site give that site less than a minute
(in fact, I've heard only 20 seconds) to answer their primary questions:

- ✔ Who are you, anyway?
- ✔ All right, so, what is your main message or mission?
- ✔ Well, then, what do you have here for me?
- ✔ Why should I believe you, pay attention to you, investigate your site? . . .

This is a pretty hard-nosed perspective, I admit. But I really believe that this
is what most Web surfers are thinking as they scan sites for information.

A study conducted by BizRate.com (`www.info-sec.com/commerce/00/`
`commerce_102300b_j.shtml`) found that as many as 75 percent of online
shoppers abandoned their shopping carts and failed to complete purchases
because pages were too slow to load. The Consumer 40 Internet Performance
Index by Keynote Systems (`www.keynote.com`) found in early March 2002
that, in a survey of 40 Web sites, the average site takes a full 21.34 seconds to
load over a 56Kbps modem. However, Web giant Ameritrade was found to be
among the fastest loading of 40 Internet sites, requiring only 4.46 seconds to
appear. Other top finishers prove that just because you have a big commercial Web site, you don't need to make it complicated: AltaVista's Web page
was clocked at 4.48 seconds and Yahoo! at 6.28 seconds.

When it comes to Web pages, it pays to put the most important elements up
front first: who you are, what you do, how you differ from any competing
sites, and how you can be contacted.

You probably can't fit every article or catalog item you have to offer right on
the first page of your site. Even if you could, you wouldn't want to: As in a
newspaper, it's better to prioritize the contents of your site so that the "top
stories" or the best contents appear at the top, and the remainder of the contents are arranged in order of importance.

Think long and hard before you decide to create one of those "splash pages" that contain only a logo or short greeting, then reload automatically and take the visitor to the main body of a site. And don't load up your home page with Flash animations or Java applets that take your prospective customers' browsers precious seconds to load. You run the risk of scaring people away needlessly rather than knocking their socks off.

Encourage visitors to click, click, click!

Imagine a bleary-eyed Web surfer staring at your Web site on a TV screen from across the living room. Make the links easy to read and in an obvious location. Having a row of links at the top of your home page, each of which points the visitor to an important area of your site, is always a good idea. Such links give visitors an idea of what your site contains in a single glance and immediately encourage viewers to click a primary subsection of your site and explore further. By placing an interactive table of contents right up front, you let often impatient surfers get right to the material they want.

The links can go at or near the top of the page on either the left or right side. The Dummies.com Technology bookstore page, shown in Figure 7-1, has a couple of links near the top banner plus links down *both* the left and right sides.

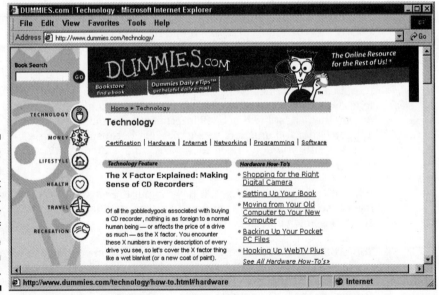

Figure 7-1:
Putting
at least
five or six
links near
the top of
your home
page is a
good idea.

Placing your site's main topics near the top of the page in a series of links has another advantage: It improves your chances of being ranked highly by search engines. Some search services index the first 50 or so words on a Web page. If you can get lots of important keywords included in that index, the chances are better that your site will be ranked highly in a list of links returned by the service in response to a search. See Chapter 11 for more on embedding keywords.

The following steps show you how to create links to local files on your Web site using Microsoft FrontPage, a popular Web page creation tool that you can test for yourself by ordering a CD containing a 30-day trial version from the Microsoft Web site (www.microsoft.com/frontpage/evaluation/default.htm). (At the time this was written, Microsoft was offering the trial version CD for free. Previously, the CD was offered for $10. Hopefully the CD will still be free when you read this.) The steps assume that you have started up the program and that the Web page you want to edit is already open:

1. **Select the text or image on your Web page that you want to serve as the jumping-off point for the link.**

   If you select a word or phrase, the text is highlighted in black. If you select an image, a black box appears around the image.

2. **Choose Insert⇨Hyperlink (or click the Insert Hyperlink toolbar button).**

   The Insert Hyperlink dialog box appears, as shown in Figure 7-2.

Figure 7-2:
If you keep all your related Web pages in the same directory, you have to enter only a simple filename as the link destination.

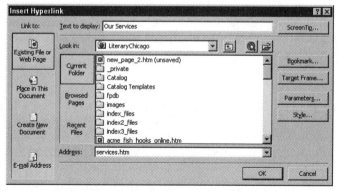

3. **In the Link To column, click Existing File or Web Page.**

4. **In the Address text box, type the name of the file that you want to link to the selected text or image.**

   If the page you want to link to is in the same directory as the page that contains the jumping-off point, you need to enter only the name of the Web page. If the page is in another directory, you need to enter a path relative to the Web page that contains the link (or locate the file in the Insert Hyperlink dialog box and select it).

5. **Click OK.**

   The Insert Hyperlink dialog box closes, and you return to the FrontPage window. If you made a textual link, the selected text is underlined and in a different color. If you made an image link, when you pass your mouse arrow over the image, the link destination appears in the status bar at the bottom of the FrontPage window.

Presenting the reader with links up front doesn't just help your search engine rankings, it also indicates that your site is content rich and worthy of exploration.

Tell us a little about yourself

One thing you need to get out in the open as soon as possible on your Web site is who you are and what you do. Profnet does this by condensing its mission statement into a single phrase:

Helping Business Professionals Find More Business

Can you identify your primary goal in a single sentence? If so, great. If not, two or three sentences will do just fine. Whatever you do, make your mission statement more specific and customer oriented than simply saying, "Out to make lots of money!" Tell prospects what you can do for them; the part about making money goes without saying.

Add a search box

One of the most effective kinds of content you can add to your site is a search box. If you can find a Web host that will help you set up one, you don't have to mess around with computer scripts and indexing tools. (See the section "Making Your Site Searchable," later in this chapter, for more information.)

Search boxes are pretty much standard on commercial Web sites. You usually find them at the top of the home page, right near the links to the major sections of the site. The Dummies.com site, shown in Figure 7-3, includes a search box.

Figure 7-3:
A search box invites visitors to interact instantly with your Web site. Many surfers prefer them to clicking links.

If you're worried about having to hire someone like me to write reams of golden prose in order to fill your pages with Pulitzer Prize content, I have news for you: Making a Web site compelling is simple. You're not writing an essay, a term paper, or a book here. Rather, you need to observe a couple of simple rules:

- ✔ Provide lots of links and hooks that readers can scan.
- ✔ Keep everything concise!

The shorter you can keep everything, the better. Keep sentences short. Limit paragraphs to one or two sentences in length. You may also want to limit each Web page to no more than one or two screens in length so that viewers don't have to scroll down too far to find what they want — even if they're on a laptop or smaller Internet appliance.

Make your content scannable

When you're writing something on paper, your contents have to be readable. On the Web, things are a little different: Content has to be scannable. This rule has to do with the way people absorb information online. Eyes that are staring at a computer screen for many minutes or many hours tend to jump around a Web page, looking for an interesting bit of information on which to rest. In this section, I suggest ways to attract those nervous eyes and guide them toward the products you have to sell or toward the services you want to provide.

I'm borrowing the term *scannable* from John Morkes and Jakob Nielsen of Sun Microsystems, who use it in their article "Concise, Scannable, and Objective: How to Write for the Web" (`www.useit.com/papers/webwriting/writing.html`). I include a link to this article in the Internet Directory portion of this book, along with other tips on enriching the content of your Web pages. See the section of the Directory called "Developing Compelling Content" for more.

Point the way with headings

One prominent Web page element that's sure to grab the attention of your readers' eyes is a heading. Every Web page needs to contain headings that direct the reader's attention to the most important contents. This book provides a good example. The chapter title (I hope) grabs your attention first. Then the section headings and subheadings direct you to the topics you want to read about.

As a general rule, I usually suggest following the convention of newspaper headlines when it comes to writing headings: Put the biggest headings at the top of the page. Most Web page editing tools designate top-level headings with the style Heading 1. Beneath this, you place one or more Heading 2 headings. Beneath each of those, you may have Heading 3 and, beneath those, Heading 4. (Headings 5 and 6 are too small to be useful, in my opinion.) The arrangement may look like this (I've indented the following headings for clarity; you don't have to indent them on your page):

Stan and Bud's Surfer Dude Paradise (Heading 1)

HangTen Surfboards (Heading 2)

The Surfer Dude Story (Heading 2)

Catch a Wave Surfin' School (Heading 2)

Registration (Heading 3)

Course Schedule (Heading 3)

New Bodysurfing Course Just Added! (Heading 4)

You can energize virtually any heading by telling your audience something specific about your business. Instead of "Fred's Shopping Mall," for example, say something like "Fred's Shopping Mall: Your One-Stop Shopping Spot for New and Used Hand Tools." Instead of simply writing a heading like "Mary Murano, Certified Public Accountant," say something specific, such as "Mary Murano: The Oldest Accounting Firm in San Diego."

Become an expert list maker

Lists are simple and effective ways to break up text and make your Web content easier to digest. They're simple to create and they give your customers' eyes more places on which they can rest. For example, suppose that you roast your own coffee and you want to offer certain varieties at a discount. Rather than bury the items you're offering within an easily overlooked paragraph, why not list them prominently so that visitors can't help but see them.

The following example shows how easy lists are to implement if you use a Web page editor, such as Microsoft FrontPage. You have your Web page document open in FrontPage, and you're at that point in the page where you want to insert a list. Just do the following:

1. **Type a heading for your list and then select the entire heading.**

   For example, you might type and then select the words **Today's Specials**.

2. **Click the triangle next to the Style drop-down menu.**

   A list of paragraph styles appears.

3. **Click a heading style, such as Heading 3, to select it from the list of styles.**

   The name of the style you chose appears in the Style menu, and your text is now formatted as a heading.

4. **Click anywhere in the FrontPage window to deselect the heading you just formatted.**

5. **Press Enter to move to a new line.**

6. **Type the first item of your list, press Enter, and then type the second item on the next line.**

   Repeat until you've entered all the items of your list.

7. **Select all the items of your list (but not the heading).**

8. **Click the Bullets toolbar button at the far right of the FrontPage Formatting menu.**

   A bullet appears next to each list item, and the items appear closer together on-screen so that they look more like a list. That's all there is to it! Figure 7-4 shows the result.

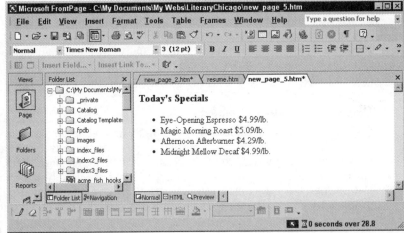

Figure 7-4:
A bulleted
list is an
easy way
to direct
customers'
attention
to special
promotions
or sale
items.

Most Web editors let you vary the appearance of the bullet that appears next to a bulleted list item. For example, you can make it a hollow circle rather than a solid black dot, or you can choose a rectangle rather than a circle.

Your Web page title: The ultimate heading

When you're dreaming up clever headings for your Web pages, don't overlook the "heading" that appears in the narrow black bar at the very top of your visitor's Web browser window: the *title* of your Web page.

The two HTML tags `<TITLE>` and `</TITLE>` contain the text that appears within the browser title bar. But you don't have to mess with these nasty HTML codes: All Web page creation programs give you an easy way to enter or edit a title for a Web page. In FrontPage, you follow these steps:

1. **With the Web page you're editing open in the FrontPage window, choose File⇨ Properties.**

   The Page Properties dialog box appears.

2. **In the Title text box, enter a title for your page.**

3. **Click OK.**

   The Page Properties dialog box closes and you return to the FrontPage window. The title doesn't automatically appear in the title area at the top of the window. When you view the page in a Web browser, however, the title is visible.

Make the title as catchy and specific as possible, but make sure that the title is no longer than 64 characters. An effective title refers to your goods or services while grabbing the viewer's attention. If your business is called Lydia's Cheesecakes, for example, you might make your title "Smile and Say Cheese! With Lydia's Cakes" (40 characters).

Lead your readers on with links

I mean for you to interpret the preceding heading literally, not figuratively. In other words, I'm not suggesting that you make promises on which you can't deliver. Rather, I mean that you should do anything you can to lead your visitors to your site and entice them to enter and explore individual pages. You can accomplish this goal with a single hyperlinked word that leads to another page on your site:

More . . .

I see this word all the time on Web pages that present a lot of content. At the bottom of a list of their products and services, businesses place that word in bold type: **More. . .** I'm always interested in finding out what more they could possibly have to offer me.

Television newscasts use the same approach. Before the newscast actually goes on the air, someone appears during a commercial break to give you a "tease" about the kinds of stories that are coming up next. You can do the same kind of thing on your Web pages. For example, which of the following links is more likely to get a response?

Next

Next: Paragon's Success Stories

Whenever possible, tell your visitors what they can expect to encounter as a benefit when they click a link. Give them a promise — and then live up to that promise.

Enhance your text with well-placed images

You can add two kinds of images to a Web page: an *inline image,* which appears in the body of your page along with your text, or an *external image,* which is a separate file that visitors access by clicking a link. The link may take the form of highlighted text or a small version of the image called a *thumbnail.*

The basic HTML tag that inserts an image in your document takes the following form:

```
<IMG SRC="URL">
```

This tag tells your browser to display an image (`<IMG>`) here. `"URL"` gives the location of the image file that serves as the source (`SRC`) for this image. Whenever possible, you should also include `WIDTH` and `HEIGHT` attributes (as follows) because they help speed up graphics display for many browsers:

```
<IMG HEIGHT=51 WIDTH=48 SRC="target.gif">
```

Most Web page editors add the WIDTH and HEIGHT attributes automatically when you insert an image. Typically, here's what happens:

1. You click the location in the Web page where you want the image to appear.

2. Then you click an Image toolbar button or choose Insert⇨Image to display an image selection dialog box.

3. Next you enter the name of the image you want to add and click OK.

   The image is added to your Web page. (For more information, see Chapter 6.)

A well-placed image points the way to text that you want people to read immediately. Think about where your own eyes go when you first connect to a Web page. Most likely, you first look at any images on the page; then you look at the headings; finally, you settle on text to read. If you can place an image next to a heading, you virtually ensure that viewers will read the heading.

Give something away for free

Raise your right hand and repeat after me. "I, [*your name*]" — no, don't say "your name," say your name. Oh, never mind. Just promise me that you'll use one of the following words in the headings on your online business site's home page:

- Free
- New
- Act (as in Act Now!)
- Sale
- Discount
- Win

Contests and sweepstakes

The word *free* and the phrase *Enter Our Contest* can give you a big bang for your buck when it comes to a business Web page. In fact, few things are as likely to get viewers to click into a site as the promise of getting something for nothing.

Giveaways have a number of hidden benefits, too: Everyone who enters sends you personal information that you can use to compile a mailing list or prepare marketing statistics. Giveaways get people involved with your site, and they invite return visits — especially if you hold contests for several weeks at a time.

Of course, in order to hold a giveaway, you need to have something to *give away*. If you make crafts or sell shoes, you can designate one of your sale items as the prize. If you can't afford to give something away, offer a deep (perhaps 50 percent) discount.

You can organize either a sweepstakes or a contest. A *sweepstakes* chooses its winner by random selection; a *contest* requires participants to compete in some way. The most effective contests on the Internet tend to be simple. If you hold one, consider including a "Rules" Web page that explains who is eligible, who selects the winner, and any rules of participation.

Be aware of the federal and state laws and regulations that cover sweepstakes and contests. Such laws often restrict illegal lotteries as well as the promotion of alcoholic beverages. Telemarketing is sometimes prohibited in connection with a contest. Following are some other points to consider:

✔ Unless you are sure that it's legal to allow Web surfers from other countries to participate, you're safest limiting your contest to U.S. residents only.

✔ On the contest rules page, be sure to clearly state the starting and ending dates for receiving entries. Some states have laws requiring you to disclose this information.

✔ Don't change the ending date of your contest, even if you receive far fewer entries than you had hoped for.

Before your contest goes online, make sure that you've observed all the legal guidelines by visiting the Arent Fox Contests and Sweepstakes site (www.arentfox.com/quickGuide/businessLines/sweeps/ contestsSweepstakes/contestssweepstakes.html).

If you do hold a contest, announce it at the top of your Web page, and hint at the prizes people can win. Use bold and big type to attract the attention of your visitors.

Expert tips and insider information

Giveaways aren't just for businesspeople in retail or wholesale salespeople who have merchandise they can offer as prizes in a contest. If your work involves professional services, you can give away something just as valuable: your knowledge. Publish a simple newsletter that you e-mail to subscribers on a periodic basis (see Chapter 10 for instructions on how to do this). Or, answer questions by e-mail. Some Web page designers (particularly, college students who are just starting out) work for next to nothing initially, until they build a client base and can charge a higher rate for their services.

Make your site searchable

A search box is one of the best kinds of content you can put on your Web site's opening page. At least, it's something I like to see. A search box is a simple text-entry field that lets a visitor enter a word or phrase. By clicking a button labeled Go, Search, or something of the sort, the search term or terms are sent to the site, where a script checks an index of the site's contents for any files that contain the terms. The script then causes a list of documents that contain the search terms to appear in the visitor's browser window.

Search boxes let visitors instantly scan the site's entire contents for a word or phrase. They instantly put visitors in control and get them to interact with your site. I highly recommend that you add one.

Yes, I recommend some sort of search utility for e-commerce sites. However, adding a search box to your site doesn't make much sense if you only have five to ten pages of content. Add search only if you have enough content to warrant searching. If your site has a sales catalog driven by a database, it makes more sense to let your customers use the database search tool rather than adding one of the site search tools that I describe in this section.

The problem is, search boxes usually require someone with knowledge of computer programming to create or implement a program called a CGI script to do the searching. Someone also has to compile an index of the documents on the Web site so that the script can search the documents. An application such as ColdFusion can do this, but it's not a program for beginners.

But you can get around having to write CGI scripts to add search capabilities to your site. Choose one of these options:

- ✔ **Let your Web host do the work:** Some hosting services will do the indexing and creation of the search utility as part of their services.

- ✔ **Use a free site search service:** The server that does the indexing of your Web pages and holds the index doesn't need to be the server that hosts your site. A number of services will make your site searchable for free. In exchange, you display advertisements or logos in the search results you return to your visitors.

✔ **Pay for a search service:** If you don't want to display ads on your search results pages, pay a monthly fee to have a company index your pages and let users conduct searches. FreeFind (`www.freefind.com`) has some economy packages, including $9 per month for a site of 500 pages or less. SiteMiner (`siteminer.mycomputer.com`) charges $19.95 per month for up to 1500 pages, but lets you customize your search box and re-index your site whenever you add new content.

Judy Vorfeld went beyond having a simple Search This Site text box on her Office Support Services Web site. As you can see in Figure 7-5, she created a Site Index page that combines the search box with a list of links to her site's most important contents.

You say you're up to making your site searchable, and you shudder at the prospect of either writing your own computer script or finding and editing someone else's script to index your site's contents and actually do the searching? Then head over to Atomz (`www.atomz.com`) to check out the application Express Search. If your site contains 500 pages or less, you can also add a search box to your Web page that lets visitors search your site. Other organizations offer similar services. Visit FreeFind (`www.freefind.com`), PicoSearch (`www.picosearch.com`), or Webinator (`www.thunderstone.com/texis/site/pages/webinator.html`).

Figure 7-5:
A Search This Site text box or Site Index page lets visitors instantly match their interests with what you have to offer.

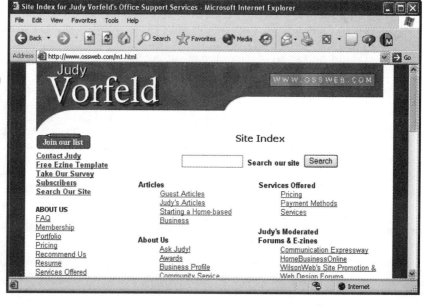

Writing for an Online Business Site

Business writing on the Web differs from the dry, linear report writing one is often called upon to compose (or, worse yet, read) in the corporate world. So loosen up your tie, kick off your pumps, and relax: You're online, where sites that are funny, authors who have a personality, and content that's quirky are most likely to succeed.

Striking the right tone

When your friend meets you at the train station, how does he pick you out from all the other passengers who have arrived on the 8:40? Maybe it's your signature haircut or that hat you'll probably take to the grave. Your business also has a personality, and the more striking you make its description on your Web page, the better. Use the tone of your text to define what makes your business unique and what distinguishes it from your competition.

Letting others speak for you

Don't go overboard with promotional prose that beats readers over the head. Web readers are looking for objective information they can evaluate for themselves. An independent review of your site or your products carries far more weight than your own ravings about how great your site is. Sure, you know your products and services are great, but you'll be more convincing if your offerings can sell themselves, or you can identify third parties to endorse them.

What's that you say? *Wired* magazine hasn't called to do an in-depth interview profiling your entrepreneurial skills? Yahoo! hasn't graced you with the coveted "glasses" icon (indicating, in the estimation of Yahoo!'s Web site reviewers, a cool site worthy of special attention) on one of its long index pages? Take a hint from what my colleagues and I do when we're writing computer books such as the one you're reading now: We fire up our e-mail and dash off messages to anyone who may want to endorse our books: our mentors, our friends, and people we admire in the industry.

People should endorse your business because they like it, not simply because you asked for an endorsement. If they have problems with your business setup, they can be a great source of objective advice on how to improve it. Then, after you make the improvements, they're more likely than ever to endorse it.

Satisfied customers are another source of endorsements. Approach your customers and ask if they're willing to provide a quote about how you helped them. If you don't yet have satisfied customers, ask someone to try your products or services for free and then, if they're happy with your wares, ask permission to use their comments on your site. Your goal is to get a pithy, positive quote that you can put on your home page or on a page specifically devoted to quotes from your clients.

Don't be afraid to knock on the doors of big-wigs, too. Send e-mail to an online reporter or someone prominent in your field, and ask for an endorsement. People love to give their opinions and see their names in print. You just may be pleasantly surprised at how ready they are to help you.

Sharing your expertise

Few things build credibility and ensure return visits like a Web site that presents "inside" tips and goodies you can't get anywhere else. The more you can make your visitors feel that they're going to find something on your site that they can't get anywhere else, the more success you'll have.

Tell what you know. Give people information about your field that they may not have. Point them to all sorts of different places with links.

Siteinspector.com (www.siteinspector.com) provides many services that Web site owners can access and use online for free. One utility sends your business URL to a variety of search engines and indexes. Another evaluates how highly your site is ranked by the major search services. After you have designed your pages, added your content, and gone online, check your pages with another online utility called Doctor HTML (www2.imagiware.com/RxHTML) to make sure that everything works efficiently.

Getting Your Customers to Talk Back

Quick, inexpensive, and *personal:* These are among the advantages that the Web has over traditional printed catalogs. The first two are obvious pluses. You don't have to wait for the ink to dry on an online catalog. On the Web, your contents are published and available to your customers right away. And, as the little birdie said, it's *cheap, cheap, cheap.* Putting a catalog on the Web eliminates (or, if publishing a catalog on the Web allows you to reduce your print run, dramatically reduces) the cost of printing, which can result in big savings.

But the fact that online catalogs can be more personal than the printed variety is perhaps the biggest advantage of all. The personal touch comes from the Web's potential for *interactivity.* Getting your customers to click links makes them actively involved with your catalog.

Inviting e-mail feedback

Don't leave your customers looking for bread crumbs to find their way to you. What's the single most important piece of content on a Web site? It could be the way you provide for your customers to interact with you so that they can reach you quickly.

Add a simple *mailto* link like this:

> Questions? Comments? Send e-mail to: info@mycompany.com

A mailto link gets its name from the HTML command that programmers use to create it. When visitors click the e-mail address, their e-mail program opens a new e-mail message window with your e-mail address already entered. That way, they have only to enter a subject line, type the message, and click Send to send you their thoughts.

Most Web page creation programs make it easy to create a mailto link. For example, if you use another popular Web page editing tool, Macromedia Dreamweaver, follow these steps:

1. **Launch Dreamweaver and open the Web page to which you want to add your e-mail link.**

2. **Position your mouse arrow and click at the spot on the page where you want the address to appear.**

   The convention is to put your e-mail address at or near the bottom of a Web page. A vertical blinking cursor appears at the location where you want to insert the address.

3. **Choose Insert⇨Email Link from the main menu.**

   The Insert Email Link dialog box appears.

4. **In the Text box, type the text that you want to appear on your Web page.**

   You don't have to type your e-mail address; you can also type **Webmaster**, **Customer Service**, or your own name.

5. **In the E-Mail box, type your e-mail address.**

6. Click OK.

The Insert Email Link dialog box closes, and you return to the Dreamweaver Document window, where your e-mail link appears in blue and is underlined to signify that it is a clickable link.

Other editors work similarly but don't give you a menu command called Email Link. For example, in World Wide Web Weaver, a shareware program for the Macintosh, you choose Tags⇨Mail. A dialog box called Mail Editor appears. Enter your e-mail address and the text you want to appear as the highlighted link and then click OK to add the mailto link to your page.

The drawback to publishing your e-mail address directly on your Web page is that you're virtually certain to get unsolicited e-mail messages (commonly called *spam*) sent to that address. Hiding your e-mail address behind generic link text (such as "Webmaster") might help reduce your chances of attracting spam.

Using Web page forms

You don't have to do much Web surfing before you become intimately acquainted with how Web page forms work, at least from the standpoint of someone who has to fill them out in order to sign up for Web hosting or to download software.

When it comes to creating your own Web site, however, you become conscious of how useful forms are as a means of gathering essential marketing information about your customers. They give your visitors a place to sound off, ask questions, and generally get involved with your online business.

Be clear and use common sense when creating your order form. Here are some general guidelines on how to organize your form and what you need to include:

✔ **Make it easy on the customer:** Whenever possible, add pull-down menus with pre-entered options to your *form fields* (text boxes that visitors use to enter information). That way, users don't have to wonder about things such as whether you want them to spell out a state or use the abbreviation.

✔ **Validate the information:** You can use a programming language called JavaScript to ensure that users enter information correctly, that all fields are completely filled out, and so on. You may have to hire someone to add the appropriate code to the order form, but it's worth it to save you from having to call customers to verify or correct information that they missed or submitted incorrectly.

✔ **Provide a help number:** Give people a number to call if they have questions or want to check on an order.

✔ **Return an acknowledgment:** Let customers know that you have received their order and will be shipping the merchandise immediately or contacting them if more information is needed.

As usual, good Web page authoring and editing programs make it a snap to create the text boxes, check boxes, buttons, and other parts of a form that the user fills out. The other part of a form, the computer script that receives the data and processes it so that you can read and use the information, is not as simple. See Chapter 10 for details.

Not so long ago, you had to write or edit a scary CGI script in order to set up forms processing on your Web site. A new alternative recently turned up that makes the process of creating a working Web page form accessible to non-programmers like you and me. Web businesses, such as Response-O-Matic (`www.response-o-matic.com`) and FormMail.To (`www.formmail.to`), will lead you through the process of setting up a form and providing you with the CGI script that receives the data and forwards it to you.

Providing a guestbook

A guestbook on a Web page performs roughly the same function as a guestbook in a hotel or at a museum: It gives your customers a place to sign in and provide some brief comments about your business. When you add a guestbook to one of your business's Web pages, your clients and other visitors can check out who else has been there and what others think about the site.

If you set out to create your own Web page guestbook from scratch, you'd have to create a form, write a script (fairly complicated code that tells a computer what to do), test the code, and so on. Lucky for you, an easier way to add a guestbook is available: You simply register with a special Web business that provides free guestbooks to users. One such organization, Lycos, offers a guestbook service through its Html Gear site (`htmlgear.lycos.com/specs/guest.html`).

If you register with Html Gear's service, you can have your own guestbook right away with no fuss. (Actually, Html Gear's guestbook program resides on one of its Web servers; you just add the text-entry portion to your own page.) Here's how to do it:

1. **Connect to the Internet, start up your Web browser, and go to** `http://htmlgear.lycos.com/specs/guest.html`.

2. **Scroll down the page and click the Get Gear! button.**

   You go to the Network Membership page.

3. **Click Sign Me Up! and follow the instructions on subsequent pages to register for the guestbook and other software on the Html Gear site.**

   The program asks you to provide your own personal information, choose a name and password for your guestbook, enter the URL of the Web page on which you want the guestbook to appear, and provide keywords that describe your page.

4. **After you've registered, a page entitled Step 2: Confirmation appears; click Get Web site add-ons now!**

   After a few seconds, a page called Create Guest Gear appears; see Figure 7-6. This page contains a form that you need to fill out in order to create the guestbook *text-entry fields* (the text boxes and other items that visitors use to submit information to you) on your Web page.

5. **Fill out the Create Guest Gear form.**

   The form lets you name your guestbook and customize how you want visitors to interact with you. For instance, you can configure the guestbook to send you an e-mail notification whenever someone posts a message.

Figure 7-6:
If you register with Html Gear, you can add a free guestbook to your own Web page.

6. **When you're done filling out the form, click Save & Create.**

   The Get Code page appears. A box contains the code you need to copy and add to the HTML for your Web page.

7. **Position your mouse arrow at the beginning of the code (just before the first line, which looks like this:** `<!- \/ GuestGEAR Code by http://htmlgear.com \/ ->`, **press and hold down your mouse button, and scroll across the code to the last line, which reads:** `<!- /\ End GuestGEAR Code /\ ->`.

   The code is highlighted to show that it has been selected.

8. **Choose Edit➪Copy to copy the selected code to your computer's clipboard.**

9. **Launch your Web editor, if it isn't running already, and open the Web page you want to edit in your Web editor window.**

   If you're working in a program (such as Dreamweaver or HotDog Pro) that shows the HTML for a Web page while you edit it, you can move on to Step 10. If, on the other hand, your editor hides the HTML from you, you have to use your editor's menu options to view the HTML source for your page. The exact menu command varies from program to program. Usually, though, the option is contained in the View menu. In FrontPage, for example, you click the HTML tab at the bottom of the window. The HTML for the Web page you want to edit then appears.

10. **Scroll down and click the spot on the page where you want to paste the HTML code for the guestbook.**

    How do you know where this spot is? Well, you have to add the code in the BODY section of a Web page. This is the part of the page that is contained between two HTML commands, `<BODY>` and `</BODY>`. You can't go wrong with pasting the code just before the `</BODY>` tag — or just before your return e-mail address or any other material you want to keep at the bottom of the page. The following example indicates the proper placement for the guestbook code:

```
<HTML>
<HEAD>
<TITLE>Sign My Guestbook</TITLE>
</HEAD>
<BODY>
The body of your Web page goes here; this is the part
        that appears on the Web.
Paste your guestbook code here!
</BODY>
</HTML>
```

11. Choose Edit⇨Paste.

The guestbook code is added to your page.

12. Close your Web editor's HTML window.

Exactly how you do this varies depending on the program. If you have a separate HTML window open, click the close box (X) in the upper-right corner of the HTML window, if you are working in a Windows environment. (If you're working on a Mac, close the window by clicking the close box in the upper-left corner of the window that displays the HTML.)

The HTML code disappears, and you return to your Web editor's main window.

13. Choose File⇨Save to save your changes.

14. Preview your work in your Web browser window.

The steps involved in previewing also vary from editor to editor. Some editors have a Preview toolbar button that you click to view your page in a Web browser. Otherwise, double-click the icon to launch your Web browser, if you haven't launched it already. Then

- If you use Netscape Navigator, choose File⇨Open Page, single-click the name of the file you just saved in the Open Page dialog box, and then click Open to open the page.

- If you use Internet Explorer, choose File⇨Open, single-click the name of the file you just saved in the Open dialog box, and then click Open to open the page.

The page opens in your Web browser, with a new Guestbook button added to it (Figure 7-7).

Figure 7-7:
Add a
guestbook
link to your
Web page.

Now, when visitors to your Web page click the highlighted Sign My Guestbook link, they go to a page that has a form they can fill out (Figure 7-8). Clicking the View My Guestbook link enables visitors to view the messages that other visitors have entered into your guestbook.

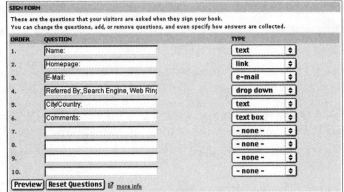

Figure 7-8:
A guest-book gives customers an easy way to provide you with feedback about your online business.

The problem with adding a link to a service that resides on another Web site is that it makes your Web pages load more slowly. First, your visitor's browser loads the text on your page. Then, it loads the images from top to bottom. Besides this, it has to make a link to the Html Gear site in order to load the guestbook. If you decide to add a guestbook, images, or other elements that reside on another Web site, be sure to test your page and make sure that you're satisfied with how long the contents take to appear. Also make sure to use the "Moderation" feature that enables you to screen postings to your guestbook. That way you can delete obscene, unfair, or libelous postings before they go online.

Gathering 'round the water cooler

You put your business online, you created some great content, and you're excited by the response you're receiving. You're getting plenty of e-mail inquiries, and once in a while someone gives you a big thrill by placing an order for your products or services.

Congratulations are certainly in order. But because I'm here to see that your online business is a real success, it's my duty to tell you not to stop there. After visitors start coming to your site, the next step is to retain those visitors. A good way to do this is by building a sense of community by posting a bulletin-board-type discussion area.

A discussion area takes the form of back-and-forth messages on topics of mutual interest. Each person can read previously posted messages and either respond or start a new topic of discussion. For an example of a discussion area that's tied to an online business, visit the Australian Fishing Shop (www.ausfish.com.au) discussion areas, one of which is shown in Figure 7-9.

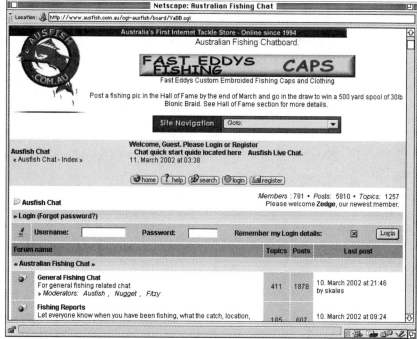

Figure 7-9:
A discussion area stimulates interest and interaction among like-minded customers.

The talk doesn't have to be about your own business per se. In fact, the discussion will be more lively if your visitors can discuss general concerns about your area of business, whether it's computers, psychotherapy, automotive repair, antiques, or whatever.

How, exactly, do you start a discussion area? Generally speaking, you need to install a special computer script on the computer that hosts your Web site. (Again, discussing this prospect with your Web hosting service beforehand is essential.) When visitors come to your site, their Web browsers access the script, enabling them to enter comments and read other messages.

Here are some specific ways to make your site discussion-ready:

✔ Install Microsoft FrontPage, which includes the scripts you need to start a discussion group. You can try out a demo version of the software for 30 days (see the section "Encourage visitors to click, click, click!" earlier in this chapter for specifics); it comes in versions for Macintosh and Windows platforms.

✔ Copy a bulletin board or discussion-group script from Extropia.com (http://www.extropia.com/applications.html) or Matt's Script Archive (www.worldwidemart.com/scripts/).

✔ Start your own forum on a service such as HyperNews, by Daniel LaLiberte, or install the HyperNews program yourself (`www.hypernews.org/HyperNews/get/hypernews.html`).

Because chat rooms and discussion groups are for a more advanced business Web site rather than one that's just starting out, I don't discuss them in detail in this book. I do, however, explore the topic in my book *Small Business Internet For Dummies*.

Chapter 8

Marketing to a Worldwide Audience

*A*s I write this, indicators continue to point to the growth of the Internet around the world. In its 2002 Information Society Index (www.worldpaper.com/2002/feb02/isi.jpg), research group IDC lists Sweden, Norway, and Finland ahead of the United States in terms of advanced information, computer, Internet, and social infrastructures. A study of how much countries around the world spend on computer and information technology (www.itaa.org/news/pr/PressRelease.cfm?ReleaseID=1014919282) lists the United States well in the lead — but also reports that its share of spending is on the decline while that of nations such as China is growing far more quickly.

Nielsen//NetRatings, in its Global Internet Trends report, reported that 14.8 million people gained home-based Internet access in the third quarter of 2001, adding that more than half the people in six of the seven Asia Pacific markets measured by Nielsen//NetRatings have Internet access from home.

What do all these lofty facts and figures mean for you, the budding Web businessperson? It means that the Web is a worldwide phenomenon, and you need to market yourself to customers and clients around the world, not just around the corner or across your own country.

One of the most exciting moments for many online merchants occurs when they receive their first order from overseas. That's when a host of new concerns pops up, too: How do I ship this order to Australia, Norway, Mexico, or Japan? How do I accept payment? After that, questions arise about how to attract more business from overseas. In this chapter, I provide pointers to help you attract and fulfill business orders, not just from around the neighborhood but also from around the world.

Speaking Their Language

What is it that attracts shoppers to your business and encourages them to place orders from thousands of miles away? It's what you have to sell and how you present it. But how can customers understand what you're selling if they speak a different language? You must make your site accessible to *all* your potential customers.

Minding your Ps and Qs (puns and quips)

Put yourself in your customer's place. Suppose that you're from Spain. You speak a little English, but Spanish is your native tongue, and other Romance languages, such as French or Italian, are definitely easier for you to understand than English. You're surfing around an Internet shopping mall and you come across sentences such as

> Hey, ratchet-jaws. Shoot me some e-mail with your handle, and steer clear of Smokeys with ears.

> Whatever. All you home boys will be down with my superfly jive.

> Like, this cable modem is totally awesome to the max.

Get the picture? Your use of slang and local dialect may have customers from your own hometown or region in stitches, but it can leave many more people scratching their heads and clicking to the next site. The first rule in making your site accessible to a worldwide audience is to keep your language simple so that people from all walks of life can understand you.

Good manners and good business practices are both important in Japan. You'll find tips covering both subjects at the Gateway Japan Web site (www.gwjapan.com).

Using the right salutations

First impressions mean a lot. The way you address someone can mean the difference between getting off on the right foot and stumbling over your shoelaces. The following useful tidbits are from the International Addresses and Salutations Web page (`www.bspage.com/address.html`), which, in turn, borrowed them from Merriam Webster's *Guide to International Business Communication*:

- ✔ In Austria, address a man as *Herr* and a woman as *Frau*; don't use *Fräulein* for business correspondence.

- ✔ In southern Belgium, use *Monsieur* or *Madame* to address someone, but the language spoken in northern Belgium is Flemish, so be sure to use *De heer* (Mr.) when addressing a man, or *Mevrouw*, abbreviated to *Mevr.* (Mrs.), when addressing a woman.

- ✔ In India, use *Shri* (Mr.) or *Shrimati* (Mrs.). Don't use a given name unless you're a relative or close friend.

- ✔ In Japan, given names aren't used in business. Use the family name followed by the job title. Or, add *-san* to the family name (for example, Fujita-san), or the even more respectful *-sama* (Fujita-sama).

Adding multilingual content to your Web site is a nice touch, particularly if you deal on a regular basis with customers or clients from a particular area. Regional differences abound, so it's prudent to find a person familiar with the area you are trying to target to read your text before you put it up on the Web. Let a friend, not the absence of orders, tell you that you've committed a cultural *faux pas*.

Making your site multilingual

One of the best ways to expand your business to other countries is to provide alternate translations of your content. You can either hire someone to prepare the text in one or more selected languages or use a computer program to do the work for you. Then provide links to the Web pages that contain the translated text right on your site's home page, like this:

```
Read this page in:
French
Spanish
German
```

The limitations of a computer translation

The problem with having a computer perform a translation is that you don't have the benefit of a real human being's judgment in choosing the right words and phrases. And in most cases, you have no idea just how good a job the program is doing in conveying your message. Suppose that you want to say your business deals in "vintage and collectible" watches, and the program says your watches are "juicy and delectable"?

To test the AltaVista online translation service, I took two paragraphs from my own business Web site and turned them into French. Then, I had my friend Caroline Dauteuille evaluate the translation. Caroline is a native French speaker and professional translator.

Here is the original text:

> Since ancient times, the stylus has been used to communicate messages. In modern recording, a stylus reads the traces left on a disk by voices or musical instruments into electronic data that can be amplified and enjoyed by many. Stylus Media takes your ideas, your words, and your products and services, and styles them into a variety of electronic media so that you can effectively communicate with customers.

When Caroline first read the AltaVista translation, she rated it a six on a scale of one to ten because she got the basic idea of what the text was trying to say. But, when she took a second look, she noticed two big mistakes:

- The program took my company's name, Stylus Media, and translated it as a regular phrase: "The media of the stylus," with no capital letters.

- The word "left" in the phrase "traces left" was translated as the direction "left" (*à gauche*) rather than a word meaning "something remaining behind."

So Caroline downgraded her rating of the translation to a three on a scale of one to ten. Although the computer program got most of the literal meanings right, the misunderstanding that could have resulted from the few big mistakes would have made a really bad impression.

Okay, I realize that this isn't a scientific test, and the results aren't surprising. Systran Systems, Inc., which provided the software used in the AltaVista translation service, has a disclaimer on its Web site stating that a computer is no match for a human translator. But if you have only a short, *very* simple bit of content that you need to translate, this is a cost-effective and quick alternative for a small business on a tight budget.

One translation utility that's particularly easy to use — and, by the way, free — is available from the search service AltaVista. Just follow these steps to get your own instant translation:

1. **Connect to the Internet, launch your Web browser, and go to** `babelfish.altavista.com`.

   The AltaVista: World/Translate page appears.

2. **If you have a specific bit of text that you want to translate, click in the text box on this page and either type in the text or paste it from a word processing program. If you want the service to translate an entire Web page, enter the URL in the text box. Be sure to include the first part of the URL (for example,** `http://www.mysite.com` **rather than just** `mysite.com`**).**

   Obviously, the shorter and simpler the text, the better your results.

3. **Choose the translation path (that is, *from* what language you want to translate) by clicking the Translate From drop-down menu.**

   At this writing, the service offers translation to or from Chinese, English, French, Korean, Spanish, German, Italian, Japanese, and Portuguese, and from Russian to English.

4. **Click the Translate button.**

   Almost as fast as you can say "Welcome to the new Tower of Babel," a new Web page appears on-screen with the foreign language version of your text. (If you selected a Web page to translate, the Web page appears in the new language. The title of the page, however, remains in the original language.)

Instead of creating a foreign-language version of your Web page, you can provide a link to the AltaVista translation page on your own page. That way, your visitors can translate your text for themselves.

You can download the software behind the AltaVista translation service, Systran Personal, from the Systran Software, Inc. Web site (`www.systrasoft.com`). The program is available for Windows only and requires at least 32MB of RAM and 20MB of hard disk space. The cost is $30 for a single pair of languages that you can translate and $49 for five language pairs. If you need translation to or from Japanese, Chinese, or Korean (or from Russian to English), look into Systran Professional Premium, which costs $999. This program has the same software requirements as the Personal package, as well as an Asian font display driver for Asian language translation.

You don't have to translate your entire Web site. In fact, just providing an alternate version of your home page may be sufficient. The important thing is to give visitors an overview of your business and a brief description of your products and services in a language they can understand easily. Most important, include a mailto link (see Chapter 7) so that people can send mail to you. However, if you aren't prepared to receive a response in Kanji or Swahili, request that your guests send their message in a language that you can read.

Although you probably don't have sufficient resources to pay for a slew of translation services, having someone translate your home page so that you can provide an alternate version may be worthwhile — especially if you sell products that are likely to be desirable to a particular market. Plenty of translation services are available online. Yahoo! has an index of translation services at `dir.yahoo.com/Business_and_Economy/Business_to_Business/ Translation_Services/Web_Site_Translation`.

If you want to try translations yourself rather than pay a professional, you can download a program called Babylon (`www.babylon.com/eng/download/ index.html`) by Babylon Ltd. The product provides single-click translations of individual words, phrases, and even computer terms. Versions are available to translate from English to Spanish, German, Portuguese, French, Italian, Dutch, Japanese, and Hebrew. The software (for Windows 95 and later) is free to download, install, and use for 30 days. After 30 days, you need to purchase Babylon Pro, which costs $17.95 for a one-year license, $28.95 for a two-year license, or $44.95 for a perpetual license.

Using the right terms

Sometimes, communicating effectively with someone from another country is a matter of knowing the terms they use to describe important items. The names of the documents you use to draw up an agreement or pay a bill are often very different in other countries than they are in your own. For example, if you're an American merchant and someone from Europe asks you to provide a proforma invoice, you may not know what the person wants. You're used to hearing the document in question called a quote.

When you and your European buyer have come to terms, a Commercial Invoice is an official form you may need to use for billing purposes. Many of these forms have to do with large-scale export/import trade, and you may never have to use them. But if you do undertake trade with someone overseas, be aware that they may require you to use their own forms, not yours, in order to seal the deal. To avoid confusion later on, ask your overseas clients about any special requirements that pertain to business documents before you proceed too far with the transaction.

Joining the International Trade Brigade

International trade may seem like something that only multinational corporations practice. But the so-called little guys like you and me can be international traders, too. In fact, the term simply refers to a transaction between two or more individuals or companies in different countries. If you're a designer living in the U.S. and you create some stationery artwork and Web pages for someone in Germany, you're involved in international trade.

Keeping up with international trade issues

If you really want to be effective in marketing yourself overseas and become an international player in world trade, you need to follow the tried-and-true business strategies: networking, education, and research. Join groups that promote international trade, become familiar with trade laws and restrictions, and generally get a feel for the best marketing practices around the world.

Here are some suggestions for places you can start:

✔ **The Enterprise Competitiveness Division - Small Business Web site** (www.entemp.ie/ecd/busi_serv.htm): This site is part of the Irish government's Department of Enterprise, Trade, and Employment.

✔ **Small Business Exporters Association** (www.sbea.org): A group of small- and mid-size business exporters devoted to networking, assistance, and advocacy.

✔ **globalEDGE** (globaledge.msu.edu/ibrd/ibrd.asp): This site (shown in Figure 8-1) is published by Michigan State University and includes hundreds of international trade links.

Be aware of export restrictions

If you're in the business of creating computer software or hardware, you need to be aware of restrictions that the U.S. government imposes on the export of some computer-related products. The restrictions were significantly relaxed in September 1999 and restrictions on exports to European Union countries were relaxed in October 2000, but some controls still exist.

According to the Clinton Administration's Encryption Policy Update of September 1999, you can now export commercial products that use encryption keys of any length without an export license to "individuals, commercial firms, and other nongovernment end users in any country except for the seven state supporters of terrorism." In some cases, however, the product must undergo a technical review that takes about a month.

In fact, you may incur a fine of more than $100,000 from the U.S. Treasury Department and the U.S. State Department for exporting to a Denied Person, Specially Designated National, or Restricted Country. The list of these people and countries changes frequently. Look for links to the current ones at www.treas.gov/ofac/index.html.

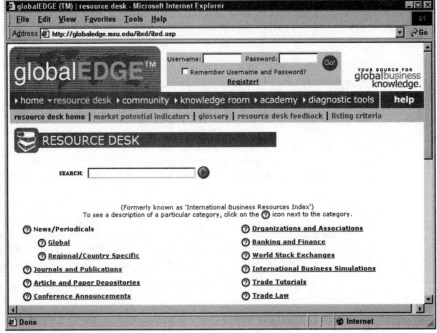

Figure 8-1:
If you want
to do busi-
ness with
overseas
customers,
globalEdge
is a must-
visit site.

The Newsletter Access Web site (www.newsletteraccess.com/subject/intertrade.html) has information on how to subscribe to hundreds of different newsletters that discuss international trade issues.

Researching specific trade laws

Instead of waiting for overseas business to come to you, take a proactive approach. First, do some research into the appropriate trade laws that apply to countries with which you might do business. The Internet has an amazing amount of information pertaining to trade practices for individual countries.

You can seek out international business by using one or more message boards designed specifically for small business owners who want to participate in international trade. These message boards let users post *trade leads*, which are messages that announce international business opportunities.

For example, at the ECCommerce.com B2B trade bulletin board (www.eceurope.com), you may find a message from a Finnish company selling surplus paint, a United States company that needs office equipment, or a

British company offering X-Ray equipment for export. Advertisements on this site typically include the URL for the business's Web site. The site charges a fee to post your own notices.

World Trade Markets (www.wtm.com) lets you post your own trade leads or search for other leads by keyword. The Trade Leads page of the extensive globalEDGE site (globaledge.msu.edu/ibrd/busresmain. asp?ResourceCategoryID=13) includes links to sites that post trade leads in countries such as Egypt, India, and Taiwan.

Exploring free trade zones

A free trade zone (FTZ) is an officially designated business or industrial area within a country where foreign and domestic goods are considered to be outside of the territory covered by customs. You don't have to pay customs duty, taxes, or tariffs on merchandise brought into, handled, or stored in an FTZ. You can find FTZs in many countries as well as in many U.S. states.

The purpose of FTZs is to reduce customs costs and make it easier for businesses to send goods into a country. You can store your items there for a while, exhibit them, and, if necessary, change them to comply with the import requirements of the country in question, until the time comes when you want to import them into the country.

A list of links to free trade zones in countries around the world is available at www.ceemail.com/free_zones.html.

Shipping Overseas Goods

It never hurts to state the obvious, so here goes: Don't depend on ground mail (appropriately nicknamed *snail mail*) to communicate with overseas customers. Use e-mail and fax to get your message across and, if you have to ship information or goods, use airmail express delivery. Surface mail can take weeks or even months to reach some regions of some countries — if it gets there at all.

Your customer may ask you to provide an estimate of your export costs by using a special set of abbreviations called *incoterms*. Incoterms (short for *international commercial trade terms*) are a set of standardized acronyms that were originally established in 1936 by the International Chamber of Commerce. They establish an international language for describing business transactions to prevent misunderstandings between buyers and sellers from different countries. Incoterms thus provide a universal vocabulary that is recognized by all international financial institutions.

Incoterms are most likely to apply to you if you're shipping a large number of items to an overseas factory rather than, for example, a single painting to an individual's home. But just in case you hit the big time, you should be aware of common incoterms, such as

- ✔ **EXW (Ex Works):** This term means that the seller fulfills his or her obligation by making the goods available to the buyer at the seller's own premises (or *works*). The seller doesn't have to load the goods onto the buyer's vehicle unless otherwise agreed.

- ✔ **FOB (Free on Board):** This term refers to the cost of shipping overseas by ship — not something you're likely to do in this high-tech day and age. But if you sell a vintage automobile to a collector in France, who knows?

- ✔ **CFR (Cost and Freight):** This term refers to the costs and freight charges necessary to transport items to a specific overseas port. CFR describes only costs related to items that are shipped by sea and inland waterways and that go to an actual port. Another incoterm, CPT (Carriage Paid To) can refer to any type of transport, not just shipping, and refers to the cost for the transport (or *carriage*) of the goods to their destination.

You'll find a detailed examination of incoterms at the International Chamber of Commerce Web site (`www.iccwbo.org/index_incoterms.asp`).

If the item you're planning to ship overseas by mail is valued at more than $2,500, the U.S. requires you to fill out and submit a Shipper's Export Declaration (SED) and submit it to a U.S. customs agent. The SED requires you to provide your name, address, and either your Social Security number or your Internal Revenue Service Employer Identification Number (EIN). You also have to describe what's being sent, where it's being sent from, and its ultimate destination. You can purchase an SED from your local U.S. customs office or from the Government Printing Office (`www.access.gpo.gov`), 202-783-3238. Detailed instructions on how to fill out the SED are available on the U.S. Census Bureau's Web site (`www.census.gov/foreign-trade/www/correct.way.html`). You can file the SED through the U.S. Customs Service's Web site (`www.customs.ustreas.gov/AES`).

Some nations require a certificate of origin or a signed statement that attests to the origin of the exported item. You can usually obtain such certificates through a local chamber of commerce.

Some purchasers or countries may also ask for a certificate of inspection stating the specifications met by the goods shipped. Inspections are performed by independent testing organizations.

Wherever you ship your items, be sure to insure them for the full amount they are worth. Tell your customers about any additional insurance charges up front. Finally, choose an insurance company that is able to respond quickly to claims made from your own country and from your customers' country.

Getting Paid in International Trade

Having an effective billing policy in place is especially important when your customers live thousands of miles away. The safest strategy is to request payment in U.S. dollars and to ask for cash in advance. This approach prevents any collection problems and gets you your money right away.

What happens if you want to receive payment in U.S. dollars from someone overseas but the purchaser is reluctant to send cash? You can ask the purchaser to send you a personal check — or, better yet, a cashier's check — but it's up to the buyer to convert the local currency to U.S. dollars. You can also suggest that the buyer obtain an International Money Order from a U.S. bank that has a branch in his or her area, and specify that the money order be payable in U.S. dollars. Suggest that your customers use an online currency conversion utility, such as the Bloomberg Online Currency Calculator (www.bloomberg.com/markets/currency/currcalc.html), to do the calculation.

You can also use an online escrow service, such as Escrow.com (www.escrow.com) or ePreview (www.epreview.net), which holds funds in escrow until you and your customer strike a deal, or Secure-Commerce (www.secure-commerce.com.au/), which specializes in transactions with Australian companies. An escrow service holds the customer's funds in a trust account so that the seller can ship an item knowing that he or she will be paid. The escrow service transfers the funds from buyer to seller after the buyer has inspected the goods and approved them.

Escrow services usually accept credit card payments from overseas purchasers; this is one way to accept credit card payments even if you don't have a merchant account yourself. The credit card company handles conversion from the local currency into U.S. dollars.

If you're going to do a lot of business overseas, consider getting export insurance to protect yourself against loss due to damage or delay in transit. Policies are available from the Export-Import Bank of the United States (`www.exim.gov`) or from other private firms that offer export insurance.

Marketing through global networking

Jeffrey Edelheit knows the potential for making connections around the world by taking advantage of the networking value of the World Wide Web. Edelheit, a business planning and development consultant based in Sebastopol, California, supports fledgling entrepreneurs' dreams of getting their businesses off the ground. He also helps established businesspeople extend their reach by looking at ways of gaining greater market exposure — including going online. In addition, Jeffrey works closely with management and staff to develop the internal systems necessary to build a strong operational base for the company.

Edelheit provides the following guidance:

✔ **Be deliberate in the creation of your Web site:** "I've worked with clients who are able to attract overseas customers and express themselves through creating their own Web sites," he says. A well-thought-out Web site can create a relationship between you and your customer; in other words, the stronger the relationship, the greater the opportunity for sales.

✔ **Know your market:** Jeffrey goes on to say, "The most important suggestion I can make is to know the overseas market that you want to reach and be aware of the issues associated with doing business there. I recommend getting contact information for an international trade group from the country's consulate."

✔ **Research shipping costs and regulations:** Shipping costs and restrictions are among the most common problems new businesspeople encounter when dealing with foreign customers, he says. "Check with the U.S. Customs Service and find out what the duty charges are before you ship overseas. Once, in the '80s, a company I was working with shipped an IBM computer to Sweden, but because there were still restrictions on exporting high-tech equipment, I nearly got arrested by the U.S. Customs for not having received the required special clearance."

✔ **Avoid being ethnocentric:** Also be aware of how consumers in other cultures regard your products, he suggests. Make sure that nothing about your products would be considered offensive or "bad luck" to someone from another part of the world.

✔ **Be visible:** Edelheit emphasizes that once you learn the inside tricks to the search engines, and cooperative links, you have unlimited potential to reach people. He believes that one of the keys to a successful Web site is providing information that your targeted market would find useful and then providing product offerings as an attractive supplement.

"The average consumer, whether in this country or overseas, wants to know who they are doing business with, and to develop a relationship with that person. A commercial Web site not only enables you to express yourself, but lets you create a 'value-added' experience for your customers," he concludes.

Part III

Promoting Your Online Business

The 5th Wave   By Rich Tennant

"See? I created a little felon figure that runs around our Web site hiding behind banner ads. On the last page, our logo puts him in a nonlethal choke hold and brings him back to the home page."

In this part . . .

*L*ike fish in the ocean, your potential customers are out there — more of them, in fact, than you can begin to count. Part III tells you everything you need to know to reel them in — hook, line, and sinker.

When you run an online business, you need to develop special strategies for getting attention and standing out from the millions of other sites that are your competitors. This means researching your market, delivering on your promises, making sure that your customers are satisfied with your goods and services, exploring all the options for advertising and publicity that are available to you, and choosing an effective marketing strategy that best meets your needs.

Nothing's more frustrating, after all, than feeling a nibble on your line and then having to content yourself with telling your friends about the one that got away.

Chapter 9

Making Your E-Commerce Site Sell

In This Chapter

▶ Understanding online consumers' purchasing needs

▶ Applying for merchant status

▶ Processing credit card data

▶ Setting up electronic purchasing systems

▶ Delivering your products and services

*S*tarting up a new business and getting it online is exciting, but believe me, the real excitement occurs when you get paid for what you do. Nothing boosts your confidence and tells you that your hard work is paying off like receiving the proverbial check in the mail or having funds transferred to your business account.

The immediacy and interactivity of selling and promoting yourself online applies to receiving payments, too. You can get paid with just a few mouse clicks and some important data entered on your customer's keyboard. But completing an electronic commerce (or, for short, *e-commerce*) transaction isn't the same as getting paid in a traditional retail store. The customer can't personally hand you cash or a check. Or, if a credit card is involved, you can't verify the user's identity through a signature or photo ID.

In order to get paid promptly and reliably online, you have to go through some extra steps to make the customer feel secure — not to mention protecting yourself, too. Successful e-commerce is about setting up the right atmosphere for making purchases, providing options for payment, and keeping sensitive information private. It's also about making sure that the goods get to the customer safely and on time. In this chapter, I describe ways in which you can implement these essential online business strategies.

What Online Customers Want

Time and again in this book, I point out how important it is to understand online shoppers' needs and habits and to do your best to address them. When it comes to e-commerce, the more effectively you can address what your customers want, the more tangible results you'll find in your bank account.

Show me that you have it for sale

Even experienced businesspeople who have a brick-and-mortar store are finding that the first thing customers want is to see the item they want listed (and better yet, depicted and described in detail) in your online catalog. More and more shoppers are taking it for granted that legitimate stores will have a Web site and an online sales catalog.

"It's not enough to just say we have this or that product line for sale. Until we actually add an individual item to our online store, with pictures and prices, we won't sell it," says Ernie Preston, co-owner of General Tool and Repair, a brick-and-mortar business that has an 84,000-item online catalog. "As soon as you put it in your online catalog, you'll get a call about it. Shopping on the Web is the convenience factor that people want."

Don't scrimp on the number of catalog items that you post online or on the amount of detail that you include about each item. For more and more businesses, having an online catalog is becoming a necessity rather than an extra service.

Tell me how much it costs, now

Don't make your customers search for a price list to find out how much an item costs. Be sure to put the cost right next to the item that you're presenting. Remember that speed and convenience are what Web shoppers want most. They don't have the patience to click through several pages. Chances are that they are comparison shopping and in a hurry.

Microsoft FrontPage 2002, which you can buy either as a standalone product or part of Office XP Developer, includes some clip art images that help highlight sales items. Figure 9-1 shows an example.

Font menu   Insert Clip Art Task Pane

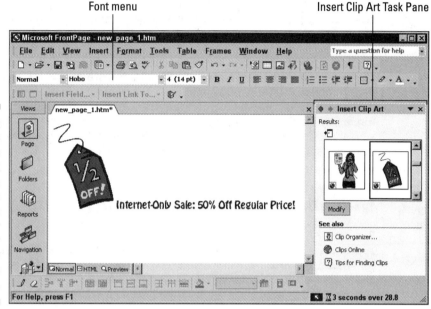

Figure 9-1:
Use
graphics
to call
attention
to the
information
your
customer
wants the
most: the
price.

Show me that I can trust you!

All business is based on trust, but for an online business, building trust is especially important. Electronic commerce is still in its early days, and many customers still have fears like these:

- ✔ How do I know that someone won't intercept my name, phone number, or credit card information and use the data to make unauthorized purchases?

- ✔ How can I be sure that your online business will actually ship me what I order and not "take the money and run?"

- ✔ Can I count on you not to sell my personal information to other businesses that will flood me with unwanted e-mail?

To get an in-depth look at how customers shop online and what constitutes "good" and "bad" shopping for many people, consult the book *Buying Online For Dummies* (published by Wiley Publishing, Inc.) by Joseph Lowery.

How do you build trust on your Web site? State your policies clearly and often. Tell people that you value their business and will do everything you can to protect their personal information. Assure them you won't give out any customer's data without that person's consent. If you plan to accept credit card orders, be sure to get an account with a Web host that provides a *secure server*, which is software that encrypts data exchanged with a browser.

If you're a member in good standing of the Better Business Bureau (www.bbb. org), you may be eligible to join the BBBOnLine program (www.bbbonline. org) to build credibility and confidence among your clients. Businesses that participate in the BBBOnLine program show their commitment to their customers by displaying a BBBOnLine Reliability Seal or Privacy Seal on their Web sites. Consumers can click the BBBOnLine seal to view a Better Business Bureau company profile on the participating business.

Give me all the information I need

Remember that one of the big advantages of operating a business online is space. You have plenty of room in which to provide full descriptions of your sale items. You also have no reason to skimp on the details that you provide about your business, your products, and your services. Here are some suggestions of how to provide information that your customer may want:

- ✔ If you sell clothing, include a page with size and measurement charts.
- ✔ If you sell food, provide weights, ingredients, and nutritional information.
- ✔ If you sell programming, Web design, or traditional graphic design, provide samples of your work, links to Web pages you've created, and testimonials from satisfied clients.
- ✔ If you're a musician, publish a link to a short sound file of your work.

Don't be reluctant to tell people ways that your products and services are better than others. Visit the Lands' End online catalog (www.landsend.com) for good examples of how this well-established marketer describes the quality of its wares.

Enabling Credit Card Purchases

Having the ability to accept and process credit card transactions makes it especially easy for your customers to follow the impulse to buy something from you. You stand to generate a lot more sales than you would otherwise.

But although credit cards are easy for shoppers to use, they make *your* life as an online merchant more complicated. I don't want to discourage you from becoming credit card-ready by any means, but you need to be aware of the steps (and the expenses) involved, many of which may not occur to you when you're just starting out. For example, you may not be aware of one or more of the following:

- ✔ **Merchant accounts:** You have to apply and be approved for a special bank account called a *merchant account* in order for a bank to process the credit card orders that you receive. If you work through traditional banks, approval can take days or weeks. However, a number of online merchant account businesses are providing hot competition, which includes streamlining the application process.

- ✔ **Fees:** Fees can be high but they vary widely, and it pays to shop around. Some banks charge a merchant application fee ($300 to $800). On the other hand, some online companies such as 1st American Card Service (www.1stamericancardservice.com) or Merchants' Choice Card Services (www.merchantschoice-usa.com) charge no application fee.

- ✔ **Discount rates:** All banks and merchant account companies charge a usage fee, deceptively called a *discount rate*. Typically, this fee ranges from 1 to 4 percent of each transaction. Plus, you may have to pay a monthly premium charge in the range of $30–$70 to the bank. Although 1st American Credit Card Service saves you money with a free application, it charges Internet businesses a 2.3 percent fee that it calls a discount rate, plus 30 cents for each transaction, a $9 monthly statement fee, and a minimum charge of $20 per month.

- ✔ **American Express and Discover:** If you want to accept payments from American Express and Discover cardholders, you must make arrangements through the companies themselves. You can apply online to be an American Express card merchant by going to the American Express Merchant Homepage (www.americanexpress.com/homepage/merchant.shtml) and clicking the Apply to accept the Card link. At the Discover Card merchant site (www.discoverbiz.com/), click the Apply Online link, which leads you to the application for credit card merchants.

- ✔ **Software and hardware:** You need software or hardware to process transactions and transmit the data to the banking system. If you plan to accept credit card numbers online only and don't need a device to handle actual "card swipes" from in-person customers, you can use your computer modem to transmit the data. 1st American Credit Card lets you use its secure Web site, called a Virtual Web Terminal, for processing transactions with your browser, but you have to either purchase this service for $429 or lease it for rates that vary from $20 to $53 per year. The hardware involved is a terminal or phone line, which you can either purchase for $525 or lease for anywhere from $24 to $53 per month, depending on the length of the lease.

You also need to watch out for credit card fraud, in which criminals use stolen numbers to make purchases. You, the merchant, end up being liable for most of the fictitious transactions. Cardholders are responsible for only $50 of fraudulent purchases. To combat this crime, before completing any transaction, verify that the shipping address supplied by the purchaser is the same (or at least in the same vicinity) as the billing address. If you're in doubt, you can phone the purchaser for verification — it's a courtesy to the customer as well as a means of protection for you. (See the later section "Verifying credit card data.") You can either do this check yourself or pay a service to do the checking.

Setting up a merchant account

The good news is that getting merchant status is becoming easier, as more banks accept the notion that businesses don't have to have an actual, physical storefront in order to be successful. Getting a merchant account approved, however, still takes a long time, and some hefty fees are involved as well. Banks look more favorably on companies that have been in business for several years and have a proven track record.

Traditional banks are reliable and experienced, and you can count on them being around for a while. The new Web-based companies that specialize in giving online businesses merchant account status welcome new businesses and give you wider options and cost savings, but they're new; their services may not be as reliable and their future is less certain.

You can find a long list of institutions that provide merchant accounts for online businesses at one of the Yahoo! index pages (`dir.yahoo.com/Business_and_Economy/Business_to_Business/Financial_Services/Transaction_Clearing/Credit_Card_Merchant_Services`). The list is so long that knowing which company to choose is difficult. I recommend visiting Wells Fargo Bank (`www.wellsfargo.com`), which has been operating online for several years and is well established. The Wells Fargo Web site provides you with a good overview of what's required to obtain a merchant account.

CollectibleX.com, the family-run business that I profile in Chapter 1 and cite in other chapters of this book, uses a Web-based merchant account company called Huntington Merchant Services (`www.huntington.com/bas/HNB2615.htm`) to set up and process its credit card transactions. This company offers credit card and debit card processing to businesses that accept payments online, for about $20 a month. CollectibleX.com switched to Huntington from a smaller company because it found that the larger company would help protect the business from customers who purchased items fraudulently.

One advantage of using one of the payment options set up by VeriSign Payment Services (`www.verisign.com/products/payment.html`) is that the system (which originated with a company called CyberCash) was well known and well regarded before VeriSign acquired it. I describe the widely used electronic payment company in the section "Online Payment Systems," later in this chapter.

In general, your chances of obtaining merchant status are enhanced if you apply to a bank that welcomes Internet businesses, and if you can provide good business records proving that you're a viable, moneymaking concern.

Be sure to ask about the discount rate that the bank charges for Internet-based transactions before you apply. Compare the rate for online transactions to the rate for conventional "card-swipe" purchases. Most banks and credit card processing companies charge 1 to 2 extra percentage points for online sales.

Do you use an accounting program such as QuickBooks or M.Y.O.B. Accounting? The manufacturers of these programs enable their users to become credit card merchants through their Web sites. See the "Accounting Software" section of this book's Internet Directory for more information.

Finding a secure server

A *secure server* is a server that uses some form of encryption, such as Secure Sockets Layer, which I describe in Chapter 12, to protect data that you receive over the Internet. Customers know that they've entered a secure area when the security key or lock icon at the bottom of the browser window is locked shut.

If you plan to receive credit card payments, you definitely want to find a Web hosting service that will protect the area of your online business that serves as the online store. In literal terms, you need secure-server software protecting the directory on your site that is to receive customer-sent forms. Some hosts charge a higher monthly fee for using a secure server; with others, the secure server is part of a basic business Web site account. Ask your host (or hosts you're considering) whether any extra charges apply.

Verifying credit card data

Unfortunately, the world is full of bad people who try to use credit card numbers that don't belong to them. The anonymity of the Web and the ability to shop anywhere in the world, combined with the ability to place orders immediately, can facilitate fraudulent orders, just as it can benefit legitimate orders.

Protecting yourself against credit card fraud is essential. Always check the billing address against the shipping address. If the two addresses are thousands of miles apart, contact the purchaser by phone to verify that the transaction is legit. Even if it is, the purchaser will appreciate your taking the time to verify the transaction.

You can use software to help check addresses. Following are three programs that perform this service:

- ✔ Authorizer (which I describe in the upcoming section, "Processing the orders")

- ✔ Win-Charge by Go Software Inc. (`www.gosoftinc.com/products/index.htm`)

- ✔ NetVERIFY, which you can purchase from ICVerify at `www.icverify.com` (call 1-800-666-5777 for current pricing on ICVerify)

Processing the orders

When someone submits credit card information to you, you need to transfer the information to the banking system. Whether you make this transfer yourself or hire another company to do it for you is up to you.

Do-it-yourself processing

To submit credit card information to your bank, you need POS (point-of-sale) hardware or software. The hardware, which you either purchase or lease from your bank, is a *terminal* — a gray box of the sort you see at many local retailers. The software is a program that contacts the bank through a modem.

The terminal or software is programmed to authorize the sale and transmit the data to the bank. The bank then credits your business or personal checking account, usually within two or three business days. The bank also deducts the discount rate from your account, either weekly, monthly, or with each transaction.

One payment processing program is called Authorizer, shown in Figure 9-2. You have a couple of options for using it: You can either purchase the program from the Atomic Software Web site (`www.atomic-software.com`) and install it on your computer or use the online version. A single-user version of Authorizer for Windows is available for $349. A multi-user version costs $549.

If you have a small scale Web site — perhaps with only one item for sale — you can use an online version of Authorizer called iAuthorizer. iAuthorizer is a payment gateway: It enables you to add a "Pay Button" to a catalog page that securely processes a customer's payment information. (In the example page shown in Figure 9-2, the button is labeled "Submit for Secure Processing.") The transaction is then processed on one of Atomic Software's secure servers. Both you and your customer receive e-mail notifications that the transaction has been completed. But you first have to set up a merchant account with a financial institution that uses the iAuthorizer service. You can find out more at www.iauthorizer.com.

Automatic processing

You can hire a company to automatically process credit card orders for you. These companies compare the shipping and billing addresses to help make sure that the purchaser is the person who actually owns the card and not someone trying to use a stolen credit card number. If everything checks out, they transmit the data directly to the bank.

You can look into the different options provided by VeriFone, Inc. (www. verifone.com) or AssureBuy (www.otginc.com) for such services.

Figure 9-2:
A software program or online service that verifies identity and processes payments is important for conducting credit card transactions.

CASE STUDY

Keeping back-office functions personal

Dave Hagan, Jr. knows the importance of credit card verification and order processing. Yet he tries to make these functions as personal as possible in keeping with the spirit of online business.

Dave is president of both York Internet Services, a Web site design company, and General Tool & Repair, Inc., a tool supplier based in York, Pennsylvania. General Tool has been in business for twelve years, but three years ago, Dave created a simple Web page on America Online to help promote the company. Within two weeks, he received an order from a customer in Florida.

Since then, Dave has expanded his e-commerce Web site using Microsoft Commerce Server, and he set up shop at www.gtr.com.

Dave estimates that General Tool's Web site receives between 10 and 40 orders each day, and average online sales amount to $35,000 to $45,000 per month. He believes the site takes the place of 50 salespeople. "This is all business we never had until two years ago, so it's basically all gravy for us," he notes happily.

Q. How do you process credit card orders?

A. Our customers send us the credit card information through our Web site, and our secure server encrypts the data. But we don't process orders online. We first check to see if we have the item in stock, and, if we do, we process the order the next business day. That way, we don't "slam" the customer's credit card without having the item ready to ship out.

Q. How do you verify the identity of customers who submit credit card numbers to you?

A. We use a program called Authorizer by Atomic Software. The program lets you check the shipping address against the address of the credit card owner. If the two addresses are in the same state, you're pretty sure that you can ship the item. Otherwise, you know that you'd better e-mail the card owner and tell the person there's a problem. Sometimes, a customer will want to purchase a gift and have it shipped out of state to a family member, and in this case you should also e-mail the customer just to be sure. We recently upgraded to the multi-merchant version of Authorizer, which lets us accept several different types of credit cards.

Q. Do you get many fraudulent credit card orders?

A. We get bogus orders all the time. Normally, you can tell because they don't have the correct "ship to" address.

Q. Whom do you use for shipping?

A. We get orders from countries like Japan and Finland, and all over the United States, too. If the customer is affiliated with the military, you're required to use the U.S. Postal Service for shipping. If we're shipping to a business address, such as an office in New York City, we use United Parcel Service because they give the option of sending a package "signature required" which, as it implies, requires someone to sign for an item before they deliver it. We add the UPS charge for "signature required" to the shipping charge, but we feel that it's worth it because we don't want any items to get lost because they were left without a signature. There have been many instances where a customer's neighbor or landlord have signed for their package without the customer's knowledge, so it really provides protection for all involved.

Q. How do you tell your customers about shipping options?

A. We offer customers three choices during the purchase process: UPS ground, second-day air, and next-day air. We also provide a comment area where shoppers can make shipping requests or provide us with special instructions regarding their orders. That way, they can choose. We don't add on flat-rate shipping or handling charges that might be excessive. There are only five of us here, and I can't justify charging someone $25 shipping and handling for a $3 set of nuts or bolts. Our products vary a great deal in price and weight, and we haven't found a way to provide a flat rate for shipping that is fair to everyone, so each order is treated individually.

Automatic credit card processing works so fast that your customer's credit card can be charged immediately, whether or not you have an item in stock. If a client receives a bill and is still waiting for an item that is on back order, the person can get very unhappy. For this reason, some business owners, such as Dave Hagan (profiled in the sidebar, "Keeping back-office functions personal"), chose not to use them.

Online Payment Systems

A number of organizations have devised ways to make e-commerce secure and convenient for shoppers and merchants alike. These alternatives fall into one of three general categories:

✔ Organizations that help you complete credit card purchases (for example, VeriSign Payment Services).

✔ Escrow services that hold your money for you in an account until shipment is received and then pay you, providing security for both you and your customers.

✔ Organizations that provide alternatives to transmitting sensitive information from one computer to another by using "virtual money" rather than real money (for example, Cartio).

In order to use one of these systems, you or your Web host has to set up special software on the computer that actually stores your Web site files. This computer is where the transactions take place. The following sections provide general instructions on how to get started with setting up each of the most popular electronic payment systems.

Reach for your wallet!

One of the terms commonly thrown around in the jargon of e-commerce is *wallet.* A wallet is software that, like a real wallet that you keep in your purse or pocket, stores available cash and other records. You reach into the cyberwallet and withdraw virtual cash rather than submitting a credit card number.

A cybershopper who uses wallet software, such as Microsoft .NET Passport (www.passport.com), is able to pay for items online in a matter of seconds, without having to transfer credit card data. What's more, some wallets can even "remember" previous purchases you have made and suggest further purchases.

Microsoft is putting a big marketing push behind its .NET services, including Passport. For consumers, .NET Passport offers a "single sign-in"

to register or make purchases on sites that support this technology. It also enables consumers to create a wallet that stores their billing and shipping information. (Credit card numbers are stored in an offline database when users sign up for a .NET Passport.) Customers can then make purchases at participating sites with the proverbial single mouse click. In order for your online business Web site to support .NET Passport, you need to download and install the .NET Passport Software Development Kit (SDK) on the server that runs your Web site. You may need some help in deploying this platform; a list of consultants as well as a link to the SDK are included on the .NET Passport home page, www.microsoft.com/myservices/passport.

Some electronic payment systems require you to set up programming languages such as Perl, C/C++, or Visual Basic on your site to work smoothly. You also have to work with techy documents called *configuration files.* This is definitely an area where paying a consultant to get your business set up saves time and headaches and gets your new transaction feature online more efficiently than if you tackle it yourself. VeriSign, for instance, provides support in setting up systems for its merchants; you can find an affiliate to help you or call the company directly. Visit the VeriSign Payment Processing page (www.verisign.com/products/payment.html) for links and phone numbers.

Shopping cart software

When you go to the supermarket or another retail outlet, you pick goodies off the shelves and put them in a shopping cart. When you go to the cash register to pay for what you've selected, you empty the cart and present your goods to the cashier.

Shopping cart software performs the same functions on an e-commerce site. Such software sets up a system that allows online shoppers to select items displayed for sale. The selections are held in a virtual shopping cart that "remembers" what the shopper has selected before checking out.

Shopping cart programs are pretty technical for nonprogrammers to set up, but if you're ambitious and want to try it, you can download and install a free program called PerlShop (www.arpanet.com/perlshop). Signing up with a Web host that provides you with shopping cart software as part of its services, however, is far easier than tackling this task yourself.

You can even supplement an e-commerce shopping cart feature with software from Net Perceptions (www.netperceptions.com) that "suggests" products that your customers might want, based on their shopping habits. Read more about "suggestive selling," shoppers' purchasing habits, and ways to protect yourself and your customers at news.cnet.com/news/0-1007-200-1430357. html?tag=st.ne.ron.lthd.1007-200-1430357.

A shopping cart is an essential part of many e-commerce Web sites, but many shoppers are put off by them. They're just as likely to abandon a purchase than follow through by submitting payment. You don't *have* to use a shopping cart on your site; lots of other e-businesses have users phone or fax in an order or fill out an online form instead.

VeriSign payment services

For several years, CyberCash (www.cybercash.com) was one of the best-known companies providing payment options for online businesses — until the company went bankrupt. Some of CyberCash's assets were purchased by another well-known Internet commerce service, the security company VeriSign, which now offers small businesses a variety of online payment solutions.

VeriSign's Payment Services site (www.verisign.com/products/payment .html) includes services such as Payflow, which lets your company accept payments online, and Commerce Site Services, which places your site on a server that uses SSL encryption as well as certificates. (See Chapter 12 for more detailed explanations of these security features.)

There's no cost to try out one of the Payflow options for 30 days to see how it works with your own business, but both options require that you have a merchant account. (If you don't have one, VeriSign suggests several financial institutions to which you can apply.) The Payflow services do carry some charges and require you to do some work, however:

✔ **Payflow Link:** The smallest and simplest of the VeriSign payment options, Payflow Link is intended for small businesses that process 500 transactions or fewer each month. You add a payment link to your online business site, and you don't have to do programming or other site development to get the payment system to work. Payflow Link requires that you use either Internet Explorer 3.0 (or later) or Netscape Navigator 4.0 (or later). You pay a $179 setup fee and a $19.95 monthly fee.

✔ **Payflow Pro:** With this service, you can process up to 1,000 transactions per month, and any additional transactions cost 10 cents each. To use this option, you begin by installing the Payflow software on the server that runs your Web site. The customer then makes a purchase on your site, and the Payflow software sends the information to VeriSign, which processes the transaction. Payflow Pro carries a $249 setup fee and costs $59.95 per month.

You can sign up for a trial of either Payflow Link or Payflow Pro on the VeriSign Payment Services page (`www.verisign.com/products/payment.html`).

PayPal

By now, you're probably wondering if there's any way to accept online payments from your customers without having to apply for a merchant account, download software, apply for online payment processing, or some combination of these steps.

Lots of entrepreneurs, particularly those who sell items through the online auction service eBay, use an online payment broker called PayPal to process payments. The system requires that both you and your customers obtain a PayPal account. If you want to sell items (including through your Web site), you sign up for a PayPal Business or Premier account. You get a PayPal button that you add to your auction listing or sales Web page. The customer clicks the button to transfer the payment from his or her PayPal account to yours and you're charged a transaction fee.

Setting up a PayPal account is free. Here's how you can set up a PayPal Business account:

1. **Go to the PayPal home page (`www.paypal.com`), and click the <u>Sign Up</u> link under the <u>Businesses</u> heading.**

   You go to the Pay Pal — Registration page.

2. **Follow the instructions on the registration form page, and set up your account with PayPal.**

   After you've filled out the registration forms, you receive an e-mail message with a link that takes you back to the PayPal Web site to confirm your e-mail address.

3. **Click the link contained in the e-mail message.**

   You go to the PayPal — Password page.

4. **Enter your password (the one you created during the registration process) in the Password box, and then click the Confirm button.**

   You go to the PayPal — My Account page.

5. **Click the Sell tab at the top of the My Account page.**

   If you want to create a shopping cart, click the <u>Shopping cart</u> link. For the purposes of this exercise, click <u>Single-item purchases</u>.

6. **Provide some information about the item you're selling:**

   • Enter a brief description of your sales item in the Item Name/Service box.

   • Enter an item number in the Item ID/Number Box.

   • Enter the price in the Price of Item/Service box.

   • Choose a button that shoppers can click to make the purchase. (You can choose either the PayPal logo button or a button that you've already created.)

7. **When you're done, click the Create Button Now button.**

   You go to the PayPal — Web Accept page shown in Figure 9-3.

8. **Copy the code in the For Web Pages box, and paste it onto the Web page that holds your sales item.**

   That's all there is to it.

The nice thing about using PayPal is that the system enables you to accept payments through your Web site without having to obtain a merchant account. It puts a burden on your customers, however; they have to become PayPal users. That said, with PayPal, your customers have many funding options: credit card, bank account or PayPal stored value account. Both you and your customers place a high level of trust in PayPal to handle your money. And the buyer still has to trust you to ship out the sale item. The additional effort might scare some shoppers off. Most shoppers are used to paying by credit card, and if you sell lots of items regularly, you'll probably want to get a merchant account sooner or later.

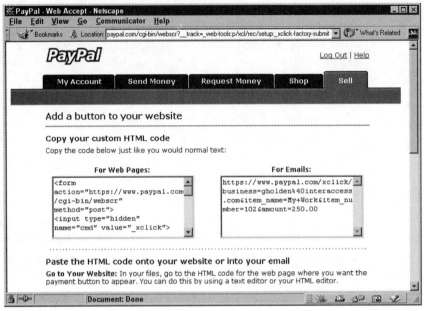

Figure 9-3:
Copy this
code to
your sales
catalog
Web page
to enable
other
PayPal
users to
transfer
purchase
money to
your
account.

Micropayments

Micropayments are very small units of currency that are exchanged by merchants and customers. The amounts involved may range from one-tenth of one cent (that's $.001) to a few dollars. Such small payments enable sites to provide content for sale on a per-click basis. In order to read articles, listen to music files, or view video clips online, some sites require micropayments in a special form of electronic cash that goes by names such as *scrip* or *eCash*.

Micropayments seemed like a good idea in theory, but they've never caught on with consumers, at least in the United States. Nevertheless, it's good for you to know what they are and how they work so you're aware of the full range of options available to you. Also, if consumers in this country ever begin to make purchases with their Web-enabled cell phones, they will probably use a micropayment system to do so.

As a vendor, you authorize a broker such as Cartio Micropayments (www.cartio.com) to sell scrip on your behalf to your customers. If a customer goes to your site and wants to purchase articles or other content, the customer has to follow a few steps. The customer first sets an electronic Cartio Wallet that contains a certain amount of scrip (say, $20) at face value from the broker. The broker then pays you, the merchant, the $20 purchase of scrip that the customer made, minus a service fee. The customer is then free to make purchases from your site by clicking items that have been assigned a certain value (say, one or two cents). The micropayment service's software causes the few cents of scrip to be automatically subtracted from the user's supply of scrip. No credit card numbers are exchanged in these micropayment transactions.

Other payment options

A number of new online payment options have appeared that let people pay for merchandise without having to submit credit card numbers or mail checks. Here are some relatively new options to consider:

- ✔ **ibill** (www.ibill.com): A service of Internet Billing Corp., ibill provides Web sites with a number of ways to accept online payments, including an innovative system called Web900 that enables customers to have a transaction billed to their phone bills instead of their credit cards.

- ✔ **Intell-A-Check** (www.icheck.com): This service enables shoppers to make purchases by sending online checks to merchants. The shopper notifies the seller about the purchase and then contacts a special secure Web site to authorize a debit from his or her checking account. The secure site then transmits the electronic check to the merchant, who can either print out the check on paper or save the check in a special format that can be transmitted to banks for immediate deposit.

Which one of these options is right for you? That depends on what you want to sell online. If you're providing articles, reports, music, or other content that you want people to pay a nominal fee to access, consider a micropayment system (see the preceding section). If your customers tend to be sophisticated, technically savvy individuals who are likely to embrace online checks or billing systems, consider ibill or Intell-A-Check. The important things are to provide customers with several options for submitting payment and to make the process as easy as possible for them.

Fulfilling Your Online Orders

Being on the Internet can help when it comes to the final step in the e-commerce dance: order fulfillment. *Fulfillment* refers to what happens after a sale is made. Typical fulfillment tasks include the following:

- ✔ Packing up the merchandise
- ✔ Shipping the merchandise

- ✔ Solving delivery problems or answering questions about orders that haven't reached their destinations
- ✔ Sending out bills
- ✔ Following up to see whether the customer is satisfied

Order fulfillment may seem like the least exciting part of running a business, online or otherwise. But from your customer's point of view, it's the most important business activity of all. The following sections suggest how you can use your presence online to help reduce any anxiety your customers may feel about receiving what they ordered.

The back-end (or, to use the Microsoft term, BackOffice) part of your online business is where order fulfillment comes in. If you have a database in which you record customer orders, link it to your Web site so that your customers can track orders. Macromedia Dreamweaver or ColdFusion can help with this. (The latest version of Dreamweaver, MX, contains built-in commands that let you link to a ColdFusion database.)

Provide links to shipping services

One advantage of being online is that you can help customers track packages after shipment. The FedEx online order-tracking feature, shown in Figure 9-4, gets thousands of requests each day and is widely known as one of the most successful marketing tools on the Web. If you use FedEx, provide a link to its online tracking page.

The other big shipping services have also created their own online tracking systems. You can link to these sites, too:

- ✔ United Parcel Service (www.ups.com)
- ✔ U.S. Postal Service Express Mail (www.usps.gov)
- ✔ Airborne Express (www.airborne.com)

Present shipping options clearly

In order fulfillment, as in receiving payment, it pays to present your clients with as many options as possible and to explain the options in detail. Because you're online, you can provide your customers with as much shipping information as they can stand. Web surfers are knowledge hounds — they can never get enough data, whether it's related to shipping or other parts of your business.

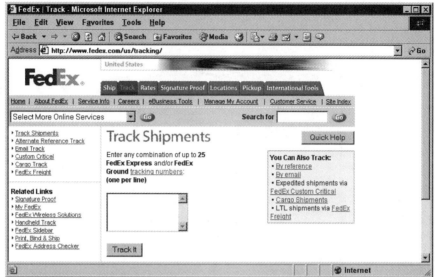

When it comes to shipping, be sure to describe the options, the cost of each, and how long each takes. (See the sidebar called "Keeping back-office functions personal," earlier in this chapter, for some good tips on when to require signatures and how to present shipping information by e-mail rather than on the Web.) Here are some more specific suggestions:

- ✔ **Compare shipping costs:** Make use of an online service such as InterShipper (www.intershipper.net), which allows you to submit the origin, destination, weight, and dimensions of a package that you want to ship via a Web page form and then returns the cheapest shipping alternatives.

- ✔ **Make sure that you can track:** Pick a service that lets you track your package's shipping status.

- ✔ **Be able to confirm receipt:** If you use the U.S. Postal Service, ship the package "return receipt requested" because tracking isn't available — unless you use Priority Mail or Express Mail. You can confirm delivery with Priority Mail (domestic) and Parcel Post.

Many online stores present shipping alternatives in table form. (*Tables*, as you probably know, are Web page design elements that let you arrange content in rows and columns, making them easier to read; refer to Chapter 4 for more on adding tables to your site.) You don't have to look very far to find an example; just visit John Wiley & Sons Web site and order a book from its online store. When you're ready to pay for your items and provide a shipping address, you see the table shown in Figure 9-5. (Although the table borders aren't visible, the prices and other details are aligned by being contained within table cells.)

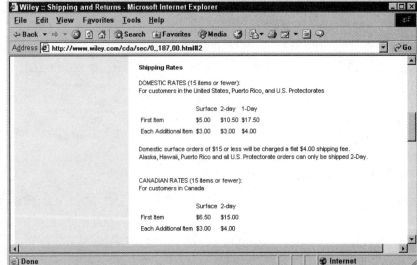

Figure 9-5:
Tables help shoppers calculate costs, keep track of purchases, and choose shipping options.

Where are the smart cards?

If you've traveled in Europe recently, you may have noticed lots of people using *smart cards*. A smart card has an embedded computer chip that stores lots of information, from personal passwords to bank account balances. A record of the owner's available cash reserves resides directly on the card, rather than being stored in the banking system.

Smart cards haven't yet caught on in the U.S., but they are available. For a few years now, American Express has offered the Blue card, which combines a traditional magnetic stripe reader with a smart chip. The card can be used with the American Express Online Wallet to make online purchases securely.

The Wallet is software that stores a user's personal information including credit card number and shipping address. When the user wants to make a purchase, he or she "opens" the wallet and it automatically submits his or her personal information to the merchant's Web site. The Wallet can be used in conjunction with the Blue card; only after running the Blue card through a special smart card reader and entering a PIN into their computers can users actually access their wallets.

Visa also has a smart card (find out about it at `www.usa.visa.com/personal/icards/visa_smart_apply2.jsp`).

So if you get any inquiries from foreign customers asking whether you accept smart cards, you should probably respond with "Not yet" rather than "Huh?"

Chapter 10

Service with a Virtual Smile

- -

In This Chapter

▶ Keeping customers satisfied through effective communication

▶ Creating forms that let your patrons talk back

▶ Encouraging involvement through discussion areas

▶ Taking steps to reach overseas customers

▶ Finalizing sales through chat-based customer service

- -

*W*hen you — or your children — have your heart set on something, receiving it on time may seem to be the most important thing in the world. That's when a customer service representative can save the day. My daughter chose a teddy bear theme for her seventh birthday party, and I was thrilled to find the perfect coloring book on Amazon.com. It was reassuring to receive the e-mail confirmation that my online order had been received and the notification of when the ten party favors had been shipped. However, as the days went by, I was concerned that they might not arrive in time, so I called the Amazon.com toll-free number. A patient person explained that I could return the merchandise if it arrived too late and my shipping charges would be refunded. Despite my pre-party jitters, the package showed up a day early. As a result, the party came off without a hitch, and I'll continue to order happily from Amazon.com.

Granted, Amazon.com isn't exactly a small business. But you can learn something from this example of a big-time success story. Customer service *is* one area in which small, entrepreneurial businesses can outshine larger competitors. It doesn't matter whether you're competing in the areas of e-trading, e-music, or e-tail sales of any sort. Tools such as e-mail and interactive forms, coupled with the fact that an online commerce site can provide information on a 24-7 basis, give you a powerful advantage when it comes to retaining customers and building loyalty.

What constitutes good online customer service, particularly for a new business that has only one or two employees? Whether your customers are broadband or dialup, you need to deal with them one at a time and connect one-to-one. But being responsive and available is half the battle. This chapter presents ways to succeed with the other half of the battle: providing information, communicating effectively, and enabling your clientele to talk back to you online.

Customer Service = Information

The more information you can provide up front, the fewer phone queries or complaints you'll receive later on. Sure, you can go the traditional route and print pamphlets and brochures that describe your products and services at length. But the cheaper and more effective route is to publish as much information as possible online.

Suppose that you hire a writer like me to compose a 1,000-word description of your new company and your products and/or services. If I were to take those words and format them to fit on a 4-x-9-inch fold-out brochure, the contents would cover several panels and take at least a few hundred dollars to print.

On the other hand, if I divide my golden prose into a few Web pages and put them online, they'd probably take up no more than 5K to 10K of disk space. The same applies if you distribute your content to a number of subscribers in the form of an e-mail newsletter. In either case, you need pay only a little, or at least next to nothing, to publish the information.

Sticking to the FAQs

A set of *frequently asked questions* (FAQs) is a familiar feature on many online business sites — so familiar, in fact, that longtime Web surfers like myself practically expect to find a FAQ page on every business site, and we have a pretty good idea of the kind of information we'll find there.

The format of FAQ pages is pretty similar from site to site, and this predictability is itself an asset. FAQ pages are generally presented in Q-and-A format, with topics appearing in the form of questions that have either literally been asked by other customers or that have been made up to resemble real questions. Each question has a brief answer that provides essential information about the business.

Because FAQ pages tend to be pretty long, listing all of the questions at the top of the page is an effective strategy. This way, by clicking a hyperlinked item in the list, the reader jumps to the spot down the page where you present the question and its answer in detail.

Not all FAQ pages are created equal. The best ones are easy to use and comprehensive. Take a look at one of the most famous of the genre, the venerable World Wide Web FAQ by Thomas Boutell (`www.boutell.com/faq/oldfaq/index.html`) to get some ideas for your own FAQ page.

How do you come up with a good FAQ? Get your own customers to do some of the work. Invite visitors to make suggestions and ask questions. Also, enlist the help of friends and family to come up with questions about your business. You may want to include questions on some of the following topics:

- **Contact information:** If I need to reach you in a hurry either by mail, fax, or phone, how do I do that? Are you available only at certain hours?
- **Instructions:** What if I need more detailed instructions on how to use your products or services? Where can I find them?
- **Service:** What do I do if the merchandise doesn't work for some reason or breaks? Do you have a return policy?
- **Sales tax:** Is sales tax added to the cost I see on-screen?
- **Shipping:** What are my shipping options?

You don't have to use the term FAQ. The retailer Lands' End, which does just about everything right in terms of e-commerce, uses the term Fact Sheet for its list of questions and answers. Go to the Lands' End home page (`www.landsend.com`) and click <u>General Information</u> to see how Lands' End presents the same type of material.

Starting an online newsletter

Sharing information with customers and potential customers through an e-mail newsletter is a great way to build credibility for yourself and your business.

For added customer service (not to mention a touch of self-promotion), consider producing a regular publication that you send out to a mailing list. You can compile your mailing list from customers and prospective customers who visit your Web site and indicate that they want to subscribe.

An e-mail newsletter does require some effort to create and distribute, but it can provide your business with great long-term benefits, including the following:

- ✔ **Customer tracking:** You can add subscribers' e-mail addresses to a mailing list that you can use for other marketing purposes, such as promoting special sales items for return customers.

- ✔ **Low-bandwidth:** An e-mail newsletter doesn't require much memory. It's great for business people who get their e-mail on the road via laptops, palm devices, or appliances that are designed specifically for sending and receiving e-mail.

- ✔ **Timeliness:** You can get breaking news into your electronic newsletter much faster than you can put it in print.

Assuming that you already have a name for your newsletter and have assembled content that you want to include, follow these steps to create your publication:

1. **Create your newsletter by typing the contents in plain-text (ASCII) format.**

   Optionally, you can also provide an HTML-formatted version. You can then include headings and graphics that will show up in e-mail programs that support HTML e-mail messages.

   If you use a plain-text newsletter, format it using capital letters; rules that consist of a row of equal signs, hyphens, or asterisks; or blank spaces to align elements.

2. **Save your file with the proper filename extension: .txt for the text version and .htm or .html if you send an HTML version.**

3. **Attach the file to an e-mail message by using your e-mail program's method of sending attachments.**

4. **Address your file to the recipients.**

   If you have lots of subscribers (many newsletters have hundreds or thousands), save their addresses in a mailing list. Use your e-mail program's address book function to do this.

5. **Send out your newsletter.**

If you have a large number of subscribers, I recommend sending your publication late at night or in several stages, rather than sending out all the e-mail messages at one time. That way, your words will reach their destination much more quickly and reliably.

Managing a mailing list can be time-consuming because you have to keep up with all the messages from people who want to subscribe, unsubscribe, or who ask for more information. You can save time and trouble by hiring a company such as SkyList (www.skylist.net) to do the day-to-day list management for you.

Helping Customers Talk Back to You

The simplest and most essential element of customer service that you can provide is your contact information. When you're online, this information can take several forms. Be sure to include

- ✔ Your mailing address
- ✔ Your e-mail address(es)
- ✔ Your phone and fax numbers, and a toll-free number (if you have one)

Because most Web hosting services (such as the types of hosts that I describe in Chapter 4) give you more than one e-mail inbox as part of your account, consider setting up more than one e-mail address. One address can be for people to communicate with you personally, and the other can be where people go for general information. You can also set up e-mail addresses that respond to messages by automatically sending a text file in response. (See "Setting up autoresponders" later in this chapter.)

Keep your site as personal and friendly as possible. A contact page is a good place to provide some brief biographical information about the people visitors can contact, namely you and any employees or partners in your company.

You don't *have* to put your contact information on a separate Web page, of course. Doing so only makes your patrons have to wait a few seconds to access it. If your contact data is simple and your Web site consists only of a few pages, by all means put it right on your home page.

Using advanced e-mail techniques

E-mail communication is a must for every online business. The more you learn about the finer technical points of e-mail, the better you're able to meet the needs of your clients. The following sections suggest ways to go beyond simply sending and receiving e-mail messages, and utilize e-mail for business publishing and marketing.

Setting up autoresponders

An *autoresponder*, which also goes by the name *mailbot*, is software that you can set up to send automatic replies to requests for information about a product or service, or to respond to people subscribing to an e-mail publication or service.

You can provide automatic responses either through your own e-mail program or through your Web host's e-mail service. If you use a Web host to provide automatic responses, you can usually purchase an extra e-mail address that can be configured to return a text file (such as a form letter) to the sender.

Look for a Web host that provides you with one or more autoresponders along with your account. Typically, your host assigns you an e-mail address that takes the form info@mycompany.com. In this case, someone at your hosting service configures the account so that when a visitor to your site sends a message to info@yourcompany.com, a file of your choice, such as a simple text document that contains background information about you and your services, automatically goes out to the sender as a reply.

If the service that hosts your Web site does not provide free autoresponders, look into SmartBotPRO, an online service that provides you with autoresponder service for free but that may send you advertising e-mail messages from time to time. Read about it at www.smartbotpro.net/newsite2/features.html.

Noting by quoting

Responding to a series of questions is easy when you use *quoting* — a feature that lets you copy quotes from a message to which you're replying. Quoting, which is available in almost all e-mail programs, is particularly useful for responding to a mailing list or newsgroup message because it indicates the specific topic being discussed.

How do you tell the difference between the quoted material and the body of the new e-mail message? The common convention is to put a greater-than (>) character in the left margin, next to each line of the quoted material.

When you tell your e-mail software to quote the original message before you type your reply, it generally quotes the entire message. To save space, you can *snip* (delete) out the part that isn't relevant. However, if you do so, it's polite to type the word <snip> to show that you've cut something out. A quoted message looks something like this:

```
Mary Agnes McDougal wrote:
>I wonder if I could get some info on <snip>
>those sterling silver widgets you have for sale...
Hi Mary Agnes,
Thank you for your interest in our premium collector's line
        of widgets. You can place an order online or call our
            toll-free number, 1-800-WIDGETS.
```

Attaching files

A quick and convenient way to transmit information from place to place is to attach a file to an e-mail message. In fact, attaching files is one of the most useful things you can do with e-mail. *Attaching*, which means that you send a document or file along with an e-mail message, allows you to include material from any file to which you have access. Attached files appear as separate documents that recipients can download to their computers.

Many e-mail clients allow users to attach files with a simple button or other command. Compressing a lengthy series of attachments by using software such as StuffIt or WinZip conserves bandwidth. Using compression is also a necessity if you ever want to send more than one attached file to someone whose e-mail account (such as an AOL account) doesn't accept multiple attachments.

Protocols such as MIME (Multipurpose Internet Mail Extensions) are sets of standards that allow you to attach graphic and other multimedia files to an e-mail message. Recipients must have an e-mail program that supports MIME (which includes almost all of the newer e-mail programs) in order to download and read MIME files in the body of an e-mail message. In case your recipient has an e-mail client that doesn't support MIME attachments, or if you aren't sure whether it does, you must encode your attachment in a format such as BinHex (if you're sending files to a Macintosh) or UUCP (if you're sending files to a newsgroup).

Creating a signature file that sells

One of the easiest and most useful tools for marketing on the Internet is called a signature file, or a sig file. A *signature file* is a text blurb that your system automatically appends to the bottom of your e-mail messages and newsgroup postings. You want your signature file to tell the readers of your message something about you and your business; you can include information such as your company name and how to contact you.

Creating a signature file takes only a little more time than putting your John Hancock on the dotted line. First, you create the signature file itself, as I describe in these steps:

1. **Open a text-editing program.**

   This example uses Notepad, which comes built in with Windows. If you're a Macintosh user, you can use SimpleText. With either program, a new blank document opens on-screen.

2. **Press and hold down the hyphen (-) or equal sign (=) key to create a dividing line that will separate your signature from the body of your message.**

   Depending on which symbol you use, a series of hyphens or equal signs forms a broken line. Don't make this line too long or it will run onto another line, which doesn't look good; 30 to 40 characters is a safe measure.

3. **Type the information about yourself that you want to appear in the signature, pressing Enter after each line.**

   Include such information as your name, job title, company name, e-mail address, and Web site URL, if you have one. A three- or four-line signature is the typical length.

   If you're feeling ambitious at this point, you can press the spacebar to arrange your text in two columns. My agent (who's an online entrepreneur himself) does this with his own signature file, as shown in Figure 10-1.

Figure 10-1:
A signature file often uses divider lines and can be arranged in columns to occupy less space on-screen.

Always include the URL to your business Web site in your signature file and be sure to include it on its own line. Why? Most e-mail programs will recognize the URL as a Web page by its prefix (`http://`). When your reader opens your message, the e-mail program displays the URL as a clickable hyperlink that, when clicked, opens your Web page in a Web browser window.

4. **Choose File⇨Save.**

   A dialog box appears, enabling you to name the file and save it in a folder on your hard disk.

5. **Enter a name for your file that ends in the filename extension** .txt.

   This extension identifies your file as a plain text document.

6. **Click the Save button.**

   Your text file is saved on your computer's hard disk.

Now that you've created a plain-text version of your electronic signature, the next step is to identify that file to the computer programs that you use to send and receive e-mail and newsgroup messages. Doing so enables the programs to make the signature file automatically appear at the bottom of your messages. The procedure for attaching a signature file varies from program to program; the following steps show you how to do this by using Microsoft Outlook Express 6:

1. **Start Outlook Express and choose Tools⇨Options.**

   The Options dialog box opens.

2. **Click the Signatures tab.**

3. **Click New.**

   The options in the Signatures and Edit Signature sections of the Signatures tab are highlighted.

4. **Click the File button at the bottom of the tab, and then click Browse.**

   The Open dialog box appears. This is a standard Windows navigation dialog box that lets you select folders and files on your computer.

5. **Locate the signature file that you created in the previous set of steps by selecting a drive or folder from the Look in drop-down list. When you locate the file, click the filename and then click the Open button.**

   The Signature File dialog box closes, and you return to the Options dialog box. The path leading to the selected file is listed in the box next to File.

6. **Click the Add signatures to all outgoing messages check box, and then click OK.**

   The Options dialog box closes, and you return to Outlook Express. Your signature file will now be automatically added to your messages.

To test your new signature file, choose File⇨New⇨Mail Message from the Outlook Express menu bar. A new message composition window opens. Your signature file should appear in the body of the message composition window. You can compose a message by clicking before the signature and starting to type.

Creating simple Web page forms

Forms are a convenient and effective way to conduct customer service. They give customers a means to provide you with feedback as well as essential marketing information. Using forms, you can find out where customers live, how old they are, and so on. Customers can also use forms to sound off and ask questions. The speed of the Internet enables your customers to dash off information right away and enables you to immediately send a response that's tailored to the individual's needs and interests.

The two components of Web page forms

Forms consist of two parts, only one of which is visible on a Web page.

The visible part includes the text-entry fields, buttons, and check boxes that an author creates with HTML commands.

The part of the form that you don't see is a computer script that resides on the server that receives the page. This script, which is typically written in a language such as Perl, AppleScript, or C++, processes the form data that a reader submits to a server and presents that data in a format that the owner or operator of the Web site can read and use.

How the data gets to you

What exactly happens when customers connect to a page on your site that contains a form? First, they fill out the text-entry fields, radio buttons, and other areas you have set up. When they finish, they click a button, often marked Submit, in order to transmit, or *post*, the data from the remote computer to your Web site.

A computer script called a Common Gateway Interface (CGI) program receives the data submitted to your site and processes it so that you can read it. The CGI may cause the data to be e-mailed to you or it may present the data in a text file in an easy-to-read format.

Optionally, you can also create a CGI program that prompts your server to send the user a Web page that acknowledges that you have received the information and thanks them for their feedback. It's a nice touch that your customers are sure to appreciate.

Writing the scripts that process form data is definitely in the province of Webmasters or computer programmers and is far beyond the scope of this book. But you don't have to hire someone to write the scripts: You can use a Web page program (such as Microsoft FrontPage or Macromedia Dreamweaver) that not only helps you create a form but also provides you with scripts that process the data for you. (If you use forms created with FrontPage, your Web host must have a set of software called FrontPage Server Extensions installed. Call your host or search the host's online Help files to see if the extensions are present.)

Some clever business people have created some really useful Web content by providing a way for nonprogrammers such as you and me to create forms online. Appropriately enough, you connect to the server's Web site and fill out a form provided by the service in order to create your form. The form has a built-in CGI that processes the data and e-mails it to you. See the "Free Forms Online" section of this book's Internet Directory to find some free form creation and processing services.

Using FrontPage to create a form

You can use the Form Page Wizard that comes with Microsoft FrontPage to create both parts of forms: the data-entry parts (such as text boxes and check boxes), as well as the behind-the-scenes scripts, called *WebBots*, that process form data. Creating your own form gives you more control over how it looks and a greater degree of independence than using a ready-made forms service.

The first step in setting up a Web page form is determining what information you want to receive from someone who fills out the form. Your Web page creation tool then gives you options for ways to ask for the information you want. Start FrontPage and choose Insert⇨Form, and a submenu appears with the following options:

- ✔ **Textbox:** This creates a single-line box where someone can type text.
- ✔ **Text Area:** This creates a scrolling text box.
- ✔ **File Upload:** This lets the user send you a text file.
- ✔ **Checkbox:** This creates a check box.
- ✔ **Option Button:** This creates a button, sometimes called a radio button.
- ✔ **Drop-Down Box:** This lets you create a drop-down list.
- ✔ **Picture:** This lets you add a graphic image to a form.

Figure 10-2 shows the most common form fields as they appear in a Web page form that you're creating.

When you choose Insert⇨Form, FrontPage inserts a dashed, marquee-style box in your document to signify that you're working on Web page form fields rather than normal Web page text.

Forms submenu

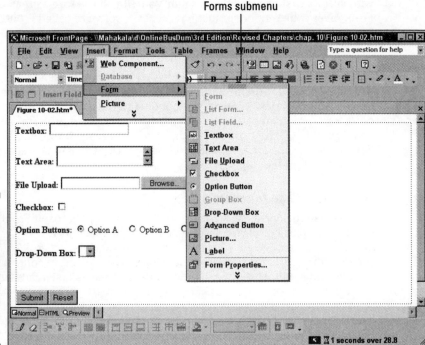

Figure 10-2:
FrontPage
provides
you with
menu
options for
creating
form
elements.

The Form Page Wizard is a great way to set up a simple form that asks for information from visitors to your Web site. It lets you concentrate on the type of data you want to collect rather than on the buttons and boxes needed to gather it. To create such a form, follow these steps:

1. **Choose Start➪Programs➪Microsoft FrontPage.**

   FrontPage starts and a blank window appears.

2. **Choose File➪New➪Page or Web.**

   The New Page or Web task pane appears.

3. **Click Page Templates.**

   The Page Templates dialog box appears.

4. **Double-click Form Page Wizard.**

   The first page of the Form Page Wizard appears. (You can click Finish at any time to see your form and begin editing it.)

5. **Click Next.**

6. **Follow the instructions presented in succeeding steps of the wizard to create your form.**

    a. **Click Add, and then select from the set of options that the wizard presents you with for the type of information you want the form to present.**

       This may include account information, ordering information, and so on.

    b. **Select specific types of information you want to solicit.**

    c. **Choose the way you want the information to be presented**.

       You have options such as a bulleted list, numbered list, and so on.

    d. **Identify how you want the user-submitted information to be saved.**

       You can choose to save information as a text file, a Web page, or with a custom CGI script if you have one.

7. **Click Finish.**

    The wizard window closes and your form appears in the FrontPage window.

When you finish, be sure to add your own description of the form and any special instructions at the top of the Web page. Also add your copyright and contact information at the bottom of the page. Follow the pattern you've set on other pages on your site. You can edit the form by using the Forms sub-menu options if you want to.

Be sure to change the background of the form page from the boring default gray that the wizard provides to a more compelling color. See Chapter 6 for more specific instructions on changing the background of Web pages you create.

Turning Customers into Members

Think about what it means to be a customer at a typical retail store: You go to the store, make a purchase, and then leave. You don't go back until you need to buy something else or make a return. Now think about what it means to be a member of a club or other organization: You meet with the group on a regular basis, hold discussions, and attend special events. You're part of a community.

Good customer service can make your customers feel like members of a community — the community of satisfied individuals who regularly use your goods and services. In the following sections, I describe some ways to make your customers feel like members who return to your site on a regular basis and interact with a community of individuals with similar interests.

CASE STUDY

Adding the personal touch that means so much

Sarah-Lou Reekie started her business out of an apartment in London, England in 1997. She developed an herbal insect repellent called Alfresco that she developed while working in a botanical and herbal research center. Since then, sales have grown quickly — often doubling each year. One key to Reekie's quick success is that there were no products in direct competition with her lotion. Another key component is her personal approach to serving her customers, who include movie stars on location and other prominent entertainers like Sir Paul McCartney.

Reekie's Web site (www.alfresco.uk.com), shown in the accompanying figure, nearly doubled sales, but she stuck to basic business practices and focused on cultivating the customer base she had already developed through selling her product by word of mouth. (The trendy term for this type of publicity is "viral marketing"; see Chapter 11 for more on this topic.) She started a fan club for Alfresco, and she has personally visited some of her best customers.

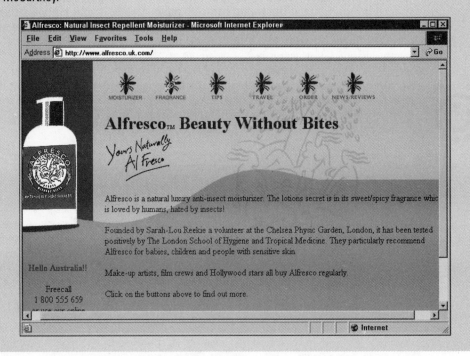

Q. How have you been able to keep a steady flow of business amid the ups and downs of the world economy?

A. We have built up a bigger and bigger customer base by constantly giving good service to customers. We send out special editions for frequent buyers, have a fan club, and encourage customers to make recommendations. We bring out new and exciting products; we care and look after our customers. We are about to do a major re-fit on our site, as well.

Q. What are the one or two most important things people should keep in mind if they are starting an online business these days?

A. It is not necessary to spend fortunes to set it up. Find a host that has been in business a number of years. (There ARE experts now.) A clean database that really works for you is vital, as your customers are the most precious things a business can have. Keep in touch with them. Treat them with care and respect.

Q. What's the single best improvement you've made to your site to attract more customers or retain the ones you've had?

A. Putting on a special code that only special customers or fan club members can access for discounts, etc. For example, Royal Bank of Scotland employees have a special code dedicated to them.

Q. Is this a good time to start an online business?

A. I actually feel it is a great time to start an e-commerce biz for a number of reasons, not least being that the technical support is now well and truly in place. Lets just say more people know what they are doing than in earlier years.

Q. What advice would you give to someone thinking of starting a new business on the Web?

A. Your customer is King, Queen, Prince, and Princess. Whatever you would like yourself is what you should aim to offer. "Do as you would like to be done by" should be your motto. Expose yourself any which way and as often as is acceptable to as many well targeted customers as possible. Most of all, keep a positive attitude. Sir Paul McCartney once said to me when I felt depressed and almost ready to give up "Always have Faith." I'm glad I listened to him!

Putting the "person" into personal service

The department store giant Nordstrom's is known for having an employee available to personally greet you at the door. On the Web, one of the challenges is providing prompt, personal response that is essential to many sales. How can you provide someone on your Web site who's available to provide live customer support?

Some Web sites do provide live support so that people can e-mail a question to someone in real-time (or close to real time) Internet technologies, such as chat and message boards. The online auction giant eBay has a New Users Board, for instance, where beginners can post questions for eBay support staff, who post answers in response.

An even more immediate sort of customer support is provided by chat, in which individuals type messages to one another over the Internet in real time. One way to add chat to your site is to start a Yahoo!Group, which I describe later in this chapter. Another method is to purchase and install a program such as ichat (www.ichat.com). Because such software is expensive and complicated, ichat provides support to customers via message boards as well as live chat sessions.

LivePerson (www.liveperson.com) provides a simpler alternative that allows small businesses to provide chat-based support. LivePerson is software that enables you to see who is connected to your site at any one time and instantly lets you chat with them, just as if you're greeting them at the front door of a brick-and-mortar store.

LivePerson works like this: First, you install the LivePerson Pro software on your own computer (not the server that runs your site). You can try out LivePerson Pro for free for 30 days, and then pay $89.50 per month thereafter. With LivePerson, you or your assistants can lead the customer through the process of making a purchase. For instance, you might help show customers what individual sale items look like by sending them an image file to view with their Web browsers.

Reaching out to overseas customers

Giving guidance to online customers who face language and cultural barriers is especially crucial if you want to extend your reach into the huge overseas markets where e-commerce is just beginning to come into its own. Making sure that products are easily and objectively described with words as well as clear images and diagrams, where necessary, is becoming increasingly important.

Keep in mind the fact that shoppers in many developing nations still prefer to shop with their five senses. So that foreign customers never have a question on how to proceed, providing them with implicit descriptions of the shopping process is essential. You should make information on ordering, payment, execution, and support available at every step.

Customer support in Asia is, in many ways, a different creature than in the West. While personalization still remains critical, language and translation gives an e-commerce site a different feel. A Western site that might work well by looking clean and well organized might have to be replaced with the more chaotic blitz of characters and options that's often found more compelling by Eastern markets. In Asia, Web sites tend to place more emphasis on color and interactivity. Many e-commerce destinations choose to dump all possible options on the front page, rather than presenting them in an orderly, sequential flow.

Creating a discussion area on your site

A small business can turn its individual customers into a cohesive group by starting its own discussion group on the Internet. Discussion groups work particularly well if you're promoting a particular type of product or if you and your customers are involved in a provocative or even controversial area of interest.

You can create three kinds of discussion groups:

- ✔ **A local group:** Some universities create their own discussion areas for their students. Other large companies set aside groups for their employees. Outsiders can't gain access because the groups aren't on the Internet but rather are on a local server within the organization.

- ✔ **A Usenet newsgroup:** Individuals are allowed to create an Internet-wide discussion group in the alt or biz categories of Usenet without having to go through the time-consuming application and approval process needed to create other newsgroups.

- ✔ **A Web-based discussion group:** Microsoft FrontPage includes easy-to-use wizards that enable you to create a discussion area on your business Web site. Users can access the area from their Web browsers without having to use special discussion-group software. Or, if you don't have FrontPage, you can start a Yahoo!Group, which I describe in the section named (surprise!) "Starting a Yahoo!Group."

Of these three alternatives, the first isn't practical for your business purposes, so I focus on the second two in the following sections.

In addition to newsgroups, many large corporations also hold interactive chats on subjects related to their area of business. Experts in various fields often moderate these chats. Small businesses can hold chats, too. The most practical way is to set up a chat room on a site that hosts chat-based discussions. I briefly discuss this process in Chapter 15.

Starting an alt discussion group

Usenet is a system of communication on the Internet that enables individual computer users to participate in group discussions about topics of mutual interest. Internet newsgroups have what's referred to as a hierarchical structure. Most groups belong to one of seven main categories: comp, misc, news, rec, sci, soc, and talk. The name of the category appears at the beginning of the group's name, such as rec.food.drink.coffee. In this section, I discuss the `alt` category, which is just about as popular as the seven I just mentioned and which enables individuals — like you — to establish their own newsgroups.

In my opinion, the `biz` discussion groups aren't taken seriously because they are widely populated by people promoting get-rich-quick schemes and simply blowing their own horns. The `alt` groups, though they can certainly address some wild and crazy topics, are at least as well-known and often address serious topics. Plus, the process of setting up an `alt` group is well documented.

The prefix `alt` didn't originally stand for *alternative*, although it has come to mean that. The term originally stood for Anarchists, Lunatics, and Terrorists. These days, `alt` is a catch-all category in which anyone can start a group, if others show interest in the creator's proposal.

The first step to creating your own `alt` discussion group is to launch your newsgroup software and access the group called `alt.config.newgroups`. This area contains general instructions on starting your own Usenet newsgroup. Also look in `news.answers` for the message "How to Start a New Usenet Newsgroup."

For instructions specific to starting a group in the `alt` category, go to Google (`www.google.com`), click Groups, and search for the message "How to Start an Alt Newsgroup." (You can also find this message at `www.visi.com/~barr/alt-creation-guide.html`.) Follow the instructions contained in this message to set up your own discussion group. Basically, the process involves the following steps:

1. **You write a brief proposal describing the purpose of the group you want to create and including an e-mail message where people can respond with comments.**

   The proposal also contains the name of your group in the correct form (`alt.groupname.moreinfo.moreinfo`). Try to keep the group name short and official-looking if it is for business purposes.

2. **You submit the proposal to the newsgroup** `alt.config`.

3. **You gather feedback to your proposal by e-mail.**

4. **You send a special message called a *control message* to the news server that gives you access to Usenet.**

   The exact form of the message varies from server to server, so you need to consult with your ISP on how to compose the message correctly.

5. **Wait a while (a few days or weeks) as news administrators (the people who operate news servers at ISPs around the world) decide whether to adopt your request and add your group to their list of newsgroups.**

Before you try to start your own group, look through the Big 7 categories (comp, misc, news, rec, sci, soc, and talk) to make sure that a group devoted to your topic doesn't already exist.

Starting a Yahoo!Group

Back in the early days of the Internet, Usenet was almost the only game in town. These days, the Web is pretty much (along with e-mail) the most popular way to communicate and share information. Starting a discussion group on the Web, then, only makes sense. A Web-based discussion group is somewhat less intimidating than others because it doesn't require a participant to use newsgroup software.

Yahoo!Groups are absolutely free to set up. (To find out how, just go to the FAQ page, help.yahoo.com/help/us/groups/index.html, and click <u>How do I start a group?</u>) They not only enable users to exchange messages, but they can also communicate in real-time using chat. And as the list operator, you can send out e-mail newsletters and other messages to your participants, too.

You need a topic of interest that encourages your customers to join. Simply operating an online store isn't enough. You need to present yourself as an authority in a particular area. The discussion group needs to concern itself primarily with that topic and give participants a chance to exchange views and tips on the topic. If people have questions about your store, they can always e-mail you directly — they don't need a discussion group to do that.

Creating a Web discussion area with FrontPage

The reason that Microsoft FrontPage is such a popular tool for creating Web sites is that it enables you to create Web page content that you would otherwise need complicated scripts to tackle. One example is the program's Discussion Group Wizard, which lets you create Web pages on which your members (as opposed to customers, remember?) can exchange messages and carry on a series of back-and-forth responses (called *threads*) on different topics. Newcomers to the group can also view articles that are arranged by a table of contents and accessible by a searchable index.

Creating the discussion area

Follow these steps to set up your own discussion group with Microsoft FrontPage 2002:

1. **After you install the program, start FrontPage by choosing Start⇨Programs⇨Microsoft FrontPage.**

   The FrontPage window opens.

   You can create a new discussion *web* (that is, a group of interlinked documents that together comprise a Web site) of Web pages by using one of the built-in wizards that come with FrontPage.

2. **To use the FrontPage Discussion Group Wizard, choose File⇨New⇨Page or Web.**

   The New Page or Web task pane appears.

3. **Click Web Site Templates.**

   The Web Site Templates dialog box appears.

4. **Select Discussion Web Wizard and then click OK.**

   A dialog box appears, stating that the new discussion web is being created. Then the first of a series of Discussion Web Wizard dialog boxes appears.

5. **Click Next.**

   The second dialog box lets you specify the features you want for your discussion web. Because this is the first time you've created a group, leave all the options checked.

6. **Click Next.**

   A dialog box appears that lets you specify a title and folder for the new discussion web. Enter a title in the box beneath Enter a descriptive title for this discussion. You can change the default folder name _disc1 if you want.

7. **Click Next.**

   The dialog box that appears lets you choose one of three options for the structure of your discussion:

   - Select Subject, Comments if you expect visitors to discuss only a single topic.

   - Select Subject, Category, Comments if you expect to conduct discussions on more than one topic.

   - Select Subject, Product, Comments if you want to invite discussions about products you produce and/or sell.

   After you select one of these options, the next Discussion Web Wizard dialog box appears. Go through this and the subsequent dialog boxes, answering the questions they present you with in order to determine what kind of discussion group you're going to have. At any time, as you go through the series of Discussion Web Wizard pages, you can click Finish to complete the process.

8. **When you're done, the pre-set pages for your discussion web appear in the FrontPage Explorer main window.**

The middle column of the FrontPage window shows the arrangement of the discussion documents. The right side of the window is a visual map that shows how the discussion group is arranged and how the pages are linked to each other.

When you set up a discussion area with FrontPage, you have the option of designing your pages as a *frameset*, or a set of Web pages that has been subdivided into separate frames. To find out more about frames, see Chapter 6.

Editing the discussion pages

After you use the Discussion Group Wizard to create your pages, the next step is to edit the pages so that they have the content you want. With your newly created pages displayed in the FrontPage window, you can start editing by double-clicking the icon for a page (such as the Welcome page, which has a filename such as `disc_welc.htm`) in your discussion web. Whatever page you double-click opens in the right column of the FrontPage window.

For instance, you might add a few sentences to the beginning of the Welcome page that you have just created in order to tell participants more about the purpose and scope of the discussion group. You can add text by clicking anywhere on the page and typing.

To edit more pages in your discussion group, choose File⇨Open. The Open File dialog box appears with a list of all the documents that make up your discussion group. You can double-click a file's name in order to edit it. When you finish editing files, choose File⇨Save to save your work.

To see how your discussion pages look, use the FrontPage Preview feature. Choose File⇨Preview in Browser, and the page you've been editing appears in your browser window.

Posting your discussion area

The final step is to transfer your discussion web of pages from your own computer to your Web host's site on the Internet. Many Web hosting services support one-step file transfers with Microsoft FrontPage. If you plan to use FrontPage often, I recommend locating a host that offers this support. (If your host doesn't support such transfers, you need to use an FTP program such as Fetch or WS_FTP to transfer your files.)

With one-step file transfers, you simply connect to the Internet, choose File⇨Publish Web from the FrontPage menu bar, and enter the URL of your directory on your host's Web server where your Web pages are published. Click OK, and your files are immediately transferred.

Chapter 11

Advertising and Publicity

· ·

In This Chapter

▶ Free advertising strategies for businesses on a budget

▶ Using newsgroups and mailing lists

▶ Keeping an electronic address book

▶ Linking and partnering with other businesses

▶ Placing banner ads — and gaining revenue by displaying ads on your own site

· ·

*E*ver heard of a low-budget movie that came out a few years ago called *The Blair Witch Project?* The cost to create this horror film was less than $100,000, and yet the movie made more than $120 million at the box office. Most of the movie's popularity was generated by word of mouth, but initially, the low-budget project got a high-tech boost thanks to some clever marketing on the Web. The film's promoters knew they would be able to use the Web to reach their target audience of young people who spend a lot of time online. A Web site featured "discovered footage" and chat rooms that enabled people to talk about the movie. The result: a "Net buzz" that helped draw viewers to the box office.

Even if your own "project" is less dramatic than a motion picture, the Web can be a cost-effective way for a small business owner such as yourself to get a potential customer's attention. In fact, the most successful advertising strategies often involve one individual connecting with another. Targeted, personalized public relations efforts work online because cyberspace is a personal place where intimate communication is possible. Blanketed advertising strategies of the sort you see in other media (most notably, display ads, commercials, or billboards) are expensive and don't always work for online businesses. Why? E-commerce is a very personal, one-to-one communications medium. Successful e-commerce sites, such as eBay, thrive not just because you can find bargains there — you can find bargains all over the Web. eBay thrives because it promotes community through its newsletter, message boards, and the positive feedback ratings that buyers leave for sellers (and vice versa) when they're satisfied with a sale.

Big companies do blanket advertising campaigns online. But they, too, use one-to-one communications approaches. For instance, in early 2002, during the March Madness college basketball championships, Volvo sponsored an NCAA sports scores site — but it was designed to reach one "wired" user at a time through wireless PDAs.

Internet advertising is becoming big business, but entrepreneurs like you can benefit from it as well. In this chapter, I describe cost-effective, do-it-yourself advertising techniques for the online entrepreneur who has a fledgling business on a tight budget. Usually, the more effort you put into attracting attention to your business, the more visits you receive. So roll up your sleeves, raise your hand, open your mouth, and prepare to be heard!

Developing a Marketing Strategy

In case you haven't figured it out by now, half the battle with running a successful online business is developing a plan for what you want to do. The next step is to get noticed. The following sections describe two strategies for making your company name more visible to online customers.

Building a brand

In business-speak, branding doesn't refer to taking a hot iron to an animal's hide. *Branding* is the process of raising awareness of a company's name and logo through advertising, public relations, or other means.

Despite the recent economic slowdowns, the Web is still a great place for developing a business brand. A December 2001 study by the Interactive Advertising Bureau (www.iab.net) reported that in the third quarter of that year online, advertising revenue (the amount businesses spend to advertise online) held steady, while at the same time more traditional ad revenue was on the decline.

Online advertising is ideal for a number of reasons. Web users tend to be fixated on their computer screens while they work, so you have a relatively captive audience. They sit only a foot or two from the screen (or only inches away, if they're using a handheld device), which means that your Web page can easily get a user's undivided attention — if your content is compelling enough, that is. Users interact with Web sites in a way that they never interact with television, so don't be reluctant to encourage interaction by giving them links to click, thumbnail images to view, and the like. Previous studies have found that Web advertising is "supported and liked" by consumers, and that brands advertised on the Web were seen as being "forward-thinking."

But don't rely on your Web page alone to spread your name. Make use of the whole Internet, including e-mail, online communities, contests, and promotions. These days, you've got plenty of options, such as the following, to get the word out about your online business:

- ✔ **Banner ads:** This type of ad is similar to the traditional print ads that you can place in a newspaper. See the section "Placing banner ads" later in this chapter for more information.

- ✔ **Classifieds:** You can advertise your goods on a classified ad site such as AOL ClassifiedPlus (ClassifiedPlus.aol.com).

- ✔ **Interstitials:** These are popup ads that appear in a separate window while a Web page is loading.

- ✔ **Keyword searches:** You can pay search services to make your site appear more prominently in search results. See "Paying for search listings" later in this chapter for more information.

- ✔ **Newsletters:** You can generate goodwill and drive business to your Web site by distributing an e-mail newsletter.

- ✔ **Partnerships:** Find businesses whose goods and services complement yours and create links on each other's Web sites. See "Striking up a business partnership" later in this chapter for further discussion of this tactic.

Remember that on the Net, your goal is to promote your brand in many different ways. For example, in early 2002, a Web site was launched to advertise Poland Spring bottled water. The site not only talks about the history of the water itself, but it functions as an interactive portal to the state of Maine, where the water comes from. Visitors can sign up to receive Maine escape postcards and forward them to friends. Poland Spring thus takes advantage of _viral marketing_ — word-of-mouth advertising that works well online.

A Web site can also promote a brand that has already become well known through traditional sales and marketing strategies. The click-and-mortar version of the Gap (Gap.com, www.gap.com) works in conjunction with the clothing retailer's brick-and-mortar stores. The Web site provides a selection of styles and sizes that's generally greater than what customers can find in stores. The National Retail Federation's Stores magazine (www.stores.org) estimates that, even though the Gap foundered financially in the fiscal year ending on July 31, 2000, customers still purchased $13 billion worth of goods from the Gap.com site, which was still 17.5 percent up from the previous year.

What does this mean for a fledgling business like yours? For the most part, it means that you should be conscious of the need to develop name awareness of your company and to realize that doing so may take a long time. You probably don't have thousands of dollars to spend on banner ads. Start with simple things, such as making sure that your signature files, your domain name, and your e-mail address all refer to your company name as closely as possible.

In some cases, dot-com domain names turn into effective brand names themselves, such as Amazon.com or shareware.com. Don't get creative with your spelling, though. Spellings that differ from the common English, such as niteline.com, are difficult for people to remember, and people who only hear the name spoken won't know how to type it in or search for it properly. Hyphens, such as in `WBX-TV-Bozo@somestation.com`, are another no-no because, again, their placement isn't obvious.

If the perfect domain name for your business is already taken, consider adding a short, easy-to-remember prefix or suffix to your existing company name. For example, if your company name is something common, such as Housing Services, try fairly recognizable names such as housing.com and housingservices.com. That way, the Web address is still easy to recall and associate with your business. Or create a "cyber" name that's related to your real name; the Art Institute of Chicago can't use `www.artinstitute.edu` because it's already taken by a group of Art Institutes to which it belongs. So the Art Institute of Chicago created the short abbreviation `www.artic.edu` that I, for one, find easy to remember.

Blanketing versus targeting

The big industrial fisheries cast huge nets that snatch up all kinds of fish, including many they aren't necessarily looking for. In contrast, the old fisherman in *The Old Man and the Sea* used a single pole and hook to catch a single Big One.

Traditional broadcast advertising, such as commercials or radio spots, are like the industrial fisheries' huge nets: They deliver short bits of information to huge numbers of people — everyone in their coverage areas who happens to be tuned in at a particular time. The Internet has its own form of broadcasting: getting your company mentioned or advertised on one of the sites that draws millions of visitors each day.

But where the Internet really excels is in one-to-one communication of the kind that TV and radio can't touch. I suggest that you try your own personalized forms of online advertising before you attempt to blanket cyberspace with banner ads. Often, you can reach small, *targeted* groups of people — or even one prospect at a time — through free, do-it-yourself marketing strategies.

Using Free Publicity Strategies

In the following sections, I describe some ways that you can publicize your online business yourself. Your big expense is in time: Prepare to devote several hours a week to corresponding by e-mail and applying to have your business listed in search services, Internet indexes, or Web sites that have a customer base similar to yours.

Building relationships, which is what many of the following strategies involve, takes energy. But the results can be great for your fledgling company. Devote some time to the care and feeding of your new business by trying these techniques before you pay to hire marketing consultants or place banner ads around the Web.

The best way to generate first-time and return visits to your business site is by providing useful information. The longer people are inclined to stay on your Web site, the more likely they are to acquire your goods or services. See Chapter 7 for some specific suggestions on generating compelling, useful content.

Getting listed in the Yahoo! index

If you want to get the most bang for your advertising buck, get your site listed on the most popular locations in cyberspace. For several years now, Yahoo!'s many sites have been ranked in the top three most popular sites on the Internet in the Media Metrix Top 50 list of Web Properties published by Jupiter Media Metrix (`www.jmm.com/xp/jmm/press/mediaMetrixTop50.xml`). Although many people think of Yahoo! primarily as a search engine, it's also a categorical index to Web sites. Getting listed on Yahoo! means being included on one if its index pages. An *index page* is a list of Web sites grouped together by category, much like what you'd find in a traditional yellow-pages phone book.

Aside from its steadily increasing size and popularity, one thing that sets Yahoo! apart is the way in which it evaluates sites for inclusion on its index pages. For the most part, real human beings do the Yahoo! indexing; they read your site description and your own suggested location and then determine what category to list your site under. Usually, Yahoo! lists sites in only one or two categories, but if Yahoo! editors feel that a site deserves its own special category, they create one for it.

The Yahoo! editors don't even attempt to process all the thousands of site applications they receive each week. Reports continue to circulate on the Web as to how long it takes to get listed on Yahoo! and how difficult it is to get listed at all. The process can take weeks, months, or even years. Danny Sullivan, the editor of *Search Engine Watch*, estimates that only about a quarter of all sites that apply get listed. That's why Yahoo! has now instituted an Express listing system — your business site will get reviewed in exchange for a $299, non-refundable annual fee, though you *still* aren't guaranteed that you'll get listed. Find out more at `help.yahoo.com/help/us/bizex/index.html`.

Search Engine Watch (searchenginewatch.com) is a great place to go for tips on how search engines and indexes work, and how to get listed on them. The site includes an article about one company's problems getting what it considers to be adequate Yahoo! coverage (searchenginewatch.com/sereport/9801-miningco.html).

What can you do to get Yahoo!-ed? I have a three-step suggestion:

1. **Make your site interesting, quirky, or somehow attention-grabbing.**

   You never know; you may just stand out from the sea of new Web sites and gain the attention of one of the Yahoo! editors.

2. **Go ahead and try applying to the main Yahoo! index.**

   You can at least say you tried!

   a. **Go to www.yahoo.com, find the category page that you think should list your site, and click the <u>Suggest a Site</u> link at the very bottom of the page.**

      The Yahoo! Suggest a Site page appears.

   b. **Click the Standard Consideration button.**

   c. **Verify that the Yahoo! category shown is the one in which you want to be included, and then click Continue.**

   d. **On the form that appears, provide your URL and a description for your site.**

      Make your description as interesting as possible while remaining within the content limit. (If you submit a description that's too long, Yahoo! asks you to revise it.)

3. **Try a local Yahoo! index.**

   Major metropolitan areas around the country, as well as in other parts of the world, have their own Yahoo! indexes. Go to the main Yahoo! page (www.yahoo.com) and review the section Local Yahoo!s near the bottom of the page. Find the local index closest to you and apply as I describe in the preceding step. Your chances are much better of getting listed locally than on the main Yahoo! site.

You can improve your listing on Yahoo! by shelling out anywhere from $25 to $300 or more per year to become a sponsored Web site. Your site is listed in the Sponsored Sites box at the top of a Yahoo! category. The exact cost depends on the popularity of the category. There is life beyond Yahoo!, too. Several Web-based services are trying to compete by providing their own way of organizing and evaluating Web sites. Try submitting a listing to Best of the Net (www.bestofthenet.ws) or contact one of the guides employed by About.com (www.about.com).

Getting listed with search services

Search services can steer lots of business to a commercial Web site, based on how often the site appears in the list of Web pages that the user sees and how high the site appears in the list. Your goal is to maximize your chances of being found by the search service.

Not so long ago, search services allowed you to list your site for free, and you could be reasonably certain of getting your site included. Not so any more. Most sites only guarantee that you'll be listed in their index if you pay a subscription fee. The fee and the terms vary from service to service. I did a quick survey of the major search sites to see what the current status is. Check out Table 11-1 to see what I discovered.

Table 11-1	Search Service Listing Policies	
Service	*Free Option*	*Paid Options*
AltaVista	Submit up to 5 URLS for consideration; results in 4-6 weeks	Submit 1 URL for $39 for six-month subscription, or 2-10 URLS for $29 each for 6 months
Google	Submit one URL at a time to Open Directory (www.dmoz.org) for consideration; results in "several weeks"	N/A
HotBot, Lycos	Submit 1 URL for consideration; results in 4-6 weeks	Guaranteed listing if you pay $18 membership fee plus $12 per URL per year to join InSite Select
Overture, WebCrawler	N/A	Minimum bid of $0.05 per clickthrough per listing plus $20/month

Some search services are part of the Overture network, but they still allow individuals to submit their sites for consideration. Here's a quick example that shows how to submit your site (for consideration) to one of the search engines that still gives you the do-it-yourself option:

1. **Connect to the Internet, start your Web browser, and go to AltaVista at** www.altavista.com.

   The AltaVista home page appears.

2. **Click the Submit a Site link.**

   The AltaVista Submit a Site page appears.

3. **Click the Express Inclusion link.**

   The AltaVista Express Inclusion page appears. (Later, you can return to the Submit a Site page if you want to add enhancements, such as logos, to your listings.)

4. **Scroll down to the bottom of the page and click the SIGN UP NOW! button.**

   You go to the AltaVista Express Inclusion page on the InfoSpider.com Web site.

5. **Enter the URL for your site's home page, and then click the Submit button.**

   Your page is added to the AltaVista database.

Businesses on the Web can get obsessed with how high their site appears on the list of search-hit pages. If a Web surfer enters the exact name of a site in the Excite search text box, for example, some people just can't understand why that site doesn't come back at the top — or even on the first page — of the list of returned sites. Of the millions of sites listed in a search service's database, the chances are good that at least one has the same name as yours (or something close to it) or that a page contains a combination of the same words that make up your organization's name. Don't be overly concerned with hitting the top of the search-hit charts. Concentrate on creating a top-notch Web site and making sales.

Paying for search listings

As you can see in Table 11-1, listing with search sites is growing more complex all the time. Some sites are part of other sites (HotBot is part of Lycos, for example). Many sites, such as Yahoo! and WebCrawler, are part of the Overture search network. You tell Overture how much you'll pay if someone clicks your listing when it appears in a list of search results. The higher you bid, the better your ranking in the results. In exchange for the fees you pay to Overture, your search listings appear in multiple search sites.

Overture (formerly called GoTo.com) has lots of options for paid listings. You can create your own listing and then pay $20 per month. You can also pay a $99 fee to have Overture write up to 20 listings for you; a $199 option is also available for which Overture will write up to 100 listings for you. In each case, you need to spend a minimum of $20 per month to be listed. You bid a minimum of five cents per click on how much you want to pay for clickthroughs — each time someone clicks your listing and goes to your site, you pay Overture. You can tell Overture that you want to have a Premium Listing at the top of the search results, but remember that the more clickthroughs you get, the higher fees you pay. Find out more at www.overture.com.

Embedding keywords in your pages

To maximize your Web site's chances of being listed in response to queries to the Internet search services, you can add special code to the underlying HTML (HyperText Markup Language) source code for your home page.

The *source code* for a Web page is the set of HTML commands that actually make the words, images, links, and other content appear correctly in a Web browser window. Every Web page has HTML source code, and all Web browsers let you take a peek "behind the curtain" of a Web page to study the source code. To do so, Netscape Navigator users choose View⇨Page Source; Internet Explorer users choose View⇨Source.

SoftBear Shareware LLC (a company that I profile in the section "Holding a contest" later in this chapter) uses this strategy to draw search engines to its site. If you look at the source for SoftBear Shareware's home page, you see the following <META> tags:

```
<META NAME="description" CONTENT="SoftBear Shareware LLC:
        free contests, software, screensavers and more!">
<META NAME="keywords" CONTENT="webpage,hosting,freebies,
        software,screensavers,contests">
```

<META> is an HTML instruction, or *tag*, that contains descriptive information about the contents of a Web page or Web site. Many search services, such as Excite and AltaVista, use computer programs that scan a Web page's <META> tags in the course of indexing that page's contents. You can include important information in <META> tags to give yourself a better chance of being indexed more effectively. In the preceding example, the "description" portion of the <META> tag provides a standard site synopsis for search engines to display when they provide a link to your site. The "keywords" portion of the <META> tag includes words that users can enter into a search engine in order to find your site.

Most <META> tags use two attributes, NAME and CONTENT. The NAME attribute identifies the property and the CONTENT attribute specifies the property's value. Attributes are terms that provide a Web browser with more specific instructions about the command it is being given and how to act on that command.

Where to put the <META> Tag

Every Web page is enclosed by the two tags <HTML> and </HTML>. These tags define the page as being an HTML document. The <HTML> tag goes at the beginning of the document and </HTML> goes at the end.

Within the <HTML> and </HTML> tags reside two main subdivisions of a Web page:

- ✔ **The header section:** This section, enclosed by the tags <HEAD> and </HEAD>, is where the <META> tags go.

- ✔ **The body section:** This section, enclosed by the tags <BODY> and </BODY>, is where the contents of the Web page — the part you actually see on-screen — go.

You don't have to include <META> tags on every page on your site; in fact, your home page is the only page where doing so makes sense.

How to create a <META> tag

The following steps show how to add your own <META> tags to a Web page by using Microsoft FrontPage 2002. (The steps are similar for other Web page editors.) These steps presume that you've already installed Internet Explorer, created your Web page, and saved it on your computer with a name like index.htm or index.html. To add <META> tags to your Web page, start FrontPage, and then follow these steps:

1. **Open the Web page document to which you want to add <META> tags by choosing File⇨Open from the FrontPage menu bar. (Alternatively, if you already have your Web site open, double-click the page in the FrontPage Folder List.)**

   The Open File dialog box appears.

2. **If the file resides on your computer's hard disk, locate the Web page file in the standard Windows navigation dialog box, and then click Open.**

3. **If the file resides on the Web, you can edit it by entering the URL for the page in the Location box of the Open File dialog box and then clicking OK. (You must be connected to the Web to display the file.)**

   The Web page opens in the Normal pane of the FrontPage window, as shown in Figure 11-1. To add the <META> tags, you must type them directly into the HTML source code for the page.

4. **Click the HTML tab near the bottom of the FrontPage window.**

   FrontPage displays the HTML source code for your Web page.

5. **Scroll to the top of your page's HTML source code, between the <HEAD> and </HEAD> tags, and enter your keywords and description by using the following format:**

   ```
   <META NAME="description" content="Your short Web site
          description goes here.">
   <META NAME="keywords" content="keyword1, keyword2,
          keyword3, and so on">
   ```

   The output appears in the View HTML window, as shown in Figure 11-2.

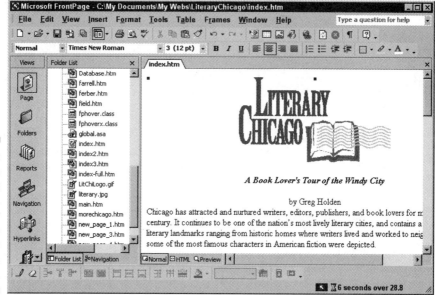

Figure 11-1:
FrontPage
may look
complex,
but it really
streamlines
the process
of editing
Web pages.

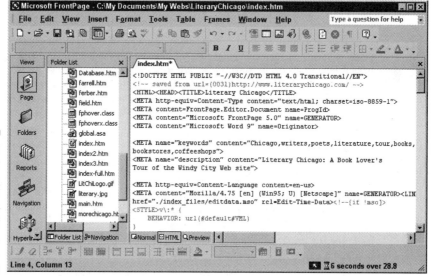

Figure 11-2:
Insert your
<META>
tags in the
HEAD
section of
your HTML
document.

6. **Click the Normal tab to close the View HTML window.**

The View HTML window closes, and you return to the FrontPage window. Your additions aren't visible on the Web page because they're intended for search engines, not visitors to your site.

7. **You can now make more changes to your page or choose File⇨Exit to close FrontPage.**

Enter the text for your <META> tags in exactly the format shown in the preceding steps. (FrontPage documents come with several <META> tags already inserted; you can just follow the same format for your own tags.) Be sure to insert a single blank space between the words META and NAME and between description and content. Separate each keyword with a comma and a blank space. Also be sure to use straight double quotation marks (double-primes) both before and after the words keywords and description. Finally, don't forget to enter the greater-than symbol (>) after each command. If you don't, the text will end up in the body of your Web page where everyone can see it.

Starting a newsletter

Back in the Dark Ages of entrepreneurship (say, six or seven years ago), the only way to publish detailed information about your new business was to create a flyer or brochure. If you were on a tight budget, you could take your simple one- or two-sheet flyer to the local copy shop and get a hundred copies duplicated on neon orange paper. If you had money to burn, you could get an actual glossy brochure designed and printed for hundreds or (more likely) thousands of dollars.

Now that you're online, you can laugh at those high printing costs and publish your own online newsletter. If you've always wanted to impress people with how much you know about what you do, now's your chance. If you've been longing to say what's on your mind without being censored, you can do it in your own publication. Online newsletters also help meet your clients' customer service needs, as I discuss in Chapter 10.

Publishing considerations

The work of producing an online newsletter is offset by the benefits you get in return. You may obtain hundreds or even thousands of subscribers who find out about you and your online business. You become an authority; you're the editor in chief; you're large and in charge.

In order for your publishing venture to run smoothly, however, you have some decisions to make:

- ✔ **What will you write about?** If you run out of your own topics to write about, don't panic. Identify magazines in your field of business so that you can quote articles. Get on the mailing list for any press releases that you can use.

- ✔ **Who will do the work?** You're busy enough running your online business and wearing other hats (parent/spouse/full-time employee . . . take your pick). Consider assigning someone to function as editor, or line up colleagues to function as contributors.

✔ **What will the publication look like?** You have two choices: You can send a plain-text version that doesn't look pretty but that everyone can read easily, or you can send a formatted HTML version that looks like a Web page but that only people who can receive formatted e-mail can read. Keep in mind, though, that many users are on corporate e-mail systems that either discourage or prohibit HTML-formatted e-mail. Others don't like HTML e-mail because it takes longer to download the graphics files.

✔ **Whom do you want to reach?** Identify your readers and make sure that your content is useful to them.

Newsletters work only if they appear on a regular basis and if they consistently maintain a high level of quality. If you decide to create a newsletter and receive subscriptions, you're making a substantial commitment. Newsletters take a great deal of work to create and update. Whether yours comes out every week, every month, or just once a year, your subscribers will expect you to re-create your publication with every new issue. Keep your newsletter simple and make sure that you have the resources to follow through.

Fire up the presses!

After you do your planning, the actual steps involved in creating your newsletter are pretty straightforward. I suggest that, because you're just starting out, you concentrate on producing only a plain-text version of your newsletter. Later on, you can think about doing an HTML version as well.

Plain old computer text isn't going to win any beauty contests, but most people who seek information online don't care; they just want the facts and they want them as fast as possible. They're satisfied with receiving inside tips and suggestions and are happy that they don't have to wait for graphics files to download. The small Chicago publishing house that published my book *Literary Chicago* uses a typical plain-text arrangement for its newsletter, which is shown in Figure 11-3.

Before you do anything, check with your ISP to make sure that you're permitted to have a mailing-list publication. Even if your newsletter is a simple announcement that you send out only once in a while (in contrast to a discussion list, which operates pretty much constantly), you're going to be sending a lot more e-mail messages through your ISP's machines than you otherwise would.

Keep your newsletters small in size; about 30K is the biggest e-mail file you can comfortably send to your recipients. If you absolutely must have a larger newsletter, break it into two or three separate e-mail messages. Reducing the file size of your newsletter keeps your readers from getting irritated because your message takes so long to download or to open. And keeping your customers happy should be one of your highest business priorities.

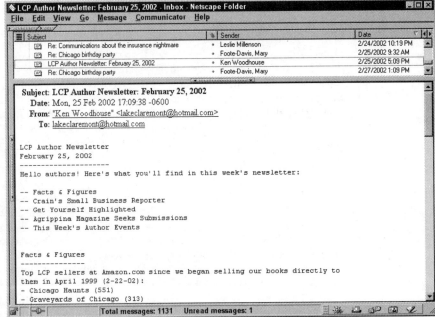

File   Edit   View   Go   Message   Communicator   Help

Subject	Sender	Date
Re: Communications about the insurance nightmare	• Leslie Millenson	2/24/2002 10:19 PM
Re: Chicago birthday party	• Foote-Davis, Mary	2/25/2002 9:32 AM
LCP Author Newsletter: February 25, 2002	• Ken Woodhouse	2/25/2002 5:09 PM
Re: Chicago birthday party	• Foote-Davis, Mary	2/27/2002 1:09 PM

Subject: LCP Author Newsletter: February 25, 2002
Date: Mon, 25 Feb 2002 17:09:38 -0600
From: "Ken Woodhouse" <lakeclaremont@hotmail.com>
To: lakeclaremont@hotmail.com

```
LCP Author Newsletter
February 25, 2002
--------------------
Hello authors! Here's what you'll find in this week's newsletter:

-- Facts & Figures
-- Crain's Small Business Reporter
-- Get Yourself Highlighted
-- Agrippina Magazine Seeks Submissions
-- This Week's Author Events


Facts & Figures
---------------
Top LCP sellers at Amazon.com since we began selling our books directly to
them in April 1999 (2-22-02):
- Chicago Haunts (551)
- Graveyards of Chicago (313)
```

Total messages: 1131   Unread messages: 1

Figure 11-3: A plain-text newsletter typically begins like this: with a heading, a horizontal divider, and a table of contents.

When you're all set with the prep work, follow these general steps for an overview of how to create and distribute your publication:

1. **Open a plain-text editor, such as Notepad (Windows) or SimpleText (Mac).**

2. **Start typing.**

   Just because your newsletter is in plain text doesn't mean that you can't format it at all. Consider the following low-tech suggestions for emphasizing text or separating one section from another:

   • **All caps:** Using ALL CAPITAL LETTERS is always useful for distinguishing the name of the newsletter or of individual article titles.

   • **Rules:** You can create your own homemade horizontal rules by typing a row of equal signs, hyphens, or asterisks to separate sections.

   • **Blank spaces:** Used carefully, that handy-dandy spacebar on your keyboard can help you center plain text or divide it into columns.

   When you finish typing, be sure to proofread the whole newsletter before sending it out. Better yet, enlist the help of an objective viewer to read over the text for you.

3. **Save your file.**

4. **Open your e-mail program's address book, select the mailing list of recipients, and compose a new message to them.**

5. **Attach your newsletter to the message, or paste it into the body of the message, and send it away.**

If you're sending many e-mail messages simultaneously, be sure to do your mailing at a time when Internet traffic isn't so heavy. Many popular newsletters, such as *eWeek News* and *HotWired*, go out on weekends, for example.

Don't flood your Internet service provider's mail server with hundreds or thousands of messages at one time; you may crash the server. Break the list into smaller batches and send them at different times. That's what Debbie Redpath Ohi did with her newsletter, *Inklings*, which attracted more than 46,000 subscribers before she decided to sell it. Inklings is no more, but you can still be inspired by the story of *Inklings* at `www.globetechnology.com/woman/archive/20010322.html`.

Be sure to mention your newsletter on your Web page and to provide an e-mail address where people can subscribe to it. In the beginning, you can ask people to send subscription requests to you. If your list swells to hundreds of members, consider automated mailing-list software or a mailing-list service to manage your list.

Help with mailing list management

When you make the decision to host and run your own mailing list, you assume the responsibility of processing requests to subscribe and unsubscribe from the list. This venture can start eating into the time that you need to spend on your other business activities.

You need to devote your energies to promoting and running your business online. When mailing lists get to be too much to handle yourself, you have a couple of options to make life easier:

✔ **Purchase special mailing-list software:** This type of program automatically adds or subtracts individuals from a mailing list in response to special e-mail messages that they send to you. You can usually manage the mailing list from your home computer. If you're a Windows NT or 2000 user, check out SLmail by BVRP Software Group (`www.bvrpusa.com/products/slmail`). Mac users can try ListSTAR by MCF Software (`www.liststar.com`).

✔ **Hire a company to run your mailing list for you:** Even though mailing-list software can help reduce the work involved in maintaining a list, you still have to install and use the software on a regular basis. So if you're really strapped for time, hiring a company to take care of your mailing list may be the way to go. Check out SKYLIST, Inc. (`www.skylist.net`) and Lyris ListHosting (`www.lyris.com/products/listhosting`) for pricing information.

Joining newsgroups and mailing lists

Many areas of the Internet can provide you with direct access to potential customers as well as a chance to interact with them. Two of the best places to market yourself directly to individuals are mailing lists and newsgroups. Mailing lists and newsgroups are highly targeted and offer unprecedented opportunities for niche marketing. Using them takes a little creativity and time on your part, but the returns can be significant.

Get started by developing a profile of your potential customer. Then join and participate in lists and newsgroups that may provide customers for your online business. For example, if you sell TV-show items (posters, T-shirts, mugs, photos of the stars, and so on) to fans online, you may want to join some newsgroups started by the fans themselves.

Where can you find these discussion forums? Topica (`www.topica.com`) maintains a mailing list directory that you can search by name or topic and that includes thousands of mailing lists. (Topica also helps you create your own e-mail newsletter, by the way.) Refdesk.com (`www.refdesk.com`) maintains links to Web sites, organized by category, that help you locate and participate in lots of newsgroups, mailing lists, and Web forums.

Mailing lists

A mailing list is a group of individuals who receive communications by e-mail. Two kinds of mailing lists are common online:

- ✔ **Discussion lists:** These are lists of people interested in a particular topic. People subscribe to the list and have messages on the topic delivered by e-mail. Each message sent to the list goes to everyone in the group. Each person can reply either to the original sender or to everyone in the group, too. The resulting series of messages on a topic is called a *thread*.

- ✔ **Announcement lists:** These lists provide only one-way communication. Recipients get a single message from the list administrator, such as an attached e-mail newsletter of the sort that I describe earlier in this chapter.

Discussion lists are often more specific in topic than newsgroups. These lists vary from very small lists to lists that include thousands of people. An example of a discussion list is ROOTS-L, which is a mailing list for individuals who are pursuing genealogical quests. People on this list exchange inquiries about ancestors that they're seeking and announce family tree information they've posted online.

By making contributions to a mailing list, you establish a presence, so when members are looking to purchase the kind of goods or services you offer, they're likely to come to you rather than to a stranger. By participating in the lists that are right for you, you also learn invaluable information about your customers' needs and desires. Use this information to fine-tune your business so that it better meets those needs and desires.

Don't directly sell your wares on mailing lists. Blatant self-promotion is frowned upon in this arena. Marketing through lists and newsgroups requires a low-key approach. Besides, participating by answering questions or contributing your opinion to ongoing discussion topics is far more effective.

Always read the welcome message and list guidelines that you receive upon joining a mailing list. Learn the rules before you post. Lurk in the background for a few weeks to get a feel for the topics and participants before you contribute. Then introduce yourself and join the discussion. Remember to stay low-key and don't directly advertise yourself. Let your four- to six-line signature file do the work for you. Also, don't forget to spell-check your messages before you send them.

Newsgroups

Newsgroups, which are often simply called discussion groups, provide a different form of online group discussion. On the Internet, you can find discussion groups in an extensive network called Usenet. America Online and CompuServe also have their own system of discussion groups that's separate from Usenet. Many large corporations and other organizations maintain their own internal discussion groups as well. In any case, you access discussion groups with your Web browser's newsgroup software. The program that comes bundled with Netscape Communicator is called Netscape Collabra; Microsoft Outlook Express has its own newsgroup software, too.

You can promote yourself and your business in discussion groups the same way that you can make use of mailing lists: by participating in the group, providing helpful advice and comments, and answering questions. Don't forget that newsgroups are great for fun and recreation, too; they're a good way to solve problems, get support, and make new friends. For more information on newsgroups, see Chapter 2.

Keeping an online little black book

If you already keep important contact information in a daily planner or other book, setting up an electronic address book on the Internet will be a piece of cake. Any good e-mail program has an address book where you can quickly record the e-mail addresses of people with whom you correspond. Use it! Every time someone sends you an inquiry, save that person's address in your online address book.

Before you know it, you'll have a mailing list of customers who have contacted you. Programs such as Microsoft Outlook Express, Netscape Messenger, and

Eudora all let you collect a bunch of e-mail addresses into a single mailing list. You can then send an announcement or a newsletter to everyone on your list at one time.

Pssst . . . can we link?

You're probably used to exchanging businesses cards and phone or fax numbers with other businesspeople. When you go online, you can exchange something else: hypertext links to your respective Web sites. These kinds of personal recommendations can carry more weight than a banner advertisement, in my opinion.

This is another way in which tried-and-true one-to-one communication can pay off handsomely. Simply call or e-mail the owner of another Web site and ask to exchange links with that person. When you ask, be friendly, brief, and to the point. Just say, "I'll put a link to your site or your e-mail address on my home page if you put a link to my site on yours."

Approaching your fiercest competitors to exchange links is probably not a good business practice. Rather, try to find a complementary business or group or organization that covers every business in your field.

Striking up a business partnership

Remember the movie *Miracle on 34th Street*, in which the owners of Macy's and Gimbel's department stores decided to send customers to each other's stores when those patrons couldn't find what they were looking for? Both merchants were depicted as reaping benefits from helping one another.

You can strike up the same sort of cooperative arrangement with your own colleagues online — one that can help you through downturns in the economy. Notice that I said *colleagues* and not competitors. I'm not talking about approaching online businesses that do exactly the same thing you do and that target the same customers. Rather, I'm talking about teaming up with another online company whose products or services complement your own. The Big Guys do this all the time: Microsoft signs an agreement with NBC; Yahoo! joins Viacom; Viacom joins CBS.

On a smaller scale, the WoodCentral site, where woodworkers go to share ideas and plans and swap tools, includes an ad for WoodFinder in a prominent location on its home page at www.woodcentral.com, shown in Figure 11-4. Conversely, if you visit WoodFinder (www.woodfinder.com), you see the same sort of referral on its home page.

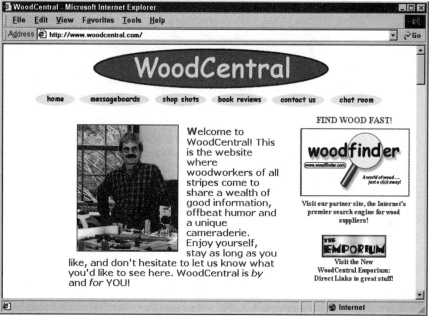

Figure 11-4:
By partnering with another organization, your small business can get more attention and reach the audience you want.

Often, you find that two businesses that have this type of symbiotic relationship are more than partners; they may be branches of the same company, or perhaps the same people created both sites. But the principle is the same: Two related businesses help one another by promoting each other's Web sites.

Trapezo (www.trapezo.com) is a company that's in the business of setting up partnerships between related companies on the Internet. Trapezo arranges partnerships between online businesses and displays one company's content on another's through a "Display Case," a small, banner ad-type area on each partner's Web pages.

Holding a contest

In Chapter 1, I describe how cartographer John Moen uses contests and other promotions to attract attention to his online business. Remember that everyone loves to receive something for free. Holding a contest can attract visitors to your Web site, where they can find out about the rest of your offerings — the ones you offer for sale, that is. (See Chapter 7 for specific details about holding a contest or sweepstakes on your Web site.)

You don't have to give away cars or trips around the world to get attention. SoftBear Shareware LLC, a company located both on America Online and the Web, gives away teddy bears and other simple items on its Web site (www.799bear.com). As you can see in Figure 11-5, its Teddy Bear contest has attracted more than 17,000 visitors over several years. When I asked SoftBear's owner, John Raddatz, whether contests had helped gain attention for his business, he responded as follows:

> *"YES, YES, YES. Contests have increased traffic to my site. The response averages about 350 entries per month. I offer contests, free screensavers and software, which still attracts quite a few people from all over the world. My number one contest draw is at Ice Puck University (www.ipucku.com) where I offer a free hockey diploma every month. My Johnny Puck Web site (www.johnnypuck.com) has spawned a local UHF TV show here in Muskegon, Michigan. All of this started with my software and Teddy Bear contest on and screensaver site (www.jrsoftbear.com). You must offer something for free to draw people in to your site. Then you can draw their attention to your main offerings."*

Elsewhere on the SoftBear Shareware site, you can see that SoftBear is enrolled in the Amazon.com Associates Program. This is another kind of cooperative link partnership you can consider for your small business. SoftBear recommends some Amazon.com books on its site and, in return, receives referral fees. Find out more by visiting www.amazon.com and clicking the Join Associates link at the bottom of the page.

Figure 11-5: Holding regular contests attracts attention to the rest of your online business, too.

Placing banner ads

I'm not as big a fan of traditional banner ads as I am of the other strategies that I discuss in this chapter, especially where small entrepreneurial businesses are concerned. Banner ads are like the traditional print ads you might take out in local newspapers. In some limited cases, banner ads are free, as long as you or a designer can create one. Otherwise, you have to pay to place them on some-one else's Web page, the same way you pay to take out an ad in a newspaper or magazine.

However, many commercial operations *do* use banner ads successfully on the Web. Banner ads can be effective promotional tools under certain circumstances:

- ✔ If you pay enough money to keep them visible in cyberspace for a long period of time
- ✔ If you pay the high rates charged by the most successful Web sites, which can steer you the most traffic

Banner ads differ from other Web-specific publicity tactics in one important respect: They publicize in a one-to-many rather than a one-to-one fashion. Banner ads broadcast the name of an organization indiscriminately, without requiring the viewer to click a link or in some respect choose to find out about the site.

Anteing up

You have to pay the piper in order to play the banner ad game. In general, Web sites have two methods of charging for banner ads:

- ✔ **CPM, or Cost Per Thousand:** This is a way of charging for advertising based on the number of people who visit the Web page on which your ad appears. The more visits the Web site gets, the higher the ad rates that site can charge.
- ✔ **CTR, or Clickthrough Rate:** A *clickthrough* occurs when someone clicks a banner ad that links to your (the advertiser's) Web site. (Virtually all banner ads are linked this way.) In this case, you are billed after the ad has run for a while and the clicks have been tallied.

Say 100,000 people visit the site on which your banner runs. If the site charges a flat $20 CPM rate, your banner ad costs $2,000 (100 × $20). If the same site charges a $1 per clickthrough rate, and 2 percent of the 100,000 visitors click through to your site (the approximate average for the industry), you pay the same: $2,000 (2,000 × $1).

Obviously, the more popular the site on which you advertise, the more your ad costs. Back in 1999, when Yahoo! was still publishing its advertising rates online, it charged a CPM rate of $20 to $50 for each 1,000 visits to the Yahoo! page on which the banner ad appears. If the page on which your banner runs received 500,000 visits, such ads could cost $10,000 to $25,000. Not all advertising sites are so expensive, of course. AdResource published a sample ad rate guide listing a variety of Web sites and average rates at `adres.internet.com/adrates/article/0,1401,,00.html`.

CPM rates are difficult to calculate because of the number of repeat visitors a site typically receives. For example, a Web page designer may visit the same site a hundred times in a day when testing scripts and creating content. If the site that hosts your ad charges a rate based on CPM, make sure that they "weed out" such repeat visits. In general, you're better off advertising on sites that charge not only on a CPM basis, but on a cost-per-click basis as well — or, better yet, *only* on a clickthrough basis. The combination of CPM and CTR is harder for the hosting site to calculate but ultimately fairer for you, the advertiser.

Positioning banner ads can be a substantial investment, so be sure that your ad appears on a page whose visitors are likely to be interested in your company. If your company sells automotive parts, for example, get on one of the Yahoo! automotive index pages.

Some new options for ad placement have gained popularity in recent years. One type of ad, an *interstitial*, appears in a small popup window while a browser is downloading the requested page. Such ads are becoming common on the Web. *Takeover ads* are less frequently seen and should probably be avoided. With a takeover ad, if the viewer clicks an ad, the browser window is taken over by a Flash animation. You can read about interstitials at `ecommerce.internet.com/solutions/ectips/article/0,1467,6311_771181,00.html`.

Just how much should you try to spend for banner ads or for other types of Internet marketing? An article in *Business Week* entitled "Who's Getting More Bang for the Marketing Buck" indicated that the most efficient online marketers spend 10 percent of their revenue in attracting customers. Read more about it at `www.businessweek.com/datedtoc/1999/9922.htm`.

Designing your ad

The standard "medium rectangle" and "large rectangle" banner ads are by far the most popular ones. A new larger "skyscraper" ad is gaining in popularity. In March 2002, the Interactive Advertising Bureau estimated that such ads comprised about 9 percent of all online ad placements. Some standard square configurations or small button-like shapes are common, too. The numeric measurements for ads usually appear in pixels. An inch contains roughly 72 pixels, so a 468 x 60-pixel ad (the most common size) is about 6.5 inches wide and about 0.875 inch in height.

Profiting from someone else's banner ads

When used economically and targeted to the right audience, banner ads can help you achieve one of your goals: attracting visitors to your Web site. Attract enough visitors, and banner ads can help you achieve another, even more important goal: making money.

If you attract thousands or (if you're lucky) even millions of visitors to your site each month, you become an attractive commodity to advertisers looking to gain eyespace for their own banner advertisements. By having another business pay you to display their ads, you can generate extra revenue with very little effort.

Of course, the effort involved in soliciting advertisers, placing ads, keeping track of how many visitors to your site click ads, and getting paid *is* considerable — but you don't have to manage ads yourself.

For John Moen, owner of a pair of map-related Web sites (including Graphic Maps, which I profile in Chapter 1), the move from marketing his own Web site to becoming an advertiser came when his worldatlas.com (www.worldatlas.com) site began to attract 3 million hits per month. He turned to advertising giant DoubleClick (www.doubleclick.com) to serve the ads and handle the maintenance.

"We place their (DoubleClick's) banner code on our pages and they pay us monthly for page impressions, direct clicks, page hits, and the like," says John. "They (DoubleClick) also provide a daily report on site traffic. With their reports I can tell which page gets the most hits and at what time of day. Banner advertising now pays very well."

The rectangular ads appear most often at the top of a Web page, so they load first while other page contents have yet to appear; smaller ads may appear anywhere on a page. (Ensuring that your ad appears at the top of a Web page is always a good idea.)

Many banner ads combine photographic images, type, and color in a graphically sophisticated way. However, simple ads can be effective as well. You can create your ad yourself if you have some experience with a graphics program such as Paint Shop Pro. (You can download a trial copy of Paint Shop Pro at www.jasc.com.)

Need some help in creating your own banner ad? If you have only a simple, text-only ad in mind and you don't have a lot of money to spend on design, try a create-your-own-banner-ad service or software program. I've had mixed results using the online banner-ad services such as The Banner Generator, provided for free by Prescient Code Solutions (www.coder.com/creations/banner). See Figure 11-6 for an ad that I created in just a couple of minutes by using a shareware program called Banner Maker Pro (www.bannermakerpro.com).

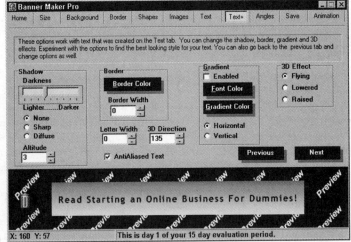

Figure 11-6:
With the right choice of color, a text-only banner ad can look good.

Part IV
Law, Security, and Accounting

The 5th Wave — By Rich Tennant

"They were selling contraband online. We broke through the door just as they were trying to flush the hard drive down the toilet."

In this part . . .

Okay, so this may not be the tastiest part of the book, but it's definitely good for you.

The bad news is that doing business online has its own set of risks and dangers; the good news is that Part IV shows you strategies to protect yourself and your business. In this part, I also include an overview of basic accounting practices for Web businesses and suggestions of software and online accounting help that you can use to keep track of your e-commerce activities.

The following chapters take the mumble-jumble out of business law and accounting, leaving you with easy-to-read, easy-to-understand steps, definitions, and do's and don'ts to keep your business merrily humming along.

Chapter 12

Security for Your Commerce Site

· ·

· ·

*W*hen a retail store closes at the end of the business day, available cash is locked in a cash box or a safe, and stock that's particularly valuable is stored in a safe area. The last employee to leave makes sure to lock the doors.

When it comes to an online store, you don't have to worry about locking up merchandise, but you need to protect data — not only your own information but also that which pertains to your customers. Security, of course, is on everyone's mind these days because of viruses like the infamous I Love You and Melissa, as well as denial of service attacks that periodically make head-lines. An online business needs to have the ability to recover data in case of disaster. You also need to protect your business from the viruses and other hack attacks that are proliferating along with the always-on broadband Internet connections, which are especially vulnerable to these intrusions.

In this chapter, I discuss some easy-to-implement technologies and strategies that can keep your data secure. Some of these measures are easy to put into practice and especially important for home-based businesspeople. Others are technically challenging to implement on your own. But even if you have your Web host or a consultant do the work, it's good to familiarize yourself with Internet security schemes. Doing so gives you the ability to make informed decisions about how to protect your online data. You can then take steps to lock your virtual doors when you need to and protect your cyberstock from hackers and other bad guys.

Basic Business Safety Strategies

Just because you work at home doesn't mean that your security problems are over. Working in a home office carries its own set of safety concerns for small-business owners. Luckily, these concerns tend to be easy to address. Safe computing practices, such as using password protection, making back-ups, and installing virus software, can go a long way toward keeping your data secure, even if you never have to get into more technical subjects such as public key encryption.

Protecting your home office privacy

Working at home is safer in many ways than driving to a remote office. You don't have to brave the highways and byways commuting from one place to another. And I probably don't need to mention that you're protected from having to deal with office politics and infighting, too.

But when your workplace is the same as your living space, you run into new challenges, not the least of which is privacy. The doorbell, the phone, and the kids all make demands on your time. Some simple steps can help you set more clearly defined boundaries so that you can concentrate on your work and thus be able to focus on pets, family, and home when the work is done.

Passing the password test

To your kids and your spouse, the computer may be a place to do homework, play games, or surf the Net. But to you, it's the central tool for operating your business. The ultimate solution is to have separate machines — one for personal use and one for business use. Then set up your system so that you have to log on to your business computer with a username and password. (For suggestions on how to devise a good password that's difficult to crack, see the section "Picking a good password," later in this chapter.)

If you have only one computer, passwords can still provide a measure of protection. Windows gives you the ability to set up different user profiles, each associated with its own password. You can assign a different profile to each member of your family. You can even make a game out of selecting profiles: Each person can pick his or her own background color and desktop arrangement for Windows. User profiles and passwords don't necessarily protect your business files, but they convey to your family members that they should use their own software, stick to their own directories, and not try to explore your company data.

You can also set up different user profiles for your copy of Netscape Communicator. That way, your kids won't receive your business e-mail while they're surfing the Internet because you'll have different e-mail inboxes. If you're on Windows, choose Start⇨Programs⇨Netscape Communicator⇨ Utilities⇨User Profile Manager. If you use Outlook Express for e-mail, choose File⇨Identities...⇨Add New Identity, to create an identity and assign a password to it.

Folder Guard, a program by WinAbility Corporation (www.winability.com/ folderguard), enables you to hide or password-protect files or folders on your computer. The software works with Windows 95/98/Me/2000/XP. You can choose from the Standard version, which is intended for home users, or the Professional version, which is designed for business customers. A 14-day trial version is available for download from the WinAbility Web site; if you want to keep the Standard version of Folder Guard, you have to pay $39.95 (or $69.95 for the Professional version). A third Lite version costs $24.95 and only lets you hide folders.

Maintaining your telephone privacy

The first step to protecting the telephone privacy of your business is to get a separate phone line for business use. Having a devoted phone line not only makes your business seem more serious but also separates your business calls from your personal calls. Additionally, if you need a phone line to connect to the Net, you then have a choice of which line to use for your modem.

The next step is to set up your business phone with its own answering machine, which has a different message from your personal answering machine. On your business answering machine, identify yourself with your business name. This arrangement builds credibility and makes you feel like a real business owner. You can then install privacy features, such as caller ID, on your business line as needed.

If you're looking for tips and news on telephone service, not only for small businesses but also for personal use, visit the Telecommunications Research & Action Center (www.trac.org). This site provides suggestions of ways to cut your phone bills and make smart decisions on telephone service.

Preparing for disaster

Your fledgling business is no Titanic. It wouldn't take a big iceberg to sink you before you reach your destination. A basic technique for safeguarding your data is to protect yourself against disasters. When it comes to online computing, one of the worst things that can happen is loss of data. Whether the culprit is a natural disaster, fire, theft, or computer virus or bug, you can take steps to prevent problems as well as to recover more easily should a problem arise.

The following sections include ways to keep from having to abandon ship and swim for the lifeboats.

Insuring against disaster

You insure your house and car, so why not protect your business investment by obtaining insurance that specifically covers you against hardware damage, theft, and loss of data? You can also go a step further and obtain a policy that covers the cost of data entry or equipment rental that would be necessary to recover your business information. Here are some specific strategies:

- ✔ Write a list of all your hardware and software and how much each item cost, and store the list in a safe place, such as a fireproof safe or safe deposit box.

- ✔ Take photos of your computer setup in case you need to make an insurance claim and store the photos in a safe location, too.

Investigate the many options available to you for insuring your computer hardware and software. Your current homeowner's or renter's insurance may offer coverage. You may also want to look into the computer hardware and software coverage provided by Safeware, The Insurance Agency Inc. (www.safeware.com).

Having a backup plan

The Gartner Group estimates that two out of five businesses that experience a major disaster will go out of business within five years. In contrast, companies that have recovery plans in place can get back up and running quickly. Even if your company is small, you need to be prepared for big trouble — not only for terrorist attacks, but natural disasters such as floods, hurricanes, or tornadoes.

First, draw up a recovery plan. This can be as simple as a paragraph or two stating what you'll do in case your office and computers become unavailable. A recovery plan includes information on the following topics:

- ✔ **Backup power systems:** What will you do if the power goes out and you can't access the Web? It might be impractical to fire up a gas-powered generator, but consider a battery backup system such as APC Back-UPS Office (www.apc.com/products/back-ups_office/index.cfm). It instantly switches your computers to battery power when the electricity goes out, so you can save your data and switch to laptops. A version that runs for 5 to 10 minutes costs about $75. Even more importantly, make sure that your ISP or Web host has a backup power supply so that your store can remain online in case of a power outage.

- ✔ **Data storage:** This is probably the most practical and essential disaster recovery step for small or home-based businesses. Back up your files on a computer that's not located in the place where you physically work. At the very least, upload your files periodically to the Web space that your hosting service gives you. Also consider storing your files with an online storage service. (See the section on online storage space in this book's

Internet Directory for suggestions, including one free storage option.) You might even copy your files to tape and store the tapes in a safe deposit box.

✔ **Telecommunications:** Having some alternate method of communication available in case your phone system goes down ensures that you're always in touch. The obvious choice is a cell phone. Also set up a voice mailbox so that customers and vendors can leave messages for you even if you can't answer the phone.

✔ **Alternate offices:** For major corporations located in large cities, locating at least one branch in a rural area provides a place to regroup and resume operations in case of trouble. For your small business, you can set up a temporary alternate office at a colleague or relative's house, at Kinko's, or at your ISP's facility, if computers are available for you to use there. Have a place in mind in case you need to get there in a hurry.

After you devise a plan, don't leave it on paper and shove it into your desk drawer. Back up your data on a regular basis, purchase additional equipment if you need it, and make arrangements to use other computers and offices if you need to — in other words, *implement* your plan. You owe it not only to yourself but also to your customers to be prepared in case of disaster.

Inoculating your computers against infection

ISCA Labs (`www.icsalabs.com/html/communities/antivirus/alerts. shtml`), which keeps track of viruses circulating around the Internet, has estimated that as many as 20,000 viruses are present online at any one time. As an online businessperson, you're going to be downloading files, receiving disks from customers and vendors, and exchanging e-mail with all sorts of people you've never met before. Surf safely by installing one of the virus protection programs that I list in Chapter 3.

Viruses change all the time, and new ones appear regularly. The virus program you install one day may not be able to handle the viruses that appear just a few weeks or months later. Pick a virus program that doesn't charge excessive amounts for regular upgrades. Also check the ICSA's weekly antivirus Product Testing Reports (`www.icsalabs.com/html/communities/antivirus/ labs.shtml`).

Getting a secure seal of approval

TRUSTe, a nonprofit organization, is seeking to boost the degree of trust that Web surfers have in the Internet. It does this through a third-party oversight "seal" program. If you demonstrate to TRUSTe that you're making efforts to keep your visitors' personal data secure, and if you pledge not to share your customers' data and to publish a privacy statement on your site, TRUSTe issues you a seal of approval that you can place on your site's home page. The TRUSTe seal is intended to function as the online equivalent of the Good Housekeeping seal of approval on a product.

By itself, the seal doesn't keep hackers from breaking into your site and stealing your data. That's still up to you. Having the seal just makes visitors feel better about using your services. The TRUSTe site provides you with a wizard that leads you through the process of generating a privacy statement for your site. The statement tells visitors how you will protect their information. Find out more by visiting the TRUSTe home page (www.truste.org) and clicking the For Businesses link.

Backing up your business treasure

Treat your business information like gold. Back up your business data two or three times a week. You can find software that automatically creates backups for you (preferably in the middle of the night, when you don't need your computer). This software means that you don't have to spend lots of valuable business time making copies of files. One of the most popular of these software packages is Retrospect Backup (www.dantz.com). You can now download a 30-day trial of a Windows version of Retrospect. Other versions work with the Mac OS.

Data that you've backed up from personal computers is most easily saved on tape drives, removable cartridges, or writeable CD-ROM drives, which I describe in Chapter 3.

You also need to protect any business information that's stored on handheld devices, laptops, or other portable computing devices that are easily lost. At the very least, make the device's storage device accessible with a password. You can also install protection software designed especially for mobile devices, such as VirusScan Wireless by McAfee.com (www.mcafee.com/myapps/vsw/default.asp).

Blocking Trojan horses and other unwanted programs

A *Trojan horse* is a program that enters your computer surreptitiously and then attempts to do something without your knowledge. Some folks say that such programs enter your system through a "backdoor" because you don't immediately know that they've entered your system. Trojan horses may come in the form of an e-mail attachment with the filename extension .exe (which stands for *executable*). I got one just a couple of weeks before I wrote this; someone widely distributed an e-mail that purported to be from Microsoft Corporation and that claimed it contained a security update. The attachment looked innocent enough, but had I saved the attachment to my computer, it would have used my computer as a staging area for distributing itself to many other e-mail addresses.

I didn't run into trouble, however. A special firewall program I installed, called Norton Internet Security, recognized the attachment and alerted me to the danger. I highly recommend that anyone who, like me, has a cable modem, DSL, or other direct connection to the Internet install one right away. A firewall is software or hardware that monitors data transmissions across a network (so you can track attempts by hackers to break in to your machine) and filters the data based on criteria that the owner sets up. You might configure your firewall to permit you to access only certain types of content — only Web pages but not chat rooms or multimedia files, for instance.

You can try out a shareware program called ZoneAlarm by Zone Labs, Inc. (`www.zonealarm.com`) that provides you with basic firewall protection, though more full-featured programs like Norton Internet Security (`www.symantec.com/product`) will probably be more effective.

Ad-aware is a useful program that detects and erases any advertising programs you may have downloaded from the Internet without knowing it. Such advertising programs might be running on your computer, consuming your processing resources and slowing down operations. Some "spyware" programs track your activities as you surf the Web; others simply report that they have been installed. Many users regard these "spyware" programs as invasions of privacy because they install themselves and do their reporting without your asking for it or even knowing they're active.

When I ran Ad-aware the first time, it detected a whopping 57 programs I didn't know about that were running on my computer and that had installed themselves when I connected to various Web sites or downloaded software. As you can see in Figure 12-1, when I ran Ad-aware while I was working on this chapter, sure enough, it found four suspicious software components running.

I highly recommend Ad-aware; you can download a version at `www.lavasoftUSA.com` and try it for free. If you decide to keep it, you pay a $15 shareware fee.

Figure 12-1: Ad-aware deletes advertising software that, many users believe, can violate your privacy.

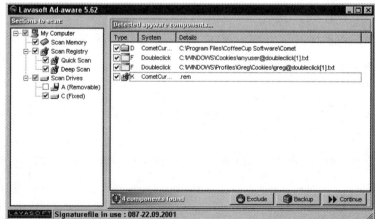

Locking down your equipment

When Web surfers and Web site owners think about keeping their online business secure, they naturally think about high-tech stuff such as encryption. But security doesn't need to start with software. The fact is, all the firewalls and passwords in the world won't help you if someone breaks into your home office and makes off with your computer and all your files.

Besides insuring your computer equipment and taking photos in case you need to get it replaced, you can also invest in locks for your home office and your machines. They might not keep someone from breaking into your house, but they'll at least make it more difficult for intruders to carry off your hardware.

Here are some suggestions for how to protect your hardware and the business data your computers contain:

✔ **Lock your office:** Install a deadbolt lock on your office door as well as the front door to your house.

✔ **Lock your computers:** Innovative Security Products (www.wesecure.com) offers several varieties of computer locking systems, as well as an ultraviolet pen that you can use to mark your equipment with your name and the serial number of your computer in case the police recover it.

✔ **Mark your modem:** An innovative theft recovery system called CompuTrace can be installed on your hard disk, where outsiders can't detect it. If your computer is stolen, the software is activated so that, when and if the thief connects its internal modem to a phone line, the authorities are notified. CompuTrace Plus (www.computrace.com) is offered by Absolute Software Corp. and costs home office users $49.95 for one year of monitoring.

✔ **Make backups:** Be sure to regularly back up your information on Zip drives or similar storage devices. Also consider signing up with a Web-based storage service: You transfer your sensitive files from your computer to a Web site that stores it securely. That way, if your computers and your extra storage disks are stolen, you'll have an online backup in a secure location. Look into @Backup (www.atbackup.com), which will give you 100MB of storage space for $99 per year.

Providing Public-Key Security for Your Business

Radio and TV childhood heroes used to give out "secret decoder rings" to their young audience members. They then broadcast coded messages that only the lucky ring bearers could decode.

Computers use the same process of encoding and decoding to protect information they exchange on the Internet. The schemes used online are far more complex and subtle than the ones used by kids, however. This section describes the security method that is used most widely on the Internet, and the one you're likely to use yourself: Secure Sockets Layer (SSL) encryption.

How public key/private key encryption works

Terms like SSL and encryption might seem as exciting as watching paint dry, but, in terms of e-commerce, they're actually very a-peeling. SSL is making it safer to do business online and boosting the trust of potential customers. And anything that makes shoppers loosen their virtual pocketbooks is something you need to know about.

The term *encryption* refers to the process of encoding data, especially sensitive data, such as credit card numbers. Information is encrypted by means of complex mathematical formulas called *algorithms*. Such a formula may transform a simple-looking bit of information into a huge block of seemingly incomprehensible numbers, letters, and characters. Only someone who has the right formula, called a *key*, which is itself a complex mass of encoded data, can decode the gobbledygook.

Here's a very simple example. Suppose that my credit card number is 12345 and I encode it by using an encryption formula into something like the following: 1aFgHx203gX4gLu5cy.

The algorithm that generated this encrypted information may say something like: "Take the first number, multiply it by some numeral, and then add some letters to it. Then take the second number, divide it by x, and add y characters to the result," and so on. (In reality, the formulas are far more complex than this, which is why you usually have to pay a license fee to use them. But this is the general idea.) Someone who has the same formula can run it in reverse, so to speak, in order to decrypt the encoded number and obtain the original number, 12345.

In practice, the encoded numbers that are generated by encryption routines and transmitted on the Internet are very large. They vary in size depending on the relative strength (or uncrackability) of the security method being used. Some methods generate keys that consist of 128 bits of data; a *data bit* is a single unit of digital information. These formulas are called *128-bit keys*.

Encryption is the cornerstone of security on the Internet. The most widely used security schemes, such as the Secure Sockets Layer protocol (SSL), the Secure Electronic Transactions protocol (SET), and Pretty Good Privacy (PGP), all use some form of encryption.

With some security methods, the party that sends the data and the party that receives it both use the same key (this method is called *symmetrical encryption*). This approach isn't considered as secure as an asymmetrical encryption method, such as public-key encryption, however.

In public-key encryption, the originating party obtains a license to use a security method. (In the following section, I show you just how to do this yourself.) As part of the license, you use the encryption algorithm to generate your own private key. You never share this key with anyone. However, you use the private key to create a separate public key. This public key goes out to visitors who connect to a secure area of your Web site. As soon as they have your public key, users can encode sensitive information and send it back to you. Only you can decode the data — by using your secret, private key.

Obtaining your own certificate

How do you know for sure whom you're dealing with on the Internet? How do you know that people are who they say they are when all you have to go on is a URL or an e-mail address? In the real world, the government issues you a passport or a state ID, and retailers use these documents to check your identity. The solution in the online world is to obtain a personal certificate that you can send to Web site visitors or append to your e-mail messages.

How certificates work

A *certificate*, which is also sometimes called a Digital ID, is an electronic document issued by a certification authority (CA). The certificate contains the owner's personal information as well as a public key that can be exchanged with others online. The public key is generated by the owner's private key, which the owner obtains during the process of applying for the certificate.

In issuing the certificate, the CA takes responsibility for saying that the owner of the document is the same as the person actually identified on the certificate. Although the public key helps establish the owner's identity, certificates do require you to put a level of trust in the agency that issues it.

A certificate helps both you and your customers. A certificate assures your customers that you're the person you say you are, plus it protects your e-mail communications by enabling you to encrypt them.

Obtaining a certificate from VeriSign

Considering how important a role certificates play in online security, it's remarkably easy to obtain one. You do so by applying and paying a licensing fee to a CA. One of the most popular CAs is VeriSign, Inc., which lets you apply for a certificate called a Class 1 Digital ID.

A Class 1 Digital ID is only useful for securing personal communications. As an e-commerce Web site owner, you may want a business-class certificate called a 128-bit SSL Global Server ID (www.verisign.com/products/site).

This form of Digital ID works only if your e-commerce site is hosted on a server that runs secure server software — software that encrypts transactions — such as Apache Stronghold. Check with your Web host to see if a secure server is available for your Web site.

A VeriSign personal certificate, which you can use to authenticate yourself in e-mail, news, and other interactions on the Net, costs $14.95 per year, and you can try out a free certificate for 60 days. Follow these steps to obtain your Digital ID:

1. **Go to the VeriSign, Inc. Digital IDs for Secure E-Mail page at** `www.verisign.com/products/class1/index.html.`

2. **Click the Buy Now button if you're certain you want an ID. Otherwise, for the purposes of this exercise, click Try a Digital ID FREE for 60 days (on the right side of the page).**

   The Personal Digital ID Enrollment page appears.

3. **Click <u>Class 1 Digital ID</u>.**

   An application form for a Digital ID appears.

4. **Complete the application form.**

   The application process is pretty simple. The form asks for your personal information and a challenge phrase that you can use in case anyone is trying to impersonate you. It also requires you to accept a license agreement. (You don't need to enter credit card information if you check the 60-day trial option.)

5. **Click the Accept button at the bottom of the screen.**

   A dialog box appears asking you to confirm your e-mail address. After you confirm by clicking OK, two dialog boxes appear, asking you to confirm that you want to use VeriSign's encryption technology to generate first an exchange key and then a private key for you. The private key is an essential ingredient in public-key/private-key technology.

6. **Click OK to have your browser generate your private key.**

   A page appears asking you to check your e-mail for further instructions. In a few minutes, you receive a message that contains a Digital ID PIN.

7. **In your e-mail program, open the new message from VeriSign Digital ID Center.**

8. **Use your mouse to highlight (select) the PIN, and then choose Edit⇨Copy to copy the PIN.**

9. **Go to the URL for the Digital ID Center that's included in the e-mail message and paste your PIN in the text box next to Enter the Digital ID Personal Identification Number (PIN).**

10. **Click Submit.**

    The certificate is generated, and the Certificate Download page appears.

11. **Click the Install button.**

    The ID from VeriSign downloads, and you're now able to view it with your browser. Figure 12-2 shows my certificate for Microsoft Internet Explorer. (Copying this ID, or anyone else's, is pointless because this is only your public key; the public key is always submitted with your private key, which is secret.)

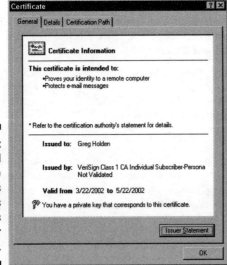

Figure 12-2:
A personal certificate assures individuals or Web sites of your identity.

After you have your Digital ID, what do you do with it? For one thing, you can use it to verify your identity to sites that accept certificate submissions. Some sites that require members to log in use secure servers that give you the option of submitting your certificate instead of entering the usual username and password to identify yourself. You can also attach your Digital ID to your e-mail messages to prove that your message is indeed coming from you. See your e-mail program's Help files for more specific instructions.

You can't encrypt or digitally sign messages on any computer other than the one to which your certificates are issued. If you're using a different computer than the one you used when you obtained your certificates, you must contact your certificate issuer and obtain a new certificate for the computer you're now using. Or, if your browser allows transfers, you can export your certificate to the new computer.

Keeping Your Sensitive Content Secure

Encryption isn't just for big businesses. Individuals who want to maintain their privacy, even while navigating the wilds of the Internet, can install special software or modify their existing e-mail programs in order to encode their online communications.

The Cyberangels Web site (www.cyberangels.org) presents some good tips and strategies for personal protection on the Internet.

Using personal encryption software

PGP (Pretty Good Privacy), a popular encryption program, has been around about as long as the Web itself. PGP lets you protect the privacy of your e-mail messages and file attachments by encrypting them so that only those with the proper authority can decipher the information. You can also digitally sign the messages and files you exchange, which assures the recipient that they come from you and that the information has not been tampered with. You can even encrypt files on your own computer, too.

PGP (web.mit.edu/network/pgp.html) is a freely available personal encryption program. PGP is a *plug-in*, an application that works with another program to provide added functionality. You can integrate the program with popular e-mail programs such as Eudora and Microsoft Outlook (although Netscape Messenger is notably absent from the list of supported applications).

In order to use either the free version of PGP or another, commercial version called PGP Personal Privacy, the first step is to obtain and install the program. After you install the program, you can use it to generate your own private-key/ public-key pair. After you create a key pair, you can begin exchanging encrypted e-mail messages with other PGP users. To do so, you need to obtain a copy of their public keys, and they need a copy of your public key. Because public keys are just blocks of text, trading keys with someone is really quite easy. You can include your public key in an e-mail message, copy it to a file, or post it on a public-key server where anyone can get a copy at any time.

After you have a copy of someone's public key, you can add it to your *public keyring*, which is a file on your own computer. Then you can begin to exchange encrypted and signed messages with that individual. If you're using an e-mail application supported by the PGP plug-ins, you can encrypt and sign your messages by selecting the appropriate options from your application's toolbar. If your e-mail program doesn't have a plug-in, you can copy your e-mail message to your computer's clipboard and encrypt it there by using PGP built-in functions. See the PGP User's Guide files for more specific instructions.

The freeware version of PGP is distributed freely by MIT with the approval of Network Associates, which owns the rights to PGP encryption technology and has incorporated it into a variety of commercial security products. A commercial product called PGP Personal Privacy is still being sold by McAfee.com for $49.95 but is no longer being actively marketed. The freeware version of PGP will run on Windows 95/98/NT/2000 and the Mac OS 7.6.1 or later. (It also ran on my Windows Me computer.)

Encrypting your e-mail messages

You can use your existing software to encrypt your mail messages rather than have to install a separate program such as PGP. In the following sections, I describe the steps involved in setting up the e-mail programs that come with the Big Two browser packages, Microsoft Internet Explorer and Netscape Communicator, to encrypt your messages.

Sending secure messages with Microsoft Outlook Express

If you use Outlook Express, you can use your Digital ID to do the following:

- ✓ **Send a digital signature:** You can digitally shrink-wrap your e-mail message by using your certificate in order to assure the recipient that the message is really from you.

- ✓ **Encrypt your message:** You can digitally encode a message to ensure that only the intended party can read it.

To better understand the technical details of how you can keep your e-mail communications secure, read the How It Works page of the VeriSign Digital ID section, which you can access at `www.verisign.com/products/class1/how.html`.

After you have a digital ID, in order to actually make use of it, you need to follow these steps:

1. **After you obtain your own Digital ID, the first step is to associate it with your e-mail account. Select Tools⇨Accounts.**

   The Internet Accounts dialog box appears.

2. **Select your e-mail account and click Properties.**

   The Properties dialog box for your e-mail account appears.

3. **Click the Security tab to bring it to the front.**

4. **Check the Select button in the Signing Certificate section; then, when the Select Default Account Digital ID dialog box appears, select your Digital ID.**

5. **Click OK to close the Select Default Account Digital ID dialog box; then click OK to close the Properties dialog box, and click Close to close the Internet Accounts dialog box.**

   You return to the main Outlook Express window.

6. **To send a digitally signed e-mail message to someone, click Create Message.**

   The New Message dialog box appears.

7. **Click either or both of the security buttons at the extreme right of the toolbar, as shown in Figure 12-3.**

   Digitally Sign Message enables you to add your Digital ID. Encrypt Message lets you encrypt your message.

Figure 12-3: When the Signed and Encrypted buttons are selected, your message goes out encrypted and with your certificate attached.

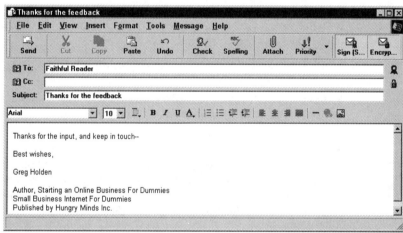

8. **Finish writing your message and then click the Send button.**

   Your encrypted or digitally signed message is sent on its way.

The preceding steps show you how to digitally sign or encrypt an individual message. You have to follow these steps every time you want to sign or encrypt a message. On the other hand, by checking one or more of the options (Encrypt Contents and Attachments for all Outgoing Messages and Digitally Sign all Outgoing Messages) on the Security tab of the Options dialog box, you activate Outlook Express's built-in security features for *all* of your outgoing messages. (You can still "turn off" the digital signature or encryption for an individual message by deselecting the Sign or Encrypt buttons in the toolbar of the New Message dialog box.)

If you use Netscape Messenger, the e-mail application that comes with Netscape Communicator, follow these steps to encrypt your e-mail messages or include your certificate with them:

1. **With Messenger running, select Communicator⇨Tools⇨Security Info (or press Ctrl+Shift+I).**

   A security information dialog box appears.

2. **Click the word Messenger in the list of topics on the left side of the Security dialog box.**

   The following security options appear in the right half of the dialog box:

   - Encrypt mail messages, when it's possible

   - Sign mail messages, when it's possible

   - Sign news messages, when it's possible

3. **In order to activate Messenger's security features, check one or more of the check boxes; then click OK.**

   The security dialog box closes. You return to the Messenger window that you were in previously.

4. **You can now address and write your message and then click the Send button in the Message Composition toolbar.**

   Your encrypted or digitally signed message is sent on its way.

By checking one or more of the options in the Security dialog box, you activate Messenger's built-in security features for all your outgoing messages. In order to actually verify or undo those features (that is, if you want a message to be unencrypted or to be sent without a digital signature), you need to follow these additional steps:

1. **With any Messenger window open (Inbox, Message Center, or Message), click the New Msg toolbar button.**

   The Message Composition window appears.

2. **In the Address area of the Message Composition window, click the Message Sending Options button, which appears at the bottom of the three buttons on the left side of the Message area.**

   The Message Sending Options appear. A check mark appears next to the Encrypted or Signed options if you previously clicked either option in the Security dialog box.

3. **If you want to undo either of these options, click the check box to deselect it.**

4. **You can now address and write your message and then click the Send button in the Message Composition toolbar.**

   Your unencrypted or digitally unsigned message is sent on its way.

Picking a good password

Whether you're protecting your own computer, downloading software, subscribing to an online publication, or applying for a certificate (as I explain earlier in this chapter), picking a password that thieves won't be able to crack is important.

One good method for choosing a password is to take a phrase that's easy for you to remember and then use the first letter of each word to form the basis of a password. For example, the phrase "Early to Bed and Early to Rise" would be ETBAETR. Then, mix uppercase and lowercase, add punctuation, and you wind up with eTb[a]ETr. If you *really* want to make a password that's hard to crack, add some numerals as well, such as the last two digits of the year you were born: eTb[a]Etr59.

Whatever you do, follow these tips for effective password etiquette:

- ✔ **Don't use passwords that are in a dictionary:** Clever hackers can run a program that tries every word in an online dictionary as your password until they eventually discover it.

- ✔ **Don't use the same password at more than one site:** I know this is difficult because you tend to accumulate lots of different passwords after you've been online for a while. But if you use the same password all the time and your password to one site on the Internet is compromised, all your password-protected accounts are in jeopardy.

- ✔ **Use at least six characters:** The more letters in your password, the more work code-crackers have to go through.

It's especially important not to re-use the same password that you enter to connect to your account on a commercial service such as America Online or CompuServe as a password to an Internet site. If a hacker discovers your password on the Internet site, that person can use it to connect to your AOL or CompuServe account, too — and you'll have to pay for the time they spend online.

Protecting content with authentication

Authentication is another common security technique used on the Web. This measure simply involves assigning approved users an official username and password that they must enter before gaining access to a protected network, computer, or directory.

Most Web servers allow you to set up areas of your Web site to be protected by username and password. Not all Web hosts allow this, however, because it requires setting up and maintaining a special password file and storing the file in a special location on the computer that holds the Web server software. If you need to make some content on your business site (such as articles you've written) available only to registered users, talk to your Web host to see whether setting up a password-protected area is possible.

Chapter 13

Keeping It All Legal

• •

In This Chapter

▶ Protecting your company's name through trademarks

▶ Paying license fees to local authorities

▶ Avoiding copyright infringement

▶ Considering the pros and cons of incorporation

▶ Avoiding major legal infractions

• •

*A*s the field of e-commerce becomes more competitive, e-litigation, e-patents, e-trademarks, and other means of legal protection multiply correspondingly. The Microsoft antitrust suit, which is still dragging on as I write this, is only the most notable example. The courts are increasingly being called upon to resolve smaller e-squabbles and, literally, lay down the e-law.

For instance, in April 2002, the popular search service Overture sued another popular search service, Google, for allegedly stealing its patented system of presenting search results based on bids placed by advertisers and Web sites. In the first few months of 2002, the WIPO Arbitration and Mediation Center had resolved more than two dozen domain name disputes. Many of these were filed by large corporations seeking to gain control over domain names that were allegedly being held by small business "cybersquatters" that hold on to multiple domain names in the hope of selling them. In late 2001, Microsoft filed a lawsuit in U.S. District Court trying to stop a company called Lindows.com for allegedly infringing on its trademarked name.

As a new business owner, you risk getting in legal trouble of one sort or another because you lack experience in business law and you don't have lots of money with which to hire lawyers and accountants. You don't want to be learning for the first time about copyright law or the concept of intellectual property when you're in the midst of a dispute. In this chapter, I give you a heads-up on legal issues that you need to know about as an online business-person. Hopefully this information will help you head off trouble before it occurs.

Trade Names and Trademarks

A *trade name* is the name by which a business is known in the marketplace. A trade name can also be *trademarked*, which means that a business has taken the extra step of registering its trade name so that others can't use it. Big corporations protect their trade names and trademarks jealously, and sometimes court battles erupt over who can legally use a name.

What does this mean for your fledgling business? Although you may never get in a trademark battle yourself, and you may never trademark a name, you need to be careful which trade name you pick and how you use it. Choose a trade name that's easy to remember so that people can associate it with your company and return to you often when they're looking for the products or services that you provide. Also, as part of taking your new business seriously and planning for success, you may want to protect your right to use your name by registering the trademark, which is a relatively easy and inexpensive process.

You can trademark any visual element that accompanies a particular tangible product or line of goods, which serves to identify and distinguish it from products sold by other sources. In other words, a trademark is not necessarily just for your business's trade name. In fact, you can trademark letters, words, names, phrases, slogans, numbers, colors, symbols, designs, or shapes. For example, take a look at the cover of the book you're reading right now. Look closely and see how many ™ or ® symbols you see. The same trademarked items are shown at the Dummies Web site, as you can see in Figure 13-1. Even though the *For Dummies* heading doesn't bear a symbol, it's a trademark — believe me.

The ™ mark can be used with items that may have been registered with a particular state but not with the U.S. Patent and Trademark Office. The ® symbol means the item has been registered with the aforementioned office.

For most small businesses, the problem with trademarks is not so much protecting your own as it is stepping on someone else's. Research the name you want to use to make sure that you don't run into trouble.

Researching a trademark

To avoid getting sued for trademark infringement and having to change your trade name or even pay damages if you lose, you should conduct a trademark search. The goal of a trademark search is to discover any potential conflicts between your trade name and someone else's. Ideally, you conduct the search before you actually use your trade name or register for an official trademark.

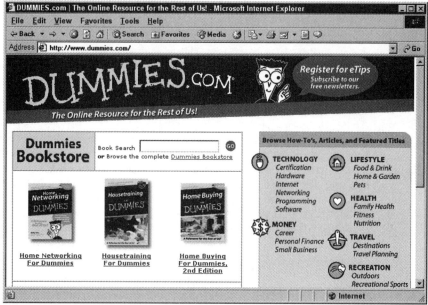

Figure 13-1:
You don't
have to use
special
symbols to
designate
logos or
phrases
on your
Web site,
but you may
want to.

You can do this search yourself the old-fashioned manual way by visiting one of the Patent and Trademark Depository Libraries (listed online at www.uspto.gov/go/ptdl/ptdlib_1.html). While time consuming, this approach doesn't cost anything.

Alternately, you can pay a professional search firm to research a trademark for you. Look for professional search firms in the Yellow Pages under Trademark Consultants or Information Brokers. You can expect to pay between $25 and $50 per mark searched. More complete searches that cover registered and unregistered marks that are similar to the one you want to use can cost several hundred dollars.

Of course, you're becoming a Cyberspace Expert, and as you may expect, you can use the Web and your own computer to help you conduct a trademark search. The best place to go is TESS, the United States Patent and Trademark Office's federal trademark database. This is the same as doing a search at a depository library, but it's more convenient because you can do the searching from the comfort of your computer. You can search the database from the Web for free at http://tess.uspto.gov/bin/gate.exe?f=tess&state=gktoq9.1.1.

Nolo.com sells a guide to doing trademark searches: Go to www.nolo.com/lawstore/atoz/a_to_z.cfm and scroll down the list of books to find Do Your Own Trademark Search. If you're on CompuServe, try searching the BizFile database of U.S. and Canadian businesses (**go:bizfile**). Also try Trademark Scan (**go:trademark**).

Cyberspace goes beyond national boundaries. A trademark search in your own country may not be enough. Most industrialized countries, including the United States, have signed international treaties that enable trademark owners in one country to enforce their rights against infringement by individuals in another country. If you are concerned about conducting business worldwide in the long term (and you should be, if you're planning for success), conduct an international trademark search. This undertaking is difficult to do yourself, so you may want to pay to have someone do the searching for you.

You may think that, just because you have a one-person business operating out of a spare room in your home, you can't possibly get in trouble by using a trademark owned by someone halfway around the world. This is dangerous thinking. The consequences of failing to conduct a reasonably thorough trademark search can be severe. In part, the consequences depend on how widely you distribute the protected item — and on the Internet, you can distribute it worldwide. If you attempt to use a trademark that has been federally registered by someone else, you could go to court and be prevented from using the mark again. You may even be liable for damages and attorney's fees. So it's best to be careful.

Protecting your trade name

In addition to a federal trademark law, each state has its own set of laws establishing when and how trademarks can be protected. You can obtain trademark rights in the states in which the mark is actually used, but you can also file an application with the United States Patent and Trademark Office.

After researching your trade name against existing trademarks, you can file an application with the Patent and Trademark Office online by following these steps:

1. **Connect to the Net, start up your browser and go to the Trademark Electronic Application System (TEAS) home page (**www.uspto.gov/teas/index.html, **shown in Figure 13-2).**

   This page includes a two-column table: The left column contains instructions on how to fill out your application online and pay by credit card; the right column explains how to print out the application form and mail it with a check to the Patent and Trademark Office.

2. **Click Apply for a NEW Mark under e-TEAS if you want to file online, or under PrinTEAS if you want to mail in your application.**

   The following steps assume that you want to file online. When you click Apply for a NEW Mark under the e-TEAS heading, a page with a list of application forms appears.

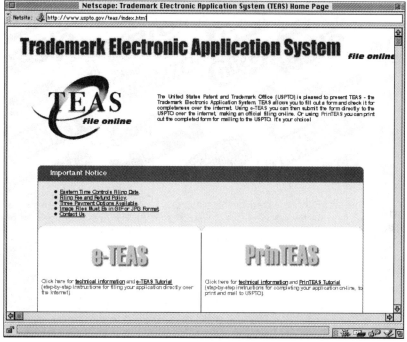

Figure 13-2:
You can quickly apply for your own federally registered trademark online using this site.

3. **Click Trademark/Servicemark Application, Principal Register.**

   The Trademark/Service Mark Application Form Wizard page appears.

4. **Select the appropriate radio buttons and menu options on this page (note that you're asked whether anyone else is already using the desired trademark because the program assumes that you've done a trademark search), and click Next at the bottom of the page.**

   An application form page appears.

5. **Fill out the required forms in the application, including your credit card data (so that you can pay the $325 per application fee) and the electronic signature fields at the bottom of the application.**

6. **You can attach a GIF or JPEG image of a symbol or logo that you want to trademark by clicking the Attach an Image link.**

   A new page appears that lets you specify the image. Even though the image you want to trademark may be in color, the image you submit with your application must be in black-and-white form.

7. **Click the Validate Form button at the bottom of the form.**

   If you filled out all the fields correctly, a Validation screen appears. If not, you return to the original form page so that you can correct it.

8. **Print the special declaration to support the adoption of the electronic signature, and retain it for your records, and then click the Submit button.**

   You receive a confirmation screen if your transmission is successful. Later, you will receive an e-mail acknowledgment of your submission.

Generally, each state has its own trademark laws, which apply only to trademarks to be used within a single state. Products that may be sold in more than one state (such as those sold on the Internet) can be protected under the federal Lanham Act, which provides for protection of registered trademarks. In order to comply with the Lanham Act, you register your trademark as described in the preceding series of steps.

Trademarks are listed in the trademarks register, last for 15 years, and are renewable. You don't have to use the ™ or ® symbol when you publish your trademark, but doing so impresses upon people how seriously you take your business and its identity.

Protecting your domain name

The practice of choosing a domain name for an online business is related to the concept of trade names and trademarks. By now, with "cybersquatters" and other businesspeople snapping up domain names since 1994 or so, it's unlikely that your ideal name is available in the popular .com domain. It's also likely that another business has a domain name very similar to yours or to the name of your business. You may well run into two common problems:

✔ Someone else has already taken the domain name related to the name of your existing business.

✔ The domain name you choose is close to one that already exists or to another company with a similar name. (Remember the Microsoft Windows/Lindows.com dispute that I mention at the beginning of this chapter?)

If the domain name that you think is perfect for your online business is already taken, you have some options. You can contact the owner of the domain name and offer to buy it. Alternatively, you can choose a domain name with another suffix. If a dot-com name isn't available, try the old standby alternatives, .org (which, in theory at least, is for nonprofit organizations), and .net (which is for network providers).

You can also choose one of the new Top-Level Domains (TLDs), a new set of domain name suffixes that have been made available, which include the following:

✔ **.biz** for businesses

✔ **.info** for general use

✔ **.name** for personal names

You can find out more about the new TLDs at the InterNIC Web site, `www.internic.net/faqs/new-tlds.html`.

You can always get around the fact that your perfect domain name isn't available by changing the name slightly. Instead of `treesurgeon.com` you might choose `tree-surgeon.com` or `treesurgery.com`. But be careful lest you violate someone else's trademark and get into a dispute with the holder of the other domain name. A court might order you to stop using the name and pay damages to the name's owner.

On the other hand, if you have been doing business for a while and have a trademarked name, and you find someone else owns the domain name, you can assert your rights and raise a dispute yourself. To resolve the dispute, you would go to a group like the WIPO Arbitration and Mediation Center (`arbiter.wipo.int/center/index.html`) or ICANN, the Internet Corporation for Assigned Names and Numbers (`www.icann.org`). But first, learn more about what constitutes trademark infringement and how to enforce a trademark. Go to Nolo.com's Legal Encyclopedia (`www.nolo.com/lawcenter/ency/index.cfm`), scroll down to click <u>Trademarks</u>, and then click <u>Using and Enforcing Trademarks</u>.

Copyright Management

What's the difference between a trademark and a copyright? Trademarks are covered by trademark law and are distinctive words, symbols, slogans, or other things that serve to identify products or services in the marketplace. Copyright, on the other hand, refers to the creator's ownership of creative works, such as writing, art, software, video, or cinema (but not names, titles, or short phrases). Copyright also provides the owner with redress in case someone copies the works without the owner's permission. Copyright is a legal device that enables the creator of a work the right to control how the work is to be used.

Although copyright protects the way ideas, systems, and processes are embodied in the book, record, photo, or whatever, it doesn't protect the idea, system, or process itself. In other words, if Thomas Jefferson were writing the Declaration of Independence today, the exact wording he chose to use in the Declaration would be copyrighted but the general ideas he expressed would not.

You may or may not consider yourself to be an intellectual, but as a business-person who produces goods and services of economic value, you may be the owner of intellectual property. *Intellectual property* refers to works of author-ship as well as certain inventions. Because intellectual property may be owned, bought, and sold just like other types of property, it's important that you know something about the copyright laws governing intellectual property. Having this information maximizes the value of your products and keeps you from throwing away potentially valuable assets or finding yourself at the wrong end of an expensive lawsuit.

What's protected by copyright

These days, the controversy regarding copyright on the Web centers on the Digital Millennium Copyright Act, which calls for Internet radio stations to pay high royalty fees to record labels for music they play. The copyright act contains at least one provision that has implications for all online businesses: Internet service providers are expected to remove material from any cus-tomer Web sites that appear to constitute copyright infringement. So it pays to know something about copyright.

Everything you see on the Net is copyrighted, whether or not a copyright notice actually appears. For example, plenty of art is available for the taking on the Web, but look before you grab. Unless an image on the Web is specified as being copyright-free, you'll be violating copyright law if you take it. HTML tags themselves aren't copyrighted, but the content of the HTML-formatted page is. General techniques for designing Web pages are not copyrighted, but certain elements (such as logos) are.

Keep in mind that it's okay to use a work for criticism, comment, news report-ing, teaching, scholarship, or research. That comes under the "fair use" limita-tion. (See the nearby sidebar, "Fair use . . . and how not to abuse it" for more information.) However, I still contend that it's best to get permission or cite your source in these cases, just to be safe.

URLs are not protected but complete lists of URLs (otherwise known as *link lists*) can be copyrighted. Don't simply copy someone else's link list wholesale and put it on one of your Web pages. Read the Copyright Web site's article on the subject at www.benedict.com/digital/webIssues/webIssues.asp.

How to protect your copyright

A copyright — which protects original works of authorship — costs nothing, applies automatically, and lasts more than 50 years. When you affix a copyright notice to your newsletter or Web site, you make your readers think twice about unauthorized copying and put them on notice that you take copyright seriously. You can go a step further and register your work with the U.S. Copyright Office.

Creating a good copyright notice

Even though any work you do is automatically protected by copyright, having some sort of notice expresses your copyright authority in a more official way. Copyright notices identify the author of a given work (such as writing or software) and then spell out the terms by which that author grants others the right (or the license) to copy that work to their computer and read it (or use it). The usual copyright notice is pretty simple and takes this form:

```
Copyright 2002 [Your Name] All rights reserved
```

You don't have to use the © symbol, but it does make your notice look more official. In order to create a copyright symbol that appears on a Web page, you have to enter a special series of characters in the HTML source code for your page. For example, Web browsers translate the characters `&copy;` as the copyright symbol, whish is displayed as © in the Web browser window. Most Web page creation tools provide menu options for inserting special symbols like this one.

Copyright notices can also be more informal, and a personal message can have extra impact. The graphic design company Echoed Sentiments Publishing (`www.espdesign.bigstep.com/`) includes both the usual copyright notice plus an extra message about digital watermarks, as shown in Figure 13-3.

Fair use . . . and how not to abuse it

Copyright law doesn't cover everything. One of the major limitations is the doctrine of *fair use*, which is described in Section 107 of the U.S. Copyright Act. The law states that fair use of a work is use that does not infringe copyright "for purposes such as criticism, comment, news reporting, teaching (including multiple copies for classroom use), scholarship, or research." You can't copy text from online magazines or newsletters and call it fair use because the text was originally news reporting.

Fair use has some big gray areas that can be traps for people who provide information on the Internet. Don't fall in to one of these traps. Shooting off a quick e-mail asking someone for permission to reproduce their work isn't difficult. Chances are, that person will be flattered and will let you make a copy as long as you give him or her credit on your site.

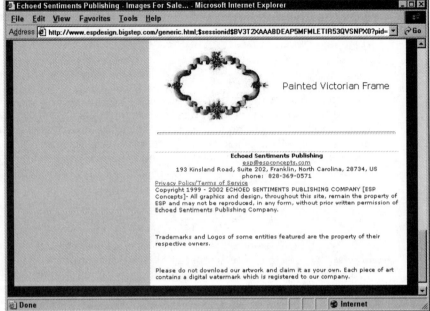

Figure 13-3:
If your
products
are
particularly
precious,
such as
unique
works of art
you want to
sell, assert
your
copyright
over them
on your
Web site.

Adding digital watermarks

In traditional offset printing, a *watermark* is a faint image embedded in stationery or other paper. The watermark usually bears the name of the paper
manufacturer, but it can also identify an organization for whom the stationery
was made.

Watermarking has its equivalent in the online world. Graphic artists sometimes
use a technique called *digital watermarking* to protect images they create.
This process involves adding copyright or other information about the
image's owner to the digital image file. The information added may or may
not be visible. (The image shown in Figure 13-3 has copyright information
added, not visible in the body of the Web page but in the image file itself.)

Digimarc, which functions as a plug-in application with the popular graphics
tools Adobe Photoshop (`www.adobe.com`) and Paint Shop Pro 7 (`www.jasc.
com`), is one of the most widely used watermarking tools.

Registering your copyright

Registering your copyright is something I recommend for small businesses
because it's inexpensive and easy to do, and it affords you an extra degree
of protection. Having registered your copyright gives your case more weight
in the event of a copyright dispute. You don't need to register, but doing so
shows a court how serious you are about obtaining protection for your work.

To register your work, you can download an application form from the U.S. Copyright Office Web site at www.loc.gov/copyright/forms/. This form is in Adobe Acrobat PDF format, so you need Acrobat Reader to view it. (Adobe Acrobat Reader is a free application that you can download from the Adobe Systems Incorporated Web site at www.adobe.com.) You can then send the form by snail mail, along with a check for $30 and a printed copy of the work you are protecting, to Library of Congress, Copyright Office, 101 Independence Avenue, S.E., Washington, DC 20559-6000.

At this writing, the Copyright Office's online registration system (which is called CORDS) is still being tested and is not yet widely available.

Licensing and Other Restrictions

Another set of legal concerns that you need to be aware of when you start an online business involves any license fees or restrictions that are levied by local agencies. Some fees are specific to businesses that have incorporated, which brings up the question of whether you should consider incorporation for your own small business. (I discuss the legal concerns and pros and cons of incorporation in the upcoming section, "Determining the Legal Form of Your Business.")

Knowing about local fees or restrictions

Before you get too far along with your online business, make sure that you have met any local licensing requirements that apply. For example, in my county in the state of Illinois, I had to pay a $10 fee to register my sole proprietorship. In return, I received a nice certificate that made everything feel official.

Other localities may have more stringent requirements, however. Check with city, county, and state licensing and/or zoning offices. Trade associations for your profession often have a wealth of information about local regulations as well. Also, check with your local chamber of commerce. If you fail to apply for a permit or license, you may find yourself paying substantial fines.

The kinds of local regulations to which a small business may be susceptible include the following:

✔ **Zoning:** Your city or town government may have *zoning ordinances* (shudder) that prevent you from conducting business in an area that is zoned for residential use, or they may charge you a fee to operate a business out of your home. This policy varies by community; even if your Web host resides in another state, your local government may still consider your home the location of your business. Check with your local zoning department.

- **Doing Business As:** If your business name is different from your own name, you may have to file a Doing Business As (DBA) certificate and publish a notice of the filing in the local newspaper. Check with your city or county clerk's office for more information.

- **Taxes:** Some states and cities levy taxes on small businesses, and some even levy property tax on business assets such as office furniture and (uh-oh) computer equipment.

Keeping up with trade restrictions

If you are planning to sell your goods and services overseas, you need to be aware of any trade restrictions that may apply to your business. In particular, you need to be careful if any of the following applies:

- You trade in foodstuffs or agricultural products.

- You sell software that uses some form of encryption.

- Your clients live in countries with which your home country has imposed trade restrictions.

For more detailed suggestions of how to research international trade law, see Chapter 8.

The Arent Fox Web site, which is run by a Washington, D.C.-based law firm, has lots of good legal information for people who want to do business online. Of particular interest is its E-TIPSheet (www.arentfox.com/publications/E-TIPSheet/e-tipsheet.html), which publishes news about trademark, licensing, and doing business internationally on the Internet.

Determining the Legal Form of Your Business

Picking a legal form for your online business enables you to describe it to city and county agencies as well as to the financial institutions with which you deal. A legal type of business is one that is recognized by taxing and licensing agencies. You have a number of options from which to choose, and the choice can affect the amount of taxes you pay and your liability in case of loss. The following sections describe your alternatives.

If you're looking for more information, Eric Tyson and Jim Schell explore the legal and financial aspects of starting and operating a small business in *Small Business For Dummies*.

Sole proprietorship

In a *sole proprietorship*, you're the only boss. You make all the decisions and you get all the benefits. On the other hand, you take all the risk, too. This is the simplest and least expensive type of business because you can run it yourself. You don't need an accountant or lawyer to help you form the business, and you don't have to answer to partners or stockholders, either. To declare a sole proprietorship, you may have to file an application with your county clerk.

Partnership

In a partnership, you share the risk and profit with at least one other person. Ideally, your partners bring skills to the endeavor that complement your own contributions. One obvious advantage to a partnership is that you can discuss decisions and problems with your partner. All partners are held personally liable for losses. The rate of taxes that each partner pays is based on his or her percentage of income from the partnership.

If you decide to strike up a partnership with someone, drawing up a Partnership Agreement is a good idea. Although you aren't legally required to do so, such an agreement clearly spells out the duration of the partnership and the responsibilities of each person involved. In the absence of such an agreement, the division of liabilities and assets is considered to be equal, regardless of how much more effort one person has put into the business than the other.

Incorporation

If sole proprietorships and partnerships are so simple to start up and operate, why would you consider incorporating? After all, you almost certainly need a lawyer to help you incorporate. Plus, you have to comply with the regulations made by federal and state agencies that oversee corporations. Besides that, you may undergo a type of *double taxation*: If your corporation earns profits, those profits are taxed at the corporate rate, and any shareholders have to pay income tax at the personal rate.

Despite these downsides, you may want to consider incorporation for the following sorts of reasons:

- If you have employees, you can deduct any health and disability insurance premiums that you pay.
- You can raise capital by offering stock for sale.

✔ Transferring ownership from one shareholder to another is easier.

✔ The company's principals are shielded from liability in case of lawsuits.

If you offer services that may be susceptible to costly lawsuits, incorporation may be the way to go. You then have two options: a C corporation or a sub-chapter S corporation. The latter is the most likely choice for small businesses.

Subchapter S corporations

One benefit of forming a subchapter S corporation is liability protection. This form of incorporation enables start-up businesses that encounter losses early on to offset those losses against their personal income. Subchapter S is intended for businesses with fewer than 75 shareholders. The income gained by an S corporation is subject only to personal tax, not corporate tax.

Sounds great, doesn't it? Before you start looking for a lawyer to get you started, consider the following:

✔ Incorporation typically costs several hundred dollars.

✔ Corporations must pay an annual tax.

✔ Attorneys' fees can be expensive.

✔ Filing for S corporation status can take weeks or months to be received and approved. (You need to meet your state's requirements for setting up a corporation, then file Form 2553 to "elect" S corporation status.)

All these facts can be daunting for a lone entrepreneur who's just starting out and has only a few customers. I recommend that you wait until you have enough income to hire an attorney and pay incorporation fees before you seriously consider incorporating, even as an S corporation.

C corporations

Many big businesses choose to become C corporations. In fact, everything about C corporations tends to be big — including profits, which are taxed at the corporate level — so I mention this legal designation only in passing because it's probably not for your small entrepreneurial business. C corpora-tions tend to be large and have lots of shareholders. In order to incorporate, all stockholders and shareholders must agree on the name of the company, the choice of the people who will manage it, and many other issues.

Limited liability corporations

The limited liability corporation (LLC) is a relatively new type of corporation that combines aspects of both S and C corporations. Limited liability corpo-rations have a number of attractive options that make them good candidates for small businesses (such as the Collectible Exchange, LLC, which is profiled in Chapter 1). Benefits include the following:

> ✔ Members have limited liability for debts and obligations of the LLC.
>
> ✔ LLCs receive favorable tax treatment.
>
> ✔ Income and losses are shared by the individual investors, who are called members.

An LLC can be a sole proprietorship, corporation, or a partnership. A similar entity, a Limited Liability Partnership (LLP) needs to be a partnership. The responsibilities of LLC members are spelled out in an operating agreement, an often complex document that should be prepared by a knowledgeable attorney.

Steering Clear of Legal Trouble

A big part of keeping your online business legal is steering clear of so-called business opportunities that can turn into big problems. You can run into trouble both at the federal or the local level. In the following sections, I highlight some areas to watch out for.

Be wary of multilevel marketing

Be careful if you undertake *multilevel marketing* (MLM), also known as *network marketing*. Multilevel marketing /network marketing is a strategy used by many reputable firms, such as Amway: You recruit some people to help you, and those people, in turn, recruit others to help them. No doubt, some network marketers are on the up-and-up. But other companies (many of which you can find online) use MLM to run an old-fashioned pyramid scheme in which the participants recruit other investors. I'm not saying that you shouldn't look into network marketing at all; I'm saying that you should be very careful about how much money you have to commit in order to play the game.

The U.S. Postal Service treats MLM businesses as lotteries; go to `www.usps.gov/websites/depart/inspect/pyramid.htm` to read the warning about them. Fraudulent pyramid schemes typically violate the Postal Lottery Statute (Title 18, United States Code, Section 1302). Yahoo! also maintains a list of Web pages that warn against MLM schemes, which you can find at `dir.yahoo.com/Business_and_Economy/Business_to_Business/Business_Opportunities/Network_Marketing/Anti_Network_Marketing/`. Don't be taken in by someone who wants you to participate in a questionable MLM-type scheme.

Steer clear of the seven dirty words

Ever heard of the "seven dirty words" made famous in a routine by comedian George Carlin? The Federal Communications Commission (FCC) has banned them from being uttered on TV and radio broadcasts. However, the FCC does not regulate the Internet. The U.S. Supreme Court struck down the Communications Decency Act, which sought to regulate "obscene" communications on the Internet. Then the Child Online Protection Act (COPA) was passed by Congress, but it was struck down in federal court.

Now, there's the Children's Internet Protection Act (CIPA), which was signed into law by President Bill Clinton in late 2001. It requires schools and libraries to filter pornography, obscenity, and other material deemed offensive to children. At this writing it, too, is being challenged in court.

It might seem like you can say whatever you want online. But you might get your site filtered out, not only by a librarian but by a parent using child-safety software. So use your judgment as a businessperson. You don't want to turn away potential customers by your choice of language. Also, make sure you don't violate your ISP's terms of use, lest you find your Web site suddenly offline.

Be aware of risks with adult content

Be careful if you provide so-called adult content. There's no doubt about it: Cyberspace is full of X-rated sites, some of which do make money. But this is a risky area. Congress continues to debate legislation that may legally require online vendors of adult material to restrict access to sites by persons less than 17 years of age. Additionally, many ISPs prohibit you from publishing Web pages that contain adult content.

If you do sell adult items online, consider working with a blocking company, such as SurfWatch (www.surfwatch.com) or Net Nanny (www.netnanny.com/home/home.asp) that can prevent minors from visiting your site.

Know about acceptable use policies

Be aware of acceptable use policies set up by agencies that control what goes out online. Usually, the company that hosts your Web site has a set of acceptable use guidelines spelling out what kind of material you can and can't publish. For example, America Online has its own policies for its members who create home pages through AOL.

Another important kind of acceptable use policy that you need to know about is the acceptable use policy issued by your Internet service provider. The most common restriction is one against *spamming* (sending out unsolicited bulk mailings). Not following your Web host's or your ISP's guidelines can get you kicked off the Internet, so make sure that you're aware of any restrictions by reading the guidelines posted on your ISP's or Web host's site.

Pay your state sales taxes

Sales tax varies from state to state. Your job as an online storeowner is to charge the sales tax rate applicable in the state in which the purchase is made — that is, the state where your customer lives, not where you live. (See Chapter 14 for a more detailed examination of the sales tax situation.)

Luckily, computer software is available to help you calculate sales taxes for every state. Many Web hosting services or ISPs also help with sales tax collection, among their other services. Shopping cart programs and some electronic storefront programs, such as the ones that I discuss in Chapter 4, help you calculate sales tax, too.

If you don't have a hosting service or ISP to provide you with e-commerce software, however, you have to download software or look up sales tax rates on your own. A wonderful utiltity called Online Sales Tax Calculator, provided by the Sales Tax Clearinghouse, will do the work for you. Just access the calculator at thestc.com/RateCalc.stm. Enter your home state and the city and state where your customer resides. Press Lookup, and the calculator will not only look up the county where the customer resides but also report any applicable local sales taxes and calculate them for you. If you need to calculate Canadian sales taxes, you can download a shareware application called Sales Tax Calculator, by Carter Computer Solutions (www.niagara.com/~mcarter/taxw.htm). You can download and try the program for 30 days; if you want to keep Sales Tax Calculator, you need to pay a modest $15 fee.

Chapter 14

Online Business Accounting Tools

*S*ome people have a gift for keeping track of expenses, recording financial information, and performing other fiscal functions. Unfortunately, I'm not one of those people. Yet I know well the value of accounting procedures, especially those that relate to an online business.

Without having at least some minimal records of your day-to-day operations, you won't have any way — other than the proverbial "gut feeling" — of knowing whether your business is truly successful. Besides that, banks and taxing authorities don't put much stock in gut feelings. When the time comes to ask for a loan or to pay taxes, you'll regret not having records close at hand.

In this chapter, I introduce you to some simple, straightforward ways to handle your online business's financial information — and all businesspeople know that accurate record keeping is essential when revenues dwindle and expenses must be reduced. Read on to discover the most important accounting practices and find out about software that can help you tackle the essential fiscal tasks that you need to undertake to keep your new business viable.

Basic Accounting Practices

The most important accounting practices for your online business can be summarized as follows:

> ✔ **Deciding what type of business you're going to be:** Are you going to be a sole proprietorship, partnership, or corporation? (See more about determining a legal form for your business in Chapter 13.)

> ✔ **Establishing good record keeping practices:** Record expenses and income in ways that will help you at tax time.
>
> ✔ **Obtaining financing when you need it:** Although getting started in business online doesn't cost a lot, you may want to expand someday, and good accounting can help you do it.

There's nothing sexy about accounting (unless, of course, you're married to an accountant; in that case, you have a financial expert at hand and can skip this chapter anyway!). Then again, there's nothing enjoyable about unexpected cash shortages or other problems that can result from bad record keeping.

Good accounting is the key to order and good management for your business. How else can you know how you're doing? Yet many new businesspeople are intimidated by the numbers game. Use the tool at hand — your computer — to help you overcome your fear: Start keeping those books!

Choosing an accounting method

Accepting that you have to keep track of your business's accounting is only half the battle; next, you need to decide how to do it. The point at which you make note of each transaction in your books and the period of time over which you record the data make a difference not only to your accountant but also to agencies such as the Internal Revenue Service. Even if you hire someone to keep the books for you, it's good to know what options are open to you.

 You don't have to take my word for all this. Consult the Internal Revenue Service Publication 334, Tax Guide for Small Businesses (www.irs.gov/pub/irs-pdf/p334.pdf). Review section 2, Accounting Periods and Methods, which explains how to do everything right when tax time comes. Also check out the Accounting System section of the CCH Business Owner's Toolkit site (www.toolkit.cch.com/text/P06_1300.asp).

Cash-basis versus accrual-basis accounting

Don't be intimidated by these terms: They are simply two methods of totaling up income and expenses. Exactly where and how you do the recording is up to you. You can take a piece of paper, divide it into two columns labeled *Income* and *Expenses*, and do it that way. (I describe some more high-tech tools later in this chapter.) These are just two standard ways of deciding when to report them:

> ✔ **Cash-basis accounting:** You report income when you actually receive it and write off expenses when you pay them. This is the easy way to report income and expenses, and probably the way most new small businesses do it.

✔ **Accrual-basis accounting:** This method is more complicated than the cash-basis method, but if your online business maintains an inventory, you must use the accrual method. You report income when you actually receive the payment; you write down expenses *when services are rendered* (even though you may not have made the cash payment yet). For example, if a payment is due on December 1, but you send the check out on December 8, you record the bill as being paid on December 1, when the payment was originally due. Accrual-basis accounting creates a more accurate picture of a business's financial situation. If a business is experiencing cash flow problems and is extending payment on some of its bills, cash-basis accounting provides an unduly rosy financial picture, whereas the accrual-basis method would be more accurate.

Choosing an accounting period

The other choice you need to make when it comes to deciding how to keep your books is the accounting period you're going to use. Here, again, you have two choices:

✔ **Calendar year:** The calendar year ends on December 31. This is the period with which you're probably most familiar and the one most small or home-based businesses choose because it's the easiest to work with.

✔ **Fiscal year:** In this case, the business picks a date other than December 31 to function as the end of the fiscal year. Many large organizations pick a date that coincides with the end of their business cycle. Some pick March 31 as the end, others June 30, and still others September 30.

If you use the fiscal-year method of accounting, you must file your tax return three and a half months after the end of the fiscal year. If the fiscal year ends on June 30, for example, you must file by October 15.

Knowing what records to keep

When you run your own business, it pays to be meticulous about recording everything that pertains to your commercial activities. The more you understand what you have to record, the more accurate your records will be — and the more deductions you can take, too. Go to the office supply store and get a financial record book called a *journal*, which is set up with columns for income and expenses.

Tracking income

Receiving checks for your goods or services is the fun part of doing business, and so income is probably the kind of data that you'll be happiest about recording.

You need to keep track of your company's income (or, as it is sometimes called, your *gross receipts*) carefully. Not all the income your business receives is taxable. What you receive as a result of sales (your *revenue*) is taxable, but loans that you receive aren't. Be sure to separate the two and pay tax only on the sales income. But keep good records: If you can't accurately report the source of income that you didn't pay taxes on, the IRS will label it *unreported income*, and you'll have to pay taxes and possibly fines and penalties on it.

Just how should you record your revenue? For each item, write down a brief, informal statement. This is a personal record that you may make on a slip of paper or even on the back of a canceled check. Be sure to include the following information:

- ✔ Amount received
- ✔ Type of payment (credit card, electronic cash, or check)
- ✔ Date of the transaction
- ✔ Name of client or customer
- ✔ Goods or services you provided in exchange for the payment

Collect all your check stubs and revenue statements in a folder labeled *Income* so that you can find them easily at tax time.

Assessing your assets

Assets are resources that your business owns, such as your office and computer equipment. *Equity* refers to your remaining assets after you pay your creditors.

Any equipment you have that contributes to your business activities constitutes your assets. Equipment that has a life span of more than a year is expected to help you generate income over its useful life; therefore, you must spread out (or, in other words, *expense*) the original cost of the equipment over its life span. Expensing the cost of an asset over the period of its useful life is called *depreciation*. In order to depreciate an item, you estimate how many years you're going to use it and then divide the original cost by the number of years. The result is the amount that you report in any given year. For example, if you purchase a computer that costs $3,000 and you expect to use it in your business for five years, you expense $600 of the cost each year.

You need to keep records of your assets that include the following information:

- ✔ Name, model number, and description
- ✔ Purchase date
- ✔ Purchase price, including fees

✔ Date the item went into service

✔ Amount of time the item is put to personal (as opposed to business) use

File these records in a safe location along with your other tax-related information.

Recording payments

Even a lone entrepreneur doesn't work in a vacuum. An online business owner needs to pay a Web host, an ISP, and possibly Web page designers and other consultants. If you take on partners or employees, things get more complicated. But in general, you need to record all payments such as these in detail as well.

Your accountant is likely to bring up the question of how you pay the people who work for you. You have two options: You can treat them either as full- or part-time employees or as independent contractors. The IRS uses a stringent series of guidelines to determine who is a contractor and who is a full-time employee. Refer to the IRS Publication 15A (`www.irs.gov/pub/irs-pdf/p15a.pdf`), which discusses the employee/independent contractor subject in detail.

Hiring independent contractors rather than salaried workers is far simpler for you: You don't have to pay benefits to independent contractors, and you don't have to withhold federal and state taxes. Just be sure to get invoices from any independent contractor who works for you. If you have full-time employees whom you pay an hourly wage, things get more complicated, and you had best consult an accountant to help you set up the salary payments.

Listing expenses

When you break down business expenses on Schedule C (Profit or Loss from Business) of your federal tax return, you need to keep track of two kinds of expenses:

✔ The first type of expenses (simply called "Expenses" in Part II of Schedule C) includes travel, business meals, advertisements, postage, and other costs that you incur in order to *produce revenue.*

✔ The second kind of expenses (grouped under "Other Expenses" in Part V of Schedule C) includes instances when you're just exchanging one asset (cash) for another (a printer or modem, for example).

The difference between "Expenses" and "Other Expenses" lies in how close the relationship is between the expense and revenue produced. In the case of the Part II "Expenses," your expenditure is directly related — you wouldn't take out an add or take a business trip if you didn't expect it to produce revenue. In the second case, the act of spending money doesn't directly result in more revenue for you. You would purchase a modem, for instance, to help you communicate and get information online, not just to boost your bottom line. You do *hope*, though, that the equipment being purchased will *eventually* help you produce revenue.

Get a big folder and use it to hold any receipts, contracts, canceled checks, credit card statements, or invoices that represent expenses. It's also a great idea to maintain a record of expenses that includes the following information:

- ✔ Date the expense occurred
- ✔ Name of the person or company that received payment from you
- ✔ Type of expense incurred (equipment, utilities, supplies, and so on)

Recalling exactly what some receipts were for is often difficult a year or even just a month after the fact. Be sure to jot down a quick note on all canceled checks and copies of receipts to remind you of what the expense involved.

Understanding the Ps and Qs of P&Ls

You're likely to hear the term *profit-and-loss statement* (also called a P&L) thrown around when discussing your online business with financial people. A P&L is a report that measures the operation of a business over a given period of time, such as a week, a month, or a year. The person who prepares the P&L (either you or your accountant) adds up your business revenues and subtracts the operating expenses. What's left are either the profits or the losses.

Most of the accounting programs listed later in this chapter and in this book's Internet Directory include some way of presenting profit-and-loss statements and enable you to customize the statements to fit your needs.

Accounting Software for Your Business

The well-known commercial accounting packages, such as Quicken, Microsoft Money, QuickBooks and M.Y.O.B., let you prepare statements and reports and even tie into a tax preparation system. Stick with these programs if you like setting up systems such as databases on your computer. Otherwise, go for a simpler method and hire an accountant to help you.

Whatever program you choose, make sure that you're able to keep accurate books and set up privacy schemes that prevent your kids from zapping your business records.

If your business is a relatively simple sole proprietorship, you can record expenses and income by hand and add them up at tax time. Then carry them through to Schedule C or IRS Form 1040. Alternatively, you can record your entries and turn them over to a tax advisor who will prepare a profit-and-loss statement and tell you the balance due on your tax payment.

If you're looking to save a few dollars and want an extra-simple accounting program that you can set up right now, look no farther than Owl Simple Business Accounting 2, available for Windows 95 or later. Mac users can try WhereDidAllMyMoneyGo? by Bert Torfs (users.pandora.be/bert.torfs/WhereIst.html).

Simple Business Accounting 2, by Owl Software (www.owlsoftware.com/sba.htm), really lives up to its name. It's so simple that even a financially impaired person like yours truly can pick it up quickly. Owl Simple Business Accounting 2 (SBA) is designed to let people with no prior accounting experience keep track of income and expenses, and it uses the single-entry accounting system favored by the IRS. You can try the program for 30 days, and then pay $39 to keep it.

The following steps illustrate how easy it is to start keeping books with SBA. These instructions assume that you have downloaded and installed the software from the Owl Software Web site.

1. **Choose Start⇨Programs⇨OWL Business Apps⇨SB Accounting 2.**

   The main Owl Simple Business Accounting window appears, as shown in Figure 14-1.

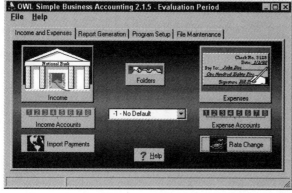

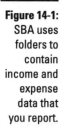

Figure 14-1: SBA uses folders to contain income and expense data that you report.

The program comes with a set of sample data already entered to help you learn its features. Choose Help⇨Help to open the SBA User's Guide help files. Click the topic Getting Started if you want an overview of how the program operates.

2. **Click the Program Setup tab to bring it to the front, and make any custom changes you may want:**

  • If you want to operate in a fiscal year different from the pre-entered January 1, enter the number for the new month that you want to set as the beginning of your fiscal year.

  • If you want your on-screen and printed reports to be in a different font than the preselected one (MS Sans Serif), click the Report Font button, choose the font you want, and then click OK to close the Font dialog box. Times New Roman is usually a good choice because it's relatively compact.

3. **Click the File Maintenance tab to bring it to the front, and then click the Erase Data button. When asked if you want to erase expense data or other information, click OK.**

  This step erases the sample data that was pre-entered to show you how the program works.

4. **Select the Income and Expenses tab to bring it to the front, and then click the Folders button to create folders for your business data.**

  The PickFol dialog box appears, as shown in Figure 14-2. This dialog box lists any folders that have been created.

Figure 14-2:
Use this dialog box to add, delete, or edit folders that hold your business data.

5. **Click New.**

  The Folder Definition dialog box appears.

6. **Enter a new name in the Description box and click Save.**

  A Confirm dialog box appears asking if you want to add another folder.

7. **If you do, click Yes and repeat Step 6; when you're done, click No.**

   The Folder Definition dialog box closes, and you return to the PickFol dialog box, where your renamed folder or folders appear.

   You may want to create separate folders for your personal or business finances, for example. After your folders are set up, you can record data as the following steps describe.

8. **Click Exit.**

   The PickFol dialog box closes and you return to the main OWL Simple Business Accounting window.

9. **Select the Income and Expenses tab to bring it to the front and then click either the Income Accounts or Expense Accounts button to create an Income or Expense Account.**

   The Select Account dialog box appears.

10. **Click New.**

    The Account Definition dialog box appears.

11. **Enter a name for the account in the Description dialog box, and then click Save.**

    A dialog box appears asking if you want to create another account.

12. **If you do, click Yes and repeat Step 11; when you're done, click No.**

    The Select Account dialog box appears, listing the items you just created.

13. **Click Exit.**

    You return to the main OWL Simple Business Accounting window.

14. **When you've created Income and Expense Accounts, click either the Income button or the Expense button, depending on the type of data you want to enter.**

    Depending on the button you clicked, the Select Income or Select Expense dialog box appears.

15. **Click New to enter a new item.**

    A dialog box named either Income or Expense appears, depending on the button you selected in Step 14.

16. **Enter the amount and description in the appropriate fields and click Save.**

    The Confirm dialog box appears asking you to confirm that you either want to add or delete a record.

17. **Click No.**

    You return to the Income or Expense dialog box, where you can make more entries.

18. **When you finish, click Save.**

    You return to the Select Item dialog box, where you can review your changes.

19. **Click Exit.**

    You return to the Income and Expenses options.

20. **When you're all finished, choose File⇨Exit to exit the program until your next accounting session.**

After entering some data, you can select the Report Generation tab, run each of the reports provided by SBA, and examine the output. SBA can generate the following reports: Expense Reports, Income Reports, Profit Reports, a General Ledger Report, and a Check Register. When running the reports, be sure to select a reporting period within the current calendar year.

Small Business Tax Concerns

After you make it through the start-up phase of your business, it's time to be concerned with taxes. Here, too, a little preparation up front can save you lots of headaches down the road. But as a hard-working entrepreneur, time is your biggest obstacle.

In an American Express survey, 26 percent reported that they wait until the last minute to start preparing their taxes, and 13.9 percent said that they usually ask for an extension. Yet advance planning is really important for taxes. In fact, Internal Revenue Code Section 6001 mandates that businesses must keep records appropriate to their trade or business. The IRS has the right to view these records if they want to audit your business's (or your personal) tax return. If your records aren't to the IRS's satisfaction, the penalties can be serious.

Should you charge sales tax?

This is one of the most frequently asked questions I receive from readers: Should I charge sales tax for what I sell online? The short answer is that it depends on whether or not your state collects sales tax at all. There's no single regulation that applies to all states equally.

If your state doesn't collect sales tax (at this writing, five states — Montana, Alaska, Delaware, New Hampshire, and Oregon — do not), you don't need to, either. However, if your state requires it, yes, you need to collect sales tax — but only from customers who live in the same state where your company has a "physical presence." A state's tax laws apply only within its own borders. If you're located in Ohio, for instance, your business is subject to Ohio sales tax regulations, but only for transactions that are completed in Ohio. If you sell to someone in, say, California, you don't need to collect sales tax from that California resident. But because tax laws change frequently, the safest thing I can tell you is to check with your own state's department of revenue to make sure.

The nature of what constitutes a "physical presence" varies. Some states define it as an office or warehouse. If you take orders only by phone or online, you don't have to collect sales tax. But again, check with your state. Also, most states require that their merchants charge sales tax on shipping and handling charges as well as the purchase price.

One good piece of news is that the President has signed a two-year extension of The Internet Tax Freedom Act, which calls for a freeze on new taxes on Internet access and e-commerce. It's in effect until October of 2003. You can read a "Plain English" version of the law as well as the latest news about it at cox.house.gov/nettax.

The Internet Tax Freedom Act does *not* mean that Internet sales are free from sales tax. It means only that states can't impose any new sales tax requirements on Internet merchants over and above what other merchants already have to collect in sales tax. To deal with this supposed loophole, most states charge a "use" tax in addition to a sales tax: If a resident of the state makes a purchase from another state, the transaction is still subject to use tax. But one state can't compel a merchant located in another state to collect its use tax — only merchants located within its own borders.

Sales tax varies from state to state, city to city, and county to county. Some states tax only sales of tangible personal property, while others tax services as well. Not only that, but some counties and municipalities levy local taxes on sales. Check with your local comptroller or department of revenue to find out for sure what your requirements are.

Federal and state taxes

Although operating a business does complicate your tax return, it's something you can handle if your business is a simple one-person operation, if you're willing to expend the time, and, finally, if you have kept the proper business records.

If you have a sole proprietorship, you need to file IRS form Schedule C along with your regular form 1040 tax return. If your sole proprietorship has net income, you're also required to file Schedule SE to determine any Social Security and FICA taxes that are due.

State taxes vary depending on where you live. You most likely need to file sales tax and income tax. If you have employees, you also need to pay employee withholding tax. Contact a local accountant in order to find out what you have to file, or contact the state tax department yourself. Most state tax offices provide guidebooks to help you understand state tax requirements.

When you start making money for yourself independently, rather than depending on a regular paycheck from an employer, you have to start doing something you've probably never done before: You have to start estimating the tax you will have to pay based on the income from your own business. You're then required to pay this tax on a quarterly basis, both to the IRS and to your state taxing agency. Estimating and paying quarterly taxes is an important part of meeting your tax obligations as a self-employed person.

A page full of links to state tax agencies is available at `www.tannedfeet.com/state_tax_agencies.htm`.

Deducing your business deductions

One of the benefits of starting a new business, even if the business isn't profitable in the beginning, is the opportunity to take business deductions and reduce your tax payments. Always keep receipts from any purchases or expenses associated with your business activities. Make sure that you're taking all the deductions for which you're eligible. I mention some of these deductions in the following sections.

Your home office

If you work at home (and I'm assuming that, as an entrepreneur, you probably do), set aside some space for a home office. This isn't just a territorial thing. It can result in some nifty business deductions, too.

Taking a home office deduction used to be difficult because a 1993 Supreme Court decision stated that, unless you met with clients, customers, or patients on a regular basis in your home office, you couldn't claim the home-office deduction. However, the 1997 tax law eliminates the client requirement and requires only that the office be used "regularly and exclusively" for business.

What you deduct depends on the amount of space in your home that's used for your business. If your office is one room in a four-room house, you can deduct 25 percent of your utilities, for example. However, if you have a separate phone line that's solely for business use, you can deduct 100 percent of that expense.

Your computer equipment

Computer equipment is probably the biggest expense related to your online business. But taking tax deductions can help offset the cost substantially. The key is showing the IRS (by reporting your income from your online business on your tax return) that you used your PC and related items, such as modems or printers, for business purposes. You track what you spend on computer equipment in the "Other Expenses" section, which is Part V of Schedule C in your federal tax return.

In case you're ever audited, be sure to keep some sort of record detailing all the ways in which you have put your computer equipment to use for business purposes. If less than half of your computer use is for your business, consider depreciating its cost over several years.

Other common business deductions

Many of the business-related expenses that you can deduct are listed on IRS form Schedule C. The following is a brief list of some of the deductions you can look for:

- ✔ Advertising fees
- ✔ Internet access charges
- ✔ Computer supplies
- ✔ Shipping and delivery
- ✔ Office supplies
- ✔ Utilities fees that pertain to your home office

The Starting an Online Business For Dummies, 3rd Edition, Internet Directory

The 5th Wave   By Rich Tennant

Cleopatra Carpet Cleaners

"So far our Web presence has been pretty good. We've gotten some orders, a few inquiries, and nine guys who want to date our logo."

In This Directory...

Trying to find a Web site or Internet resource can be like trying to get a drink out of a fire hydrant. You're sure that what you want is out there in cyberspace somewhere, but every time you try to find it, you get deluged.

The following directory does the sorting for you. The flood of choices has been quality tested, labeled, and organized, just like rows of bottled water neatly arranged and waiting for your enjoyment. My research assistant and I scouted out hundreds of possibilities in order to provide you with the definitive collection of online resources, especially for online entrepreneurs.

One thing on the Web leads to another, and you're sure to find plenty on your own when you get started. The following directory is intended to serve as a set of starting points. So jump in whenever you're ready. The water's fine!

- ✔ Downloading software to help you construct your commercial site
- ✔ Finding out about Web design and e-commerce
- ✔ Marketing and advertising your business online
- ✔ Finding business networks and groups you can join
- ✔ Using Internet resources designed for start-ups like yours

About This Directory

When it comes to finding sources of support as you start your new business, the best place to turn is the Internet itself. The *Starting an Online Business For Dummies Internet Directory* is a comprehensive Yellow Pages-style list of Web sites and other resources to give you a jump-start.

To help you judge at a glance whether a site may be useful for you, this directory includes some handy miniature icons (otherwise known as *micons*). Here's an explanation of what each micon means:

$ You have to pay a fee to access some services at this site.

    This site gives you a chance to talk to fellow entrepreneurs, business authorities, or potential customers online.

    You can download software or other files at this site.

    This site lets you access Web-based services, like those provided by an Application Service Provider (ASP).

    This site provides some services for free.

    Information about electronic commerce or shopping-cart software is available at this site.

    This site has particularly good hyperlinks, which can be very useful for business research.

★★ ★★   This site is truly worthy of a four-star rating. It's a particularly valuable resource due to its content, links, free software, or all of these.

Accounting Software

"You mean I have to keep *track* of all this stuff?" Yes, my entrepreneurial friend, owning and managing a small business, whether it's located online or not, requires good accounting practices and solid record keeping. It's even more important to keep close watch on your expenses in the current era of tight budgets. Here are some powerful, yet user-friendly, accounting software programs that can help you organize and control your finances. The Web sites associated with these products often include links to related sites where you can perform financial operations online, such as basic record keeping or payroll.

Quicken 2002

www.shopintuit.com/Q2002/Consumer/ Home.asp

Quicken 2002 for Windows isn't a single product but rather a family of accounting software packages, each with a different purpose. For example, you can order Quicken Home and Business 2002, which enables you to manage both your personal and business finances; create business invoices with your company logo, reports, and graphs, and business plans; and take advantage of financial services, including online banking and online payment and investment tracking. Quicken Deluxe 2002 for Macintosh is available for Mac users with OS 9 or later. A related site, Intuit Online Financial Services (www.intuit. com/ofs/) enables current Quicken 2002 users to do online banking, pay bills, and track investments.

QuickBooks

www.quickbooks.com

The QuickBooks products, like Quicken, are produced by Intuit, Inc. Whereas Quicken emphasizes personal finance — and includes features that you can use to manage your home accounts — QuickBooks is more of a straight business product. The software comes in four versions: Basic, Pro, Premier, and QuickBooks for the Web. Another difference between Quicken and QuickBooks is that you can order a trial CD of QuickBooks Basic from the Intuit Web site or try out QuickBooks for the Web, which lets you or your coworkers access your books from any location that's connected to the Web. Current users of QuickBooks can find plenty of support on this site, including user discussion forums, ways to contact QuickBooks Professional Advisors, free e-mail newsletters, a set of Frequently Asked Questions, and tips, tools, and advice designed for specific types of industries. You can also take advantage of a new Merchant Account Service that sets up businesses to accept credit card payments. The QuickBooks Web site contains links to Payroll.com, which contains Frequently Asked Questions as well as live support for small business managers who manage their own payroll service.

Peachtree Office Accounting

www.peachtree.com

If you're looking for accounting software that's specifically designed for a small business, Peachtree Software products may just be right for you. Peachtree Office Accounting and Peachtree Complete Accounting allow you to work seamlessly with Microsoft Office products such as Excel and Word. A new product, Peachtree First Accounting, is designed for businesspeople who are converting a personal financial system to a small business system. The Peachtree Software site is distinguished from its competitors' sites by providing easy-to-find business services built around its software. Services include payroll and tax filing, bill payment, banking, and Web site building. You can export product inventory directly from your Peachtree accounting program into your Web site catalog and process orders and customer information from your Web site into your accounting software. (Peachtree Office Accounting and Peachtree Complete Accounting are available for Windows users only.)

Microsoft Money 2002 Web Site

www.microsoft.com/money

One of the distinguishing features of Microsoft Money is its level of integration with the Internet. You can get automatic updates on stock prices and other information, as well as suggestions of online resources, through this Web site. For example, you can check to see whether your bank is online, and then set up online banking. You can learn how to control your business finances through the Money Academy and Money Wise Web sites. You can also download a trial version of Microsoft Money 2002 Deluxe & Business, the version targeted toward small businesses. (A new version — Microsoft Money for the Pocket PC — is now available for mobile users.) Current users of Microsoft Money will find a set of Frequently Asked Questions, an offer for a free year of online data backups, and links to financial institutions that support Microsoft Money bill payments.

M.Y.O.B. Web Site

www.bestware.com

This program, by BestWare, comes in versions for Macintosh and Windows. From this site, you can order a version of the program on CD-ROM that will be shipped to you. Links to the M.Y.O.B. eBusiness Gateway enable you to establish yourself as an American Express credit card merchant or automatically bill your customers. Accountants who use M.Y.O.B. can join the M.Y.O.B. Accountant Club, a group that provides products and services to help them advise and support their clients. Other users can find technical support in the Support Services area of the site (www.myob.com/us/service/).

Other Stuff to Check Out

www.owlsoftware.com
www.pegasus.co.uk
www.palo-alto.com
www.1040.com

Advertising Your Site on the Web

Advertising on the Web is a broad subject that encompasses traditional banner advertising, the use of search engines and linking, as well as a variety of combined approaches that are unique to online business. What follows is a list of sample sites related to the use of two of the most important Web advertising methods — banners and linking. I also include a reference page that provides a well-maintained list of Web advertising resources.

bCentral Traffic Builder

**www.bcentral.com/products/tb/
default.asp**

You don't have to host your Web site with the Microsoft bCentral hosting service in order to use this set of advertising and marketing tools. For a monthly subscription fee (rates start at $24.95 per month), Traffic Builder automates many of the processes associated with publicizing a business site online. Traffic Builder lets you place an ad in a banner ad exchange network, create a mailing list of prospective and current customers so that you can send them news about promotions, and submits your site's URL to a variety of search engines.

Internet Advertising Report

www.internetnews.com/IAR/

If you want the latest headlines about the state of Internet advertising and marketing — at least, as it applies to big commercial Web sites — this is the place to go. You can get news on industry trends that might apply to your small operation.

The Banner Generator

www.coder.com/creations/banner/

With The Banner Generator, you can create your own custom animated banner for free. Rather than using a graphics program to create the banner, you do all the work with your Web browser. You begin by specifying the textual message that you want the banner to convey. Then you choose the banner's size, colors, and typefaces. Finally, you're given the chance to add special effects, such as embossing. When you're ready, you click a Submit Banner button. You can then save the banner to your own computer.

Other Stuff to Check Out

www.iab.net
www.markwelch.com/bannerad
www.exchange-it.com

Auctions

Online auctions give small business owners a place to find bargain equipment, unload excess inventory, and sell products in a location other than their online store. Auctions give you access to the entire international Web community. Making a bid or offering something for sale usually requires a registration process. Trading is public, which adds interest and keeps the forum honest. eBay, for one, has a feedback forum, where users can indicate whether a trade was a positive or negative experience.

eBay

www.ebay.com

$

eBay is certainly one of the largest person-to-person trading areas on the Internet, offering millions of items in more than 1,000 categories of auction classifieds. eBay is known to many for selling precious or collectible items at auction, but you can also find computer equipment, phones, and other small business essentials. You can browse the listings or search by specific item, bid on anything, or offer something for sale. Viewing, bidding, and buying items are free; listing and selling items incur insertion fees and final value fees.

Yahoo! Auctions

auctions.yahoo.com

Yahoo! allows you to browse its auction categories in order to identify auction Web sites or search for a particular item available at a current auction site. It doesn't cost a thing to sell, bid on, or purchase an item.

Other Stuff to Check Out

www.auctions.msn.com
auctions.yahoo.com
auctions.amazon.com
dir.yahoo.com/Business_and_Economy/
Shopping_and_Services/Auctions/

Business Resources on the Web

The Web offers a vast resource for the entrepreneur. An overwhelming amount of information is available on every conceivable topic related to the starting and growing of a small business. So the question isn't "Does the Web have useful information for me?" but rather "Where on the Web do I find the best information for my needs?" The following sites are either guides to small-business sites on the Web or are themselves some of the better business sites available.

CCH Business Owners Toolkit

www.toolkit.cch.com

This site offers model business plans and other business documents that you can download and use, an "Ask Alice" advice column, and useful articles about starting and running a small business. Also find thousands of pages of articles from a guidebook for small office/home office workers.

About.com Guide to Small Business Information

sbinformation.about.com

This is a great guide to small-business information on the Web — provided you can endure the pop-up ads that appear whenever you click a link. The About.com guide presents links to a comprehensive list of articles targeted at small businesses/home-based business owners.

Netscape Netbusiness

netbusiness.netscape.com

Netscape provides a short page with news headlines pertaining to small business issues. A list of links leads you to resources of interest to entrepreneurs. Click the Community link, and you go to a page that leads you to message boards where you can get advice from other small business owners. Click the Manage My Business link, and you go to a page containing links that help you handle the everyday tasks associated with running a business.

Entrepreneurial Edge

edge.lowe.org

Sponsored by the Edward Lowe Foundation, Entrepreneurial Edge claims to have "Over 1,415 ideas to grow your company." You can search a digital library of links, articles, and books containing useful information for the small-business owner.

Morebusiness.com

www.morebusiness.com

This is another site that collects articles about planning, managing, and marketing a small business. However, Morebusiness.com goes a step further. It also offers business tools you can download or use online, such as a calculator, sample business agreements, business and marketing plan templates, and even an interactive travel agent.

OPEN: The Small business Network

www.americanexpress.com/homepage/
    smallbusiness.shtml

This site is primarily devoted to giving American Express business card holders a place to learn more about running a business and paying their credit card bills online. Perhaps the best thing about this site is the Community area. You can post a question that other entrepreneurs will answer. Previous questions and answers are organized by subject, so you can browse the list to see whether someone has already posed a question like yours.

Startupjournal.com

startupjournal.com

This site describes itself as The Wall Street Journal Center for Entrepreneurs, and it is affiliated with the Journal's Web site, WSJ.com. It presents a variety of columnists who provide advice on starting up a new business. An online toolkit includes a MiniPlan tool that you can use before you write a full-fledged business plan, as well as a trademark search utility. The articles apply to startups whether they're online or not, but online business owners should find them of value.

Yahoo! Small Business

smallbusiness.yahoo.com

Yahoo! Small Business topics include Starting a Business, Finance, Technology & E-Commerce, Legal and Government Services, Sales and Marketing, Human Resources, Startup Basics, and Franchises. Other links on this page enable you to send a job to an online printer, find business supplies and services, and track packages you've shipped.

Other Stuff to Check Out

www.office.com
www.entrepreneurmag.com
www.fastcompany.com
www.techsoup.org

Classifieds

The Web offers countless sources for advertising via classified ads. In this section, I've included guides to the many sites that offer this service, some of which are free and some require payment. Obviously, the beauty of the Web is that you reach a lot more people than you would by advertising in your local newspaper. On the Web, the whole world of online users can be your potential buyers.

The Grandfather of All Links Free Advertising Directory

ecki.com/links/oclass.shtml

This huge listing of free classified advertising sites takes forever to load, but it is updated regularly and is current. Sites are sorted alphabetically and grouped by how long you can run the ad and whether the ad is city- or state-specific. The Grandfather of All Links also includes a directory of non-English sites.

Yahoo! Classifieds

dir.yahoo.com/Business_and_Economy/
   Classifieds

As usual, Yahoo! is a great starting point if you're looking for just about anything — in this case, sites where you can place your classified ads online. Yahoo! allows you to browse by region or by category. Also listed are general classified sites that can include additional services, such as chat rooms, personal ads, and auctions.

Other Stuff to Check Out

www.villagesclassified.com
www.classifieds2000.com

Computer Equipment Bargains

Anyone who manages an online business needs to be budget conscious these days. You can save money by buying equipment at auction. Sometimes, the goods are refurbished rather than new, but the point is that you get what you need at a price that fits your budget.

Dell Small Business Center

www.dell.com/us/en/bsd/default.htm

Dude: If you're looking for a Dell, the Dell Computer Web site for small business owners presents you with a variety of

options. First, specials are advertised on this site's home page. Then, there's the Refurbished Systems link, which you'll find under the Quick Links section on the left side of the home page. You can also use the Computer Finder, an interactive tool in which you specify the features you want and then receive a suggestion of the type of machine that fits the bill. You can also shop by the model name of the machine you're looking for, or get a quote from a representative.

FairAuction.com

www.fairauction.com

This online auction site deals not just in computers but also in individual computer components. If you're looking for a DVD drive, internal modem, or other add-on and you or an associate have the skills needed to install it, this is the place to go. You can also find bargains on monitors, digital cameras, and other necessities.

UBid

www.ubid.com

uBid specializes in selling brand-name computer and electronics equipment at up to 70 percent less than the retail price. Sometimes the material is refurbished; other times, it's overstock items. But items are backed either by uBid or by the manufacturer's warranty. The format is a Dutch auction; a certain number of items are available, and the highest number of successful bidders wins. (For instance, if 17 items are up for auction, and the 17 highest bidders have bid $135 or more, all 17 win and each pays just $135.)

Other Stuff to Check Out

shopping.yahoo.com/
   shop?d=browse&id=21754470
shopper.cnet.com/shopping/0-1257.html
www.outpost.com
www.gateway.com/work/smb/index.shtml

Developing Compelling Content

As a fledgling Web entrepreneur, you may find yourself preoccupied with the technical issues of this relatively new medium — page design, layout, graphic elements, icons, browsers, ease of navigation, animation — but when it comes to the user, content is king. Bottom line: People go to the Web to find information. Studies show that users don't read, but rather *scan* the page, and that they prefer scannable, objective writing to the promotional and over-hyped language that's tolerated and expected in other media. The following sites contain guidance to help you create Web content that's concise and effective.

"Concise, Scannable, and Objective: How to Write for the Web"

www.useit.com/papers/webwriting/writing.html

John Morkes and Web usability expert Jakob Nielsen provide this scholarly but very readable article on how to write effectively for the Web. It's as pertinent now as it was when it first appeared in 1997. Their studies suggest that effective Web writing has to be *scannable*, that users want to be able to pick out what they need in a few sentences, that the writing has to be short and to the point, and that it must provide factual information rather than marketing fluff.

Contentious

www.contentious.com

Contentious is a monthly Web-zine primarily intended for professional writers and editors who create content for the Web and other online media. *Contentious* regularly examines key content-related issues, such

as the differences between writing for the Web and writing for print, and what rules are emerging for the editorial aspects of online media. However, the readers of this journal aren't just writers but all kinds of online publishers, from ezines to business Web sites, and anyone interested in effective online writing.

E-write

www.ewriteonline.com

The owners of E-write started the company when they realized that e-mail and the Internet were reinventing the way people communicate with their customers, coworkers, and suppliers. They understand that good writing is key to using e-mail effectively, as well as developing user-friendly Web content. The site includes articles for the small-business entrepreneur on writing competitive e-mail that allows you to communicate quickly and frequently with your customer.

Web Central's Web Writing Style Resources

www.cio.com/central/style.html

Web Central, the Web site affiliated with *CIO Magazine*, is a rich resource for anyone involved in online business, whether you're a Fortune 500 company or a small-business owner. In one little corner of this large site, you can find "Web Writing Style Resources," a collection of articles that provide various writing style guides for developing the written content of your Web site. Most of the articles combine the discussion of effective written communication with tips for user-friendly Web design.

"Writing for the Web, Parts I & II"

in3.org/articles/wftw1.htm

This down-to-earth, nuts-and-bolts article by Jack Powers can perhaps now be called a classic because it dates back to 1996. Powers explains why text on the Web cannot just be "re-purposed print material squirted out through an HTML word processor." He explains very clearly why print and the Web are entirely different mediums requiring entirely different writing strategies.

Domain Names

Your domain name is really an alias that functions as the online version of your street address and phone number. In the URL www.gregholden.com, for example, gregholden.com is the domain name. The *suffix*, or filename extension at the end of a domain name — that is, the part that comes after the dot — identifies the type of organization that owns the domain name. Dot-com (.com) usually means a commercial enterprise, and dot-org (.org) often means a not-for-profit organization.

Your domain name may or may not be the same as your actual company name, although most businesspeople like the two to be identical so that customers can easily remember the URL. If someone already owns the name you want, you may explore buying that name through a broker. Your chances of finding the name you want are better these days because many of the domain name "tycoons" who had been holding on to scores of names in hopes of selling them for top dollar have now had to let them expire. On top of that, new domains such as .name and .biz are now available.

FAQs on New Top-Level Domains

www.internic.net/faqs/new-tlds.html

This is a good place to start if you're confused about just how many domain-name suffixes are available to put at the end of your own site's URL. Until recently, only six suffixes were available (.com, .edu, .gov, .mil, .net, and .org). Not long ago, a group called The Internet Corporation for Assigned Names and Numbers (ICANN) approved new domain name suffixes

(.aero, .biz, .coop, .info, .museum, .name, and .pro). At this writing, .biz, .info, and .name were accepting registrations. Check this page for the current status of the new suffixes and for links to a list of companies called registrars where you can pick out a name and register it.

Network Solutions

www.networksolutions.com

$

Years ago, Network Solutions was the only place where you could register a domain name for a Web site. Now, dozens of companies all over the world are certified as registrars, but Network Solutions is the oldest and best-known of the bunch. You can perform a quick search for your domain name of choice here and see whether it's available. You can then register the name (or a similar one, if your ideal choice is taken) and even set up your Web site through Network Solutions.

E-Commerce Service Providers

You might be your online company's only employee, but that doesn't mean you have to do everything yourself. A number of companies are offering packaged services and software to entrepreneurs who want to get their business online quickly and with the support of experts. They provide a broad range of services, from the simple to the complex, that can include site hosting, shopping cart and credit card services, consultation on design, content, and marketing.

AOL Hometown

hometown.aol.com

You don't have to be a member of America Online (AOL) to create a Web site through its hosting service. One nice thing about this service is that AOL targets it at rank beginners, so if you're at all nervous about creating Web pages, this may be a good option. You can choose from 100 Web page templates to help kick-start your design. You can use a Web-based page creation tool to start creating your site. Another really nice thing is that you get a site with 12MB of storage space for free.

Bigstep.com

www.bigstep.com

$

Bigstep is a typical Web hosting service for small businesses. First, you can sign up to host your online store for a free 30-day trial period. Then, you can choose one of three hosting packages that cost $9.95, $24.95, or $34.95 per month respectively. The $9.95 per month option lets you sell 30 catalog items in an online catalog; the other two allow you to maintain bigger sales catalogs. If you want to use an interactive shopping cart and have the ability to accept credit card payments, you need to sign up for a Bigstep Store account starting at $44.90 per month. The advantage of using a service like Bigstep is that you get help obtaining a domain name, maintaining a backup copy of your site for security purposes, and marketing your business.

Microsoft bCentral

www.bCentral.com

$

If you use Microsoft FrontPage to create your Web site, consider using Microsoft bCentral to host your online business. As a bCentral customer, you get to use the FrontPage Server Extensions, a set of server software that enables you to do one-step publishing as well as set up online forms. FrontPage 2002 is equipped with an E-commerce Add-In that streamlines the process of publishing an online catalog to bCentral. You also gain access to the

bCentral tools for tracking visitors, publicizing your site, and managing customer contact information.

Yahoo! Store

store.yahoo.com/index.html

$

Yahoo! bills itself as the fastest, easiest way to open an online store. You create your site on its server using nothing more than the browser you're using to read its page. This isn't a free service; hosting costs are based on the number of items that you sell per month. However, it's a good solution for those of us who are nontechnical and want to get a presence on the Web in a quick, affordable way. Yahoo! Store has built-in searches, statistical tools, and flexible pricing options.

Other Stuff to Check Out

www.icverify.com
www.intershop.com
www.homestead.com
www.verifone.com

Fax Services

Need to receive a fax but don't have a fax machine? That's no longer a problem. These services allow you to receive faxes and view them on your e-mail. Some of these services have a free trial period, while others are advertiser supported, like all free stuff on the Web. Some services also send faxes for you for free. Limits often apply to the amount of activity you can perform, so watch for stipulations.

eFax

www.efax.com

$

eFax documents look and work just like e-mails with attachments. People dial your eFax number on their fax machines and send documents to you. The fax is received by eFax and compressed (optionally protected with a password) and sent to your e-mail address as an attachment. You open the attachment by using eFax Messenger Plus software (which you have to download and install beforehand) and see your fax on-screen. You can then print it or forward it to other e-mail addresses. You can send two trial faxes for free; after that, the service costs $9.99 per month.

FaxWave

www.callwave.com/faxwave/index.aspF

FaxWave gives you a personal fax number you can use to receive faxes. The FaxWave service receives the fax, converts it to a computer file, and sends it to you as an e-mail attachment. The service is free, but you have to provide registration information to FaxWave and you're required to view text ads in the e-mail message that accompanies the fax.

Onebox.com

www.onebox.comF

This site gives you free voicemail, e-mail, and fax, all in one place, through a phone number that you obtain for free from Onebox. You also get a Onebox e-mail address. You can listen to voice messages, read your e-mail, or view your faxes through the Onebox Web site or by dialing your Onebox phone number. E-mail messages are spoken, not typed. You can also send voice e-mail, e-mail, or faxes. Phone numbers may not be available in your home area code, however, so anyone who phones or faxes you at your Onebox number may be subject to long-distance charges.

Other Stuff to Check Out

www.callwave.com
www.phonenumbers.net
www.tpc.int

Finance

You say you're brimming with great ideas but have no money with which to turn them into reality? Never fear. The Web has some resources to help you find the capital you need for your online business.

Idea Cafe's Financing Your Business

**www.businessownersideacafe.com/
getmoney/financing.html**

★★
★★

Idea Cafe offers more than 40 Web pages full of tips to help you secure the money that your business needs. This site provides a vast range of information on finance. Topics include how to borrow money, attract investors, or find alternate funding sources. It also holds moderated forums on credit card use, bank financing, government funding, borrowing from family and friends, women and money, and much more. Try the All-in-One Budget Calculator to find out how much money you really need. A must-visit site!

CFOL.com

www.cfol.com

CFOL.com, which stands for Commercial Finance ONLINE!, modestly describes itself as The World's Largest Business Finance Search Engine. Because so few — if any — business finance search engines are around, it might just be right. This site allows you to search a database of funding sources for business capital and to apply for funding online.

Small Business Administration

www.sba.gov/financing

The SBA site offers extensive information on financing your business, including tips on taking out a loan and working with lenders. You can download an online library full of shareware programs designed to help you manage your small business. You can even enroll in an online workshop called "Financing Options: All You Should Know."

Other Stuff to Check Out

www.businessfinance.com
www.garage.com
www.moneyhunter.com
www.entrepreneur.com/Your_Business/
   YB_Node/0,4507,368,00.html

Free and Low-Cost Business Web Sites

In the previous edition of this book, I called this section "Free Business Web Sites." Although freebies are hard to find on the Web these days, you can still get bargains. These sites offer affordable tools, links, information, or services tailored to online businesspeople.

Hypermart

www.hypermart.com

Hypermart provides free business Web site hosting, as well as solutions to other business needs. The turnkey, browser-based creation package allows you to make a Web site without HTML experience. Hypermart Web site members are required to display banner ads. Hypermart registers your site with search engines and also has a small business center that provides office supplies, books on business, communications services such as cellular and long distance, professional services such as trademark search and TM registration, and financial services to help you with

payroll, credit cards, and the IRS. Other features include a robot that checks for dead links on your page, bad HTML tags and syntax, and browser compatibility.

CNET's Quick SiteBuilder

www.bcity.com

$

Quick SiteBuilder, part of the online news service CNET, hosts Web sites for businesses, entrepreneurs, and nonprofit organizations, and allows you to create a site in 5 minutes with no knowledge of HTML. You can try the service for free for 30 days, and then pay $49.95 per year thereafter. Quick SiteBuilder gives you 25MB of storage space and access to online courses in Web development. Banner ads are *not* displayed on Web sites.

Free Merchant

www.freemerchant.com

FreeMerchant.com used to provide Web hosting for free; its hosting options now range from $14.95 to $99.95 per month. Most of the hosting options (except the low-cost one) include search engine submission and membership in an Internet shopping mall among the benefits for members. All hosting packages offer access to a secure shopping cart, an "Internet store builder," catalogs, traffic logs, e-mail accounts, merchant message boards, merchant banner exchange, shipping calculator, tax calculator, discounted corporate services and offers, and tech support.

FreeNet

www.freenet.com.my

FreeNet Business Solutions offers services such as application development, network advisory, an e-commerce consultant, Internet hosting services, and so on. Services aren't actually free, however — hosting plans start at about $8 per month depending on exchange rates. This Malaysian site (the .my in the URL stands for Malaysia) specializes in Web hosting for business sites.

Netfirms
www.netfirms.com

For absolutely no monthly fee, you get 25MB of Web space, e-mail service, and technical support. The catch? You're required to display banner ads on your Web site. You can also process Web page forms by using CGI scripts. For only $5 per month, you can remove the banner ads by upgrading to the Netfirms premium service.

Other Sites to Check Out

www.freeservers.com
www.tripod.lycos.com
geocities.yahoo.com
angelfire.lycos.com

Free E-mail and Newsgroup Accounts

Free e-mail and news accounts come in two flavors: Web-based and non-Web-based. Both options have their advantages. You can check the Web-based accounts from anywhere, and you don't need Internet access to use the non-Web-based accounts. Most services are semi-secure, and a few actually specialize in securing your transmissions.

Juno
www.juno.com

Juno's free Web access service offers free e-mail service as well. Juno, however,

provides you with a way to access your e-mail account from the Web. You download the software from the Web site and then dial directly with your modem. The Juno site itself offers numerous Web guides, features, and links.

Eudora Web-Mail
www.eudoramail.com

Eudora Web-Mail is a free Web-based e-mail. Features include an address book, attachments without long downloads, automatic response to people when you're away, and the ability to create signature files. It also offers special filters that block incoming mail from a list you specify, from known "spammers," or from all addresses except those that you preapprove. You can also configure your Eudora account to access all your POP mail accounts, which allows you to consolidate your e-mail in one location. It's pretty comprehensive as far as free e-mail goes.

Yahoo!
login.yahoo.com

Is there anything Yahoo! doesn't do? With Yahoo!, you can get free Web-based e-mail. With the account, you get free Yahoo! Messenger instant messaging service, which lets you instantly contact friends and colleagues. You also have free access to other Yahoo! offerings.

Google Groups
groups.google.com

Google, the Internet search engine, also lets you access USENET discussion groups for free through this site. All you need is a Web browser; you don't need to install special newsgroup software. Amazingly, Google Groups not only presents current newsgroup postings, but it also maintains an archive of millions of newsgroup messages that stretches back a full 20 years.

Freenewsgroups.com

www.freenewsgroups.com

This site provides you with a list of servers that allow free access to newsgroups — whether or not its administrators actually intend to permit free access. The list specifies which servers allow you to post news messages and which ones are "read-only." The list changes frequently, so check back often.

Hushmail

www.hushmail.com

Hushmail is a fully encrypted, free, Web-based e-mail service. Despite the convenience of giving you both a Web-based and secure e-mail account, however, Hushmail carries with it a number of requirements and stipulations. The encryption service works only if you send mail to another Hushmail user. Hushmail is not available to Mac users, limits the size of e-mail, and the free version offers only a limited amount of message storage. (A premium version of Hushmail gives you more storage space.) Still, this service is worth checking out, if nothing else for its incredibly detailed explanations of encryption and secure e-mail in general. It has also been well received by the technology press.

Mail.com

www.mail.com

Mail.com offers free Web-based e-mail that has a generous 2MB e-mail message limit and 10MB of e-mail storage space. Mail.com says it has anti-spam policies that will (hopefully) keep junk e-mail from clogging your inbox.

1on1Lite

www.1on1mail.com

1on1Lite offers free e-mail accounts in a secure channel environment and uses encryption. 1on1 also guarantees delivery and receipt of mail by tracking and reporting the delivery of all e-mails. 1on1 isn't Web-based, so you can work offline until you're ready to send or receive. The software can be downloaded or will be provided on CD-ROM. The software is free because 1on1 is supported by advertising. The site also has good links regarding privacy on the Web.

Other Sites to Check Out

www.emailaddresses.com
www.flashmail.com
www.caremail.com

Free Forms Online

You don't need to be a programmer, or have access to one, in order to create forms that actually do something — that is, forms that accept user-submitted data, format it, and present it to you in a readable format. The following Web resources will lead you painlessly through the process of creating your own form that comes with its own CGI script.

FormMail.To

www.formmail.to

At FormMail.To, you can create your own Web browser e-mail form and the data that you enter on this form will be sent to your e-mail account. You don't need any CGI programming on your Web site to use FormMail.To. On your form, you can specify whatever data you need. You can use pull-down menu selections and check boxes to make your forms easier to use and to control the allowed entries. The form data can be sent to multiple e-mail address, so you can use FormMail.To as a private mailing list program. You can specify a URL to transfer to after your form is submitted or you can insert a form between two of your existing pages to capture information from visitors as they click through your site. FormMail.To is supported by advertising in the form of one banner on the bottom of your form.

Response-O-Matic

www.response-o-matic.com

Response-O-Matic allows you to use forms on your Web site without any programming knowledge or programming tools. Response-O-Matic works with any home page hosted by any Web host, including AOL, GeoCities, Earthlink, and others. After you create your forms with Response-O-Matic, you can move them to any Web site on any server. Response-o-Matic is free.

Other Sites to Check Out

www.tou.com/cgi/form
www.responders.net

Free Internet Access

A few sites still offer free access to the Internet, which can come in handy if you're on the road and not able to connect to your own provider — or if you just want to save a few bucks and get online on the cheap. You might only get a few hours of free access per month, and you might have to view online ads, but if you really want to get online for free, here are some options.

Access-4-Free

www.access-4-free.com

Access-4-Free is distinguished from its competition by its promise of service that's free of banner ads. The company provides 10 hours of Internet access for free each month after you pay a $4.95 one-time setup fee. If you go over that amount of usage, you are charged $1 per hour; however, the most you pay is $10 per month. Access-4-Free doesn't provide local access numbers for every part of the country. Check with your phone company to make sure the area code you're dialing doesn't carry toll charges.

America Online

www.aol.com

America Online is big and successful enough that it can offer new members a substantial amount of time online in order to try out its software. At the time this was written, America Online was offering a whopping 1,000 hours of free Internet access.

Juno

www.juno.com

Juno offers free access to the Internet — apparently without time limits. You don't use a Web browser, however; you download Juno's own software that is used to browse the Web and send and receive e-mail. The software is reliable and easy to use, but it isn't compatible with Macs. In summer 2001, Juno merged with its main competitor, NetZero, and, at this writing, it isn't yet clear how the merger will affect the service that each company offers.

NetZero

www.netzero.com

NetZero offers 10 hours of free Internet access per month with access numbers across the country. You have to download software from the Web site, including a dialer that makes the connection with the NetZero system and loads a floating ad window on your desktop. NetZero sells advertising that is displayed in the desktop window, which works just like the banner ads that you see on Web pages. NetZero also offers free e-mail.

Other Sites to Check Out

www.address.com/main.asp
free-isp-internet-access.net/isp.shtml
www.thefreesite.com/Free_Internet_
Access

Free Phone Service

These services allow you to get a few minutes of free phone calls to anywhere in the United States, sometimes in exchange for listening to ads. In some cases, you make a phone call through your computer, and the quality of your connection depends on your processor speed and bandwidth. If you don't mind a little echo or sound breakup from time to time or the ads, you can save substantially on long-distance phone charges.

Dialpad

www.dialpad.com

Dialpad lets you download software for free that enables your PC to make phone calls to other PCs or phones around the world. Your computer needs to be equipped with a sound card, microphone, and speakers or

headphones. You also have to pay the cost of the phone call. Check the rates on the Dialpad Web site before you have your computer dial that number.

PGPfone

web.mit.edu/network/pgpfone/

The clever folks at the Massachusetts Institute of Technology who created Pretty Good Privacy also provide free software that turns your PC into a phone. PGPfone enables a user with a sound-equipped PC (a PC with a sound card, microphone, and speakers) to communicate by voice with other PC users.

PhoneFree.com

www.phonefree.com

PhoneFree provides you with software you download and install free of charge. The software enables you to make a call to a phone or another PC from your PC, provided you have a sound card, speakers or a headset, and a microphone. If you have a slow Internet connection, you may find that the sound quality suffers. PhoneFree isn't available for the Mac. On the other hand, the company says that its system is entirely free of ads.

Other Sites to Check Out

www.hottelephone.com
messenger.msn.com

Free Web Page Tools

In order to keep up with all the competition among e-commerce sites, you need to make yours work. You need forms that work, graphics that look professional, newsletters that are well-designed, and more. The following Web sites allow you to obtain free tools to help you build your Web pages and make them stand out from the crowd.

Bellsnwhistles.com

www.bellsnwhistles.com

The page design may look a little amateurish, but who cares? It's Web page add-ons you want, and this site has them in abundance. And they're all free, too. You'll find Java applets, DHTML effects, software programs, and graphics.

Dynamic Drive

dynamicdrive.com

Looking for scripts? Dynamic Drive offers free, original DHTML (dynamic HTML) scripts, text editors, and fonts. All scripts use the latest in JavaScript and DHTML technology, with emphasis on practicality and *backward compatibility* (functionality with earlier versions of browsers and other software, not just the latest versions). Dynamic Drive also offers a Web hosting service, a menu bar maker, Web graphics, traffic reports, and a newsletter.

Html Gear

www.htmlgear.lycos.com

Html Gear organizes its Web site add-ons by the purpose they're supposed to perform. You can find several options for gathering feedback from your visitors; for example, you can take a poll, create an interactive form, or send automatic responses. You have to join the Lycos Network in order to download the goodies, but membership is free.

Reallybig.com

www.reallybig.com

Reallybig.com is a network of links to sites that offer Web site building tools. There's a very large collection of free Web page tools to be had. Resources include free clip art, CGI scripts, counters, fonts, HTML, Java, animation, backgrounds, icons, WYSIWYG editors, buttons, photos, site promotion, Server-Side Includes (add-ons such as the current time and date), log analyzers, hit counters, and tutorials. Really Big also has a newsletter to learn about what's going on in the Reallybig.com Web Builder network, and offers interviews of top Web designers. This site can help you find out where to get pretty much anything and everything.

Other Sites to Check Out

www.freesitetools.com
www.freestuffcentral.com/
   webmaster.php
www.sitebuildingtools.com

Glossaries, Dictionaries, and Encyclopedias

You may want to bookmark these handy reference sites for those times when you find yourself knee-deep in computer, Internet, or Web terms you have never heard before. Rest assured: New terms are being created even as we speak.

Computing Dictionary

wombat.doc.ic.ac.uk/foldoc/index.html

Enter a computer word or phrase in the box at the top of the page and click Search for free access to this online dictionary of computing.

Dictionary.com/Thesaurus.com

www.dictionary.com/www.thesaurus.com

These two sites are interrelated. When you search for a word on one site, you're given the opportunity to look it up in either the dictionary or the thesaurus. Dictionary definitions are gathered from a variety of different sources, which are given after each listing. Thesaurus listings are extensive and full of hyperlinked cross-references.

New York Times Glossary of Internet Terms

www.nytimes.com/library/cyber/ reference/glossary.html

From Archie and ARPAnet to Zine, this list of techy terms is a useful resource for the Web entrepreneur. Terms are listed alphabetically and cross-referenced. Entries are thorough and up-to-date. You have to register to use the site by choosing a username and password, but registration is free.

The Webmaster's Lexicon

www.wdvl.com/WebRef/Lexicon

This is an easy-to-use alphabetical listing of key words and phrases that you will inevitably come across in your new role as online business owner.

Government

As an online businessperson, you will at times need government information. The following are a few useful sites in this area. Be sure to check out the Small Business Administration site and the site run by the Secretariat for Electronic Commerce.

Internal Revenue Service: Forms

www.irs.ustreas.gov

The new-and-improved IRS provides this Web site, where you can download or print any form you want in a choice of four different file formats. You've got a couple of options for finding forms. You can either enter the name in the Forms Finder box near the top of the home page or click the Forms and Publications link farther down the home page under the Resources heading.

SCORE: Service Corps of Retired Executives

www.score.org

The SCORE Association, in partnership with the U.S. Small Business Administration, provides confidential business counseling free of charge by e-mail. SCORE also offers workshops and free satellite conferences. The SCORE Web site provides many additional resources worth exploring, including a way to get business counseling by e-mail.

State and Local Government on the Net

www.statelocalgov.net/index.cfm

This up-to-date site has extensive lists of links to state and local government sites, multi-state sites, and some federal resources. It also includes listings of national organizations related to government and other miscellaneous government resources.

United States Government Electronic Commerce Policy

www.ecommerce.gov

This site is maintained by the Secretariat for Electronic Commerce, U.S. Department of Commerce. The reports and documents that are available to read and download provide an important framework for understanding the phenomenal growth of online business and the emerging digital economy, both globally and nationally. This site also includes links to related international sites and links to examples of electronic commerce.

U.S. Small Business Administration

www.sba.gov

The U.S. Small Business Administration site offers a huge amount of information useful to the small-business person, as well as an online library and a listing of programs offering various kinds of assistance.

HTML and Link-Checking Tools

Even though you don't have to actually learn HTML in order to create a Web page — in fact, precisely *because* you may not know HTML — it pays to have a Web-based service do an evaluation of your pages to make sure that they're written correctly. Here are some Web page "tune-up" sites that you can try.

Doctor HTML

www2.imagiware.com/RxHTML

Doctor HTML is a Web page analysis tool that retrieves an HTML page and reports any problems that it finds. The online version of Doctor HTML is free and will analyze a single Web page. You may also purchase a license to use the program on an internal intranet.

NetMechanic

netmechanic.com/index.htm

NetMechanic has three sets of utilities that analyze different aspects of a Web site's

performance. NetMechanic HTML Toolbox is an online verification and validation tool that can help you find broken links or other errors in your site. Search Engine Power Pack helps promote your site, and Server Check Pro monitors your hosting service's performance.

Web Site Garage

www.websitegarage.com

$

This site enables you to run critical performance diagnostics on your entire Web site, ensure browser compatibility by seeing your site as viewed by 18 different browsers, and speed up your site by optimizing your images. All services are available for a fee.

Other Stuff to Check Out

www.linklint.orgwatson.addy.com
www.cen.uiuc.edu/cgi-bin/weblint

Legal Resources

You don't need to be in legal trouble in order to research the many legal resources in cyberspace. Small-business owners often need to know about copyright and trademark issues, as well as international trade law and state laws.

The Copyright Website

www.benedict.com

This site endeavors to inject a measure of humor into the sometimes dry subject of copyright. It has a section on Fair Use and Public Domain and a chat group on copyright issues. You can use a Copyright Wizard to register your Web site content.

The Internet Legal Resource Guide

www.ilrg.com

This is a good general starting point if you're looking for legal information. The ILRG includes an index of lawyers and law firms, in case you're in need of help. It also has extensive databases of legal information, articles, and links.

Nolo.com

www.nolo.com

The Web site of this well-known publisher in the field of self-help law contains a number of Law Centers. The Small Business Law Center contains articles on starting and naming a small business. A page on copyrights and trademarks points you to lots of good information on intellectual property terminology, as well.

THOMAS

thomas.loc.gov

THOMAS (which is named after Thomas Jefferson) is the official Web site of the U.S. Congress. Administered by the Library of Congress, THOMAS lets you check on the status of pending legislation before the Congress. You can search by bill number, title, or keyword.

The United States Copyright Office

lcweb.loc.gov/copyright

★★
★★

This is an outstanding resource on a topic of interest to everyone who wants to start an online business. This is the place to go if you want to apply to register for copyright for your Web site. Registering your copyright gives you an extra level of protection for your business site contents, even though copyright law provides for online material to be protected as soon as it is published.

Other Stuff to Check Out

www.doc.gov
dir.yahoo.com/Government/Law
www.eff.org
www.findlaw.com/01topics/10cyberspace
www.findlaw.com
www.globalcontact.com

Online Schedulers

You say you don't have the money to employ a personal secretary? You don't even have the funds for one of those snazzy scheduling packages? You're in luck: The following Web sites will help you record appointments and keep track of upcoming events.

ScheduleOnline

www.scheduleonline.com

$

ScheduleOnline is a service that lets you have your own private calendar, which lists meetings, tasks, to-dos, and notes about what you scheduled for yourself. You can access and update your calendar information online from any computer. For businesses that require group scheduling, different members of your organization can have different access levels to the scheduling information. Attendees can view their calendars, create their own to-do lists and notes, and schedule tasks for themselves, but they may not schedule meetings. Administrators can set up and administer departments, people, and resources with ScheduleOnline.

Evite

www.evite.com

Evite puts a twist on the online scheduling idea: It focuses on enabling users to invite others to specific events. If your guests are connected to the Internet, you can quickly assemble a list and invite them to gatherings such as parties, TV nights, or movie outings.

HotDiary

www.hotdiary.com

★★
★★

At HotDiary, you can get an online organizer, community events calendar, Jazzed calendar management that runs on your domain, and a Jivelt site builder for custom calendars that run on any Web site. Features include an integrated online organizer, personal and group calendars, pager/fax/e-mail reminders of important appointments for both personal and group use, address book, personal and group memos, personal and group to-do's, group chat, event invitation capability, subscriptions to local calendars, summary lists, and calendar management and access control. You can promote and advertise your business by using the HotDiary public community event calendars. HotDiary is a winner of CNET/Windows Best Business Site Award.

Netscape Calendar

calendar.netscape.com

This is an easy-to-use online calendar that lets you record upcoming events. You can view monthly, weekly, daily events, or set up an "Event Calendar" that lists upcoming events that you've recorded. You can quickly e-mail events to others if you want to invite or just notify them. If you already have an America Online screen name, you can use it to register for Netscape Calendar.

Other Sites to Check Out

calendar.yahoo.com/
www.supercalendar.com
www.abrio.com/
www.calendars.net

Online Storage Space

Storing your electronic data on a server that's connected to the Internet is a good safety measure, one that can help you rebuild your business quickly in case of fire, theft, or other disasters. Online storage space is also a great way to get access to your files from anywhere. You don't need to be on your home computer or even have a floppy disk. It helps if you need to keep backups, need to send large files to others, or keep files in a safe place during a transition, such as when you're moving files between computers. Some online storage sites give group access to files so that numerous people can share a document.

E-ttach

www.e-ttach.net

When you upload a file to your space on E-ttach, you can optionally specify that someone be notified by e-mail that the file is available, so the individual can easily click a link in the e-mail message to download the file. You can try out the service for free for 30 days. After that, a personal license for 500MB of storage space costs $14.95 per month.

FilesAnywhere

www.filesanywhere.com

★★
★★

At FilesAnywhere, you get 50MB of storage space for a free 30-day trial period. You can then upgrade to 100MB for $3.95 per month. (Larger packages are available.)

Besides file storage, you can send large files with the E-Send feature, which confirms delivery. E-Send allows you to attach larger files than e-mail does and allows you to send multiple files at one time. Custom messages can accompany files and appear in a user's Inbox, just like e-mail. The site has GroupShares, which are personal folders shared for private group access so that all members of a business team can work off the same document. Files Anywhere has automated daily backup and a recovery service. With that, you know your files are safe even if you delete one by accident.

IBackup

www.ibackup.com

IBackup provides backup, storage, and file sharing space plus a number of innovative ways to access and manage your data. You can, for instance, map your IBackup storage area as though it's a local drive on your own computer. You can also schedule file transfers for specific future dates and times. Data is protected using SSL encryption. Storage options begin at 50MB for $3 per month or $30 per year. Both Windows and Macintosh systems are supported.

StorageVault

www.storagevault.net

This is one of few storage sites that includes a free storage option. You can sign up for 10MB of free space. Of course, StorageVault would probably prefer that you sign up for one of its storage plans that range from 50MB to 5GB and carry either monthly or annual charges. You move files from your computer to your StorageVault space by dragging and dropping them into Web Folders you set up.

Other Sites to Check Out

www.lockboxx.com
www.freedrive.com
www.globedesk.com
java.isavvix.com/freeback.jsp

Search Engines

You're probably already familiar with search engines from the standpoint of a consumer. You can find information on just about any topic by using an Internet search service. When it comes to running an online business, your perspective is different. You need to visit these sites to find out how to get your business listed so that customers can find you more easily. Each site has information that explains how to include your site on its index.

AltaVista

www.altavista.com

AltaVista is fast, and it provides users with a wide range of shortcuts to narrow down the information you want. Like other search services, AltaVista presents a directory of Internet sites on a topic-by-topic basis. Its Business and Finance category includes sites for Regulation and Government and Small Businesses. One nice touch is that you can search in a variety of languages other than English — even Estonian, Icelandic, and Finnish.

Google

www.google.com

This is my current search engine of choice. Search results tend to be very focused and useful. Google also maintains a good Yahoo! -style index to Web sites and other resources throughout the Internet.

HotBot

www.hotbot.com

HotBot's colorful artwork reflects its creator, Wired Digital, which is now part of the Lycos Network. HotBot is especially good if you're searching for links to your own Web site: Enter your own URL in the search text box, and select "links to this site" from the first drop-down menu under Options. If you're looking for your own free home page or e-mail address, HotBot even provides hosting, too.

My Excite

www.excite.com

Excite lets users create their own personalized Web pages so that they can receive the news and business information of their choosing. The Excite home page contains lots of current news, weather, and stock information as well as an Internet search box.

My Lycos

my.lycos.com

Lycos is one of the oldest search engines on the Web. Lycos has a category listing for small-business resources that you may find useful. It lets you search not only the usual categories like the Web and newsgroups, but also stocks, weather, and even recipes. The site attempts to detect your geographic location so that it can present you with contents that are tailored to where you live, such as links to local newspapers and the local weather report.

WebCrawler

www.webcrawler.com

WebCrawler began as a student project in 1994 and has since turned into a mini-industry of its own. One good thing about WebCrawler is that it lets you (or your customers) search through Internet classifieds for particular items. Look at the fine print at the bottom of the page for a surprise: The Excite search engine's owner, Excite, Inc., owns WebCrawler.

Yahoo!

www.yahoo.com

★★
★★

Yahoo! is probably the most popular and best-known site on the Web. It's the place to go if you want to find information about almost anything. Yahoo! is at once a search engine that helps you find sites on the Web and a well-organized index to Web sites arranged by topic. In addition, Yahoo! Store is a good place to create a business Web site. I probably end up turning to Yahoo! once or twice on almost every surfing session, and I always seem to find something of interest.

Small-Business Associations

There's nothing like a little help when you're sitting all alone at your kitchen table or in your office, wondering how to make your business a success. The following organizations provide information, support, and much-needed health insurance and other benefits for the self-employed.

American Home Business Association, Inc.

www.homebusiness.com

This is a friendly site from a friendly organization offering home-based business resources. You can get good deals on Internet access, long-distance phone service, and more. A Hotline area provides tips on running an online business.

American Association of Home-Based Businesses

www.aahbb.org

AAHBB is a not-for-profit organization offering a variety of benefits to members, including discounts on long-distance service, discounted prepaid legal services, access to merchant banking services, discounted cellular phone services, and health and business insurance. The site's home page includes a link to a talk show devoted to small business that's broadcast every weekday morning.

Home Office Association of America

www.hoaa.com

HOAA offers health insurance, UPS discounts, a newsletter that monitors new equipment and software developments, help with improving your business skills, low-cost long-distance phone service, home-business equipment insurance, air-line discounts, a collection agency for bad accounts, and free or discounted software. As an HOAA member, you can apply for group health insurance, too.

National Association for the Self-Employed

www.nase.org

NASE provides a variety of member benefits and advocacy efforts for the self-employed person, including health insurance, dis-counted delivery services, and tax advice.

SOHO America

www.soho.org

According to SOHO (Small Office/Home Office), 43 million people work from their homes. SOHO was founded to provide ref-erence tools and technical support, bene-fits, and news affecting small and home offices and to represent your interests as a small-business owner.

Yahoo! Guide to Small Business Organizations

dir.yahoo.com/Business_and_Economy/ Business_to_Business/Small_Business_ Information/Organizations/

If you want to take the wide view, Yahoo! provides you with a listing of small-business support organizations that you can join. Note that some organizations are regional or for specific ethnic or age groups.

Web Authoring Tools

An increasingly powerful group of WYSI-WYG (what-you-see-is-what-you-get) Web authoring tools makes it easier to produce your own Web page. Check out The Web Tools Guide for a comprehensive list of every conceivable Web tool, authoring software, and more. The most recent authoring products on the market are simi-lar to print page-layout programs and allow you to design Web pages with special effects plus forms and other interactive features. If you want to learn HTML, you have the option of using an HTML editor, such as BBEdit. Most of these companies allow you to download a preview copy from their sites before you buy the products.

BBEdit

www.barebones.com

The Bare Bones Software motto has always been "It doesn't suck." Not long ago, the motto was revised to "It still doesn't suck." BBEdit is a high performance text and HTML editor for the Macintosh. It is designed for the editing, searching, transformation, and manipulation of text. Features are too numerous to list, but they include a Web-safe color palette, drag-and-drop HTML tools, PageMill cleaner tool, and one-button preview in any browser. The Bare Bones Web site provides you with ways to down-load, purchase, and update the software. You'll find extensive technical support links, including links to discussion groups related to Bare Bones products, and a searchable archive of past discussion group comments.

Dreamweaver

www.macromedia.com/software/ dreamweaver

Dreamweaver is a powerful (and expen-sive) professional design tool that includes a customizable interface and support for dynamic HTML. The Dreamweaver source code features color syntax highlighting and appears in a separate window so that you can tile your WYSIWYG and source views and watch the code appear as you add ele-ments visually. The Macromedia Web site leads you to a "feature tour" illustrating the program's features, areas to download a trial version or purchase a version of the program, and a set of extensions that expand Dreamweaver's functionality. These extensions let you add connectivity to databases, create music and sound, add e-commerce shopping carts, and perform many other useful tasks.

FrontPage 2002

www.microsoft.com/frontpage

FrontPage 2002 is an inexpensive yet very complete WYSIWYG tool that works well with other Microsoft products. You can purchase FrontPage either as a standalone product or bundled with Microsoft Office XP Professional Special Edition or Developer. To really get the most out of FrontPage, you need a Microsoft Web server and your users need to have the latest Microsoft browser. This FrontPage site includes ways to order the product online, links to Web site hosting services, and instructions on how to use FrontPage on an internal intranet, among other things.

Macromedia HomeSite

www.macromedia.com/software/ homesite

Like BBEdit for the Macintosh, Macromedia HomeSite is a fine tool for working directly with HTML code. The program has a built-in tag editor, a tag inspector, and a find-and-replace tool. One advantage of Macromedia HomeSite is that it's configured to help you work with some specialized versions of XML, such as Wireless Markup Language (WML) and Synchronized Multimedia Integration Language (SMIL). From this site, you can download a trial version of Macromedia HomeSite or purchase a fully registered version of the program.

Other Stuff to Check Out

www.sausage.com
www.miracleinc.com/Products

Web and Business Publications Online

If you're relatively new to the online world, you'll want to know about the latest news and developments so that you can keep up with both your competitors and your customers. The following cybermedia outlets provide you with daily business news, as well as the latest technological developments.

CIO E-Business Research Center

www.cio.com/research/ec

This print publication with an online presence provides substantive articles and resources for larger companies, but it also has much for the small-business entrepreneur to use. Previous articles include "Designing Principles: An online catalog is only as good as its design," and "Flash is Trash: Forget the spinning logos and blinking lights. Real people want real information, and they want it fast."

Down To Business

www.frugalfun.com/dtb.html

Down To Business is a no-frills online magazine for entrepreneurs and marketers. It's published by Shel Horowitz, author and publisher of *Marketing Without Megabucks: How to Sell Anything on a Shoestring.* It offers articles from some of the leading lights in the entrepreneurial niche and is a gold mine for the small operator. You will find articles on the use of e-mail, Internet strategies, the World Wide Web, technologies and trends, speaking in person and on the media, marketing and sales, and interpersonal relationships and family business. Bookmark this site.

Inc. Online

www.inc.com

The online version of the print magazine *Inc.* provides great reading for the small-business person. Expect good reporting on Web businesses and Web marketing, as well as solid articles on all aspects of business.

Internet World

www.iw.com

★★
★★

Internet World is one of the best online publications for the online entrepreneur. All articles in this daily ezine are geared toward electronic business or Web development. *Internet World* deserves a bookmark and frequent visits.

New York Times: E-Business

www.nytimes.com/pages/technology/ebusiness/index.html

This is one of the best daily sources of current information on all aspects of the Web and the Internet. This section features original columns and articles produced expressly for the Web. Special features include E-Commerce Report and New Economy.

Wired

www.wired.com/wired/

Wired offers an irreverent and hip look at new media, online economy, new technology, and policy regarding the Internet and the World Wide Web. You can browse the archives of past issues on these topics. Wired News, HotWired, LiveWired HotBot, and Suck.com are all linked from this site.

Other Stuff to Check Out

enews.com
www.eweek.com

Web Design and Graphics

If you're planning to design and create your own Web site, this section is for you. But even if you're planning to hire someone to do the job for you, it's still useful to find out as much as you can about Web page design. Understanding what goes into making an attractive and compelling site is crucial for anyone hoping to have a successful online business. Knowing some of the technical and design issues involved in the production of a Web site goes a long way in helping you communicate effectively with a designer.

BigNoseBird

★★
★★

www.bignosebird.com

A fantastic Web authoring resources site with a strange name and a great sense of humor, BigNoseBird offers tutorials on a huge range of subjects. This site boasts an overwhelming amount of information and is worth many visits. If you get lost, try the search engine.

Lynda.com

www.lynda.com

Lynda Weinman, author of *Designing Web Graphics: How to Prepare Images and Media for the Web*, hosts this site. In addition to promoting her books and workshops, she provides information and links related to the use of graphics and color on Web pages. If you plan to develop your own graphics, her books are well worth reading.

MediaBuilder

www.mediabuilder.com/abm.html

With Media Builder, you can create your own custom animated banner for free. After choosing the animation effects and the type of text, you click the Make Banner button. You can then save the banner to your own computer. This site also offers a button-maker and a host of image files, fonts, and software tools.

Reallybig.com

reallybig.com/default.shtml

This great site offers more than 3,000 resources for Web builders, including clip art, hit counters, fonts, HTML, animations, backgrounds, icons, and buttons. Whew! Besides these Web page goodies, this site also offers a selection of WYSIWYG Web page editors. On top of this, you can get help with promoting your Web site here, too.

useit.com

www.useit.com

Jacob Nielsen, author of *Designing Excellent Websites: Secrets of an Information Architect*, presents some excellent advice about the art of Web design with an emphasis on usability.

Webmonkey

www.hotwired.com/webmonkey

Hotwired's Webmonkey is a "How-to Guide for Web Developers." This is a well-designed, very hip site that offers information on e-business, design, HTML, dynamic HTML, stylesheets, graphics and fonts, multimedia, browsers, Java, Javascript, Perl, and Backend. This site pulls relevant articles from Wired News. You have the option to have the front page of this site delivered to your e-mailbox everyday, subscribe to a weekly newsletter, and/or join a mailing list for Web designers.

Web Review

★ ★
★ ★

webreview.com

Web Review is a huge and important site for the Web designer/developer. Visiting the site is free, but you are asked to register to receive additional benefits, including a free weekly newsletter and special offers on new Web products. Web Review offers 30 different departments, all loaded with up-to-date, valuable information. An absolute must visit.

Yale C/AIM Web Style Guide

info.med.yale.edu/caim/manual/graphics/
    graphics.html

This comprehensive resource guide can help you optimize the look and efficiency of your Web page graphics. The Style Guide covers color displays, graphic file formats, GIFs, JPEG graphics, information on optimizing graphics, colored backgrounds, and image maps.

Other Stuff to Check Out

www.webdeveloper.com
usableweb.com
www.killersites.com/core.html
www.webreference.com

Web Marketing

Marketing and advertising are two different activities, to my mind, at least. *Advertising* involves spreading your URL and banner ads around the Web, either to a wide variety of sites or a narrowly selected audience. *Marketing* involves building credibility for yourself and your site through content, participation in newsgroups, effective e-mail use, and a number of other strategies. The following sites either market your online business for you or suggest ways you can spread the word yourself.

CyberAtlas

cyberatlas.internet.com

CyberAtlas is a reference desk for Web marketers that provides valuable statistics and demographic information, as well as advertising, e-commerce, and site-building resources. This is a well-organized site for the online entrepreneur who wants an edge in understanding Web marketing.

eMarketer

www.emarketer.com

A handsome, well-organized site that inspires with its design as well as its content, eMarketer offers an impressive menu of resources and information and boasts having the best online statistics available. One of the most valuable parts of the site is eCommunity, a variety of discussion groups where you can meet other online marketers and compare notes.

Web Marketing Today

www.wilsonweb.com/webmarket

Wilson Internet Services is a Web consulting firm that provides a free and substantial Internet marketing resource with links to hundreds of online articles. This site offers a clickable index, a keyword search, and claims that its E-Commerce Research Room is the Internet's largest and most

comprehensive e-commerce resource and portal site. This is an excellent, not-to-be missed site.

Other Stuff to Check Out

adres.internet.com

www.marketingsource.com

pandecta.com/marketing_resources.html

Part V
The Part of Tens

The 5th Wave   By Rich Tennant

"Sales on the Web site are down. I figure the server's chi is blocked, so we're fudgin' around the feng shui in the computer room, and if that doesn't work, Ronnie's got a chant that should do it."

In this part . . .

*I*f you're like me, you have one drawer in the kitchen filled with utensils and other assorted objects that don't belong anywhere else. Strangely enough, that's the place I can almost always find something to perform the task at hand.

Part VI of this book is called "The Part of Tens" because it's a collection of miscellaneous secrets arranged in sets of ten. Filled with tips, cautions, suggestions, and examples, this part presents many kinds of information that can help you plan and create your own business presence on the Internet.

Chapter 15

Ten Ways to Boost Your Online Business

In This Chapter

▶ Planning for success and getting off to a good start

▶ Devising a well-defined business plan

▶ Developing a personalized marketing strategy

▶ Networking through effective e-mail techniques

▶ Revising and improving your business Web site

*T*he Internet may seem like a place for loners, but it's not. Sure, you sit at your computer by yourself (or possibly with a family member or partner) when you create your Web pages. You also answer your e-mail by yourself, but you aren't in a vacuum, not by a long shot. Just open your eyes and look around at what other ontrepreneurs (online entrepreneurs) have done and are doing. Ask a few questions, and suddenly, you have plenty of advice and support. You're networking!

In the course of writing this and other books, I've accumulated many tips from individuals who are conducting successful online businesses. In this chapter, I reveal the secrets they've passed on to me about what separates an exciting, money-making project from one that induces a great big virtual yawn. Many of these tips aren't really secrets at all, but just common-sense practices that you may overlook while you're busy hooking up modems, dialing access numbers, filling out Web page forms, and doing other nuts-and-bolts tasks.

In this chapter, I omit both the most obvious tips and the tips that I include elsewhere in this book; instead, I concentrate on strategies that may not occur to you right away. If you can add even just a few of these strategies to your bag of tricks, you'll be boosting your business (that is, getting more visits and inquiries, receiving more positive feedback, and making more sales) faster than you can say, "How many of those do you want to order?"

Think Positive!

Seem obvious? I don't think so. After all, maintaining a rosy outlook is difficult when dot-coms are going belly-up and the economy is fluctuating wildly. This maxim really hit home when I interviewed Dan Podraza, the head of the family of ontrepreneurs who started the super-successful trading site (CollectibleX.com) that I describe in Chapter 1.

When I asked Dan about the problems that he encountered starting the online business, he told me, "We operated on a low budget in the beginning, and we didn't have the inventory that people wanted. People need to plan to be successful, and they need to be confident in what they are doing. We weren't exactly as confident as we could have been, but we were lucky because Beanie Babies are so popular."

Although choosing a product to sell that is eagerly desired by a passionately committed group of users is certainly important, what's really important is your frame of mind going into your online business project. If you have a positive frame of mind, you can sell just about anything. If you plan ahead to be successful, you *will* be successful.

How, exactly, do you plan to be successful, and how does your attitude affect your actual success? If you've never been terribly successful before, this is a good question. Here are some strategies for success that are based on my own experience and on what online business owners have told me over the years:

- **Believe in what you have to sell:** Love your product or the service that you provide and promote it energetically and enthusiastically. Come up with catchy slogans, and put them into your e-mail signature file. Take humorous photos of yourself and your product, which can imply that you're confident enough to have fun with your business. Your own enthusiasm about your product or service will radiate to your prospective customers or clients.

- **Order sufficient inventory:** You may have the option of going overboard in this area, especially on a limited budget, but don't be caught short in case you start getting tons of orders. Keep a modest surplus on hand in case of success. If necessary, you can always give extra products away as promotions.

- **Don't skimp on your computer setup:** Time and time again, I've tried to cut corners by buying a bargain computer with a small storage area. When money is limited, you may also be tempted to get the least expensive Internet connection that you can find, but in all likelihood you'll end up having to change to a faster connection with better services later on. Plan for success by paying a little extra upfront for the most memory, the fastest processor, the speediest modem, and the Web hosting service with the most features. A year from now, you'll be thanking yourself instead of kicking yourself!

Get Your Ducks in a Row, and Then Stick to Your Plan

So you say you have a bright idea for a business, and the Internet would be a cool place to start it? Whoa there, partner. Having an inspiration is only half the battle. In fact, too many people try to start an online commerce site with only a hunch or rough idea of what they plan to do. Unless they're extremely lucky, these would-be Rockefellers are asking for trouble.

Before you sign up with a Web host and start to make Web pages, sit down for a moment and discuss (with your family, your friends, your partners, or yourself) exactly what you want to do. Specifically, you should consider the following:

- ✔ **Know whom you want to reach:** Look through Usenet newsgroups where people in your market hang out. Find out what they like and dislike — and more important, what they need that they aren't getting now.

- ✔ **Know what you want to accomplish:** Be clear about the goal(s) of your online business.

- ✔ **Know your competition:** Research your competition by visiting their Web sites. Make a list of things they do that you can do better.

- ✔ **Know the structure of your Web site:** Map out and organize your Web site and determine whether you want to develop your site in stages or all at one time.

- ✔ **Know your product:** Make a list of the goods and/or services you plan to provide.

Sarah-Lou Reekie notes (see Chapter 10) that she spent months getting herself known and building up her offline customer base among film crews and other professionals before starting her online business, Alfresco (Beauty Without Bites).

I've heard it said that, if you have no idea where you're going, you're guaranteed to get there. Don't end up with your cyberbusiness going nowhere. Have a clear idea of your goal and develop the strategies to reach it. And if times get tough, don't abandon ship. Many of the ontrepreneurs that I spoke to for this book were coping with a mini-recession by expanding, rather than contracting, their online business offerings.

The important thing is not to rush online with an idea that isn't well thought out. The danger is that your good idea will drop like the proverbial lead balloon, and you'll get discouraged and give up on it. If you have a business plan ready, a line-up of the strategies you need to carry it through, and personal contacts with people who will help you along, you're more likely to stay with your business project through any ups and downs that you may encounter.

Get Personal with Your Marketing Plan

Web sites work when they offer a personalized experience. The personal touch starts before you even go online. First, determine whom you want to attract. Draw up descriptions of two or three typical customers, complete with their names, ages, occupations, modes of dress, and so on. With a well-defined image of customers you want to reach, you can tailor your Web site's headings, text, and sales promotions — your whole marketing approach — to reach those individuals.

Then, figure out a plan for how to get the attention of your likely customers and how to get people to come to your site through e-mail, promotions, or advertisements. Be sure to include a plan for getting listed on search engines and indexes, as I describe in Chapter 11.

Beginning your marketing efforts before your business goes online never hurts. Although you can't advertise your site before it's available, you can market yourself by participating in online discussions as well as trade shows and conferences.

Make It Easy on Your Customers

Your chances of receiving orders and making transactions increase in direct proportion to how easily visitors can browse through your site in order to locate and order what they want. Specifically, most Web site consultants agree that you have to attract a visitor's attention and get your message across in less than a minute — in fact, I would say in less than 20 seconds. At the point of making a sale, your site needs to be easy enough to use so that an impulse buyer can follow his or her immediate desire and make an order or purchase instantly.

How do you do it? Follow these basic rules to make your site more user-friendly:

- **Remember the KISS principle:** That's Keep It Simple, Stupid. A music file that plays in the background while your Web page is loading may seem clever, but save it for your personal home page, not your business site — such add-ons can take time to download over a slow connection and distract customers who either hate background music in general or your choice of music in particular. Stay away from Java applets and complex image files that users with slow connections will have to wait for precious seconds (or minutes) to download.

- **Tell all up front:** Explain who you are, what you do, why you do it, and how you can be contacted right on your home page.

- ✔ **Make shopping easy:** Find a Web host that lets you create a shopping-cart system that customers can use to pick out items. Provide a simple Web form that visitors can fill out quickly in order to make purchases, convey shipping information, and send credit card numbers.

- ✔ **Make shoppers feel safe:** Sign up with a host that has a secure server that can protect customers' credit card information. Stress security and integrity on your site. Provide a low-tech alternative, such as mailing in a check, for people who don't want to use a credit card. Many shoppers are still squeamish about ordering over the Internet, so making them feel safe is essential.

If you do decide to accept credit card purchases from your customers, you need to set up a merchant account with a bank, as I discuss in Chapter 9. A secure server, which I cover in more detail in Chapter 12, is also essential, and most Web hosts charge extra for this. To protect yourself from someone submitting false credit card information, pay a little more to use a service such as iAuthorizer (www.iauthorizer.com) to verify your credit card transactions.

Give Something Away for Free

Nothing drums up business inquiries for an online company like freebies. Shoppers on the Web love getting something for nothing. In fact, I think that they're so used to the convenience of finding freebies online that they *expect* to get something for free when they visit a commercial Web site.

Don't disappoint your customers. Give 'em what they want. If your online business provides products for sale, set aside one or two items to give away in a contest. An additional benefit of doing this is that you can use the e-mail addresses you receive with entries for future mailings.

If you're in the business of providing information or services online, consider doing some work for free. Share your expertise freely on mailing lists, and offer to let people try out your services for nothing if they say that they're "on the fence" and aren't sure about contracting with you.

Keep Your Web Site Fresh and New

Nothing says "Don't Shop Here!" louder than a site with a "last updated" date that's a year or two old, or a site that still advertises products for sale that have been unavailable for months.

One way to avoid being out-of-date (you might call this Phase One) is not to use dates on your site at all, unless you plan to update your content regularly. You can also minimize the frequency and extent of updates by starting with only three to six Web pages for your online business and by concentrating on providing a few good products or services for sale.

After a few months, move to Phase Two of your online business project. Add six to ten more Web pages. One or more of these can be devoted to Breaking News, Weekly Specials, or some other type of timely information. The others can describe such topics as

- ✔ Who you are and why you love what you do
- ✔ How people can get customer service information if they need it
- ✔ Testimonials from satisfied customers
- ✔ Links to related resources online where people can find out more about your field

Phase Two can also involve a redesign of your Web pages. Turn your headings into graphic images that use striking typefaces. Scan more photos of your work or your items for sale. After six months, you can move on to Phase Three, which may include an expansion of your online sales catalog. The important thing is to regard your online business as an ongoing project that you continually revise and improve.

Master the Art of Effective E-Mail

E-mail is right up there with Web sites as the most important part of an online business. In fact, if I were asked to say which is more important, I don't think I could pick one or the other. If you learn to use these two parts of the Internet to communicate, you'll find that they complement one another beautifully.

Don't throw away your old e-mail messages; rather, organize the most important messages into folders so that you can track correspondence with your Very Important People later on. Also, be sure to use your e-mail software's Address Book function to save the e-mail addresses of people with whom you correspond frequently.

Get into the habit of checking your e-mail every day. If work or other responsibilities prevent you from checking your e-mail daily, this can be a good job for a spouse, an assistant, or an older son or daughter. Don't let e-mail inquiries sit for days on end. Each day you wait increases the likelihood that people who were interested will find another resource.

Even if you don't have the product or service that someone is looking for, send a message back informing that person of that fact and encouraging him or her to check back in the future. You may even consider suggesting the URL of another site that may be useful to people you can't help. The goodwill you generate might bring someone back to you for a future transaction.

Reaching Out through Newsgroups, Mailing Lists, and Offline Media

Time and time again, I've discovered that the most successful businesspeople are the ones who devote the most energy to connecting with other individuals. It never fails: If I send out ten e-mails requesting interviews or other information, the ones who get back to me the quickest are the ones who are also the busiest and most successful businesspeople.

The contact you make with potential clients doesn't necessarily have to be on the Internet. It can also be through trade shows, conferences, classified ads in newspapers or magazines, or simply getting back to people on the phone.

Don't stick solely to the Web or search engines for your Web site promotion. Use the whole Internet, including subscribing to mailing lists, posting on bulletin boards, contributing to discussions on Usenet, and participating in online chats. The more frequently you drop your name and voice your comments out there in cyberspace, the better your chances of making a sale or closing a business deal. (Chapters 9 and 11 contain more ways to promote your business on the Internet.)

Get Your Business Listed in All the Right Places

This is one of those online business tips that gets mentioned all the time, not only in books such as this but also by companies that want to host your Web site. So I won't belabor the point. But on the other hand, getting yourself listed with the big Internet search services — many of which charge fees and give preferential treatment to paying customers — is becoming more difficult. You can still get exposure by rolling up your sleeves and doing things to publicize your business for free:

- ✔ List your site on your own by filling out as many free search engines, indexes, and Internet Yellow Pages application forms as possible.

- ✔ Add meta keywords to your Web pages, making your site more likely to turn up on search engine pages. (See Chapter 11 for more information on using meta keywords.)

- ✔ Promote links to your site from businesses whose products and services complement yours.

- ✔ Make sure that your site is listed on both local and national versions of Yahoo!

Give Your Customers Instant Service

Get back to people as fast as you can. Many things in cyberspace seem to happen more quickly than they do in the offline world. That applies to a fickle Internet shopper's time frame for decision-making, too. You have only a very narrow window of time to grab somebody's attention and business.

Remember that Web surfers are used to instant gratification. If they want to know the answer to a homework or trivia question, they have only to turn to search services or online encyclopedias, and the answer appears in a few minutes. If they want a software program, they can probably find something available immediately in the shareware archives.

What does this mean for you, the provider of goods and services to these hungry, impatient consumers? It means that you need to do the following:

- ✔ Check your e-mail daily, or once every couple of days.

- ✔ Sign up with a Web hosting service that provides you with *autoresponders*. These are e-mail addresses (such as `info@company.com`) that automatically respond to e-mail inquiries by sending back a standard response to the effect of, "We have received your request and we'll be getting back to you right away." You can also set up autoresponders to send an attached text file that provides information about your company or a particular line of products.

- ✔ Provide some sort of customer service information on your site. This can be as simple as a single page that instructs customers on how to contact you if they have problems, complaints, or questions. Or you can create individual pages that provide background information about specific items or services.

If you're the type of person who loves to keep in touch by telephone and hates to miss messages, look into the Internet paging options from Arch Wireless (`content.arch.com`). You can forward e-mail messages to your pager rather than your e-mail inbox.

Chapter 16

Ten Recession-Proof Online Business Strategies

In This Chapter

▶ Contributing your own sweat equity to keep your business afloat

▶ Sticking to proven business principles that work in good times or bad

▶ Diversifying and making alliances to expand sales channels

▶ Treating your best business assets — your customers — like royalty

*I*f you're lucky, your online business will continue to attract customers even if the economy slows down. In most cases, though, you're likely to feel some impact from either a slowdown or a full-fledged recession, but that doesn't mean your business has to go up and down with every dip and peak of the stock market ticker. You can follow some good practices to smooth out your economic ups and downs.

Some of the tips that I cover in this chapter were conveyed to me by online businesspeople who responded to my question, "Are there some recession-proof strategies that you follow when times get tough?" Others tips are just commonsense practices that every business, whether on the Net or offline, can do to thrive amid boom or bust.

Contribute Your Own Sweat Equity

Wouldn't it be great if you could find someone who would work for reduced pay when business slows down? I'm talking about someone who works evenings and weekends for no extra compensation, someone who works just as hard (perhaps even harder) when the going gets tough, and doesn't even think about "going" — the perfect employee, in other words.

Chances are you're lucky enough to know one such person, and you'll find that person staring back at you when you turn off your computer monitor.

People think that running a Web-based business is easier than running another type of business. People have the impression that you can set up the Web pages, test them to make sure everything works right, and pretty much sit back and let the money roll in. On the contrary, running your own online business requires a substantial investment in terms of sweat equity. This is especially true when the economy slows to a crawl, when you have to speed up and work even harder.

Mark Cramer is owner of an Illinois-based business called MePage.com, and operator of a Web site (www.eballoon.com) that functions as a portal (or more accurately, a *sportal*) for the North American Balloon Association of sport ballooning enthusiasts. Mark reports that his business continues to grow, due in no small part to his own hard work.

"We provide coverage of sanctioned sport ballooning events and also offer marketing and advertising on the sportal, as well as at events throughout the United States," says Mark. "This allows us exclusive exposure to two million online and another five million at the events.

"Personal equity is often overlooked when determining the value of a company," he adds. "Anyone with a brick and mortar business learns early on that just because your doors aren't open to the public doesn't mean there isn't work to be done. Our hours per week vary from 35 to 84 hours per week depending on our goal for that week. Many people who start online businesses think that this discipline isn't needed. The truth is the discipline is important in any business, online or offline."

Raise Your Performance Bar

You might think that, when business slows down, it's time to hibernate: Crawl into a cave, assume the fetal position, and shrink your product line to a handful of best-selling products.

Shrinking your sales line is likely to slow your revenue even further. Worse, it prevents you from rebounding quickly when the economy swings back toward prosperity. Smart online businesspeople do the opposite of hunkering down: They actively confront slow sales by branching out, developing new sales channels, and otherwise fighting back.

CollectibleX.com, which I discuss in Chapter 1, struggled through the winter of 2001–2002 like the rest of us. Then, in February 2002, the company unveiled a new Web site and several new product lines. The moral of the story: Don't get stuck in one place when business slows down — keep pushing yourself to do better.

How do you determine what product lines to expand? Analyze how people use your Web site, and develop the areas that people visit most frequently. Your Web host should be able to give you access to your site's *log files* — computer documents that record how many visits each part of your site receives and where your visitors have been before they come to your site. Sign up with a host that uses software that makes the data in the log files easier to understand. Some of the flashier programs, such as WebTrends (`www.webtrends.com`), provide data in graphs and pie charts that are great to print out and show to your business colleagues.

Cut Your Business Expenses

One of the most important ways to weather a recession or other economic downtown is to eliminate unnecessary expenses. Because you're connected to the Internet, you have plenty of chances to buy what you need or do what you need to do more affordably. Here are some suggestions:

- ✔ **Cut down on advertising costs:** Many online businesses that weren't managed well failed, in part, because of overspending on expensive ads and marketing campaigns. Use word of mouth to spread the word about your site through newsgroups, chat rooms, and e-mail.

- ✔ **Buy used, refurbished, or auctioned equipment:** When you need hardware, software, or furniture, try an online auction site or a discount warehouse before you buy new.

- ✔ **Try bartering:** Before you buy business supplies, offer to trade goods or services with a supplier.

For me, personally, phone charges are the biggest of all my expenses. Whether analog, digital, or wireless, phone connections are indispensable not only to communicate with customers but also to get yourself connected to the Internet, to do faxes, and to communicate with the merchant network to authorize credit cards. Anything you can do to cut down on phone charges is a good thing. Check out Epinions.com (`www.epinions.com`) where you can compare cellular as well as long-distance phone plans, read reviews submitted by individual consumers, and pick the best plan for you.

Don't Put All Your Eggs in One Basket

There are plenty of ways to sell your goods and services. The smart online businessperson makes a Web site part of an overall business plan rather than its sole focus.

Just because the big players in e-commerce design huge Web sites with database back-end systems, personalization, and cookies, that doesn't mean you have to assume that's the only way to sell what you have to offer. Sell some of your goods at auction; open a storefront-office where you can sell your wares in a physical location as well as online; open a virtual storefront in an online mall; build your telephone sales skills; cultivate your existing customers through giveaways and other promotions.

Stick to Proven Business Principles

Many of the early dot-coms turned out to be dot-bombs because they forgot (or perhaps never knew) how to do business. They spent money they didn't really have, and they blew their budgets on expensive advertising and costly promotions rather than on slowly building a base of satisfied return customers. Focusing on the basics will help you succeed whether the economy is growing or slowing.

John Counsel is owner of The Profit Clinic (www.profitclinic.com), an Australian company that provides tips, sales advice, and Web design for small and home-based businesses. The Profit Clinic's own business has grown steadily since going online in 1996, and continued to thrive through the downturn of 2001–02.

"Stick to proven business principles that work offline as well as online," advises Counsel. "There have been no changes to the rules of what works and what doesn't. The revolutionaries who claimed that the wheel had turned in favor of the dot-coms have now gone where they were always destined to go, and reality has descended to expose the lack of clothing worn by these would-be emperors.

"My most successful decision was not to rush in prematurely . . . that it would pay me to watch and learn, and to build awareness and credibility for myself and my ideas by contributing to forums, ezines, discussion lists, newsgroups, etc.," says Counsel. "This has paid off handsomely. The Profit Clinic is still one of the 'stickiest' sites on the Web, with a median visitor stay of almost *three hours* (and visits of six to ten hours commonplace)."

Connect with a Brick-and-Mortar Business

Pure plays (businesses that exist only online, not in a physical store that shoppers can actually visit) can work, but your chances of withstanding economic ups and downs are greatly enhanced if your Web site is a sales channel for a real, physical business.

"What I find is that the Internet has worked best as an adjunct to an existing brick-and-mortar business," says business planning and Web design consultant Jeffrey E. Edelheit. "The keys to a successful Internet venture is to have a niche market, and having it be an adjunct to an existing business, so it becomes value added and finding a good way to generate viable traffic. It is no different than the rules of having a successful brick-and-mortar venture."

You say you don't have the money to open up your own brick-and-mortar store? Consider selling your products in someone else's store or a chain of stores. Timbuk2 Designs does this very well. This company sells several popular lines of bike messenger bags, both through its Web site (`www.timbuk2.com`) and through local stores in the San Francisco area.

Timbuk2 Designs lets Web-savvy customers place orders online through the Build Your Own Bag area of its Web site. It's also trying to reach shoppers who do their browsing the old-fashioned way, by walking through brick-and-mortar outlets. Timbuk2 has actually installed interactive computer screens called *kiosks* in many of those stores so that shoppers can use the Build Your Own Bag feature there.

"Most retailers have been resistant to e-commerce as it was viewed as more of a threat than an opportunity," says Brennan Mulligan, president of Timbuk2 Designs. "Now, with the demise of so many Internet-only retailers, the threat is mostly gone. Retailers have taken a collective sigh of relief and are now excited about getting involved in what e-commerce software can offer."

Do One Thing Well, but Do Others, Too

When times are good, resting on your laurels is easy. If you have one client or one activity that's functioning like the proverbial gravy train, you may easily rely on that one source of income while ignoring others. This isn't a smart business tactic, however. Look around and diversify. Developing other sales channels and cultivating other clients will help you in down times.

Startup Journal, the Wall Street Journal online center for entrepreneurs, has at least two articles profiling businesspeople who confronted economic slowdowns by expanding and moving forward. "Small Company Rethinks One-Customer Strategy" profiles the owner of a staffing firm who was forced to diversify (www.startupjournal.com/runbusiness/survival/20011205-bailey.html). "Using the Recession to Grow Your Company" is at www.startupjournal.com/runbusiness/survival/20020128-merle.html.

Handle Your Customers with TLC

Sam Walton, founder of Wal-Mart, once said, "High expectations are the key to everything." In other words, one of the tasks of any successful businessperson is to exceed customer expectations. Give better service than anyone else in your area of expertise; let the customer drive your business.

Your customers are your most important resource. Managing them is one thing you can always do when times get tough. Having a solid base of faithful customers who will return to your business again and again is perhaps the best business resource that you can have. Keep your customers' contact information in a database, maintain detailed records of what they buy, and get back to them as quickly as you can.

Consider giving your regular customers premium content, such as personal tips or extra-reduced items, that only they can access with a special code. It makes them feel special and builds loyalty.

Make Yourself a Resource

Suppose you have a business and your product sales go down. Is it time to close up shop? Not necessarily. Supplement your product sales by generating income through advertising. The key is to make your site a resource that people will want to visit again and again.

When I first wrote about Graphic Maps, the company had just started up a service in which it answered geography questions submitted by students. This had nothing to do with the other part of its business — creating maps for businesses — but it had everything to do with word-of-mouth advertising. Today, the Graphic Maps site (worldatlas.com) gets more than three million hits per month, and its banner advertising generates lots of revenue.

Remember to Keep the Faith!

Getting discouraged is easy; and when your income drops, you have a real reason for anxiety. This is when you need to balance out your fear with faith in the future.

Listen to Sarah-Lou Reekie, who was working as a volunteer at a botanical garden when she came up with the idea for her natural mosquito repellent Alfresco, and who spent years trying to develop just the right formula. I discuss her story in Chapter 10; Reekie is the one who received encouragement from Sir Paul McCartney as well as movie stars who have used Alfresco on location. Says Reekie: "Remember, success is never ever going to be easy or quick! Be prepared for long hours and difficult times. But if you have an idea you believe in along with the seriousness and commitment together with realistic resources and the courage of your conviction, *go for it now.*"

Index

• D •

Notes

Notes

FOR DUMMIES®

The easy way to get more done and have more fun

FOR DUMMIES®

A world of resources to help you grow

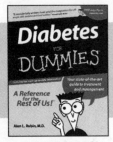